GENERAL PSYCHOLOGY

GENERAL PSYCHOLOGY

By WAYLAND F. VAUGHAN, Ph. D.

Professor of Psychology, Boston University

DOUBLEDAY, DORAN & COMPANY, INC.

Garden City, New York

PRINTED AT THE *Country Life Press*, GARDEN CITY, N. Y., U. S. A.

TO

MY FATHER

PREFACE

IT IS the conviction of the author that a textbook in *General Psychology* should acquaint the beginning student with the subject matter of psychology without burdening him with a host of technical details which are of interest primarily to advanced students. The elementary course should give the individual an accurate knowledge of the fundamental problems of psychology, and a working grasp of the terms used to describe the data involved in psychological experimentation. The student who masters this textbook should be capable of discussing psychological matters intelligently and of planning and executing experimentation in a sound fashion. He should, furthermore, appreciate what is meant by the scientific approach to the study of human nature.

The author has supplied many illustrations to clarify the presentation of the subject. An effort has been made to provide an interesting textbook without sacrificing the inclusion of facts traditionally considered essential to an understanding of *General Psychology.*

Some of the chapters are longer than the chapters appearing in many contemporary textbooks in psychology. The author feels that the arrangement of the chapters should be planned to promote comprehension of the subject rather than to facilitate convenience of assignment. For example, *Attending* and *Perceiving* are grouped into a single chapter because they belong together psychologically. In many textbooks, they are presented separately as *Attention* and *Perception*, with the possible result that the student fails to appreciate their vital connection. Due to the length of some of the chapters in the present book, assignments will obviously have to be made by pages or topics rather than by chapters—a plan that should involve no serious complications.

Less space is given to the nervous system and to the topic of sensation than is given in some textbooks in the field, because the author considers that other aspects of the elementary course are more distinctly of vital concern to the student of psychology.

The author has restricted himself largely to human psychology because he feels that the inclusion of extensive material from animal psychology imposes an excessive burden on the elementary student. There is only as much of the subject as can be adequately grasped in a single course. It is assumed that a thorough understanding of a limited field is more worth while than a careless perusal of a wider range of material.

There are many facts that have been discovered by psychology. At the same time, there are many theories that are mistaken for facts. The author feels that it is important, on this account, to warn the student that the subject should be approached critically. It is satisfying, to be sure, to realize what is already known; but it is exciting to discover what is not yet known, for there are many unsolved problems beckoning the curious investigator.

The author represents no particular school of psychology. He has no axe to grind. It is hoped the eclectic viewpoint which has been adopted will serve to orient the reader in a comprehensive manner to the sundry issues which make this science a growing enterprise.

Experiments to be performed by the student are included in the body of the text. Further experiments and projects will be found at the end of the book.

Appreciation for help in preparing the present book is due to Donald Durrell, J. Rea Butler, Lowell Trowbridge, Muriel Barrie, Dorothy Rose, Nancy Petty, Olive Colby, Jeanette

Goldberg, Leota Marshall, Elizabeth Smith, Richard M. Vaughan, Richard F. Vaughan, and Clara Colton Vaughan. The author is especially indebted to Ruth and Karl Kunze.

W. F. V.

Needham, Mass.
August, 1935.

CONTENTS

PART I

INTRODUCTION

Part I introduces the reader to the subject of Psychology by providing in Chapter I a survey of three kinds of Psychology now widely recognized, and a sketch of the pre-scientific Psychology that culminated in our modern scientific approach to human nature. A *Background* of this nature is necessary to appreciate the modern trends in the field.

CHAPTER I

BACKGROUND

THE term *psychology* conveys different meanings to different people, for some think of psychology as an easy way to social and financial success; others think of it as living in the light of ordinary common sense; and still others think of it as a technical study in the realm of natural science, associated with laboratories and learned experimentation. It is with this last kind of psychology, scientific psychology, that we shall be primarily concerned. A brief sketch of magical psychology and common-sense psychology, however, may serve as a ready introduction to our main interest.

I. PSYCHOLOGY AS MAGIC

To the public at large "psychology" is a branch of mysterious magic. The "psychologist" belongs in the same category with clairvoyants, palmists, and astrologists. One charlatan describes himself, in the grand style, as "numerologist, biographer, psychologist, astrologer, crystal seer, psychic, and prince of mystics." Like the witch doctor and the sword-swallower the "psychologist" is naïvely supposed to have at his command secret powers which enable him to perform miracles. He may not be able to pierce a two-inch board with his magic eye but he is erroneously credited with having a bag full of tricks no less astonishing to the credulous onlooker. For reimbursement proportional to the remarkable capacities he claims, the quack "psychologist" fraudulently promises to

3

reveal to you the secret of getting what you want to get, be it money, luxury, success, or love.[1]

Human nature, according to the magical point of view adopted by such mountebanks, is essentially electrical. You have probably felt a tingle when your foot was asleep, or when you held hands with your beloved. Such experiences are interpreted for the gullible public as manifestations of a mysterious electrical force by which, if you are in the "know-how," you too can develop instantaneous personal magnetism. After you have learned to project magnetism through your finger tips, sparks will fly from you when you shake hands. A million-dollar personality is yours if you buy the book.[2] "Folks," we are told, "are never the same after reading this book."

One of the priceless documents in this world of dreams come true is *Spunk*. The author, whose photograph adorns his advertisement, modestly hails himself as "the greatest psychologist that any age has developed. The press, the pulpit, and psychological investigators attest to that. . . . For he has taken this amazing study where James left it and has added tier upon tier of knowledge to its fascinating structure." *Spunk* tells us that "anybody can have spunk, if he will." It's all in the mind. Think "success" and you'll be a success. *Spunk* goes on to assure us that "as a rule, the more defeats a man has the greater will be his power in the end." Early failure, according to this spurious logic, is a presage of later success, for Washington, Lincoln, Grant, and Wrigley were disappointing in the early stages of their careers. "When you are down in the mouth, remember Jonah. He came out all right. . . . It is always darkest just before dawn." All you need to achieve success, young man, is spunk—ability might come in handy but it is not essential. "If you are get-

[1]See D. H. Yates: *Psychological Racketeers*. 1932.
[2]Edmund Shaftesbury: *Instantaneous Personal Magnetism*. 1926.

ting plenty of knocks, kicks, thumps, black eyes, and jolts, it probably is due to the fact that you are an unusual man."[1] Here is optimism, plenty of optimism, but I fear it is too superficial to encourage the critical reader.

The wide appeal of the quack psychology which promises a short cut to happiness and success is indicative of a vital need which academic psychology has too long ignored. There is no doubt that we are all harassed by emotional stresses which deprive us of that courage and energy which are necessary for the victorious life. Psychology can be an aid in the daily routine, but one must beware of get-rich-quick schemes that promise bigger returns than the assets of average human nature warrant. I cannot promise to tell you in this book how to make a fortune, but I can promise to give you a new interest in human experience which will lend more fascination than ever to that enigma which puzzles all of us, laymen and psychologists alike—human nature.

II. PSYCHOLOGY AS COMMON SENSE

Every mature human being acquires a working knowledge of psychology without undertaking a formal study of the subject. The student who begins a course in physics or chemistry starts with an initial ignorance which is more or less complete. On the other hand, the person who commences a formal study of psychology discovers many facts which are already familiar to him. Southey was practicing psychology when he discovered that his insomnia could be cured by recalling the lecture room of his college days, and the professor parading his soporific erudition before the yawning students. He was merely using that common sense of which we all possess some share. Psychology is to some extent a matter of good old plain "horse sense."

Modern psychology, according to Bertrand Russell, consists

---

[1] David V. Bush: *Spunk.* 1924.

of the discovery by the professors of what everybody else has always known. It is always reassuring to the man in the street to have the scientists burst into print with the brilliant discovery that it is wet when it rains, and that two and two do not make five. In order to impress the naïve person that psychology is something more than mere common sense, the professors have invented a technical terminology by the use of which they can describe the obvious in incomprehensible terms. They convert common sense into science through the medium of premeditated ambiguities.

An understanding of human nature is an important factor for success in any field of endeavor. A person need not take a course in psychology to become an effective psychologist. Consider the following example. Everybody learns by experience that a person blushes when he is embarrassed, but seldom is this knowledge applied with such telling effect as it was by Knute Rockne when his Notre Dame team defeated the Army in football in 1926. Rockne tells the story: "Notre Dame's defence against West Point was impregnable. As far as anyone could tell it was simply a case of superb defensive football. But the reason for this ability to stop the Army—and particularly Harry Wilson, their All-America back—was because every time the quarter back called Wilson's number, his face got red. The result was that every time Wilson blushed, the Notre Dame team concentrated on him and smothered him. . . . After the game I foolishly told Coach Biff Jones about this and thought no more of it. . . . But what happened the next year? Notre Dame received the surprise of its life and the Army backs had a field day. . . . Evidently during the year some psychiatrist had worked on the Army back-field, because on that fall day in 1927 every time the Army quarter back barked out some numbers the faces of all four Army back-field men turned red and, of course, the Notre Dame defence was thrown into confusion. . . .

Incidentally, this is the first football contest on record where the game was won by four-flushing."

Every parent is a psychologist when he faces the problem of training his children; every child is a psychologist when he confronts the task of eluding parental discipline; all husbands and wives are psychologists when they work out their mutual adjustments for the best interests of the family. The proper rearing of children is a problem in psychology. Suppose your child has developed an aversion for its bath by swallowing some of the soapy water. Common sense and psychology agree that it is wise not to take the child to the bathroom for a time. Give it a sponge bath in the nursery for a day or two; then use a wash basin with a little water in it. Increase the water in the basin. Begin to use a wetter sponge. In a few days you can take the child back again to its regular bath. It is cruel and disastrous to force the child into the tub of water, as some unthinking parents do, since violence only serves to aggravate the fear and thus to retard its eradication, results which are undesirable for all concerned.[1]

In all our human relationships we discover that there are certain principles of conduct which it is wise to follow if we want to get along happily with our fellow beings. These principles may not become articulate—indeed we may know without knowing that we know—we just "feel" that a certain mode of behavior is wise. Some call it instinct, some call it intuition, and some call it psychology.

With all its practical advantages, there are several limitations to the everyday psychology of common sense. First, it is not critical enough. We all notice complex phenomena but we do not pause to analyze them to find out what are the essential elements and what the non-essential. If we trust to a mere casual observation, we may miss the point entirely.

---

[1]See J. B. Watson: *The Psychological Care of the Infant and Child*, pp. 67–68. 1928.

Thus the ambitious young lawyer may imitate the superficial mannerisms of the successful barrister rather than the more important habits of systematic study and precise thinking. Most of us imitate in the same way as the little girl beside her father who was pulling the weeds out of the lawn—she knelt beside him and pulled up everything she could gather in her fists, good grass and all. She had not matured enough to imitate intelligently. Her behavior was uncritical.

A second deficiency in everyday psychology is the lack of painstaking research and hard thinking. Since common-sense psychology is interested only in what is immediately practical, there is a tendency to neglect technical problems which are important scientifically, even though their significance may be less obvious than problems of everyday concern. How many people, for example, ever wonder how it is that we see an object as one object although we look at it with two eyes? The natural reaction to such a question is nonchalance, for what difference does it make as long as one can see all right? Investigation of such problems requires more than a casual interest in psychology.

A third drawback of common-sense psychology is its haphazardness, its lack of organization. Scientific knowledge can only be established by the collection and classification of miscellaneous observations. Huxley defined science as "perfected common sense." Science can only develop when we set out to gather facts in an exact fashion, and when we organize those facts into a system of knowledge. As we shall see later, psychology has only become a science by adhering to definite rules of investigation and systematization.

III. PSYCHOLOGY AS SCIENCE

If psychology is not to be identified with magic or common sense, what body of facts is the concern of the psychologist? What, precisely, is the subject matter of psychology? Before the reader can fully appreciate the psychology of our own scientific era, it will be necessary to trace the stages in the historical evolution of scientific psychology from prescientific psychology.

In tracing the historical development of psychology through its most significant phases, we find that the subject matter investigated by psychologists has changed from time to time. Psychology was originally a study of the soul (*psyche*); it later devoted its attention to the mind; and latest of all it has concentrated upon that aspect of experience which we call behavior. We shall trace this evolution.

A. Soul. Psychology was, in the beginning, a study of the nature and activities of the soul. The notion of the soul originated in various experiences. Primitive man lay down in his cave to sleep and he had a dream. He dreamt that he was wandering in strange places, and yet he felt fairly certain that his body remained all the while exactly where it had reclined when sleep came. His natural conclusion was that his soul left his body in dreams and returned when he awakened. Hence arose the superstition that you should not arouse a person suddenly from his slumber lest his soul fail to return. The soul also explained a man's shadow, his reflection in a pool of water, and the mystery of death when the soul (*anima* or breath) departed from the body for a better dwelling place. On the basis of such experiences the soul came to be conceived as the essence, substance, or actuating cause of individual life, the vehicle of individual existence, separable from the body both in its nature and in its existence.

Psychology remained for centuries a speculative branch of learning indulged in by philosophers who located the soul anatomically without the aid of vivisection or laboratory technique. One man's guess was as good as another's. Time was consumed pronouncing on the origin and destiny of man's divine nature, laying down the last word on such questions as

whether animals, infants, or women possessed souls.   Even in
the United States in 1924 we have a theological psychologist
telling us that the soul is spiritual,

> it is real,
>
> it is immortal,
>
> it is rational,
>
> it is moral,
>
> it is religious,
>
> it is priceless,

and mixing his theology and modern physiological charts with
the most astounding lack of discrimination.[1]   It is no wonder
that modern psychology, in striving to become a real science,
is reacting against the philosophical and theological approaches
to human nature.   Psychology in its effort to purge itself of
non-scientific stigma has thrown the soul overboard or, even
worse, defined it as "merely an emotion created by the secretion of our ductless glands."

According to my own notion the soul is merely the spiritual
or moral aspect of mind.   When a person's mind is directed
toward ends which are ethically worthy, his soul may be said
to be lovely.   Personally, I think the term "soul" could be
well discarded because it has so many connotations, and because the term "mind" suffices to describe the phenomena
attributed to a soul.   We, as human beings, do not consist of
mind, soul, and body, but of mind and body.   A dualism is
enough of a puzzle without trying to solve a trinity.[2]

B. Mind.   Having rid itself of the soul, psychology turned
its investigation to the mind.   What is mind?   Mind, according to my conception of it, may be defined as conscious
experience.   The mental life is made up of such processes as
perceptions, desires, thoughts, and actions, in so far as they
involve "awareness."   There are different degrees of awareness

---

[1] O. M. Norlie: *An Elementary Christian Psychology.*   1924.

[2] Survival, accordingly, would be the continuance of the mind.

ranging from indistinctness to clearness. When an experience is clear, I call it conscious; when it is indistinct, I call it subconscious. Strictly speaking, there is no unconscious mind, for I restrict the term "mental" to conscious states. The term "unconscious" is useful, however, for describing the behavior of an individual who may be momentarily unaware of what he is doing or of the motives impelling him, and for referring to physiological activities of a neural or glandular character which modify our reactions without producing noticeable mental effects.

Though conscious states are subjective and cannot, therefore, be described in objective terms, every one who is alive knows what is meant by "conscious," for we are all conscious beings. This process which I call my consciousness is all that I know immediately in this universe, since it is the medium through which I become aware of all phenomena. I reach out and touch an object. My tactual perception tells me there is an actual object present. In accepting the existence of the object, I must rely upon my consciousness which is reporting its reality. When I feel sure that my consciousness is telling me the truth, I call the phenomenon a fact.

Consciousness may be awareness of external objects, or it may be awareness of one's own awareness which is spoken of as self-consciousness. The capacity for self-consciousness is supposed to be limited to human beings who have matured two years or so. The infant is not conscious of himself; he is an individual but he does not know it yet—it is said, therefore, that he has not become a self or personality. The child discovers himself when he learns that the experience evoked by his own body differs from the experience aroused by external stimuli, either in the form of other persons or objects. When he touches a toy, he gets the tactual sensation which means "toy"; when he touches his own foot, he gets the sensation in the hand which means "foot" and he gets, besides, the sensa-

tion of being touched on the foot by his hand.   His experience
is that of himself touching himself, an experience which is
different from his touching something external or something
"not-self."   The child is coming to realize that he is an individual.

All experience is the experience of some subject.   Conscious
states belong together in a unique way giving a unity to the
mind.   Your experience is experienced by you as yours; my
experience is experienced by me as mine.   Experience is for
each individual a unitary affair in which the past, the present,
and even the future are felt to hang together in an intimate
personal way.   Mind belongs to a self which is aware of the
unique character of its individual experience.   Perceptions,
emotions, thoughts, and actions belong to the mental life of
somebody.

It is difficult to state just what consciousness is because it is
intangible, but perhaps it will suffice to say that consciousness
is what you know as awareness or as your experience.   The ultimate nature of matter or mind is still a mystery.   All of us
think, but who knows what thoughts are, or just how thinking
is done?   A two-year-old child is extremely animistic (attributing life to inanimate objects).   When hot oatmeal is poured
on the man in the bottom of her dish, she sets up a howl; she
feeds her cereal to the Rastus man on the carton; she lays her
doll down tenderly for her nap.   She could not explain the
animistic tendency in her thinking.   So though we are conscious, we are at a loss to tell what consciousness is, except to
say, "we are conscious."

It is difficult to state what the mind is beyond the certainty
that consciousness is experience.   Our ignorance upon this
metaphysical question is no excuse for denying the existence
of mind, as is done by such a writer as Dorsey who asserts:
"There is no such thing as mind.   Every psychologist for
6000 years has written or talked on 'mind' and none of them

agree as to what it is. So let us discard the term as being meaningless." The mind, therefore, has been cast overboard by some psychologists to join the soul.

C. Behavior. About the beginning of the twentieth century a movement was inaugurated by a number of psychologists to ignore the mind and to emphasize, instead, the study of behavior. These psychologists had become convinced that the study of the intangible realm of consciousness was an impractical pursuit. The progress of research into animal behavior revealed the possibility of developing psychology without resort to "mind." Animals could not give verbal reports on their "mental states." Investigators, accordingly, concentrated upon the observation and description of animal behavior. Animal psychology succeeded so well without referring to "mind" that it commended the same approach to human psychology. Psychology has, consequently, for some psychologists, turned its attention entirely to the description of behavior, and no longer deals with some mysterious entity called "Soul" or "Mind" or "Consciousness" but, instead, observes the ways in which the human animal reacts to the situations of its environment. Thus as a natural science, psychology aims to keep as strictly to the natural-history point of view as do physiology and biology.

In order to establish itself among the sciences, psychology has made a conscious effort to divorce itself from the contaminating influence of those speculative philosophers who for so many centuries stunted its growth. Modern psychology, however, has committed a tragic error in trying so insistently to separate itself from philosophy.[1] The revolt has had its wholesome effects in stimulating the development of experimental psychology, but scientific psychology must not

---

[1]Philosophy is concerned with the ultimate nature of things. A part of its program is the formulation of basic principles for a unified interpretation of the universe.

forget that the basis of any science depends upon a sane philosophical background. The psychologist must remember that he is not simply dealing with facts, but that he is interpreting them in accordance with certain assumed principles. Since psychology, like every other science, must begin with certain premises, it will do well to ground itself in philosophy in order that its development may be initiated in the right direction.

One philosophical point of view which will guide us in summarizing the present discussion is the synoptic principle: that any study should have regard for all the phenomena under its survey if it is not to be one-sided and inaccurate in its conclusions. From this standpoint, psychology must respect the fact of mind as well as the fact of behavior.

In our study of the human being, we shall endeavor to satisfy the synoptic ideal, by including the various aspects of human experience without regard for any single limited point of view. We shall be interested in the world of subjective facts, which we call the mental life, as well as in the world of objective facts, which we designate as behavior.[1]

---

[1]Reading and experimental projects for each chapter will be found in supplementary sections at the end of the book. The student is urged to consult these sections constantly for additional material.

PART II
ORIENTATION

The student of psychology must get his bearings with respect to what is being done at present in this branch of science before he is ready to proceed to the mastery of the fundamental concepts involved in an elementary course. Such a preparation is intended as an *Orientation*. Chapter II, *The Science of Psychology*, as a résumé of experimental methods now in use for testing various aspects of the human being, is a demonstration of the practical value of the work being done by psychologists. The various so-called schools of psychology present a confusing chaos of data unless it is clearly realized that this variety is the result of different *Points of View*. Acquaintance with the problems and outlooks in present-day psychology will help us to assimilate the exposition of fundamentals presented in the main portion of the book.

CHAPTER II

THE SCIENCE OF PSYCHOLOGY

WITH the historical background in mind, the present status of psychology may be duly appreciated. In order to establish itself as a science, divorced, on the one hand, from speculative philosophy, and on the other, from practical quackery, psychology has found it necessary to emphasize its scientific aspects. Psychology has entered the laboratory where experiments have been conducted in accordance with the demands of science, and psychology feels today that it is worthy of being classed among the sciences.[1]

I. SCIENCE IN GENERAL

There are two important characteristics of any science—the scientific spirit and the scientific method. Psychology acknowledges their validity, and has endeavored to develop a technique that scrupulously recognizes those characteristics in its practice.

A. The Scientific Spirit. The scientific spirit is one of open-minded inquiry. A scientist does not set out to find evidence that will support a dogma he has set his heart on proving. His attitude is objective. He is ready to take the facts as they come, reserving his conclusions until all the data are in. He has no pet theories for the sake of which he is anxious to overlook contradictory evidence. He is willing to discard an hypothesis when experiment indicates its inadequacies. Charles Darwin exemplified the scientific spirit in

---

[1]See H. P. Weld: *Psychology as Science.* 1928; also C. E. Ayres: *Science, the False Messiah.* 1927.

his remark that whenever he discovered a fact which ran
counter to his opinion or belief at the time, he made a specially
careful note of it, because, as he said, we are so prone to dismiss
unwelcome facts from our minds. The scientist enters an experiment with the intention of taking it seriously. He is not
willing to toy with facts. He is cautious in avoiding premature
conclusions. The scientific spirit has been defined as "an
intelligent and disciplined Missourianism"—that is, the
scientist is not going to believe a thing is so until the evidence
is overwhelmingly in favor of its being so. Science, wherever
it has flourished, has been characterized by a cautious, un-
biased, curious search for the facts.

B. The Scientific Method. The scientific method involves three essential steps: first, the formulation of an hypothesis; second, the testing of that hypothesis by experiment,
through the gathering and classification of data; third, the
revision of the initial hypothesis in the light of experimental
findings.

There has been a persistent effort on the part of scientists
to refuse to recognize psychology as a science, because it deals
with the intangible stuff of consciousness which cannot be
studied with the same accuracy as objective phenomena. A
scholar describes his experience in looking for Einstein's mas-
terpiece on relativity: "Recently I went to one of the biggest
scientific bookstores in New York, and asked for one of Einstein's books. The clerk said that they didn't keep it in their
general scientific department. When I asked him why, he
explained that they didn't consider Einstein sufficiently scientific, and that I would find his books in their psychological
department." The story is a simple illustration of the widespread feeling that psychology is merely a pseudo-science because it deals with the mysterious forces of the mind. One
consequence of this hostile attitude has been the shift to
behaviorism—to the study of behavior as objective material

for observation and description. An alternative solution, however, is ready at hand in the work of Karl Pearson. Pearson laid down the dictum that "the unity of all science consists alone in its method, not in its material."[1] If we accept Pearson's conception of science, then psychology can qualify as a science by applying the scientific method either to the study of conscious states or to the study of explicit behavior. We shall observe how psychology has succeeded in its application of the scientific method.

II. EXPERIMENTAL PSYCHOLOGY

The recent development of psychology has been due to its emphasis on experiment. Psychology has resorted to the laboratory where phenomena can be observed under control. Since Wundt established his laboratory at Leipzig in 1879 and James set up his "brass instrument" investigations at Harvard, a host of laboratories have been equipped, where psychology is studied on an experimental basis. Experiments are rigidly controlled, varied, and repeated.

Control in experiment means the isolation of that factor in a situation which is of primary interest to the investigator. A common form of control is attained by the division of the subjects into two groups. Identical conditions must be maintained for both groups except for the one factor which is being isolated. Suppose you want to ascertain the effect of a prospective bonus upon the efficiency of your employees. Group I will work without the incentive of a bonus. This group is known as the "control." Group II will operate under conditions identical with those to which Group I is subject, except for the peculiar inducement of the bonus. A perfect control would involve an identical amount of sleep, the same diet, equally happy home conditions, and the like. Unless these factors remain constant, the investigator cannot tell whether

---

[1] Karl Pearson: *The Grammar of Science* (3rd ed.), Part I, p. 12. 1911.

superior performance is due to the promised bonus, or perhaps to happier home conditions. Such a perfect control in most experiments can only be approximated, but for practical purposes it is sufficient to control the significant factors.

Control in psychological experiments demands that the instructions to the observer be definitely the same in all cases, and that, wherever possible, the stimulus be presented without the presence of the experimenter, since a smile or a variation in movement on his part may so affect the observer as to confuse the results.

The perfection of instruments has done much to improve the factor of control. Instruments have been devised for the mechanical presentation of stimuli, and for the mechanical recording of reactions which make accurate measurements possible. In addition, trained observers, who are expert in reporting their experiences, are used. A given experiment is described in great detail so that the investigation may be carried out under identical conditions and the results checked with precision. The grave danger in the experimental method, as it is applied not only in psychology but in every science, lies, not in the gathering of the data, but in the interpretations of the evidence. This opportunity for error, as I have said, is not peculiar to psychology, but is found in any field where diagnosis is involved.

The scientific method can be used in psychology. The most convincing evidence may be found in a description of certain outstanding experiments.

A. The Conditioned Response. The first experiment we shall describe is the investigation of the conditioned salivary reflex by the famous Russian scientist, Pavlov.[1] We are all acquainted with the fact that our "mouths water" when we see or smell delicious food, especially if we are suffering from the pangs of hunger. The watering of the mouth is the popular

---

[1] I. P. Pavlov: *Lectures on Conditioned Reflexes.* 1928.

expression to describe the secretion of saliva by the salivary gland which takes place automatically (reflex) upon the presentation of food.   Pavlov wanted to ascertain whether certain stimuli which had become associated with food by repeated experience would likewise cause the flow of saliva.   This was his hypothesis.   The next step was to put the question to the test of experiment.

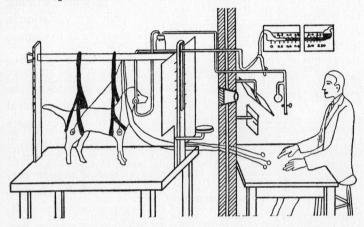

Pavlov conducted his investigation about 1900 under rigorously scientific conditions.   The dog to be studied was placed in a sound-proof room.[1]   The experimenter made his observations through peepholes, presented the stimuli by means of controls located outside the room, and employed apparatus to record mechanically the time and amount of salivary secretion. The salivary flow was usually released by feeding the dog powdered meat.   The salivary response is an unlearned or unconditioned response since no past experience is required for the secretion to occur.   Food is spoken of as the adequate stimulus, since it is capable of evoking the response upon the initial presentation.   Food "just naturally" made the dog's

[1]Diagram from Ivan Pavlov: *op. cit.*, p. 271.   By permission of Oxford University Press.

mouth water. Next Pavlov rang a bell to find out whether the sound of the bell would cause the flow of saliva. No saliva appeared. The bell is referred to as an inadequate stimulus. Next the bell was rung every time the meat was offered to the dog and this procedure was repeated a number of times. Then the bell was rung without the presentation of food, and the saliva flowed. The bell, an inadequate stimulus, had become adequate by association with the adequate stimulus, the food, and the flow of saliva in response to the bell was called a conditioned reflex. Similarly, in our own experience, we find that the sound of the noon whistle starts the secretion of saliva because noontime through long experience has acquired the meaning "meal-time."

Pavlov's experiments confirmed his hypothesis, but unfortunately the conditioned reflex was immediately hailed as the explanation for all behavior, animal and human, whether simple or complex. "Who would have thought that the salivation of one dog in Petrograd would have inspired the . . . comprehensive . . . assurance that there is nothing in all this mental mystery to explain, except a simply conditioned reflex? It isn't men, so much as psychologists, who are fearfully and wonderfully made."[1] It would be more accurate for psychologists to use the term "response" rather than "reflex," and to restrict the principle of conditioning only to the explanation of the fact that a response to one situation may be conditioned or attached to a new situation by association. The complexities of association still remain to be accounted for, and they should not be neglected in an adequate explanation of behavior. There is no fault to find with Pavlov's experiment—the errors have crept into the interpretation of his findings and their application to various modes of behavior.

Pavlov's studies of the conditioned reflex in animals furnished Watson with the idea that many of the activities of the

[1]Joseph Jastrow in the *Forum*, November, 1927.

human infant which had been attributed to instinct (native equipment) were really conditioned responses. To test his hypothesis, Watson studied the emotional reactions in a boy, Albert, who was eleven months old.[1]   Experiment showed that a white rat, a rabbit, a dog, a monkey, and burning newspaper

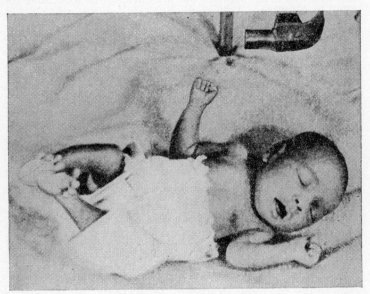

PICTURE OF INFANT IN FEAR[2]

did not evoke fear reactions.   Knowing that a loud noise was an adequate stimulus for arousing fear, Watson struck a steel bar just behind his victim.   The child started violently, his breathing was checked, and his arms were raised in a characteristic manner.   On the second stimulation the same thing occurred, and in addition his lips began to pucker and tremble. On the third stimulation the child broke into a sudden crying fit.   Albert was now ready for the conditioning process.

[1]J. B. Watson and R. Rayner: "Conditioned Emotional Reactions," *Journal of Experimental Psychology*, 1920, 31, 1–14.

[2]Reproduced by permission of J. B. Watson and W. W. Norton and Company.

A white rat was presented to Albert. He reached for it without any sign of fear. Just as his hand touched the animal, the bar was struck immediately behind his head. The joint presentation of the two stimuli, rat and noise, was repeated several times and, a week later, several more times, until Albert began to whimper. Finally, to abbreviate the account of the experiment, the presentation of the rat without the noise was sufficient to evoke crying and other reactions indicative of fear. Thus, through association of an inadequate stimulus with an adequate stimulus, a fear response had been conditioned in Albert.[1] Watson was satisfied that he had confirmed experimentally the principle of the conditioned response advanced by Pavlov. The study of Albert was carried on under laboratory conditions of strict control and with the same scientific spirit that pervades any objective investigation among the physical sciences. Watson's studies have thrown considerable light on child training.

B. Measuring. Psychology has endeavored to approximate the exactness of the physical sciences by measuring the variables with which it deals. This attempt at quantitative precision is accompanied by an interest in descriptive or qualitative delineations. In many branches of psychology, especially those studying the more esoteric forces of the personality, the qualitative approach predominates. If, for example, another person's automobile collided with yours, it would be important to measure the time expiring before you could become aware of your predicament, and to determine the magnitude of the changes in your circulatory system; in addition, it would be of concern to ascertain the quality of the emotion evoked in you, and the nature of the thoughts that might be running through your mind.

Because of the influence of the allied sciences, psychologists,

---

[1] J. B. Watson: *The Psychological Care of Infant and Child*, p. 26.

perhaps, have been too hasty in their zeal for subjecting their data to quantitative measurement or numerical relationships. This overemphasis upon measurement was most marked in the middle and last half of the nineteenth century when the psychophysical method of testing was gaining popularity. At this time the measuring devices received more attention than the subjects of the experiments; and variables were measured before they were clearly defined.

1. Measurement of Perceptual Capacities. The problem of measuring the sensitivity of the organism to external stimuli excited the interest of the psychologists in the middle of the nineteenth century. E. H. Weber's name is associated with this attempt to employ experimental methods in psychology. His efforts resulted in the psychophysical method which studies the effect of physical stimuli upon an organism. Weber investigated sensory perception to determine the smallest noticeable difference between two impressions, such as impressions of sight, hearing, and touch. He discovered that in lifting weights with the hands, a difference of one ounce could be discerned if a thirty-ounce weight was used as a standard; that is, a twenty-nine and a thirty-one ounce weight could be respectively perceived as lighter and heavier than the standard. Weber found that the just noticeable difference (j.n.d.) was not a constant unit and that, as the stimulus increased in magnitude, a greater increment was required to produce an awareness of difference. Noticing that the j.n.d. could be expressed as a proportion of the magnitude of the standard stimulus, he formulated a principle known as "Weber's Law," a satisfactory explanation of which is still forthcoming. He explained that the j.n.d. is not an absolute unit unrelated to the stimulus, and that the magnitude of increase in the stimulus necessary to bring about an awareness of a difference bears a constant relationship with the standard stimulus. Fechner modified Weber's Law by describing the relationship as one between the sensory processes and the magnitude of the stimulus, in which the stimulus must be increased logarithmically, and not arithmetically, to produce a series of j.n.d.'s. Since experimental data do not comply exactly with the demands of the Weber-Fechner law, many psychologists now consider the law to be merely a generalization of historical interest.[1] For our purposes it is sufficient to know that if an observer is subjected to an intense stimulus, more of an increment must be added to produce an appreciation of a difference than if he were attending to a weak stimulus. This generalization may be applied, in a sense, to everyday life. If all the money you possessed were ten cents you would notice the loss of a penny, but if you were affluent to the extent of ten dollars, this loss might be overlooked.

Psychophysical methods are frequently used for the measurement of perceptual capacities. Much confusion has resulted from the countless variations of, and numerous names given to, psychophysical methods. However, there are three fundamental methods, and these will be explained briefly. All the methods involve a standard and a comparison stimulus. The comparison stimulus is judged in terms of the standard. The three methods involve different presentations of the variable stimulus.

a. The Method of Limits. In the Method of Limits, the variable or comparison stimulus is set by the experimenter so that it is noticeably different in magnitude from the standard. Let us say that the experiment involves the judgment of the saturation (nearness to black) of one gray as compared with another. A revolving disc is used with the standard gray in the middle and the variable outside.

The saturation of the variable can be regulated by varying

---

[1] For a modern interpretation of this law, see H. Hoagland: "The Weber-Fechner Law and the All-or-none Theory," *Journal of General Psychology,* 1930, 3, 351–373.

the proportion of black and white; the two colors produce an impression of gray when the disc is rotated.

Let us start with the variable considerably more saturated (darker) than the standard gray. The variable is gradually

MAXWELL DISC ROTATOR

(Reproduced by courtesy of the Marietta Apparatus Company.)

rendered less and less saturated by increasing the proportion of the white to the black, until a point is reached, before arriving at the standard gray, where the variable is judged to be equal in saturation to the standard.

The next step is to begin with the variable equal to the standard, and gradually to increase the saturation of the variable, by increasing the proportion of the black to the white, until the variable becomes just saturated enough to be distinguishable from the standard.

Steps I and II are repeated until a number of measurements are obtained for each step. The average for step I is com-

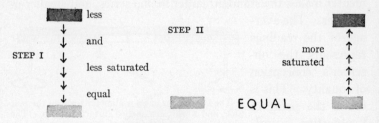

puted and then the average for step II. The average of these two averages is the j.n.d. (or difference limen) between the standard saturation and the greater saturation, that is, between the standard gray and a darker gray.

A similar procedure will establish the j.n.d. between the standard saturation and less saturation, that is, between the standard gray and a lighter gray.

The two j.n.d.'s thus determined represent the amount of variation there must be in saturation from the standard for the observer to appreciate a distinction between the standard and the variable with respect to saturation; or, in other words, the j.n.d.'s represent how much lighter or darker the gray of the variable must become to be distinguishable from the gray of the standard.

b. *The Method of Average Error.* In the Method of Average Error the stimuli are unequal, and the subject is asked to alter the variable stimulus in some way or another until he believes the two stimuli are the same. An appreciation of visual extents is measured in this way. The observer is asked to regulate one side of the Galton Bar so that the white space on that side approximates the length of the white space on the other side, which is the standard. When he judges the variable to be identical to the space of the standard, he so states, and the recorder takes his reading from the scale. The subject is not informed of the results until the test is over. The right and left sides are used alternately as standards; and the experimenter makes the standard larger in one series, and smaller in another. The average of the readings represents the observer's conception of equality. This is called the point of "subjective equality." The average amount by which the observer misses the

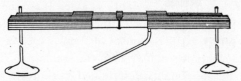

The Galton bar has a millimeter scale on the rear side, and a white enamelled surface in front. The observer regulates the size of the white surface on one side by adjusting a black metal covering with the aid of a revolving rod. (Reproduced by courtesy of the Marietta Apparatus Company.)

right measurement indicates his ability or lack of ability to judge visual extents with precision.

c. The Method of Constant Stimuli. This method uses a series of comparison stimuli, equal distances apart with respect to some characteristic. If we wish to determine the sensitivity of an observer to lifted weights, we use this method. In a lifted weights experiment, six weights are usually prepared, say, of 108, 104, 100, 96, 92, and 88 grams. The standard is presented first. The standard should be a little more than the average weight of the comparison stimuli, if a nearly equal number of "greater" and "less" judgments are to be obtained, since observers tend to depreciate the value of the first stimulus presented. In our case, therefore, a standard weight of 100 is used.

The observer lifts the standard weight and then the comparison weight. He judges whether the comparison weight seems greater, equal, or less in weight in relation to the standard. The comparison stimuli are presented in haphazard order to obviate the influence that expectation might exert on the observer's judgments. The experiment is conducted until the subject has compared each weight of the series with the standard 50 or 100 times.

The point on the scale of the comparison stimuli at which the observer gives responses of "greater" 50% of the time is the j.n.d. for weights heavier than the standard, while the point on the scale of the comparison stimuli at which the observer gives responses of "less" 50% of the time is the j.n.d. for weights lighter than the standard. The respective j.n.d.'s may be roughly determined by plotting the distribution of the responses on a graph with the frequency of judgments in per cents on the ordinate and the weights of the comparison stimuli on the abscissa.[1] For purposes of computation, the experimenter sometimes divides the "equal" responses, distributing half of them to the "greater" category and half of them to the "less" category.

2. Measurements of Motor Abilities. Tests of Motor Abilities have become popularized by the emphasis of present-day schools upon athletic games requiring physical agility and skill, and by the recognition of the value of these tests in industry. The interest in this type of testing may also be due to the comparative simplicity of the tests and apparatus, and the definiteness of the results. In personality tests, and in tests of the higher mental processes, psychologists experience difficulty not only in obtaining results that are valid and reliable, but also in accurately defining that characteristic which is measured. Motor Tests measure relatively elementary and homogeneous processes that can be isolated and controlled with some degree of success. The tests measure rapidity and accuracy of movement and the coördination of perceptual processes. Some of these tests are:

a. Tapping Tests. The Tapping Test measures the rapidity

---

[1] For a more detailed description of the computations, see E. G. Boring, H. S. Langfeld, and H. P. Weld: *Psychology*, pp. 55–56. 1935.

with which a person can tap on a hard surface. In the laboratory a stylus (a pencil-shaped instrument with a metal end) is held in the hand and a metal surface is tapped. The two pieces of apparatus are wired in such a way that when the stylus touches the steel plate a contact is made that turns an electric counter.

TAPPING TEST

(Reproduced by courtesy of the Marietta Apparatus Company.)

This test can be performed with a blunt pencil and a piece of heavy paper. In this case the test should be of short duration, say a few seconds, to avoid the placing of dots over one another.

Certain types of Tapping Tests are effective in measuring muscular control and eye coördination as well as speed. The Three-Hole Test is an example of this. Three holes are located in a triangular position on a board tipped at a 45° angle from the horizontal. The subject is told to place accurately and quickly a stylus in the holes in a fixed order until a certain time has expired. Some Three-Hole Tests have an electrified surface around the holes so that the errors can be recorded on an electric counter. This test can be duplicated with a fair degree of success by drawing squares or circles on a piece of paper and instructing the subject to place a pencil dot in the center of each figure. The test can be made complicated by distributing the figures over the paper in haphazard manner, or varying their sizes.

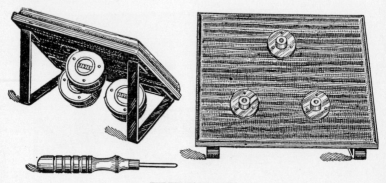

THREE-HOLE TEST
(Reproduced by courtesy of the C. H. Stoelting Company.)

Tests closely related to those just mentioned have been devised to determine a person's skill in aiming at objects. Considerable variability from person to person will be shown in these measuring devices, because in many individuals who take the tests past experience plays a more important part than it does in the Three-Hole Test. Examples of this kind of test would be experiments involving the throwing of rings on a peg or post, the hitting of targets with darts, or the throwing of balls into holes.

b. Steadiness Tests measure the voluntary control of the tremors of the hand and arm. In the Nine-Hole Test, the subject is first instructed to place a stylus into the largest hole. When he has done so, the experimenter says "go" and the subject attempts to keep the stylus in the hole for fifteen seconds without touching the rim. This procedure is repeated with the other holes, care being taken that the subject does not rest his arm or hand on any support.   When the stylus touches a rim a contact is made and the electric counter records the error.   This test has been used successfully as an aid in select-

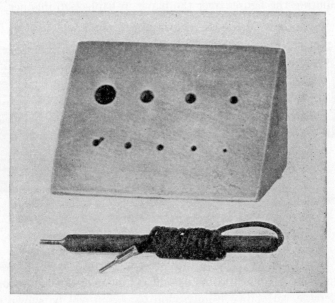

STEADINESS TEST
(Reproduced by courtesy of the Marietta Apparatus Company.)

ing men for industries where manual dexterity is involved, as in the work of watch assemblers and repairers, type setters, and engravers.

Tracing Tests, requiring the subject to trace a pointed instrument, such as a pencil or stylus, along a very narrow area, measure steadiness and motor coördination.   If the tracing board illustrated below is used, the subject is told to insert the stylus in the wide end of the groove and pull it toward himself without touching the sides.   The subject may continue along the groove until he strikes one of the sides, or he may be instructed to draw the stylus from one end to the other. In the former case the points on the scale where the contacts occur are recorded, and an average is taken of several trials. In the latter procedure, the total number of contacts is used as an indication of the subject's ability to perform the test.

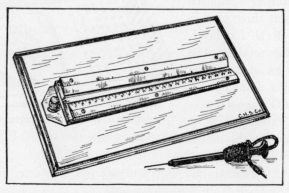

TRACING BOARD
(Reproduced by courtesy of the C. H. Stoelting Company.)

The reader may set up his own Steadiness Test by drawing diagrams similar to the one given below. Steadiness will be measured in terms of the total time consumed in completing the test, and the number of times the subject touches or goes beyond the guiding lines. Eye-hand coördination is involved.

c. Dexterity Tests. Johnson O'Connor has devised two tests for measuring finger and hand dexterity. The O'Connor Finger Dexterity Test consists of a board on which 100 holes have been drilled at equal spaces apart and a tray containing slightly over 300 pins. The subject is required to insert three pins in each of the 100 holes, and the total time is taken as an indication of finger dexterity.

The O'Connor Twee-zer Dexterity Test is similar to the finger test with the excep-tions that tweezers are used and one pin is inserted in each hole.

O'CONNOR FINGER DEXTERITY TEST

(Reproduced by courtesy of the C. H. Stoelting Company.)

d. Other Tests. The pursuitmeter, as built by the Marietta Apparatus Company, is very effective in measuring eye-hand coördination in a rapidly changing situation. The instrument has the appearance of a table gramophone with a rotating metal disc about 12 inches in diameter on top. On the surface of this disc, and flush with it, is a smaller circle somewhat off center that rotates at a speed at variance with the disc that surrounds it. On the surface of this disc, and also off center, is a black disc one-half inch in diameter that is the only portion of the entire surface that is a non-conductor of electricity. The sub-ject attempts to keep the stylus on the black spot, and when he fails to do so, an electric counter indicates his errors.

Another device indicates the total time off and on the spot. This little point follows such a complicated pattern that it is difficult to anticipate its movements.

The author has devised a simple test that roughly measures (1) the ability to retain a visual impression after the eyes have been closed and (2) the ability to appreciate distance without the aid of the eyes. (See page 37.) Place the point of your pencil in the circle and look over the situation. Keep your non-writing hand at your side. Without moving the pencil, plan the route that you are going to trace, proceeding vertically

EPICYCLOID PURSUITMETER
(Reproduced by courtesy of the Marietta Apparatus Company.)

from the circle to x, turning to the right and following the aisle all the way around until you return to x, and then heading directly for the circle. Close your eyes when you are ready and trace the above route as accurately as you can. The task is more difficult than it seems at first notice. Study your performance and then repeat the experiment with a colored pencil to see if you can improve your accuracy.

A few concluding remarks may be made in regard to tests of motor abilities. No one test is of paramount importance because each test measures only a small part of the motor system. To determine a person's motor capacities, a battery of tests must be employed, the selection of the individual tests being dependent upon the purpose of the study. Chamberlin, by experimentation and elimination, found that in the selection of finishers in an electrotype company, the Nine-Hole Steadiness Test, the Three-Hole Motor Coördination Test, and the

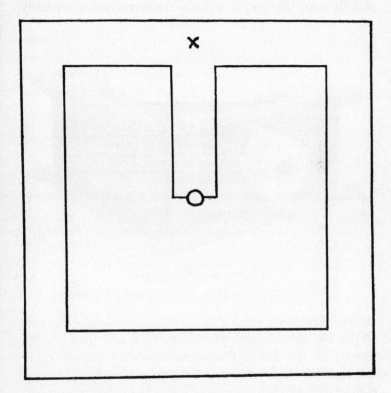

Pursuitmeter Test give results upon which, when other data as to the subject's observational ability and mental alertness are considered, a reliable judgment can be made as to the likelihood of the applicant's success on the job. Of course, the test must be weighted properly, that is, in the statistical treatment some tests are recognized as more influential than others in the determination of the rating of the subject.

3. *Measurement of Perceptual-Motor Ability: Reaction Time.* No absolute distinction can be drawn between Perceptual, Motor, or Perceptual-Motor Tests since the exercise of motor capacities ordinarily involves the cues supplied by the various sense organs. The subject sees the groove through which he pushes a stylus or the holes in which he attempts to insert pins. Nevertheless, we are following the usual classification of such tests as a convenient one. The Reaction Time Test is commonly considered as a measure of the ability to coördinate the perception of a stimulus with a rapid response to it.

It is a matter of common knowledge that some people respond quickly to stimuli, whereas other people, like the proverbial Englishman responding to a joke, need plenty of time. Repartee has been defined as the knack of saying instantly what you think of tomorrow. Many of us are so slow that our friends never suspect that we are clever.

The scientific study of reaction time grew out of a problem in astronomical observation. At the Greenwich observatory in 1796 an assistant named Kinnebrook differed 8/10 of a second from the royal astronomer, Maskelyne, in his record of the stellar transits. Though Kinnebrook had been warned to improve his accuracy, his "error" persisted, and so Maskelyne, taking his own times as the norm, decided to dismiss Kinnebrook from the observatory. In 1816 the German astronomer Bessel, after reading about Kinnebrook's case, began to wonder whether trained observers would agree in their astronomical records. He conducted experiments at Königsberg which definitely indicated the fact of individual differences, a fact which came to be known as the personal equation. Wherever subjective measurements are made the results must be corrected in the light of possible variations among the individuals who are doing the measuring. Bessel's studies stimulated considerable interest in the personal equation, and further investigations were made with which we need not concern ourselves here.

In 1840 Wheatstone constructed a chronoscope, an instrument for measuring and recording time. The chronoscope has since been perfected so that the investigator can determine the speed of reaction down to one sigma (1/1000 of a second). In a typical experiment in reaction time the observer presses a finger key when he perceives the stimulus. The stimulus, the key, and the chronoscope are connected electrically so that the time is accurately recorded. Experiments have indicated a wider variation in speed of reaction than had been anticipated.

Not long ago an express train left the rails near Mülheim in Baden and fourteen persons were killed. The cause of the accident was the speed with which the train passed over a dangerous structure. The engine-driver had gone to sleep and had, therefore, passed signals without stopping or checking the speed of the train. There was no doubt about the man's guilt. But according to the law in Baden, it was the duty of the conductor likewise to give heed to the signals. When he observed that the driver had passed them without making the slightest alteration in the speed of the train, it was his duty to set the emergency brake. If he had done this at a suitably short interval after the stop signal was passed, the train might still have been saved.

The speed of the train was 110 kilometers (about 68 miles) per hour, and twenty-two seconds were required to cover the distance between the signal at the entrance to this stretch of the road and the point of danger. The government authorities in charge of the case put the following questions to a well-known psychologist, Professor Marbe:

Did the twenty-two seconds give to the conductor sufficient time:
1. To see that the engine-driver was negligent and did not set the brake;

2. To perceive the danger to the train;
3. To remember his duty to take action;
4. To decide to set the emergency brake;
5. To carry out his decision?

Obviously the guilt or innocence of the conductor hung upon the answer to this query. Professor Marbe was able to demonstrate by exact experiment that the performance of these various mental operations required only four seconds at the utmost; consequently the man's guilt was established and he was duly sentenced.

Reaction time is a practical problem, as we have just observed in connection with the railroad accident. Taxi drivers are now tested for their speed of reaction, since taxicab companies prefer to spend their money on tests rather than on lawsuits over damaged property. A friend of mine is very slow in his motor reactions. He bought a car, and in the space of a year ran into so many obstacles that he decided it would be wiser to travel on foot in deference to the public safety, if not his own. When he was driving and a car suddenly darted out from a side street, he knew what to do but he always did it too late.

Another practical application of reaction time is found in athletics. If a man is slow, he should take up golf where he can take all the time he wants before hitting the ball. It would be an additional help if he has the sort of temperament that allows him to ignore what the golfers behind him are saying about him as they trail him around the course. Baseball, on the other hand, requires quick reactions. The batter has no time to deliberate when the pitcher delivers the ball. Babe Ruth is fast in his reaction time while Walter Hagen is not so rapid. Each man has specialized in the sport for which he is particularly qualified.

4. The Measurement of Affectivity. The term affectivity is used in a broad sense to include mental states, such as pleasantness and unpleasantness, joy and sorrow, elation and depression, and their emotional concomitants. There are all levels of affectivity from the mildest state of depression to the deepest feeling of despair. Even an isolated spot of color, a curved line, or a single tone may produce a mild affective state, although usually more complicated and meaningful patterns present themselves as stimuli for human reactions. There are two possible techniques for the study of affectivity: one is investigating an individual's subjective reactions to a stimulus situation in terms of his feelings, and the other is measuring emotional responses by the stimulus situation in terms of the physiological concomitants. The first method is called the Method of Impression, and the second, the Method of Expression.

a. Methods of Impression. The Method of Impression deals principally with one's preference for some objects over others.

(1) The Order of Merit Method. The Order of Merit Method requires the subject to rank a number of items according to his preference. If we were planning to produce an attractive box for a new breakfast cereal, we would have a number of boxes prepared with different designs and colors, and ask many home owners and housewives to choose the most attractive box, the second best, the third best, etc., down to the least attractive; then we would use the box design that had the highest average rating.

It is apparent that in this method, as in most other methods of Impression, we can only determine the relative standing of an item. With this technique it is not possible to determine the absolute extent of a person's likes or dislikes, because the results are simply in terms of preference relative to the series under consideration. We determine the preference for an item not by the degree of affectivity aroused by it in a subject, but by the number of instances that the item is given a high rating. *The Method of Choice,* in which the most preferred item is chosen and the others afterwards disregarded, the *Method of Use* in which the extent of the use of the object is taken as an index, and the *Method of Production*, in which the most preferred item is produced by the subject, are so similar to the Order of Merit Method that separate treatment is unwarranted. In seeking to determine the most pleasing variation of a form or figure, we might ask a number of people to produce their own conceptions on a piece of paper. This would be an example of the Method of Production.

(2) *The Method of Paired Comparison*. In the Method of Paired Comparison each item is compared with every other, and the observer is instructed to choose one of two items with respect to some characteristic. We might use this method to advantage in selecting the most attractive automobile from six models. We would place car no. 1 alongside of car no. 2, then, after judgment was made, place it alongside of nos. 3, 4, 5, and 6. Car no. 2 would be placed alongside of cars no. 3, 4, 5, and 6; car no. 2 was judged in terms of car no. 1 in the first series.

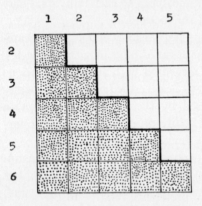

The number of judgments necessary is shown by the shaded area of the graph on the left. It may be determined mathematically by applying the formula $\frac{n(n-1)}{2}$, where n represents the number of items. In our case the formula is:

$$\frac{6(6-1)}{2} \text{ or } \frac{6 \times 5}{2} = 15$$

If the objects being judged are not excessively heavy or bulky, it is advisable to present the pairs in haphazard sequence. The object chosen as the best the greatest number of times will obviously be considered the most preferred.

(*3*) *The Method of Single Stimuli.*   In the Method of Single Stimuli the subject attends to one stimulus only, and either states his opinion in his own words or checks one of a series of categorical descriptions.   The categories may be:

+3.   Exceptionally pleasant
+2.   Moderately pleasant
+1.   Slightly pleasant
0.   Neutral
—1.   Slightly unpleasant
—2.   Moderately unpleasant
—3.   Exceptionally unpleasant

This technique could be employed to advantage in ascertaining the reactions of a sample group of people to various foods, odors, or musical chords.   This method is the only one that gives results in terms of an absolute unit.   In all the other methods, judgments are made relative to the other objects in the group, but in the Method of Single Stimuli, reference is made directly to inner states of feeling.   That the categories may convey slightly different meanings to each individual may be considered a weakness of the method.

b. Methods of Expression.   Expression connotes the manifestation of affectivity in the form of physiological activities. These bodily responses are measured with the aid of various instruments, some of which will be described presently.   Many of these instruments are used by the medical profession to determine whether or not a bodily process is functioning normally, and to what extent it deviates from the normal.

(*1*) *Pneumograph.*   The pneumograph is used to measure respiratory or breathing movements.   It consists of a rubber tube about an inch in diameter with a loose spring inside. To one side of the tube is fastened a small rubber tube that leads to a recording tambour.

The pneumograph is fastened to the chest or abdomen of the subject by means of a chain that goes around his back.

When the subject inhales, the space inside of the pneumograph is increased, causing a vacuum which pulls the rubber on the

recording tambour inward, moving the registering needle or stylus accordingly. A tambour is a rimmed or pan-shaped disc with a thin rubber covering over the open end. A record-

RECORDING TAMBOUR

(Reproduced by courtesy of the C. H. Stoelting Company.)

ing stylus is so attached to the center of this rubber sheet that one point of it can record pressure variations on the smoked drum of a kymograph.

A kymograph is a motor-driven cylinder of about six inches in diameter and six inches in height, on which smoked paper is placed. When the stylus touches this paper it produces a white line. Waxed paper, together with an electrically warmed stylus, constitutes a recent improvement in the technique.

(2) *Plethysmograph.* The plethysmograph is designed to measure the displacement of a particular part of the body submerged in liquid. The forearm or hand, in ordinary practice, is inserted in the chamber which is

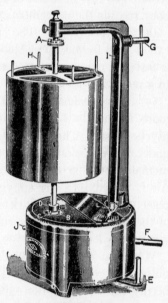

KYMOGRAPH

(Reproduced by courtesy of the C. H. Stoelting Company.)

connected with the tambour that records the variations of displacement due to changes in blood volume. Care must be taken to exclude irrelevant variables, such as alterations of room temperature and changes in the extent to which the arm or hand is submerged.

(3) *Automatograph.* The automatograph records involuntary movements of the body. There are various types of instruments adapted for different parts of the body. The automatograph for the arm consists of a flat wooden surface suspended from the ceiling in such a way that movements in all horizontal positions are possible. A pencil attached to the bottom of the board records the movements on a piece of paper. For finger and hand movements, the subject is instructed to rest his hand or finger on a rubber bulb. A tambour records the movements by pneumatic transmission.

(4) *Sphygmograph.* The sphygmograph records the form, extent, and frequency of blood pulsations. A receiving drum is fastened over an artery and the variations are transmitted to a recording device.

(5) *Sphygmomanometer.* The sphygmomanometer is used more frequently by physicians and physiologists than by psychologists. The cuff-sphygmometer (see the photograph under the discussion of Lie Detection, page 46), a type of sphygmomanometer, is wound around the arm above the elbow. Air is forced into the sphygmometer until wrist pulsations cease. Blood pressure is determined by air-pressure readings of the sphygmometer at various stages of the recovery of the wrist pulsations.

When a person lies, changes occur in his blood pressure, his pulse, his breathing, and his glandular secretions which may betray his deceit to the expert examiner. Leonarde Keeler tested 500 convicts at the Joliet Penitentiary in Illinois, in 1929, and discovered that blood-pressure and respiration changes during deception were as distinguishable in the hardened criminal as in the virtuous citizen. Even two old-time "poker-face" card sharks were readily detected.

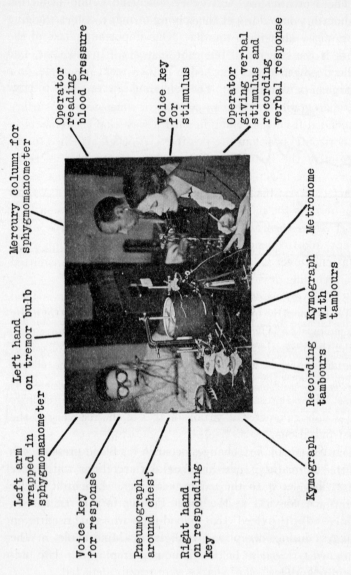

Operator
reading
blood pressure

Voice key
for
stimulus

Operator
giving verbal
stimulus and
recording
verbal response

Mercury column for
sphygmomanometer

Left hand
on tremor bulb

Left arm
wrapped in
sphygmomanometer

Voice key
for response

Pneumograph
around chest

Right hand
on responding
key

Kymograph

Recording
tambours

Kymograph
with
tambours

Metronome

The Lie Detector

The Northwestern University Scientific Crime Detection Laboratory has aided in the solving of many crimes, ranging from petty larceny to murder.   One important phase of the work is the clearing of innocent suspects.   In one case, two collection agents were arrested in Black Creek, Wisconsin, on a charge of bank robbery.   The defending lawyer asked to have

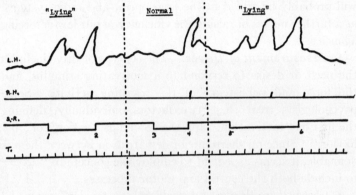

SAMPLE RECORD OF LIE DETECTION

Two features of this record which reveal efforts to conceal guilt are the tremors of the left hand (L. H., the top line) and the delay of the verbal response (S–R the line next to the bottom).   On the S–R line (1) denotes the presentation of the stimulus and (2) the response; (3) the stimulus, (4) the response; (5) the stimulus and (6) the response.   Time is indicated on the bottom line (T).   Note that the 1–2 interval and the 5–6 interval are longer than the 3–4 interval. When the stimulus word with "guilty" connections is presented, the subject gets nervous; involuntary movements of the hand betray his tension and the longer reaction time is a "give-away" of an attempt to elude detection by a resort to a misleading response.   Further analysis of such a record, including the pressure of a key by the right hand (R. H., the next to the top line), would disclose other significant features we need not mention here.

them examined on the "lie detector."   Both suspects submitted to the polygraph examination and a report to the effect that the men were innocent was supplemented by a demonstration before the judge, but he saw fit to rule out the evidence.   On the third day, two robbers who confessed to the Black Creek robbery were caught in Minneapolis.   When they were brought before the bank employees, they were definitely identified.

Though the polygraph deception test has been used successfully since the early 1920's on thousands of criminal suspects and others, a great deal of research remains to be done. The apparatus is being improved and the technique is being perfected to a high degree of reliability. In the near future some form of deception test based on the recording of bodily changes will probably be added to the finger-print and radio systems, as a further means of raising the efficiency of our law-enforcing agencies.

5. Measurement of Drives. The concept of drive includes the need or desire to respond to a motivating stimulus, and the force and persistence of the resulting activity. Some psychologists treat these two factors individually, defining the first as "motivation," and the second as "action" or "behavior." Since no sharp line of demarcation between them is definable, it seems expedient to employ the concept of "drive" to include both the central and motor processes.

a. Obstruction Method. Considerable tension may be aroused in an animal by depriving him of something he wants badly. The craving may be whetted until there is an intense urge to seek possession of the object desired. The strength of the longing may be determined by interposing measurable obstructions in the path of the search. This method of measurement is called the *obstruction* or *resistance* method.

"Any animal drive may be measured in terms of the resistance overcome, provided the strength of the resistance is known; or, where the strength of the drive is known and that of the resistance is not, the resistance may be measured in terms of the drive. . . . If white rats are kept without food for some time and placed in section A of the experiment box, whether they will cross the electric plates in B to go to the food in section C depends upon two things—how hungry they are and how strong the current is on the electric plates; *i.e.,* upon the strength of the drive as balanced against the strength of the resistance. If the animals have had sufficient contact with the plates before to know what to expect, and if there is sufficient current on the plates, they will not attempt to cross, unless impelled by a very strong hunger drive. This was demonstrated in a series of experiments, keeping the animals without food for from twelve to one hundred and forty-four hours and keeping the current on the plates at twenty-eight

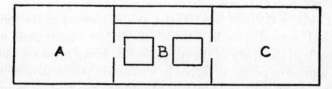

volts. Less than 5% of the animals had sufficient hunger drive to overcome the resistance necessary to go to the food at the close of a twenty-four-hour hunger period. The drive increased within the next twelve hours, so that approximately twenty per cent crossed at that time. By forty-eight hours, the drive was sufficiently strong in half the cases to overcome the resistance, and the rats crossed to the food. And by seventy-two hours, the hunger drive overcame the resistance in eighty per cent of the cases. By ninety-six hours, ninety-five per cent of the rats had crossed, and by one hundred and forty-four hours, every rat in the group had crossed. . . .

"From the above, it will readily appear that the animals may be induced to cross for the food either by increasing the drive by keeping them without food for a longer time, or by reducing the resistance in the form of the electric current which they have to overcome to get to the food."[1]

b. Topological Method. Another objective approach to the study of drives, in addition to the *obstruction* method, is the

---

[1]F. A. Moss: *Applications of Psychology*, pp. 7–10. 1929. Quoted by permission of and by arrangement with Houghton Mifflin Company.

topological method. Some modern psychologists who want to apply some of the concepts of mathematics and physics to psychology, prefer the topological viewpoint because it may serve to improve the accuracy of experimental description. This method enables the psychologist to measure and describe objectively the changes brought about when an organism responsively adapts itself to a stimulating environment. Topology is to be the basic mathematical discipline for the presentation of psychology in dynamic terms.

Lewin, a German psychologist, is an exponent of the topological method since he finds it affords him a systematic approach to the study of the psychological forces involved when an animal or person is placed in a situation provocative of action. Subjective and objective conditions must be taken into account. Heredity and environment being interdependent, they must both "work in the same direction to effect a certain mode of behavior."[1] The manner in which a person reacts is dependent upon (1) his momentary needs, desires, or subjective set, and (2) the existing environmental situation. One of these factors is meaningless without the other.

Lewin asserts that when the psychologist is studying the reactions of an individual, it is important that no parts of the environmental setting be ignored. A setting must be viewed as a dynamic whole, and not as a sum of unrelated elements. For example, a chocolate bar has a different meaning to a child if it is out of his reach, or if other things more tempting to him are available.

The method Lewin employs in studying the organism and its environment has much in common with one of the methods used by physics today. A situation is analyzed from a psychological standpoint and then it is reproduced diagram-

---

[1]K. Lewin: *A Dynamic Theory of Personality*. 1935. See also K. Lewin: "Environmental Forces," Chapter XIV in *A Handbook of Child Psychology*, C. Murchison, Editor. Second edition revised, 1933.

matically, the forces being indicated by arrows. According
to Lewin, a force possesses three significant properties: (1)
direction, (2) strength, and (3) point of application. The
direction and strength of a force are both subsumed under one
concept, that of *vector*, which is represented by an arrow. The
length of the arrow is used frequently to designate the strength
or intensity of the force. The head of the arrow is directed
toward the point of application. The power that an object
possesses to attract or repel the subject is called *valence*
(*Aufforderungscharaktere*), and an object is said to have positive (+) or negative (—) valence. Figures 1 and 2 represent
positive and negative valence respectively:

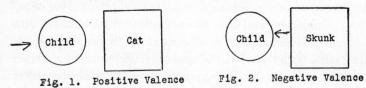

Fig. 1.   Positive Valence   Fig. 2.   Negative Valence

There are forces not resident in the object under consideration which frequently enhance, depreciate, or completely determine the value of an object as a stimulus. One of these
forces has to do with the needs of the individual himself.
These needs may be the result of a disequilibrium of the subject's physical structure, such as a need for food, liquid, sleep,
or sex satisfaction; or the needs may be the result of psychological urges such as the desire to be successful, or the wish to
obtain wealth. There may be still other forces which result
from barriers that frustrate or impede the progress of the
individual in some way. A barrier is a physical or psychological boundary which limits the activity of the person concerned. In the case of a child it may be a fence, wall, or door.
Such boundaries define the amount of space available for the
child. Social forces are also usually operative. These are
the commands and prohibitions imposed by the group. As a

child grows older he becomes increasingly aware of these restrictions. Many social demands, of course, become so much a part of the individual as to function automatically.

Lewin brings out the importance of direction in his *detour problems*, in which a child must first move away from a desired object before he can attain it. Suppose a child is separated from a doll by a hedge over which he cannot climb. In order to obtain the doll he must execute a movement at variance with the direction of the force. Lewin demonstrates the importance of direction by explaining that an increase of the valence makes it harder rather than easier to move in a direction opposite to that of the force.

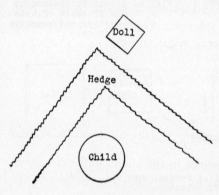

From this same topological viewpoint, a conflict is described as an opposition of approximately equal forces. There are three principal types of conflict: (1) When an individual is confronted with two positive valences, (2) when he is subjected to an object possessing both positive and negative valences, (3) when two negative valences are operating.

In Figure 3, the child has a choice of either the theater or the seashore. Both appeal to him and he must sacrifice one for the other. This kind of decision is comparatively easy because in either case pleasantness is the final result. In Figure 4, a child wants a toy that is in a dark room. If the child dislikes dark rooms the room offers positive (the toy) and negative valences. In Figure 5, the child has been placed between two negative valences, washing the dishes or going to bed. The vertical arrow delineates a force acting to remove the child from the entire situation.

Lewin's method of defining psychological processes in terms of mathematics and diagrams is commendable in that it offers a definite and clear exposition of the behavior of an individual

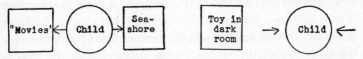

Fig. 3. A conflict between two positive valences

Fig. 4. A conflict caused by the presence of both positive and negative valences.

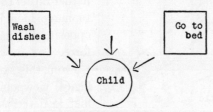

Fig. 5. A conflict between two negative valences.

under certain conditions. However, as settings become cumbersome and complicated, diagrams take on a resulting vagueness and complicatedness, and it becomes obvious that a multi-dimensional system cannot be reproduced in diagrams restricted to two dimensions.

For purposes of measurement it is convenient to consider drives in terms of behavior alone. We must not lose sight of the fact, however, that the behavior we are observing is merely an outward manifestation of a dynamically integrated subjective process. The subjective process can be studied indirectly by the methods of expression already mentioned, or directly by introspection (immediate observation of one's own consciousness).

6. The Measurement of Aptitudes. Some people seem to excel in a particular line of endeavor. Though not versatile in their capacities, they have a "gift" or knack for performing certain acts of skill with facility and finesse. Such persons are said to possess a special ability or aptitude.

a. Mechanical Aptitude. Psychologists have devised tests which measure these skills with considerable accuracy. There are tests, for example, which measure *mechanical aptitude.* Manual dexterity, eye-hand coördination, and precision of movement are involved; and in addition, acquired skill, and cultivated interest in the handling of tools and machinery.

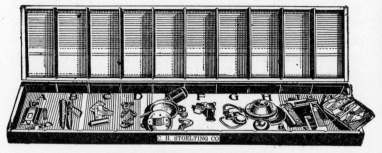

THE STENQUIST ASSEMBLING TEST
(Reproduced by courtesy of the C. H. Stoelting Company.)

(*1*) *The Stenquist Test.* The *Stenquist Assembling Tests* consist of a box divided into ten compartments. Each compartment contains a disjoined mechanical device, such as a bicycle bell or a mouse trap, which is to be assembled by the subject. The time required for putting the parts together is measured.

(*2*) *The Minnesota Test.* The Stenquist Assembling Tests have been revised at the University of Minnesota. The *Minnesota Assembling Tests* retain some of the Stenquist Tests and several new ones have been added. The Assembling Test is just one of a battery of tests which make up the Minnesota Mechanical Ability Tests. The battery aims to measure *quality* of mechanical work as judged by experts, *quantity* of mechanical work when a given standard of excellence is maintained, *creativeness* in mechanical work as demonstrated by devising new methods or by utilizing old methods in novel ways, and *critical appreciation* which involves good judgment of mechanical products and a keen interest in mechanical things.[1]

b. Musical Aptitude. Another special aptitude that is now measured scientifically is *musical ability*. Time and money are often wasted in providing a musical education for persons whose capacities do not justify such intensive training. Frequently, individuals who have a real talent for music do not take music lessons because they are unaware, until it is too late, of their hidden aptitude. It is obvious that adequate tests for measuring musical talent can prove invaluable in selecting those persons who merit a musical education.

Seashore has analyzed musical aptitude into its component skills, and has devised tests for measuring each one of them: the sense of pitch, the sense of consonance, the sense of rhythm, the sense of time, the sense of intensity, and tonal memory. The tests are presented by playing phonograph records prepared under Seashore's direction. The subject is instructed to listen for certain notes and to report his judgments.

In determining the *sense of pitch*, the subject is told that he will hear several pairs of tones, and that he is to judge whether the second tone of the pair is higher or lower in pitch than the first. In the *consonance test* the subject compares the consonance of the second of two pairs of dyads with the first. *Sense of rhythm* is tested by the presentation of pairs of rhythmic patterns, and the auditor must judge whether the second is the same as, or different from, the first. The *sense of time* test attempts to ascertain the minutest difference in time that

---

[1]D. G. Paterson, R. M. Elliott, *et al.: Minnesota Mechanical Ability Tests.* 1930.

can be perceived by a person. Three clicks are given which
mark off two intervals of time. The second interval is judged
with respect to the first. One hundred judgments of this sort
are made. In the *sense of intensity* test the auditor listens to
two tones and decides whether the second is more or less intense than the first. Two tonal sequences are sounded in the
test for *tonal memory* and the subject is required to state which
note of the second series differs from the first. The sequences
have two, three, four, five, and six tones.[1]

Though the Seashore Tests are subject to some serious crit-
icisms, they have been found to be of real value in the discovery of musical talent. Hazel M. Stanton has found over a
period of ten years at the Eastman School of Music that the
Seashore Tests are of considerable predictive value. These
data are encouraging from a scientific standpoint, especially
when we realize the complexity of the art with which we are
dealing.

c. Artistic Aptitude. Tests also have been standardized
that measure *ability in the visual arts.* One of these tests is the
Meier-Seashore Art Judgment Test, which consists of 125 pairs
of pictures printed in phototone. The pictures of each pair
differ in one respect only, in shading, heaviness of lines, balance, presence or absence of objects, and so forth. This difference is described on the record sheet given to the subject taking
the test. The problem is to decide which picture of each pair
is the more pleasing, or more artistic, or more satisfying. If
the left-hand picture is preferred, L is circled; if the right-hand,
R is circled. The test determines one's ability to choose the
kind of arrangement, shading, and the like, as judged to be the
more artistic by authorities on art. Meier contends that this
ability is indispensable to the artist. The high correlations
obtained between success as an artist and scores on the test
suggest that Meier's assertion is correct.

[1] C. E. Seashore: *The Psychology of Musical Talent.* 1919.

Tests such as we have just described are especially valuable for vocational guidance. The aim of the vocational counselor is to see that individuals are trained for the vocations particularly suited to their special aptitudes; with square pegs in square holes and round pegs in round holes, we shall be assured of more efficiency and more happiness.

7. Personality Tests. Personality is an intangible something in terms of which we describe the social stimulus value of the individual.[1] Thus we speak of a person as being sociable, or aggressive, or coöperative, or conscientious, or reliable, or resourceful, or stubborn. These qualities are sometimes referred to as *personality traits*. They are investigated by studying how the individual behaves in particular concrete situations, as usually represented by verbal means for paper and pencil tests. It must be noted, however, that people behave differently in different sorts of situations; for example, a man may be stubborn in his home relationships, but malleable in his club relationships. With this fact in mind, it is justifiable to use the term trait only with qualifications when we wish to describe the way in which the individual generally behaves in situations that involve the quality in question.

The organization of all these behavior patterns in the individual makes up what we call his personality on the reaction side; the responses which others make to him in social situations—to his quality of voice, his choice of language, his physique, and his manners—constitute his personality on the stimulus side. It is suggested by May that "personality might be characterized as that total organization of reaction tendencies, habit patterns, and physical qualities which determine the individual's social effectiveness."[2]

Allport, who approaches personality from the behavioristic

---

[1]See M. A. May: "The Foundations of Personality," Chapter IV in *Psychology at Work*, P. S. Achilles, Editor.

[2]*Ibid.*

angle, naturally stresses the reaction patterns.   He analyzes
personality into the following traits:

1. Intelligence
     Problem-solving Ability
     Memory and Learning Ability
     Perceptual Ability
     Constructive Imagination
     Special Abilities
     Soundness of Judgment
     General Adaptability
2. Motility
     Hyperkinesis—Hypokinesis
     Impulsion—Inhibition (Control)
     Tenacity
     Skill
     Style
3. Temperament
     Emotional Frequency and Change
     Emotional Breadth
     Emotional Strength
     Characteristic Mood
     Emotional Attitude
4. Self-Expression
     Drive
     Compensation
     Extroversion—Introversion
     Insight
     Ascendance—Submission
     Expansion—Reclusion
5. Sociality
     Susceptibility to Social Stimulation
     Socialization—Self-Seeking (Aggression)
        Social Participation
     Character[1]

The above outline reveals the nature of the problems with
which psychology is faced in its study of personality.

------

[1]F. H. Allport: *Social Psychology*, p. 103.   1924.   Quoted by permission of
and by arrangement with Houghton Mifflin Company.

Scientific psychology is interested in measuring the different aspects of personality with as much exactness as possible. Various methods have been devised for this purpose. Two methods in common use are the *Rating Scale* and the *Questionnaire*.

a. The Rating Scale. The *Rating Scale* as a method is related to two experimental methods: order of merit and paired comparisons. In the *order of merit* method, individuals are arranged in consecutive order from highest to lowest with respect to some trait, while in the method of *paired comparisons* each individual is compared separately twice over with the other members of the group, once as a standard, and once as a comparison stimulus. The number of preferences for each person determines his position in the final order of merit for the series.

(1) Man-to-Man Rating Scale. Rating scales may be of several types. The *Man-to-Man Rating Scale* involves the selection of the five key men rating highest, high, middle, low, and lowest; and then all the other members of the group are rated with reference to them, a numerical plan being used.[1]

(2) The Graphic Rating Scale consists of a straight line representing the range of a trait. Brief descriptive terms are located along the line to indicate various degrees of the quality. The rater marks the line with a check to designate his estimate of the individual.[2]

Coöperativeness—Consider ability to work with others

————|————————|———————|—————·————|————————

| Coöperative | Falls in line | Difficult to handle | Obstructive |

[1] W. D. Scott and R. C. Clothier: *Personnel Management.* 1923.

[2] M. A. Bills: "A Method for Classifying the Jobs and Rating the Efficiency of Clerical Workers," *Journal of Personnel Research*, 1923, 1, 384–393.

(*3*) *The Percentage Rating Scale* involves the rating of individuals on a percentage basis from 100% (high degree of the quality) down to 10% or lower (low degree of the quality). This method is in common use in the marking of ability as revealed on school examinations.

(*4*) *The Descriptive or Adjective Scale* is widely used by agencies which desire references concerning candidates applying for jobs. A prospective teacher, for example, may be rated on his ability to maintain discipline as "very poor," "poor," "medium," "good," or "excellent."[1]

A rating scale in wide use is the *Personality Rating Scale, Committee on Personality Measurement, American Council on Education.*[2] Five traits are to be rated on a graphic scale: appearance and manner, industry, ability to control others, emotional control, and distribution of time and energy. Space is provided for "behaviorgrams," that is, concrete instances to support the rater's judgment. Revision A is scored by checking along a straight line which is subdivided into ten sections. Revision B is scored by checking one of six alternatives.

b. The Questionnaire. The *Questionnaire* method calls for a systematic report of the individual's attitudes and reaction patterns. The quantitative estimates of the rating scale are not involved. The questionnaire method has been employed to secure personal data with reference to feelings of inadequacy and other symptoms of maladjustment, to discover systematic interests people may have in sports, vocations, or social activities, and to reveal attitudes or convictions about social, economic, or religious issues. Since data of such a nature are not open to direct measurement, they may be conveniently investigated by the questionnaire method.

---

[1] For an excellent presentation of these rating methods, see H. E. Garrett and M. R. Schneck: *Psychological Tests, Methods, and Results*, Part II, Chapter III, "The Measurement of Personality and Temperament." 1933.

[2] Published by the American Council on Education, 744 Jackson Place, Washington, D. C.

(*1*) *Traits.* There are a number of personality inventories which have been widely used for the study of personal traits. Woodworth's *Personal Data Sheet* aims to estimate psychoneurotic tendencies in terms of social and emotional inadequacies. 116 questions are to be answered by Yes or No, such as:

Do you usually feel strong and well?
Were you shy with other boys?
Does it make you uneasy to go into a tunnel or subway?

The score is interpreted according to standardized norms.[1] Ellen Mathews has revised Woodworth's test to measure emotional stability in children.[2]

Neymann and Kohlstedt have devised a *Diagnostic Test for Introversion—Extroversion* which consists of fifty statements to be answered by underlining Yes or No, such as:

Always be calm and collected.
Rewrite social letters.

Tendencies toward extroversion or introversion are revealed by whether the subject agrees or disagrees with the ideas expressed in the statements.[3]

A Scale for Measuring Ascendance—Submission in Personality has been designed by the Allports to "discover the disposition of an individual to dominate his fellows (or to be dominated by them) in various face-to-face relationships of everyday life." Separate forms are available for men and women. Situations or problems are presented to which the subject

---

[1]R. S. Woodworth: *Personal Data Sheet.* 1917. The C. H. Stoelting Company.

[2]Ellen Mathews: *Revision of the Woodworth P. D. Sheet.* 1923. The C. H. Stoelting Company.
See E. Mathews: "A Study of Emotional Stability in Children," *Journal of Delinquency*, 1923, 8, 1–40.

[3]C. A. Neymann and K. D. Kohlstedt: *Diagnostic Test for Introversion—Extroversion.* 1928. The C. H. Stoelting Company. A manual is also procurable.

indicates his reaction by checking one of the two to five alternatives provided.

Thus:

> At church, a lecture, or entertainment, if you arrive after the program has commenced and find that there are people standing, but also that there are front seats available which might be secured without "piggishness" or discourtesy, but with considerable conspicuousness, do you take the seats?
> habitually . . .
> occasionally . . .
> never . . .

Numerical values are assigned the answers in the scoring. Norms have been established.[1]

A more comprehensive test has been arranged by Bernreuter who has combined questions from Allport, Thurstone, Laird, and others in his *Personality Inventory*. The test is designed to measure neurotic tendencies, self-sufficiency, introversion—extroversion, dominance—submission, confidence in oneself, and sociability, which are scored on separate scales. The questions are to be answered by Yes, No, or ? (undecided).

> Do you consider yourself a nervous person?
> Are you much affected by the praise or blame of many people?
> Would you rather work for yourself than carry out the program of a superior whom you respect?
> Do you usually try to avoid dictatorial or "bossy" people?

Percentile norms have been established for each scale.[2]

(2) *Interests.* A person's interests reveal the nature of his personality and thus serve as a basis for prediction of his future educational and vocational pursuits and as an index of the life accomplishments in store for him. Various interest question-

---

[1] G. W. Allport and F. H. Allport: *A Scale for Measuring Ascendance—Submission in Personality (The A-S Reaction Study).* By permission of and by arrangement with Houghton Mifflin Company.

[2] R. G. Bernreuter: *Manual for the Personality Inventory.* 1935. Stanford University Press, Palo Alto, California.

naires have been devised, among which is Strong's *Vocational Interest Blank*. The subject indicates whether he likes (L), is indifferent to (I), or dislikes (D) various occupations, amusements, school subjects, certain kinds of people, and the like. The blank is scored separately for each occupation.[1]

Brainard and Stewart have designed a *Specific Interest Inventory* for the discovery and analysis of interests, to serve as a basis for vocational guidance. The tests cover mechanical, literary, æsthetic, commercial, and other interests. The subject is asked:

How do you like—

To wrap parcels, cover or repair books, making neat folds.

	Dislike	N.	Like	
1	2	3	4	5

The final score is the sum of all the numbers circled. Subtotal scores are useful in the analysis of the various interests. The directions for interpreting the scores are given in a manual.[2]

(3) Attitudes. An individual's personality may also be understood in terms of his attitudes. Opinions on religious and economic issues may be examined by Goodwin Watson's *Test of Public Opinion*. The purpose of the test is to show the extent and strength of the individual's prejudices. The different forms of the test deal with opinions on social, religious, and economic questions; the certainty of opinion on these issues; the extent to which the individual is willing to commit himself on moot questions; and the subject's willingness to generalize his opinions on controversial issues. Extreme opinions,

---

[1] E. K. Strong: *Vocational Interest Blank*. 1927. Stanford University Press, Palo Alto, California. A manual can also be secured.

E. K. Strong: "Diagnostic Value of the Vocational Interest Test," *Educational Record*, 1929, 10, 59–68.

E. K. Strong: *Change of Interests with Age*. 1931.

[2] F. J. Stewart and P. Brainard: *Specific Interest Inventory*. 1932. Psychological Corporation, 522 Fifth Ave., New York City.

D. Fryer: *The Measurement of Interests*. 1931.

whether *pro* or *con*, are scored as evidences of prejudice. The gross total represents the general level of prejudice, and an analytic score indicates the direction of prejudice.[1]

Thurstone and Chave have developed a test to reveal attitudes toward the Church, called *Experimental Study of Attitudes toward the Church*. Forty-five statements, ranging from statements very favorable to the Church to statements very unfavorable, give the subject an opportunity to indicate his sympathy or antagonism. Norms have been worked out for various groups such as college freshmen, divinity students, and non-churchgoers.[2]

Another test for measuring attitudes is *A Study of Values*, developed by Allport and Vernon.[3] Part I consists of statements or questions with two alternative answers. Agreement and disagreement are checked numerically; "3" in the first column and "o" in the second column indicate a decided preference for the first alternative, while "2" in the first column and "1" in the second column indicate a slight preference for the first alternative. Thus:

7. In a paper such as the New York Sunday *Times*, are you more interested in the section on picture galleries and exhibitions than in the real estate sections and the account of the stock market?
 (a) Yes; (b) No.   (a)   (b)
                                      3   o

The answer indicates a decided preference for the section on picture galleries and exhibitions: æsthetic concerns are felt to be more important than economic concerns.

---

[1]Goodwin Watson: *A Test of Public Opinion* (*A Survey of Public Opinion on Some Religious and Economic Issues*). 1923. Bureau of Publications, Teachers College, Columbia University, New York. A manual is available.
 Goodwin Watson: *The Measurement of Fair-Mindedness*. 1925.

[2]L. L. Thurstone and E. J. Chave: *Experimental Study of Attitudes toward the Church*. 1929. University of Chicago Press, Chicago, Illinois.
 L. L. Thurstone and E. J. Chave: *The Measurement of Attitude*. 1929.

[3]G. W. Allport and P. E. Vernon: *A Study of Values*. 1931. Houghton Mifflin Company.

Part II of *A Study of Values* consists of situations or questions followed by four possible attitudes or answers. Preference is registered by writing the number:

1 . . . beside the answer that appeals to you most.
2 . . . beside the answer which is next most important to you.
3 . . . beside the next, and
4 . . . beside the answer that least represents your interest or preference.

Thus:

13. To what extent do the following famous persons interest or attract you—

  2 a. Florence Nightingale

. . . .

  4 b. Napoleon

. . . .

  3 c. Henry Ford

. . . .

  1 d. Charles Darwin

. . . .

The answers of the subject indicate his sentiments about the relative importance of various attitudes toward life. Various tests involve attitudes such as theoretical, economic, æsthetic, social, political, and religious. These six basic interests are found in varying degrees in every personality, according to Eduard Spranger, a German psychologist, who has described them in his *Types of Men* (1928). Let us contrast two types by way of illustration. The person whose dominant attitude is economic will look upon a friend as a prospect for a sale, while the person whose dominant attitude is religious will look upon a friend as a prospective convert for whom to pray.

The relative importance of the different attitudes may be determined by a computation of the separate scores. The representation of the scores on a *profile* makes it easy to see at a glance the relations of the various interests in the individual's personality.

A *profile* represents the distribution of the scores of a test as they are plotted on a graph. The complete diagram is called a *psychograph*. It is a convenient way of describing the personality compactly in its various aspects. The profile is plotted as follows. The vertical scale represents the complete absence of a characteristic at the bottom and a gradual increase of the characteristic to the greatest amount at the top. The horizontal line in the middle represents the "average" between the extremes. The traits in which the individual is superior to the average will be represented on the graph by the fact that the plotting line (scores) is above the average line, and the traits in which he is inferior will be represented below the median.[1] The following psychograph represents two individuals, A and B.

If you were considering applicants for positions as salesmen in your organization, and you wanted an extroverted person superior in social intelligence, education, intelligence, self-sufficiency, dominance, sociability, and motivation, you would probably choose A in preference to B, in spite of the fact that A is self-conscious, for A has a much better chance of becoming a successful salesman.

The psychograph is useful in personality evaluation. It makes it possible to compare scores computed in different units; it would be impossible to compare directly the number of years of education with the amount of self-consciousness. Then, too, the psychograph gives a convenient picture of the individual's relative development with respect to various functions. His superiorities and deficiencies become graphically apparent.

There are certain limitations which must be kept in mind when the graph is interpreted. These precautions are re-

---

[1]This description does not apply to a trait like extroversion where the extremes represent the limits of the range between extroversion and introversion rather than the limits of increase or decrease in the amount of the trait.

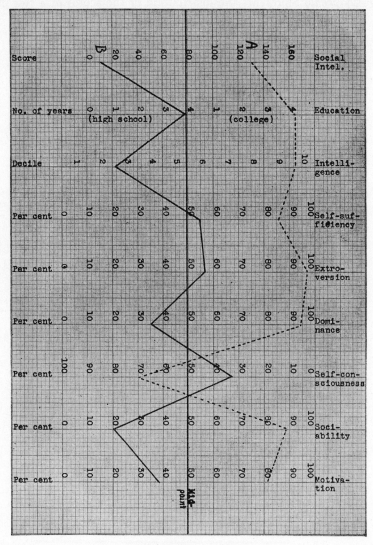

PSYCHOGRAPH: A AND B

67

spected by the expert psychologist. For our purposes, we need not analyze them here.

The psychograph gives us a description of a person as he is. It does not tell us "how he got that way." An investigation into the genesis of the various traits is needed to render the psychographic method really effective in the analysis of personality.

C. Statistical Treatment of Data. We have described the various methods by means of which scientific psychology measures the different aspects of mind and behavior. The interpretation of the data obtained by experimental investigation depends upon a mathematical treatment of the figures that measurement has yielded. This is the function of statistics. It is sufficient for our purposes to limit ourselves to a brief survey of the fundamental factors involved in the application of statistical methods.

1. The Distribution Curve. Suppose we measure the reaction times of a large number of people. We find that a few people are very fast, a few people are very slow, and most people are neither fast nor slow but fall somewhere in between the extremes. The range of individual differences in this case may be represented by a *distribution* or *frequency curve*. If we assume that the distribution is uniform, we have a "normal curve" like the following, on which the amount of time re-

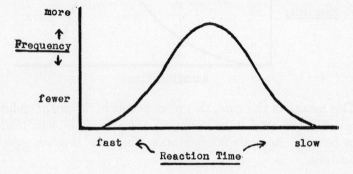

quired for reaction is plotted along the horizontal line and frequency (number of individuals) along the vertical line.

In everyday thinking, we often describe some people as fast and other people as slow. In other words, we classify people into two types, the fast and the slow. If there were such types, the curve would look like this:

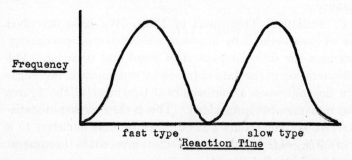

Since no such curve is obtained by actual investigation, we are forced to conclude that people do not fall into discrete types. Instead, people taken *en masse* range by gradual steps or degrees from fast through average to slow.

In actual practice the normal curve is only approximated. Sometimes the curve is *skewed*. Thus:

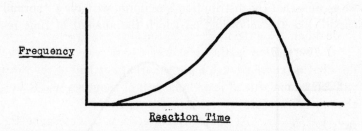

This means, in this case, that more people in the group under investigation tend to be slow than there are those who tend to be fast. Accurate interpretation, therefore, involves some analysis.

a. The Central Tendency. The *central tendency* in our case represents the grouping of the majority of the people toward fastness or slowness. It is analyzed in terms of the *mean*, the *mode*, and the *median*.

(*1*) *The mean* is determined by adding the reaction times of all the people tested, and then dividing this total by the number of people involved. Thus:[1]

A . . . takes 3 seconds to react to a stimulus
B . . . 4
C . . . 5
D . . . 6
E . . . 7

The total time in seconds is 25. Divide this by 5 (the number of people). The resulting figure, 5, is the mean.

(*2*) *The mode* is the area on the curve where the largest number of people is grouped. Thus:

A . . . 3 seconds
B . . . 4
C . . . 5
D . . . 6
E . . . 6
F . . . 6
G . . . 7

In this case, 6 is the mode. When the curve is skewed, the mode differs from the mean, as in the above sample.

(*3*) *The median* is the line drawn vertically through the distribution curve in such a position that one half of the cases will fall on one side of it and one half of the cases will fall on the other side of it.

b. Variability. At times it is necessary to determine the amounts by which people differ, so that we must proceed beyond the mere computation of the central tendency. The central tendency represents the *center* of distribution. The

---

[1]We are taking a small group for the sake of simplicity. In actual practice, larger groups are necessary to get significant conclusions.

amount of *scatter* is computed in terms of *deviation*. The *average deviation* (A.D.) is computed by calculating the distances of all the individuals from the average, adding up these deviations and dividing by the number of people. Thus:

A . . . 2 seconds
B . . . 4
C . . . 4
D . . . 7
E . . . 7
F . . . 8
G . . . 10

The average in this case is $\frac{42}{7}$ or 6. The average deviation is derived by computing how much each individual's score differs from the average of 6, adding the amounts of deviation, and dividing the total by the number of cases. Thus:

Ave.	*Score* on reaction time test	Deviation (d)
6	2 (A)	4
6	4 (B)	2
6	4 (C)	2
6	7 (D)	1
6	7 (E)	1
6	8 (F)	2
6	10 (G)	4

The sum of the deviations is 16. The A.D. is 16 divided by 7 (the number of cases) or 2.29. Where the scatter is more extensive than in our illustration, the A.D. sheds important light on the nature of the distribution. For accurate computation, the *standard deviation* (S.D.) is used rather than the A.D., for reasons which do not concern us here. The S.D. is obtained by squaring each individual deviation, then adding them, dividing by the number of cases and finally extracting the square root. The theory underlying these computations is highly technical in nature.

Scatter is often represented conveniently on a *scattergram* in cases where people are measured with respect to two functions. We shall explain how this is done in connection with correlation.

2. Correlation. Let us suppose that the individuals we are investigating are given, in addition to the test in reaction time, a test on intelligence. It will be of interest to determine how the scores attained in the one test correspond to the scores attained in the second test. This relationship is measured by means of *correlation*. Thus we will be able to answer the question as to whether the same individuals make high scores in both speed and intelligence (in which case speed is probably a factor in intelligence), or whether individuals who are slow are the high scorers in the test of intelligence.

An exact representation of the relative standing of each individual on the two tests may be accomplished by means of a scattergram.

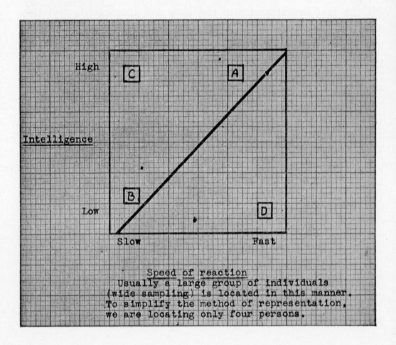

Usually a large group of individuals (wide sampling) is located in this manner. To simplify the method of representation, we are locating only four persons.

A fast person will be located to the right of the diagram and a slow person to the left. An intelligent person will be located near the top of the diagram and a stupid person near the bottom. One cross will locate a person with respect to both scores. The diagonal represents the central tendency. Interpreting our scattergram, we see that:

A is fast and intelligent. B is slow and stupid. C is slow and intelligent. D is fast and stupid.

a. Coefficient of Correlation. The correlation chart or scattergram gives us only a rough picture of the relationship between speed and intelligence. A more accurate answer to our question can be secured by computing the *coefficient of correlation*. If the fast are intelligent and the slow are stupid, and this distribution is uniform all along the line, the correlation is perfect. It is 100%, represented in practice by + 1.00. If the fast are stupid and the slow are intelligent, and this distribution is uniform all along the line, the coefficient is represented by —1.00. If the fast and slow fall in a uniform fashion on both sides of the average intelligence, the coefficient is represented by 0. Correlation may thus range from + 1.00 through 0 to —1.00. Actually, a + 1.00 or —1.00 correlation is practically never obtained. A coefficient of about .30 is usually considered to be significant.

Let us take a simple example to illustrate how the coefficient of correlation is obtained. The individuals under investigation are ranked in their order of achievement on the two tests. Thus:

	Speed	Intelligence
A	1	2
B	2	3
C	3	1
D	4	5
E	5	4
F	6	6

The following formula worked out by Spearman may be used.

$$r = 1 - \frac{6 \Sigma (d^2)}{n (n^2 - 1)}$$

r: coefficient

Σ: sum of

d: deviation (difference in rank order between the two scales)

n: number of cases

Computation is carried out thus:

	Speed	Intelligence	d	d²
A	1	2	1	1
B	2	3	1	1
C	3	1	2	4
D	4	5	1	1
E	5	4	1	1
F	6	6	0	0

The sum of the d²'s is 8. Therefore,

$$r = 1 - \frac{6 \times 8}{6 (36 - 1)}$$

$$r = 1 - \frac{48}{210}$$

$$r = 1 - .23$$

$r = + .77$, which means that there is a considerable tendency for the fast to be intelligent and the slow to be stupid, in our particular sample.

The Method of Rank Differences we have just used in applying the Spearman formula is apt to be somewhat inaccurate, since it takes account of relative position only. For example, suppose A, B, C react 1, 2, 3 with reference to speed. A takes 1 second; B takes 2 seconds; C takes 5 seconds. The differences in rank are seen to be unequal. For greater accuracy, therefore, the Product Moment Method of Pearson, which correlates actual scores, is used. The use of the Pearson formula is explained on pages 578–580.

b. Probable Error. In order to be sure that the coefficient of correlation between two tests is significant, the *probable error* must be computed. The extent of this error indicates the probability as to whether nearly the same coefficient of correlation will be obtained if the same tests are administered to another group under identical conditions, or to the same group under identical conditions at another time.

c. Reliability and Validity. A test is *reliable* if an individual obtains approximately the same score upon taking the same test at another time, or if he obtains equivalent scores on equivalent tests. A thoroughly reliable test should correlate as high as + .90 or above.

A test is valid if it measures what it is designed to measure. Thus a test for salesmanship is valid if the persons who score high on the test succeed in selling, whereas those who score low on the test fail in selling. Success in the activity for which the test is planned is taken as the *criterion* against which the test must be checked. If the test is valid, it will have a high correlation with the particular criterion chosen.

Exercises are supplied in the section on Experiments, beginning on page 574, to provide practice in the application of the various statistical methods. Formulæ are supplied, with an explanation of how they are to be used.

III. SUMMARY

The scientific approach to Psychology has resulted in the evolution of exact methods for measuring the data discovered by painstaking investigation. Improvements in experimental technique are being steadily introduced. Statistical treatment of the data derived from experimentation is becoming gradually more extensive. Psychology is no longer a matter of theoretical guesswork; it has become an exact science.

CHAPTER III

POINTS OF VIEW

THE essential method of psychology, as of other sciences, is observation, for it is only through the systematic assemblage of facts that a scientific insight into human nature can be secured. Since the human being is a very complex creature, it is not strange that a variety of views have been advanced in regard to mental life and its manifestations in behavior. What a psychologist will observe depends, of course, upon what he is looking for. Scientific observation must start, like any other observation, with a particular bias. The adoption of a particular viewpoint involves the selection of particular phenomena for study.

I. METHODS OF OBSERVING THE MIND

The first method of observing the mind is introspection (looking within)—the immediate inspection of one's own experience. Introspection can only be used to reveal the content of one's own mind.

The second method of approaching the mind is to observe behavior, and then to infer what is going on in the mind of the person under observation. This method is used primarily in getting at the mind of another person, since direct observation of the mind of somebody else is impossible.

A. Introspection: the Contents of the Mind. The study of one's own experiences is known as introspection (looking within). The method of introspection is to be distinguished from the kind of observation employed in the physical sciences which we may call inspection (looking at). Introspection as a method of observation is peculiar to the science of psychology, for it is only in psychology that a person is interested in the nature of his own experiences *per se*.

In an introspective experiment the subject, or observer, as he is called, is given the opportunity to watch his own mental states under conditions which are so controlled that they may be repeated, isolated, and varied. Instructions are given in a standardized form and manner to prepare the observer for the presentation of the stimulus. The subject is requested to observe the stimulus, and then to give a full report of his experience. Suppose a bottle of camphor is submitted for him to smell for a minute with both nostrils. The observer maintains the opening of the bottle in a definite position with respect to his nose, and breathes deeply at a prescribed rate. The introspective report involves a description of the sensations, feelings, and ideas aroused by the stimulus—how the nasal membranes smart, how the sensation fades gradually or suddenly, whether the experience is pleasant, and how his ideas turn to closets and moth balls, and so on.

An introspective experiment involves one peculiar difficulty in that the subject is at once both the observer and the observed. The person who is observing a chemical reaction can write down a description of what he is seeing during the course of the reaction, but the observer in an introspective experiment finds that the effort to observe interferes with the experience that is being observed. The activity of observation affects the experience under examination. The observer is in a predicament analogous to that of the small girl who stood in front of a mirror with her eyes closed to see how she looked when she was asleep. As soon as the subject observes he tends to substitute the state of mind "look" for the state of mind "smell of camphor," let us say. One way to obviate this difficulty in introspection is to allow the experience to run its course as freely as possible and then to recall it and describe it from memory, repeating the experiment to check carefully all the data recalled. Introspection is thus carried out by resorting to retrospection; introspective examination becomes *post mortem* examination. Trained observers, however, learn to take mental notes while the observation is in progress without interfering with consciousness. Expert introspection can be achieved only by long training.

Experience may be analyzed into its elements, or it may be described as a whole.

1. Elementarism. One school of psychology prefers the method of analysis, patterning its method upon the analytic approach adopted by investigators in the physical sciences where an understanding of the nature of matter has been gained by breaking matter down into molecules, atoms, electrons, protons, and so on. Titchener, long a professor of psychology at Cornell, was a leading exponent of the view that the best way to understand consciousness is to take it apart and describe it in terms of its elements and the relations among the elements. We may speak of the Titchenerian viewpoint as *Elementarism*, since the primary aim of its introspective method is to analyze consciousness into its elements.

The elements of consciousness are sensations, images, and affections. Sensations are familiar to every one, in the perception of stimuli—the sensation of a blister on the finger, or of a bright light glaring in the eyes. Images are the mental pictures involved in the memory of past experiences, or in the anticipation of the future. They are the elements of our ideas. Affections constitute the elements of our emotional life, such as love, fear, and anger.

Sensation has a number of attributes, among them, quality, intensity, and duration. The quality of a sensation is its distinctive attribute: yellow, hot, bitter. Intensity is the attribute described by such terms as stronger, louder, and brighter. Duration is the attribute which has reference to the course of a sensation with respect to time. Sensations may appear, fade, and reappear in successive moments, with the stimulus constantly present.

The qualitative attributes of sensation are as follows:

1. Sense of vision (visual modality)
   Hue
   Tint (brightness)
   Chroma (saturation)
2. Sense of hearing (auditory modality)
   Pitch
   Volume
   Tonality
   Vocality
3. Sense of taste (gustatory modality)
   Bitter
   Sweet
   Sour
   Salt
4. Sense of smell (olfactory modality)
   Fragrant
   Ethereal
   Spicy
   Resinous
   Putrid
   Burned
5. Sense of touch (tactual modality)
   Pressure
   Pain
   Cold
   Warm

There are more than five senses. Additional modalities will be described later.

In Titchener's system sensation was regarded as an elementary process. Rahn suggested a very apt criticism when he pointed out that sensation could not be an element since it was further analyzable into its attributes.[1] The attribute, therefore, should be regarded as the simplest mental process instead of the sensation. Experimental evidence supports Rahn's contention by showing that the attributes are independently variable. For example, consider a certain tone, say of 256 vibrations (quality of middle C) and of a certain intensity. The same tone (quality) may be experienced even though the intensity is altered and, in the same manner, a different tone (quality) may be perceived though the intensity remain the same. The attributes, being independently variable, should be regarded as elementary, or at least as more elementary than sensations.

2. Configurationism. Another school of psychology emphasizing the introspective technique, though not limiting itself to this method, as did the Titchenerians, is *Configurationism*. The best critique of Titchener's introspective psychology is to be found in the works of Köhler and Koffka who belong to the school of *Gestalt Psychologie*, known in America as Configurationism.[2] The noun *Gestalt* has two meanings: it connotes "shape" or "form," or a thing having a shape or form as one of its attributes. Thus any structure may be said to be a *Gestalt*, in that it possesses form.

The *Gestalt* psychologists emphasize the fact of organization in experience. The whole, say the Configurationists, is prior to the parts in experience. A two-year-old child will not recognize a picture of his mother's nose because his mother's nose is not a separate item to him, but an integral part of her face. Her nose is not a nose but a nose-on-a-face. I remember a game which afforded considerable amusement to a

---

[1] C. Rahn: *The Relation of Sensation to Other Categories in Psychology; A Study in the Psychology of Thinking.* 1913.

[2] See W. Köhler: *The Mentality of Apes.* 1925. *Gestalt Psychology.* 1929. K. Koffka: *The Growth of the Mind.* 1924.

group of married couples who were being entertained by a professor. The women all retired to a separate room. One woman at a time, so well concealed behind a portière as to be *incognito*, extended one of her hands to be examined by the men. Each man was to judge whether the particular hand belonged to his wife. Considerable confusion reigned when the men revealed the wildness of their guesswork. Some of the errors, I suspect, later incurred the rebukes they deserved from embarrassed and humiliated wives. The men should hardly be given much credit as far as intelligence is concerned for exposing themselves to such a dangerous ordeal, but they should, of course, have been pardoned for their mistakes in identification, since a woman's hand belongs to a woman and is not just a hand. A hand is a part, it is true, but a *part of the whole woman*.

To what whole a part belongs, depends upon the process of grouping which is an inherent aspect of the perceptual process. The figure below may be seen in various arrangements of the parts.[1]

 It may be seen as or

On one occasion, assigning a part to a wrong whole resulted in an amusing incident for radio listeners.

> Stein Song Not a Part
> of W.C.T.U. Program
> Those persons who tuned in on sta-
> tion WNAC Wednesday to hear the
> W.C.T.U. radio forum and thought
> that the program was opened by the
> stirring strains of the Stein Song of the

---

[1]From W. Köhler: *Gestalt Psychology.* The representations of the variations are mine. By permission of Liveright Publishing Corporation.

See also Gardner Murphy: "The Geometry of Mind," *Harper's Magazine,* October, 1931.

> University of Maine, should have their
> watches adjusted, because they really
> tuned in ahead of time. They heard
> the Stein Song all right, but it was the
> closing number of the Berry Spring
> Mineral Water Company entertainers.
> The dry broadcast started at the sched-
> uled time—3:45 P.M.—and was an all-
> speaking program.[1]

The whole, says the *Gestalt* psychologist, is more than the
sum of its parts. Take four lines

and arrange them in a particular relationship and there has
evolved the quality (*Gestaltqualität*) of squareness which

does not exist in any of the four lines. Squareness only appears when the parts are related to each other in a certain
structure. A still better illustration is found in a melody.
The melody does not depend upon the parts but upon the
structure, for the parts may all be changed by transposing to
another key, and yet the melody remains intact. The parts
have all been altered, the whole is still the same. If a note is
sung flat or sharp, the musical listener immediately detects
the fault, since the tone is not merely a tone but a tone in a
melody, deriving its properties, to some degree, from the whole
to which it belongs.

If you alter any one part, you change the whole. Suppose
you furnish a living room with a suite fitted with reversible
cushions. If you reverse one cushion, you alter the whole
room.

An interesting phenomenon involving the part-whole re-

[1]The Boston *Herald*, April 18, 1930.

lationship is the process of closure: given a part of a familiar whole, the individual completes the structure himself.   If I supply the figure

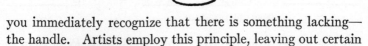

you immediately recognize that there is something lacking— the handle.   Artists employ this principle, leaving out certain lines for the observer to fill in for himself.

(Drawn by R. Wilson Hammell.)

The same process of closure, by which the observer makes subjective additions to the figures, occurs in seen movement—what the Configurationists call the *phi phenomenon*.[1] By means of a tachistoscope,[2] the figures at the top of page 84 are successively exposed to view at intervals of about 60 sigma. There is a discrete displacement actually but the observer sees the lines move from position 1 to position 2. The phenomenon of movement is appreciated still more clearly if human figures are exposed in a situation calling for motion, such as a person hammering a nail, or a woman hammering her husband.   Closure is the basis for the apprehension of the stroboscopic movements involved in motion pictures.

[1]See H. R. De Silva: "An Experimental Investigation of the Determinants of Apparent Visual Movement," *American Journal of Psychology*, 1926, 37, 469–501.

[2]An apparatus for exposing stimuli for a very brief duration.

The principle of closure is likewise applicable to explicit behavior. The pursuit of a goal may be described as a pro-

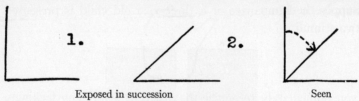

1.　　　　　　　2.

Exposed in succession　　　　　　　Seen

gression from preparatory to consummatory responses, in Woodworth's terms, or as a progression from non-closure, in

Gestalt terms. The Configurationists, as I said before, do not confine themselves, by any means, to introspection.

When a person learns to behave in response to certain

stimuli, it is not to the separate stimuli but to structures that the individual is reacting, since experience is pattern-wise. Suppose a chimpanzee or a three-year-old child is presented two stimuli

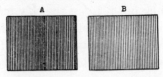

one of which is a dark gray and the other a lighter gray.   The subjects are taught to go to "B" by a conditioning process— being rewarded when they go to "B" and punished when they go to "A."   To make sure that the subjects are not going to the right-hand stimulus in preference to the left, "B" is some-times presented to the left of "A."   The subjects apparently have learned to go to "B"—they have contracted the "B" habit, so to speak.   When "B" is presented with another stimulus "C" (a still lighter gray than "B"),

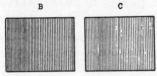

they should go to "B."   Do they?   No.   The subjects go to "C."   The experiment demonstrates that the chimpanzee and the child did not learn to go to "B," but to go to the lighter gray.   "B" was simply, from the experiential point of view, the lighter gray in a structure in which it was related to the darker gray "A."   It was to the whole rather than to the parts that the subjects were reacting.   So when "B" and "C" were exposed, "C" was chosen as the lighter gray in the new struc-ture.   The behavior in this experiment is good evidence that experience comes in wholes, in structures, in *Gestalten*.

The *Gestalt* psychologists do not object to the method of analysis as such, but they do protest against the assertion that the elements constitute the essence of experience. There are parts to experience but they are parts subordinated to a whole, and when experience is observed naïvely (naturally), it is structures and not elements that are noted. Analysis is a justifiable procedure but it is not the only method of scientific psychology. The psychologist who has observed only the elements has ignored a very important aspect of his experience —and that is the fact that the elements *belong together* in a pattern. The controversy between Titchener and the Configurationists can be reconciled, it seems to me, in terms of attitude. If you assume the analytic attitude in introspection, you can describe the elements of experience. If you assume the naïve attitude of everyday experience, you will get a total impression of patterns. Each method of observation is *equally scientific*. Experience must be complex in order to be analyzed. The error in analytic introspection has been committed by the observer who forgets, after analysis, the whole which he has been picking to pieces. Take experience as it comes in wholes (*Gestalt*), or take it as it comes in wholes and analyze it into its constituent elements (*Elementarism*)—either method is legitimate—both methods are necessary to an adequate psychology.

3. Criticism. The introspective approach to the study of the mind is subject to a number of limitations. The interference of the introspective attitude with the course of consciousness has already been mentioned. Other limitations of the method are equally serious.

a. Privacy of Consciousness. Since consciousness is a strictly private affair, your introspection must of necessity be limited to a direct examination of your own conscious processes. The privacy of mental life is illustrated in the story of the young boy who was observed in the act of scratching himself. A gentleman who was witnessing the performance could not restrain his curiosity. "Johnnie," he asked, "why are you scratching yourself?" "Because," the youth replied, "no one knows better than I do where I itch." The scope of introspective psychology is limited considerably by what we might call the individuality of experience—each one of us is the sole judge, as far as consciousness is concerned, of where he itches.

Science depends upon knowledge which can be validated by common agreement among investigators. Introspection being a private affair, how can a scientific psychology be established on the basis of personal beliefs and individual opinions promulgated through introspective reports? How can the private experience of one person be checked against the private experience of another? Can there be any common ground for validation of private impressions?

There are reasonable grounds for inferring that other human beings have experiences of the same nature as are immediately known to you. One basis for inference is similarity of physical structure. Since we all have the same type of nervous system, it is safe to assume that the mental life which is dependent in some way upon the nervous system is uniform in its character, as well. Human minds resemble each other precisely as human bodies do. Another ground of inference is the uniformity of behavior. The fact that human beings act more or less similarly in adjusting themselves to environmental stimuli, justifies the observer in drawing the conclusion, within the limits of probability, that the minds which are manifesting themselves in action are also akin. The development of language bears witness to the kinship of other minds with whom experiences can be shared. A number of observers, in describing their experiences in a given situation, will be in fundamental agreement. The more data collected, of course, the more exact will be the results. Thus, in spite of the difficulties involved in the private nature of consciousness, a reasonably accurate science of psychology may be established through the introspective method by testing one man's experience with that of others. You cannot probe another's consciousness directly, but you can infer with some certainty that there is something going on in his mind closely similar to the experience you undergo under like conditions.

b. Inadequacy of Language. Another serious drawback to introspective psychology is the inadequacy of language as a medium of description. Introspective reports must be verbal. Anybody who has tried to describe his own experiences under experimental conditions comes to realize the paucity of terms for rendering an accurate account of his feelings, images, and sensations. Try to describe the taste of grapefruit or the smell of iodine, and you will be convinced that there are no words to express exactly what you want to say. When a trained psychologist is asked to describe the states of pleasantness and unpleasantness, and the best he can do is to say that pleasantness is a "bright pressure" and unpleasantness a "dull pressure," you readily understand what I mean. Take an experiment. Two figures, ∟ and ∠, are exposed in rapid succession. Expert observers offer the following introspections:

ZE characterized the experience of movement, that is to say, what was taking place in the arc of movement, as a "change in brightness, change of intensity. Something seems to happen there. Not black and not white. Like heat rising on a hot day from the pavement. But we can usually see heat waves better. This thing is much faster and more elusive." Upon being asked if he had anything more to say about the nature of the movement he remarked that "it was very difficult to see and much more difficult to describe."

CP adopted an analytical attitude of his own accord and gives us a much completer report: "I can only describe the movement by analogy. The pure movement has an appearance more of an imaginal type. Something more like the trail of a match in the dark. I can't follow the movement of the line through space. I can get something in terms of imagery, a fuzzy sort of thing that comes in the arc of the movement. It is different from the blackness of the line. It isn't as black and as 'clear-cut.'" Later on: "a kind of blurring after-effect." CP also remarked upon the extraordinary difficulty of ever being able properly to get at it descriptively. He seemed to think of the actual stimulus as being almost beyond the ability of the sense-organs and the perceptive process to grasp.[1]

It is the vagueness of such introspective reports which has prompted some psychologists to discard all reference to consciousness.

c. Incapacity for Self-observation. The chief limitation upon the method of introspection is the natural incapacity for self-observation. Not only is language inadequate as a medium of description, but the actual observation, aside from the report, is inexpert even in the most capable observers.

Recall, for example, the sort of vagueness that seizes you when an optometrist tells you to stare at a chart and state which diagonal appears darkest to you. You don't know but you tell him something for fear of appearing stupid, and then he makes you some lenses you can hardly see through. The doctor who begs you to say where you feel a pain 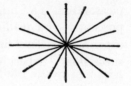 when he pushes on you is distressed at your introspective ineptness. The young man who pursues the elusive maiden for an answer, finds her "torn by a tumult of contrary emotions," so that she must confess she "doesn't know her mind" and can only reply, "Yes and No."

Personality tests which require a self-estimate demand a more expert introspective capacity than the average person possesses. Consider, for example, the following questions:[2]

1. Do I get discouraged rather easily, and have moods and occasional fits of depression? Yes No

---

[1] H. R. De Silva: *loc. cit.*

[2] J. G. Frederick: *What Is Your Emotional Age? A Book of 65 Amusing Psychological Tests.* Business Bourse, New York, 1928.

2. Am I rather fond of "cutting a dash" with my clothes and enjoy attracting attention to myself with my dress or manner?   Yes   No

3. Am I cool and self-possessed in emergencies?   Yes   No

4. Am I inclined to being very positive, irritable, and dogmatic when I am arguing a question against strong opposition?   Yes   No

5. Is solitude or being alone enjoyable to me?   Yes   No

6. Do I often say things which I later regret?   Yes   No

7. Are my relations with my family peaceful and sweet?   Yes   No

8. Do I frequently take offence at the words or actions of others?   Yes   No

9. Do I readily admit I am wrong when I know I am wrong?   Yes   No

10. Am I inclined to blame others for my failures and mistakes?   Yes   No

11. Do I place myself first in nearly all my relationships?   Yes   No

12. Is it my idea that I haven't had a very good "break" from life?   Yes   No

13. Am I inclined to live beyond my means?   Yes   No

14. Have I an underlying sense of inferiority or lack of confidence in myself, which I try to hide?   Yes   No

15. Do I incline toward tears when attending an emotional play?   Yes   No

16. Do little annoyances tend to "get my goat"?   Yes   No

17. Am I inclined toward impressing my superiority on other people?   Yes   No

18. Am I domineering?   Yes   No

19. Do I have "tantrums" when I am upset or displeased?   Yes   No

20. Am I frequently looking for sympathy from others?   Yes   No

21. Am I a "good hater"?   (someone who has active dislikes and antagonisms toward some people?)   Yes   No

22. Do I get pangs of envy and jealousy when others I know have successes?   Yes   No

23. Am I very considerate of the feelings of other people?   Yes   No

24. Do I get angry or "peeved" frequently, or have "tiffs" with people?   Yes   No

25. Have I ever thought of murdering someone, or committing suicide?   Yes   No

Think over the questions and underline either "Yes" or "No." For the present, let the self-analysis bring home to you the difficulty of accurate introspection. We shall refer back to the significance of your answers in a later chapter.

B. Introspection Plus Observation of Behavior—Activities of the Mind and Body. Another group of psychologists are definitely committed in their interest to a study of the individual in action. They center their attention in introspecting upon what the mind is doing, but they rely less on introspection and more on the observation of objective behavior which is regarded as the manifestation of mind. Psychology thus adopts a dynamic viewpoint.

Inasmuch as psychology is concerned with activities, its terms should be predominately verbs and adverbs. One noun, individual, is essential as the subject for the verbs. The use of nouns to represent the activities of the subject is confusing. Intelligence, memory, attention should be thought of as verbs and not nouns. Accurately speaking, the individual behaves intelligently, he remembers well, he sees the stimulus clearly. Such a description is more exact than to state that the person has a superior intelligence, that he has a good memory, that he is blessed with a well-trained attention, since the employment of nouns encourages the student to forget that he is observing, not things, but activities. In keeping with this suggestion, to stress activity by the use of verbs, subsequent chapter titles are called "Attending and Perceiving," "Remembering and Anticipating," instead of "Attention," "Perception," "Memory," and "Imagination," the usage in some older textbooks.[1]

[1] See R. S. Woodworth: *Psychology*, pp. 29–30. Revised edition, 1934.

1. Functionalism. The Functional psychologist is interested in the activities of the mind. It is mental activity which has immediate significance for thought and conduct. A simple situation will illustrate the difference between the Introspectionist and the Functionalist. Something begins to crawl down the psychologist's back—the Introspectionist lets it continue to crawl and describes his sensations—the Functionalist faces the situation as a problem and figures out what he should do by way of solving it. For the Functionalist consciousness is not an item to be described but an instrument to be used. The task of psychology is not simply to describe, but to investigate the relation of consciousness to behavior and the interpretation of consciousness from the standpoint of behavior. Mind is in the last analysis action—the action of human beings adjusting themselves to their environment. Mind as a manifestation of life is essentially an activity. Mind and behavior are inseparable processes in effecting an adjustment between the organism and its environment. Some of this action we call thinking, some we call feeling, some we call skill.

Functionalism grew out of the influence of Darwin upon psychology. Its chief exponents in the early stages were James, Dewey, and Angell. The fundamental question which they proposed to answer was: what is the biological *function* of mind? The function of consciousness is to solve the problems involved in adapting the organism to its environment. Mind is to be defined in terms of its use. Mind is an instrument by which the organism adjusts itself to the complex variations of the environment. Thus the mental life is treated in terms of its evolutionary value.

Psychology, from the Functional point of view, is a biological science. The biological significance of consciousness is its value in securing adaptation to novel situations. When a conflict, a crisis, an emergency, a new situation arises, consciousness steps in to effect a new and better adjustment—to help the individual in accommodating himself to the changing demands of the environment in the most efficient way. After the individual has repeated the new mode of adaptation in response to the recurring situation, consciousness steps out and habit takes care of the behavior. Thus the individual is permitted to make progress in his adjustments, for while habit operates to handle old problems, the person's full attention may be turned to the solution of further emergencies.

A few examples will illustrate how economy of effort is secured through the formation of appropriate habits. Ask a person which sock he puts on first in the morning and probably he will not be able to tell you. He solved that problem long ago, so that it no longer is an issue demanding his time for deliberation. But suppose that in slipping on his socks he discovers a hole in one of them, and suppose that all the rest of his socks are in the wash. He now has to pause and think things out. Perhaps he solves the problem by coloring his ankle with ink so that the hole is camouflaged, or he calls on his wife to mend the hole. Let us say he chooses the second alternative—which is the easier way out of the dilemma, if his wife likes to darn socks (which is improbable). The next time he meets the same crisis, he may go through the same process of deliberation, but after more repetitions he gets the habit of calling upon his wife for aid. So, at last, he just relies upon his wife's help without "thinking a thing of it." A hole in his sock is no longer a perplexing problem.

Functionalism has been especially fruitful in the field of education. Education is the process through which appropriate habits are formed. The individual who is properly educated has such a command of the ordinary situations of life that he can devote his entire attention to the more complex problems that baffle human endeavor. Dewey, especially, has emphasized the importance of habit formation in the educative process.[1]

Functional psychology is dynamic. In describing the activities of the mind, it deals with impulses, desires, drives, instincts, feelings. It is a purposive psychology in that it considers the mind as working toward the goal of adjustment. The pursuance of future ends and the choice of means for their attainment are the fundamental activities of the mind. Consciousness, according to James, is a fighter for ends.[2] Functionalism is very close to the viewpoint of Hormism which we shall now consider.

2. Hormism.[3] Hormic psychology stresses the conative (striving) aspect of mind. Mental life is interpreted in terms of energy (vitalism[4]) which is directed toward the attainment of certain goals. The Hormic approach to human nature is thus dynamic and purposive (teleological[5]). McDougall is a prominent exponent of the Hormic, purposive view of mind; the psychoanalysts, Freud and Jung, with their conceptions of the libido, adopt a scheme for interpreting mental life, likewise Hormic in its fundamentals.

McDougall takes purposive striving as his fundamental category. Human nature is described in terms of impulses which require for their satisfaction the achievement of definite perceptible ends. The motive behind behavior is always some instinctive urge, which may be conveniently defined as an innate propensity to seek a certain goal—for instance, the sex urge, which impels a person to seek a mate. The instincts, for McDougall, are the prime movers of all human activity,

---

[1]See John Dewey: *Human Nature and Conduct.* 1922.

[2]W. James: *Principles of Psychology.* 1890.

[3]The word "hormic" is from the Greek word *horme* which means a vital impulse or urge to action.

[4]Vitalism posits a force which is characteristic of living creatures. Hans Driesch and Henri Bergson are outstanding vitalists.

[5]Teleological is from the Greek word *telos* which means "end" or "goal."

initiating and sustaining thought and action. The highly developed processes of the human mind are instrumental in devising the most adequate means for attaining the ends which bring satisfaction to instinctive cravings; reasoning, for example, is the servant of instinct, and, as such, functions as a guide to striving—the motivating force, in all cases, being an innate urge to achieve some particular sort of goal.

Wherever we find that behavior is varied in its striving toward some end, there we have evidence of that capacity for purposive adaptation which is the essential function of mind. Purposive behavior is directed toward the realization of some end anticipated by the individual. In so far as behavior is teleological, it may be regarded as an expression of mind.

The psychoanalysts, Freud and Jung, may be classified in the Hormic school. Freud describes the mental life in terms of *libido*, a concept which represents the energy of the sex instinct.[1] Psychology for Freud is mainly unconscious, in contrast to the Introspectionists who consider psychology in terms of consciousness. The libido is like the oil in a well—you only see its manifestations as it spouts to the surface to express itself through normal love, or, perhaps, through abnormal interest, on the part of the unwedded, in marriages, births, and scandals.

Mental phenomena are interpreted in terms of energy. Instead of stating that a boy becomes attached to his mother, the Freudian says his libido becomes fixated upon the mother object (the Œdipus complex). When the son grows up and the time comes for him to select a mate, he cannot find one who suits him because his libido is still fixated on his mother, and he cannot release it from her and transfer it to a sweetheart. A girl may be enamored of her father in the same way (the Electra complex)—she cannot find a man like dear old Dad.

---

[1] S. Freud: *A General Introduction to Psychoanalysis*. Thirteenth edition, 1924.

Now suppose a girl suffering from an Electra complex finally does succeed in falling in love with a young man who convinces her that, while he is not the man her father is, still he will do as a substitute. When they get married and establish a home of their own, she discovers that her husband does not press his own trousers (as Father used to do), and that he hates to work around the house (Father loved to mow the lawn and repair the faucets). In short, difficulties have arisen which call for an effort at adjustment. She cannot endure the strained relationship, so she "runs home to Father." Or, as Freud says, her libido regresses (goes back) to its earlier object (the father)—it regresses to the point of fixation. The stronger the fixation, the more likely the regression.

Jung likewise interprets mental life in terms of a hypothetical fundamental striving which he designates *libido*.[1] The word "interest," as Jung suggests, might be a psychological equivalent for libido. Jung's view differs from Freud's in that Jung thinks of the libido as including more than the sexual urge; for Jung the libido is the life energy manifesting itself in nutrition, growth, sexuality, and all the human activities and interests. Freud, in treating a patient suffering from mental disorder, looks for a maladjustment in the sex life; Jung searches the individual's character over a wider range to discover if he is satisfied in his love life, if he is contented with his job, if he has won the esteem of his fellowmen.

Jung, like Freud, describes at length the mechanisms of fixation and regression. The contribution for which Jung is probably best known is his description of the mechanisms of extroversion and introversion. An extrovert is a person whose libido is turned outward—he is interested chiefly in the external world—he is the doer, the hustler, the mixer, the Behaviorist. An introvert is one whose libido is turned inward—he is inter-

[1] C. G. Jung: *Collected Papers On Analytical Psychology*. 1922.

ested in his own states of mind—he is the thinker, the poet, the philosopher, the Introspectionist.

The mind is described in terms of its activities by the Functional and Hormic schools. It is an easy transition to the next approach to psychology, Behaviorism, which deals, not with the activities of the mind, but with the activities of the physical organism.

C. Behavior of the Organism. We have dealt with the mind as content and with the mind as activity—we now come to a psychology which leaves the mind out of account and concentrates its whole attention upon the behavior of the organism.[1]

1. Behaviorism. In 1903 John B. Watson made a study at the University of Chicago of the white rat in a maze.[2] His researches on the rat, and later, on the noddy tern, raised the whole subject of animal experimentation to a new technical level. In the course of his investigations in animal psychology, Watson ran head-on into a puzzling problem. It had been the custom among psychologists to try to reconstruct the consciousness of the animal from the evidence of his behavior.[3] What is going on in the rat's mind when he is finding his way through the maze? In the phraseology of Briggs' cartoons, "I wonder what a rat thinks about" in such a situation, would be the question the psychologist would posit for himself. You can ask a human being to introspect, and he can give you a verbal report on his mental processes. But a rodent, lacking language, must remain a speechless mystery. The only step that seemed to be left was for the psychologist to make believe

---

[1] It should be stated that in our account of Behaviorism we shall deal primarily with the Watsonian variety.

[2] J. B. Watson: *Kinæsthetic and Organic Sensation: Their Rôle in the Reactions of the White Rat to the Maze.* Psychological Monographs, 1907, 8, No. 2.

[3] E. L. Thorndike, in 1898, had described his investigations of animal behavior without resorting to mental concepts, thus being a pioneer in the advocacy of the viewpoint adopted by Watson. See "Animal Intelligence," *Psychological Review Monograph Supplement*, Volume 2, Number 4.

he was a rat, and then conjecture that probably the rat would feel about the same way as he himself, in the same predicament. The psychologist would resemble that simple-minded lad who was the only one to succeed in locating the farmer's ass which had wandered away. The simpleton soon found the lost animal. In describing the method he used, he explained: "I asked myself, 'Which way would an ass naturally go?' Well, I went there and there he was." While it was no task at all for the moron to identify himself with the ass, it was not so easy for the psychologist to picture the mental life of a rat as seen from the inside. Watson realized the dangers and difficulties in an anthropomorphic animal psychology, but what was he to do? If he ceased to study consciousness, he would be resigning, according to the standards of his time, from the ranks of psychology. It was a crisis in his career.

Watson met the challenge of the problem by coming out openly in favor of limiting animal psychology to the observation and description of behavior, and then insisted that this objective method which ignored consciousness was psychology just as truly as the old Introspectionism was psychology. Animal psychologists were urged to abandon the absurd position of attempting to construct the conscious content of an animal whose behavior was under observation. This stand on Watson's part necessitated an elaboration of his views in defence of his position. He extended his Behavioristic hypothesis to include the human being, for if the behavior of a rat can be studied to advantage without reference to mind, why not *homo sapiens*, too? It was on this count that Watson came into conflict with the Introspectionists, and before the air had cleared, he had not merely stated that consciousness was no subject matter for a scientific psychology, but had majestically ruled it out of existence. While the controversy was raging, Watson attacked some of the vulnerable spots in Introspective psychology which we have already mentioned. In addition he objected strenuously to the barrenness of Introspective psychology, which, he charged, had failed to contribute anything of a scientifically usable kind to human nature—in helping people to understand why they behave as they do and how to modify their behavior.

Consciousness cannot be accurately reported. All terms which savor of such a mysterious entity as mind must be discarded. Consciousness, sensation, perception, image, will, and like terms are avoided because Watson believes that no one can use such terms in a comprehensible fashion. He himself has found that psychology can be adequately presented without them. Scientific psychology, therefore, should confine its interest to objective behavior which can be readily observed and described.

The method of Behaviorism may best be described by referring to three of its aspects: its mechanistic conception of the human being, its analytic approach, and finally its interest in prediction and control.

a. Mechanism. Man is viewed by the behaviorist as a machine going through certain performances which may be readily observed and described. Behaviorism is anti-teleological. A machine just behaves—it has no end in view. If a mechanical animal is constructed which turns toward a light, one might be tempted to say he heeds the light because he is curious. "To say that he goes to the light because of curiosity is to say that he goes to the light because he goes to it. Curiosity is a way of behaving, not a non-physical force that directs behavior."[1] The same dictum of course applies to *real* animals and *real* human beings for they too are robots, though more complicated, mechanically speaking.

---

[1] C. N. Rexroad: *General Psychology*, p. 29. 1929. As for myself, I can honestly say that I not only behave curiously (out of curiosity) at times, but that also now and then I *feel* curious as well.

b. Analysis. Thoroughly scientific in its spirit, Behaviorism adopts the analytic method for studying human behavior. The psychologist finds two factors in behavior which are open to observation—the *stimulus* which affects the individual and the *response* which the individual makes to the stimulus. What happens in between the stimulus and the response (in the so-called mind) is completely ignored because it belongs to the realm of the unseen. Man's physical structure—the apparatus by means of which he behaves—is analyzed into its most minute parts, with special attention to the receptors (sense organs which pick up stimuli), nervous system, and effectors (muscles and glands which carry out the responses). Behavior is analytically reduced to reflexes by the Behaviorists just as consciousness is reduced to sensations, feelings, and images by the Introspectionists.[1]

c. Prediction and Control. What is the purpose behind the analysis of behavior? What end can be gained by studying the relation between stimulus and response? If a given stimulus would always evoke a given response in a given individual, then it would be possible to predict what the response would be when a certain stimulus is applied, or to know what stimulus should be presented to call out a desired response. The best we can do, as the Behaviorist himself admits, is to predict in terms of probability, for an observer can never be absolutely positive that a particular stimulation will always affect a certain individual in the same way. Probability may be a matter of the general human ignorance which limits all scientific knowledge. In addition to this factor of ignorance, and the factor of individual differences,[2] there is, as I see it, the variability of the human mind to take into account a

---

[1]*Gestalt* psychology objects to the analytic method of the Behaviorists. To the Configurationist behavior is a total pattern. See R. H. Wheeler: *The Science of Psychology.* 1929.

[2]The fact that individuals differ from each other in structure and function.

variable factor which is interposed between the stimulus and the response:

Stimulus—response (Behaviorist)
Stimulus—(mind)—response.

Watson regards psychology as a purely objective branch of natural science; the goal of which is the prediction and control of behavior, without reference to any introspective data from the realm of consciousness. Behavioristic psychology seeks to discover through systematic observation and experimentation the laws and principles which govern man's behavior. Two problems are involved in this program—the one of uncovering the situation evoking a certain response, the other of predicting the response likely to be called out by a given situation. An adequate knowledge of these factors would make possible a control over behavior which is a practical goal worthy of our best scientific efforts.

One problem is the ferreting out of the situation responsible for a given response. When Frances St. John Smith disappeared from Smith College, a psychoanalyst was summoned to investigate the personality of the girl in order to ascertain whether she was the sort of person who would commit suicide, or whether there were any circumstances that might incline a person of her temperament to run away. The response, disappearing, was given; the question was, why did she disappear? The answer to that question, the authorities believed, might help them in tracing the missing girl.[1]

The other problem is predicting the response likely to be evoked by a given situation. An official at a college in the Middle West sued his wife for divorce after he had uncovered her unsavory past. He learned that he was her fifth husband, that she had divorced her first two husbands, murdered her third husband, and sent her fourth husband to prison, where

[1]The Boston *Advertiser*, January 31, 1928.

he remained long enough for his wife to divorce him. He, the fifth in line, was somewhat unnerved by his wife's past. He began to fear for his own safety. Given a husband and given the marital situation, he was led naturally to wonder what would be his wife's reaction.[1]

Knowledge promises foresight, and foresight means control because it renders prediction possible. The problems of prediction and control, upon which Behaviorism lays so much stress, are the most important ones for psychology to study, as they bear upon human conduct. Psychologists of all schools must be frank to admit that they are baffled by the complexity of the task.

2. Criticism. The Behavioristic method is a valuable one but it is not the only approach to psychology. Its main deficiency, to my mind, is its inadequate account of motivation, for when the psychologist, as a student of human nature, has observed a person's behavior and described it in every least detail, we do not feel that he has revealed all we want to know about the person in question. The Behaviorist is satisfied when he has secured an exhaustive description of what the individual is doing. The collection of data on behavior is valuable, essentially, as evidence for inferring what has been going on in the mind of the performer. We not only want to know what he is doing but also why he is doing it. In other words, we suffer from an insatiable curiosity to learn what was the *motive* behind the behavior. Until we have ascertained the motive responsible for the action we are not satisfied that we know all we are eager to learn about the individual who is behaving in the particular situation. In order to understand a person, we must also know the person. To know the person, we must find out all we can about his organism, it is true—but we must also undertake the more difficult task of delving into his mental processes—particularly his motives. We are still

---

[1]The Boston *Sunday Herald*, November 12, 1927.

far from the real man when we merely observe his behavior. An understanding of the man calls for a penetration beyond the behavior to the personality expressing itself in the pursuance of its ideals. The view here suggested implies that human nature consists of both body and mind. If we desire to gain a complete view of any person we must realize that there is a subjective phase to human nature, thoughts, feelings, and desires, the inner world of *mind*, and there is, in addition, an objective phase to human nature, the outer world of *behavior*. The conviction that an understanding of behavior necessitates an investigation of the mental states behind actions has practical consequences of real importance. Take, for example, the problem of training a child. It is important that parents understand the motives responsible for the conduct of their children, since the motives are the fundamental matter rather than the conduct itself. A child who may appear, on the surface, to be engaged in malicious behavior may really be actuated by a desire to be helpful, as in the case of the little girl who sprinkled Dutch Cleanser all over the dining room after watching the maid clean the tiled bathroom in that manner.

Unless the observer discovers what is going on in a person's mind, he is quite likely to misinterpret the behavior of that individual. The cartoon on page 104 illustrates the point.

The importance of probing beyond behavior to motives was evident in the trial of Sacco and Vanzetti. One of the indictments upon which the prosecution rested was that Sacco and Vanzetti, on the day they were arrested, manifested behavior showing "consciousness of guilt." There was no doubt as to their behavior upon the occasion of their arrest. The Behaviorist might have given an exact description of their every move, but legal action must go further—it must find out what it was in the minds of these two men which would account for their behavior. The ascertainment of the motive was no

(Reproduced by permission of Walter Schmidt.)

easy task.   The court fell into grave error in attacking the problem.   Prince pointed out clearly the fallacies committed:

As to behavior showing "consciousness of guilt" as evidence of a particular crime upon which Judge Thayer laid great stress in his charge to the jury, I do not hesitate to say that though learned in law, Judge Thayer, like almost all lawyers, shows a lamentable ignorance of the science of modern dynamic psychology.   Behavior showing a consciousness of guilt involves motives of behavior.
There is no more difficult problem in psychology than the determination of the motive or motives that impel to behavior.
The convicting behavior of Sacco and Vanzetti was lying and (as alleged) attempting to draw a gun while in the motor car after arrest.   As everyone knows, the same conduct may be determined by many motives, and when the motive is fear of punishment, a person may be guilty of more than one punishable act.   Sacco, as a notorious anarchist, was . . . guilty of activities for which he feared arrest and the fate of deportation . . .   He was actually sought by the United States government.   All this Sacco knew and feared.
What did Sacco fear?   That could only be told by delving deep into his mind and discovering what meaning arrest had for him.[1]

It seems that the Behaviorist, in ignoring "mind," cannot develop an adequate psychology of motivation.   This shortcoming seriously detracts from the value of Behaviorism as a methodology for studying human conduct.

II.   THE SYNOPTIC APPROACH

An adequate study of psychology should include the various approaches represented by the different schools.   It does not seem wise to limit ourselves to any single school.   Since elementary students should be privileged to acquaint themselves with different points of view, the elementary course may profitably be made eclectic.   Consequently, in our study of experience and behavior we shall draw upon all the schools

---

[1]Morton Prince: The Boston *Herald*, October 30, 1926.   It is important to distinguish between motive and intention.
See W. McDougall: *Outline of Psychology*, pp. 121–122.

so that we may gain an adequate picture of human nature, in the conviction that a better understanding of the conscious life will promote a better control over behavior.[1]

[1]Among the writers who adopt the eclectic viewpoint in elementary psychology are: E. G. Boring, H. S. Langfeld, H. P. Weld *et al.*, *Psychology. A Factual Textbook*, 1935; J. W. Bridges, *Psychology—Normal and Abnormal*, 1930; S. I. Franz and K. Gordon, *Psychology*, 1933; A. I. Gates, *Elementary Psychology*, Revised edition, 1928; J. H. Griffiths, *The Psychology of Human Behavior*, 1935; C. H. Judd, *Psychology—General Introduction*, Revised edition, 1917; F. H. Lund, *Psychology—The Science of Mental Activity*, 1927; G. Murphy, *General Psychology*, 1933, and *Briefer General Psychology*, 1935; W. B. Pillsbury, *Fundamentals of Psychology*, 1923; E. S. Robinson, *Practical Psychology*, 1926, and *Man As Psychology Sees Him*, 1932; M. Schoen, *Human Nature—A First Book in Psychology*, 1930; C. E. Seashore, *Introduction to Psychology*, 1924; R. S. Woodworth, *Psychology*, Third edition, 1934.

PART III

THE PHYSICAL MECHANISM

Experience depends on the nature of the physical organism. Part III provides a description of *The Physical Mechanism*, with special emphasis on its relation to the mental life. Chapter IV describes the *Sensory Equipment* by means of which we are informed of the events transpiring in our world. Chapter V depicts the organizing functions of *The Nervous System*. Chapter VI is an account of the *Motor Equipment* through which we effect our responses to the stimulating situations that have aroused our awareness.

CHAPTER IV

SENSORY EQUIPMENT

PSYCHOLOGY is the study of the modes of behavior by means of which living beings adapt themselves to the urgent demands of the environment. Survival in the struggle for existence necessitates a continuous adjustment between the needs of the organism and the physical medium through which those cravings may be satisfied. Adaptation is effected by a *response* to a *stimulus* of which the creature has become aware.

I. WHY PSYCHOLOGY IS CONCERNED WITH PHYSIOLOGY

The psychologist must become acquainted with the physiological mechanisms underlying the stimulus-response process in order to secure an adequate picture of mental life in relation to the behavior patterns through which the mind gains its ends.

The first step in adaptation, as I have said, is awareness. The individual must be cognizant of what is going on around him before he can perform the acts appropriate to his immediate environment. He must experience, become conscious of, become aware of the stimuli constantly impinging upon him. Protoplasm, the substance of all living matter, possesses a characteristic excitability. The unicellular organism, the amoeba, is excitable, but only in a vague, diffuse way. In the higher organisms, during the course of evolution, specific sense organs (receptors) developed which permit an accurate reception of a wide variety of complex stimuli. Instead of being vaguely aware of its surroundings, the organism becomes specifically conscious through its specialized receptors of a certain class of objects or occurrences. Thus, the eyes, for example, render visual experience possible—we do not just *feel* there is something going on, we definitely *see* it. The ears, likewise, pick up a specific type of stimulus—sounds. Through the eyes and ears, alone, we are affected by an elaborate range of stimuli.

Indeed we may say that the variety of experience stands in direct proportion to the differentiation of the sense organs. We are aware in just as many distinct ways as our receptors will allow—we see, hear, smell, taste, experience pain, heat, tickle, as the case may be.

Our sensory mechanisms determine not only the kinds of consciousness to which we are subject, but also the extent of each special kind of experience. There is a certain degree of sensitiveness to certain stimuli under certain conditions— there are air vibrations which never become sounds or sights because our sense organs are not delicate enough to register them. Psychologically, we say such phenomena remain subliminal, that is, lie below the threshold of consciousness. Man has supplemented the deficiencies of his receptors by the construction of instruments which permit him to study the stars (telescope), or to extract music from the air (radio). Thus the eye is enabled to see things which otherwise would have passed unseen, and the ear to detect occurrences in the world of nature which otherwise would have escaped our notice.

Awareness of surrounding stimuli is of value, of course, only as it supplies the information upon the basis of which adaptive responses can be effected. Just as, in the course of evolution, a differentiation of the sense organs has steadily progressed, so there has been developed a specialized motor equipment which makes possible the exact reactions necessary to efficient adjustment. The main effectors (motor apparatus) are the striped (skeletal) muscles, the unstriped (smooth) muscles, and the glands. The striped muscles are the muscles which you see and admire in the professional strong man—the arms, shoulders, chest, stomach, and legs. They are applied to manipulation and movement. When you pick up a heavy weight, you use the biceps, which are striped muscles. The unstriped muscles take care of the internal processes, such as the dilation and contraction of the blood vessels. The glands are of two types—the duct glands which secrete externally or into the alimentary canal, such as the sweat glands and the salivary glands; and the ductless glands which secrete into the blood stream, such as the adrenal glands and the thyroid glands. Through these various muscles and glands we make our responses to the stimuli which impinge upon us.

In addition to excitability, protoplasm exhibits the traits of conductivity and integration. The nerve is a specialized form of protoplasm evolved to conduct and integrate with the maximum effectiveness. Nerves are arranged in a system, the nervous system, which constitutes the link between the stimulus and the response. Were the stimulus to lead immediately to the response, our range of activities would be very limited. Our adaptation would be effective only for a simple environment. The introduction of the complex intermediate nerve processes between the receptor and the effector makes possible the complicated modes of behavior which constitute intelligence.

The incoming stimulus, picked up by a receptor, is conducted by the nerves to the spinal cord or further to the brain. When the impulse reaches the higher nervous centers conscious experience occurs. Just what the relation is between consciousness and brain activity is unknown. It is one of the tasks of psychology to investigate this intimate relation and to correlate nervous and conscious phenomena as accurately as possible within the bounds of our limited knowledge.

In the brain the nerve impulse is conducted through a very complex set of nerves before it proceeds down the nerve tracts to the effectors. The nervous system through its organizing functions renders possible a systematic response. Our activities must be coördinated if they are to produce an efficient adjustment.

The function of the nervous system is thus to form the organizing link between the stimulus and the response. The elaborate nervous system of the human being, connecting, as it does, a specialized set of receptors with a specialized set of effectors, is the basis for specific types of behavior exactly appropriate to the particular needs which the individual stimuli represent.

In the human being protoplasm has become highly differentiated into specialized receptors, specialized conductors, and specialized effectors. Through the complex bodily mechanism specific functions are performed efficiently, and a high degree of integration is achieved. Action is thus both widely diversified and effectively organized.

II. SENSE ORGANS AND EXPERIENCE

Receptors fall into three general groups, classified according to the source of stimulation: (1) Exteroceptors, which respond to stimuli outside the body, such as the eyes and ears (distance receptors) and taste organs (contact receptors).

(2) Propioceptors, a system of sense organs found in the muscles, tendons, joints, and so forth, whose function is to help regulate the movements evoked by the stimulation of the exteroceptors.

(3) Interoceptors, or visceral receptive organs, which respond only to stimulation arising within the body, chiefly in connection with the processes of nutrition, excretion, and so forth.

Since the exteroceptive field exceeds the others in its wealth of receptor organs, and since more is known of the exteroceptors, we shall devote most of our attention to the traditional five senses with their respective organs, eye, ear, nose, tongue, and skin (all exteroceptors). Our chief interest will lie in the sorts of experience to which we are prone by virtue of our special sense organs.

A. Vision. The receptor for visual sensations is the eye, poetically described as "the window of the soul." It should be clearly understood that our eyes do not see—they merely detect the stimulus and transmit the message along the optic nerve to the back portion of the brain. We see, not with our eyes, but with our minds. In a perfectly normal condition we may have "eyes which see not," as we look, for example, at the face of a friend while we are thinking of something else. It will be, indeed, as though he were not there. Only when we make an effort to "fix" the impression, and relate it through an act of memory to the person whom we see, does the image in our eyes have any meaning for us. Reading disability is often attributed to defective eyes, when the actual source of the difficulty is faulty training in observation. Remedial teaching, which corrects the faulty habits of observing, enables the child to see better and thus to improve his reading capacities.

The eyes are end-organs which have become specialized in their sensitivity to stimuli. Photochemical substances have been evolved which are delicately sensitive to light, and lenses have been developed to facilitate exact registration. Further, the eye is mounted in a socket which permits ready turning in many directions, thus saving wear and tear on the neck. The eye may be compared to a camera, though the former is infinitely more complicated than the latter.

The structure of the eye may be represented by a simplified diagram:

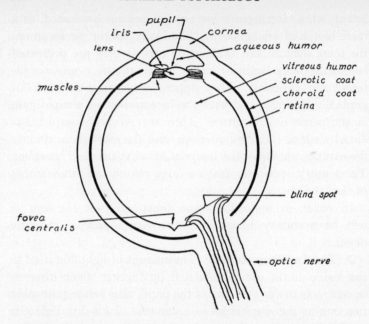

The fact that we have *two* eyes adds considerably to the complexity of experience. The importance of binocular vision will be noted when we consider the visual factors in the perception of distance. A person with one eye is handicapped in his adjustments, because his reception of stimuli is inaccurate as compared with that of the normal person.

1. How Babies Learn to See. During the first three weeks of infancy the visual apparatus is not yet complete, so that the new-born baby who seems to be staring fixedly at his adoring father is actually seeing nothing. The eyeballs move vaguely at first, and during the early days they look almost blindly around them. They are unseeing eyes. Until there is answering intelligence within, the image of the object before the child conveys nothing to him. A lamp held before the face of the child will, in the course of a week or so, be followed by the eyes waveringly and indefinitely. It probably appears to the infant, whose intelligence has not yet become awakened, as a mere blotch of orange color. Gradually, as the weeks go on, the more definite and brilliant objects as they are presented before the baby begin to excite feebly at first a sense of interest and curiosity. They appear very faint at first, but gradually increase, and with the increase comes a rapid gain in the perceptive faculties. Thus the receptors furnish the data by which the mind develops, and the more the conscious life evolves, the more the material of sense takes on meaning. The sensory apparatus plays a large rôle in the nourishment of the intelligence.

In order to understand the functioning of the eye it will be necessary to consider the visual process in some detail.

2. The Pupillary Reflex. The amount of light admitted to the inside of the eye is regulated by the iris which expands or contracts to vary the size of the pupil, thus serving the same function as the diaphragm in a camera. In a dim light the pupil is larger than in a bright light. The regulation of the size of the pupil is automatic (reflex). The pupil may be seen contracting by turning a flash-light directly upon the eye.

3. Accommodation. In order that the stimulus may be properly registered, the light rays must be focused upon the retina. The lens performs this function through the process of accommodation.

In the fish eye the lens is fixed and the retina is movable.

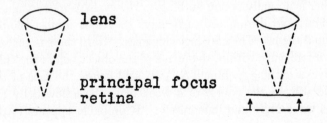

In the human eye focusing is not effected by altering the distance between lens and plate (retina), but by changing the curvature of the lens:

The curvature of the lens is regulated by means of muscles attached to each end—the lens is accommodated. Defects in the lens are compensated by the wearing of glasses which make it possible to focus properly without undue strain. If a person with normal vision puts on glasses worn by a near-sighted individual, everything will be a blur—since the rays no longer are focused on the retina. With advancing age the ligaments of the lens lose their elasticity—hence an elderly person who has misplaced his spectacles will hold a book at full arm's length in order to see it clearly.

When light rays are passed through a convex lens the image is inverted:

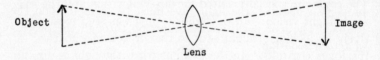

The image is upside down on the retina. Why, one may ask, then, do we not see the world upside down? The answer is simple enough—we have never seen the world right side up, so we are not conscious that we see it upside down. If you were to wear glasses which would cause the image to be upright on the retina (a totally new experience), the world would appear inverted. After a few days you would become adjusted so that the environment would lose its topsy-turvy appearance. Then if you removed the glasses, giving you the inverted image again, the world would appear upside down until an adjustment had been made.[1]

4. The Retina. Within the retina lie sensitive photochemical substances, cones and rods. It is to these specific organs that we must turn for an explanation of most visual phenomena. Light waves set up chemical changes in these receptors, which are transmitted to the optic nerve.

The point of clearest vision is directly behind the nodal point of the lens, the fovea centralis, where there are only cones. The cones become fewer and the rods more numerous toward the periphery—on the outermost periphery there are only rods.

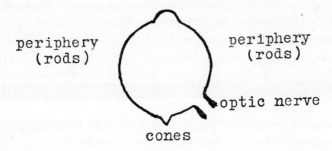

periphery (rods)   periphery (rods)

optic nerve

cones

The cones are specially suited for daylight vision and the rods for twilight vision. In daylight an object is seen most effectively by looking straight at it so that it becomes focused on the fovea centralis. In the twilight when the light is dim an object may be seen best by looking to one side of it so that it becomes focused upon the periphery.

Where the optic nerve leaves the eye, there are neither rods nor cones. This region is known as the blind spot. You

[1]G. M. Stratton: "Vision without Inversion of the Retinal Image," *Psychological Review*, 1897, 4, 341.
G. T. Ladd & R. S. Woodworth: *Elements of Physiological Psychology*, pp. 454–455. 1911.

may demonstrate the presence of the blind spot to yourself by a simple experiment:

Hold the diagram about six inches in front of you so that the cross is directly in front of the right eye. Close the right eye. Keep the left eye fixated on the cross while you move the book away. At a certain distance the dot will disappear, as the image of the dot falls on the blind spot.

We are not usually conscious of the blind spot because our eyes are constantly in motion, because the image does not fall on the blind spots of both eyes simultaneously, and because we fill in, out of our imagination, the gap in our vision. The subjective addition to perception may be discovered by the following experiment:

Close the left eye. Bring the left V close up to the right eye, and gradually move the book away, keeping the gaze fixed on the top of the left V. At a certain point, the right V will disappear, because it falls on the blind spot. Now, still keeping the gaze fixed on the top of the left V, examine the rest of the line to the right. Do you see it continuous to the end? If so, you are filling out a part of the line for which there is no image on the retina.[1]

We shall now note further aspects of visual experience and attempt to explain them in terms of the structure of the retina.

a. Spectrum. The colors which may be seen with the naked

[1] Taken from G. Humphrey: *The Story of Man's Mind,* opposite p. 58. 1923. By permission of Dodd Mead and Company.

eye range all the way from red on the long-wave end to violet
on the short. Color is not a physical thing, but a psychological
response to physical vibrations. There are many vibrations
of which we never become aware—without the aid of instruments—the infra-red and ultra-violet rays—because the retina
is not constructed to receive the light waves on the two extremes. Ultra-violet rays do not excite visual sensations because there are no substances in the retina sensitive enough to
detect them. If your radio set is not built to pick up certain
stations, the waves transmitted by those stations will go unnoticed. The structure of the eye similarly imposes limits
upon our experience. A striking illustration of this fact is
found in color-blindness.

b. Color-blindness. Color-blindness usually is only partial,
in the form of red-green blindness. It is very uncommon
among women but present in about three per cent of the men.
A person who is partially color-blind may mistake red for a dull
yellow and purple for a dull blue. His experience is a good
example of the statement, previously made, that color is a
psychological response to physical vibrations—the same
vibrations may provoke the experience of red in a normal person and dull yellow in a color-blind person. Color-blindness
is native and cannot be corrected by training. It is a serious
deficiency in motorists, paper hangers, and railway engineers.

How is color-blindness to be explained? The eye may be
plotted into color zones thus:

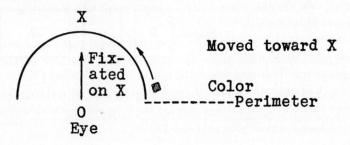

Any color moved along the perimeter will be seen as different colors according to this general plan. Red, for example, appears as a variation of gray when it is seen from the "corner of the eye." The periphery of the retina is almost totally color-blind. In this region there are only rods. A totally color-blind person would probably have no cones, only rods. A partially color-blind person would be defective in certain cones usually present in the region about the

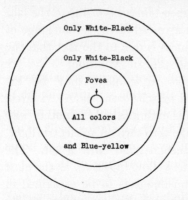

Only White-Black

Only White-Black

Fovea

All colors

and Blue-yellow

fovea, lacking the cones necessary for seeing red and green. It is likely, on the basis of these phenomena, that the rods take care of achromatic vision and the cones of chromatic vision. It is also probable that there are special substances in the cones for red-green and for blue-yellow, both types being present in the central zone, only the blue-yellow in the intermediate zone.

In terms of the Ladd-Franklin theory,[1] the retina has evolved through three stages. In the earliest stage the visual re-

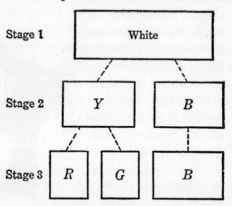

Stage 1 — White

Stage 2 — Y — B

Stage 3 — R — G — B

sponse was limited to white and black, no matter what the wave length of the stimulus; in the second stage, the visual response was differentiated into yellow for the long waves and blue for

---

[1] C. Ladd-Franklin: *Colour and Colour Theories.* 1929.

the short waves; in the third stage, the yellow response was split into red for the longest waves and green for the medium waves. According to this theory, red-green blindness is due to the fact that the central retinal zone is arrested in the second stage of evolution and total color-blindness is due to the fact that the whole retina remains in the first stage of evolution.

c. After-images. The positive after-image may be experienced by whirling a lighted match in the dark. A circle of fire remains after the match is extinguished. Another way to obtain the positive after-image is to turn on an electric light, stare at it for about thirty seconds, and turn it off. The image persists and is of the same yellow (positive) as the glow of the bulb. The positive after-image is to be explained in terms of inertia—the retinal process, having started on its way, continues of its own momentum.

A more striking phenomenon is the negative after-image (successive contrast). Look steadily at the boy's nose in the center of the picture for about thirty seconds. Then stare at a blank wall, preferably, keeping the gaze fixated on one spot, until the after-image looms into view. Note that the white and black portions have shifted, the white turned to black and the black to white (hence the term negative).[1]

Stare at the green square on the gray square in the diagram facing page 122 for about thirty seconds. Then cover the left-hand figure with a paper and transfer your gaze to the

[1]Courtesy of Snyder's Stores.

gray square on the right. A red after-image will appear on the gray background. The negative after-image is always of the complementary color.

Hering's theory of vision explains the negative after-image in terms of equilibrium. According to Hering there are three types of organs in the retina and each pair of complementary colors is produced by antagonistic changes in the same organ:

Anabolism induced by	*Katabolism induced by*
Green	Red
Blue	Yellow
Black	White

A light wave, for example, which sets up an anabolistic process in the Green-Red organ will evoke the sensation of green. The equilibrium is upset. Katabolism sets in to restore the organ to its normal state, thus giving rise to the after-image of red. The equilibratory nature of the visual process may be seen by looking at a lamp with a green shade and then turning out the light. In the darkness a red after-image will appear (negative), then a green after-image will come (positive), then a red after-image will reappear, and so on through a series of oscillations until the shifting process achieves a state of rest or equilibrium.

d. Contrast. The negative after-image is a case of successive contrast. Another contrast phenomenon is simultaneous contrast, which may be observed in the following experiments: The three gray squares in the diagram facing page 123 are the same gray. Note that the gray square on the green background has a pinkish (complementary color) appearance. Cover the figure with tissue paper and the effect will be exaggerated, since the contrast is enhanced by obscuring the contours.

The two grays are the same, yet the one on the black back-

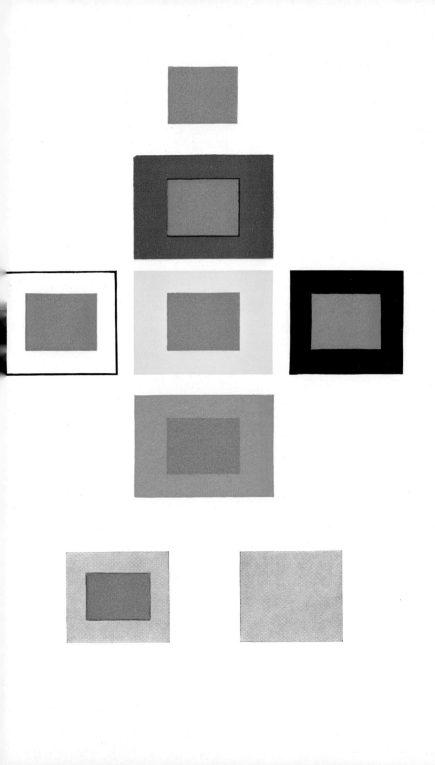

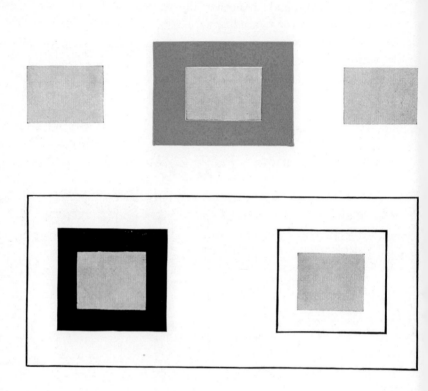

ground appears much lighter, by contrast, than the gray on the white background. Another illustration of brightness contrast is seen in the figure below.[1] Note the apparent shadows at the intersections of the white strips.

Simultaneous contrast (or retinal induction) occurs as the retinal substances tend toward equilibrium over the whole area of stimulation in such a way as to be directly affected at one point and indirectly —and oppositely—affected at all other points, though most noticeably in the immediate neighborhood of the stimulus.

e. Color Mixture. If complementary colors are mixed in the right proportions, a sensation of gray will result. Blue and yellow, for example, will produce a gray. You may remember in your schooldays that you mixed blue and yellow pigments in order to get green. The pigments are not pure colors, the blue containing some green and the yellow some green. Paints in reflecting the light waves absorb some of the waves, thus affecting the consequent sensation.

If blue and yellow are mixed, according to the Hering theory the anabolistic and katabolistic processes should balance each other and leave nothing as a result. But actually a gray remains. To account for this fact Müller postulated a cortical gray—a gray produced by the cortical cells, the central organ for vision in the occipital lobe. Blind persons, if not blind from birth, always see this gray.

One type of color harmony used in interior decoration is

---

[1]M. Luckiesh: *Visual Illusions,* p. 118.   1922.   Courtesy of D. Van ... rand Co.

complementary.   The effect of environment upon the appearance of colors is shown by the figures facing page 122.   A particular color must be selected with an eye for its relation to
the other colors in the scheme.   A wheel is sometimes used
in which complementary colors are arranged directly opposite
each other.   If you are matching a linoleum to your kitchen
woodwork, you look up the color of the wood as represented
on the wheel, and then the desirable color for the linoleum is
readily discovered.   Make-up testers, for matching cosmetic
colors in exterior decoration, are bringing the psychology of
color down to a science.   Correct color in decoration is a
valuable asset.

  f. Adaptation.   One of life's most embarrassing situations
confronts the individual who deserts the sunlight for the dark
shadows of the theater.   The process of locating a seat is
rendered hazardous by the simple fact that one can see neither
the aisle nor the people one is stumbling over.

  This phenomenon is to be explained by the fact that in the
sunlight or other bright light, the visual purple in the rods of
the retina is bleached.   In the theater, twilight conditions
prevail so that it is principally the rods which come into use.
The visual purple is regenerated in the dark, thereby, in some
way, increasing the sensitivity of the chemical substances in
the rods.   While the regeneration is proceeding, vision gradually improves until objects begin to take on definite outlines.
After one has been in a dark room for several hours and the
visual purple has been considerably restored, sudden emergence into bright light hurts the eyes which are then unduly
sensitive.   Bleaching of the purple must occur to some degree
before it is comfortable to expose the eyes steadily to the surroundings.   The bleaching and regenerating of the visual
purple in the rods constitutes one process of adaptation.
Adaptation to colors also occurs, though not so often in daily
experience.   The retina becomes adapted, if one stares at a

color, so that it gradually tends toward gray. The explanation for this phenomenon lies in the arousal of the antagonistic processes involved in the maintenance of retinal equilibrium.

5. The Importance of Color in Our Experience. That colors profoundly affect us may be illustrated by the employment of colors in medical treatment. Zeller was one of the pioneers in this field. Convinced of the recuperative value of colored light in the case of persons affected with nervous disorders, he set up sun parlors with ruby, violet, amber, and opal window-panes in the Peoria, Illinois, State Hospital, with walls, artificial lights, and bedclothing colored in harmony. Zeller was transferred to another field of activity, and his successor, who considered the entire color scheme nonsensical, removed all the colored panes and replaced them with clear glass. On his return, eight years later, Zeller partially reinstated color treatment. Color, he discovered, acts in three distinct ways—as a stimulant, as a sedative, and as a recuperative. Color is a sedative when it has the power to induce contemplation, indifference, and melancholy. It is said to be recuperative when it creates conditions of change, generosity, and contentment. Stimulative colors excite hope, ecstasy, desire, aspiration, ambition, and action. Yellow has proved to be stimulating. Red must be used with the same discretion as morphine. It is highly stimulating. Too much red can disturb the mental balance of a delicately poised mind. When violent patients are placed in a room in which the red ray predominates, they rapidly become worse. When placed under the influence of the blue ray, they become calm and quiet. Ponza, a French psychiatrist, placed a patient afflicted with morbid taciturnity in a red chamber. After a period of three hours, the patient became gay and affable. Another patient who had refused all food until he had reached the danger point asked for breakfast after twenty-four hours in the red room. In the blue chamber Ponza placed a patient so highly excited that he was confined in a strait-jacket.   It is recorded that one hour later there was a decided change for the better.

6. Some Effects of Poor Vision.   Poor vision which is due to ocular defects may seriously affect the development of personality.   Children who do not see adequately may be considered unintelligent by teachers who fail to recognize the sensory inferiority.   A woman with weak eyes refused to wear her glasses because she felt they impaired her charm.   She frequently failed to recognize friends on the street, and consequently she gained a reputation for being "high-hat." Sometimes the ability to concentrate is facilitated by a narrow field of vision, since stimuli which might distract the person with normal visual acuity remain unnoticed.

A man entered the front of a lecture hall where he sought to catch the attention of his wife who was in the audience. Nearly everyone saw him except his wife.   She was intently listening to the speaker, and, according to her husband, the primary reason for her close attention to the lecturer was the fact that without her glasses the gesticulations of her frantic mate lay outside the field of her ordinary vision.

7. The World of the Blind.   The value of the eyes for the business of living is easily appreciated by observing how the deprivation of sight reduces the range of experience in the blind.[1] A blind person must rely upon other senses which are not so efficient as vision for receptive purposes.   Hearing, for example, has serious limitations, being far less selective than sight.   Sight impressions can be focused so that only the data are noticed which are of particular interest to the observer, whereas sound impressions from every point within audible range are received, whether or not the listener wishes to heed them.   Considerable effort is necessary to "tune out" extraneous sounds.   To the blind hearing is like a radio set which permits all stations to be heard simultaneously, and leaves it

[1] See P. Villey: *The World of the Blind; a Psychological Study.*   1930.

to the audience to concentrate on the one that is of special interest. The constant demand on voluntary attention is tiring. The inability to shift from hearing to sight when the former is fatigued imposes an additional hardship. Then, too, the ears cannot be closed as readily as the eyes in order to retreat momentarily from the bustling world, or to exclude an intense stimulus. It is a mistake to think that the sound conditions most agreeable to the blind are quietness or absolute silence. According to the testimony of one person, some stimulation is desirable:

I find that any unusual quietness produces a depression strikingly like that which gloom produces on the seeing. The dead of night or isolated spots make me strangely dull and uneasy. There is apparently a minimum of received stimuli necessary for mental alertness, which hearing must supply in the case of the blind.[1]

The experiences of an eighteen-year-old girl[2] who had been blind from birth and who suddenly gained her sight may shed some light on the early visual impressions of the infant. When she first caught sight of her black-spotted dog, she was alarmed at what she took to be holes in the poor animal. Sunbeams baffled her, for even as she reached for them, they eluded her touch. She had walked so long without the aid of her eyes that her mother had to teach her how to coördinate her steps with her visual cues. She found the process so difficult that when she wished to hurry she closed her eyes and felt her way about, in keeping with the habits of coördination thoroughly established over a period of years. "You can't tell a person how anything looks unless he has once had eyes that saw," she says. "The words don't mean a thing to him."

8. The Significance of Visual Experience in the Evolution of the Human Mind. The vast significance of the visual factor in evolution is not adequately appreciated. Vision, primi-

---

[1] C. M. Adams: "The World and the Blind Man," *The Atlantic Monthly*, 1924, 134, 595–602.

[2] Miss Joan Getaz of Lincoln, Nebraska.

tively a rival of smell, came to be the dominant sense in the human being.   Sight has contributed in an important way to the appreciation of æsthetic values, and thus to sexual selection; and it has played a large rôle as a means of intercommunication, through the interpretation of gestures and facial

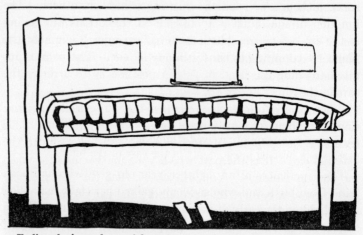

Feeling the ivory keys of her piano and her own smooth, shiny teeth, Miss Joan had pictured the keyboard as resembling a human mouth with parted lips and large teeth.[1]

expressions.   The world and most of what is happening in it are made known to us by sight.   Vision is the essential instrument for observation and experimentation.   Such words as "insight" and "foresight" are testimony to the fact that man's increasing reliance upon visual guidance made possible the emergence of those expanding powers of discrimination which underlie the superior intelligence of the human being.

B. Audition.   The receiving apparatus for auditory sensations is a pair of ears.   Two ears, of course, can render more effective service in the detection of stimuli than one ear, especially in the matter of determining the direction from which sounds originate.

[1]Printed by permission of the *American Weekly*, Inc., 1928.

When the ear is mentioned the average person thinks merely of the external ear, the part that flaps so prominently on the donkey. Some human beings can wiggle the pinna, as it is called, arousing thereby suspicions of evolutionary kinship, but most of us are unable to resemble the donkey in this respect, although we succeed too well, perhaps, in others. The function of the pinna is to collect the vibrations proceeding in the air. A person who is hard of hearing will augment the pinna by cupping his hand behind the ear. The neck is rotated to bring the head in such a position as to arrange the ears in the direct line of the sound.

When you wish to exclude the penetrating noises of civilization, you sometimes stick your fingers into your ears. This section is the external auditory meatus, also belonging to the external ear. It is the part which your mother used to wash for you on Sundays. You will notice that the passage way goes around a corner, thus protecting the ear drum from objects which might puncture it.

The middle ear begins with the eardrum or tympanic membrane, which vibrates something like the disk on a telephone receiver, in response to air waves. The vibration is then passed on to the malleus, the first of the three ossicles (bones), which is in contact with the drum. The malleus is so called because it resembles a hammer. From the malleus the vibration is imparted to the incus (anvil) and then to the stapes (stirrup). The ossicles—malleus, incus, and stapes—function as a transformer, decreasing the amplitude of the waves and magnifying their intensity. The middle ear is connected with the throat by means of the Eustachian tube. The tube is opened by the act of swallowing so that air is admitted to the middle ear, thus maintaining a balance of air pressure on both sides of the drum. The air pressure on the inside of the drum may be felt by holding the nose and then attempting to exhale through the nasal passage.

The sensitive receptor for sounds lies in the internal ear, in the cochlea, so called because it resembles a snail in its spiral form. Vibrations of perilymph in the cochlea set up by the stapes are picked up by the basilar membrane which is a part of the Organ of Corti located in the cochlea, then imparted by the membrane to the hair cells, thence communicating the

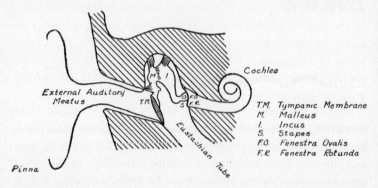

impulse to the auditory nerve fibres which conduct the impulse to the temporal lobe of the cortex. It is not until this final stage is reached that a wave motion becomes a sound. The tectorial membrane acts as a damper.[1]

1. Some Phenomena. The structure of the ear renders possible a certain variety of auditory experience within a limited range.

a. Pitch. Tones are characterized by a quality called pitch which refers to the "highness" or "lowness" of the sound. The pitch of a tone is determined by the vibration frequency of the air wave. In other words, the low frequency of vibration in a bass voice evokes one experience while the high frequency of a soprano gives rise to another. A singer learns to emit an air wave of a specific vibration frequency in order to

---

[1]A number of these statements are subject to controversy. It is not advisable to raise too many issues as the subject is difficult enough without adding confusion to complication.

produce a specific experience in the hearer—256 vibrations to create the impression of middle "C."

The limits of our experience, whether it be visual, auditory, or any other, are represented by the term *limen* or threshold.

low   low tone
frequency

high   high tone
frequency

Infra-red and ultra-violet rays are invisible to the naked eye, because our visual apparatus is not constructed in such a way as to register these stimuli with enough sensitivity to penetrate consciousness. An experience must be sufficiently clear before it becomes conscious. The limen represents the amount of clearness which a given experience must attain to arouse awareness.

The lowest frequency which the average person can hear is 16 vibrations per second. This threshold is technically called the R.L. (stimulus limen). It is fortunate, in some ways, that sounds below the R.L. cannot be detected, for if the ears were sensitive to waves slower than the lowest audible sounds, we should perceive at a distance the swaying of trees in the wind, the oscillations of barometric pressure, and the slow movements of the earth beneath our feet. Experience would become one "blooming, buzzing confusion." If our ears were so sensitive that we did not need the assistance of a radio set to pick up the programs over the air, life would become the boisterous noise that it now is in some apartment houses where all the radios are booming at once.

The limited sensitivity of our receptors promotes the selectivity of experience by eliminating an overwhelming multiplicity of stimuli.

The average human being can hear a frequency as high as 20,000. This is known as the T.R. (terminal limen)—the highest degree of any stimulus which is perceptible.

Between 16 and 20,000 vibrations, the human listener can distinguish about 11,000 different pitches. The D.L. (differential limen) is the least amount of difference between two stimuli which permits them still to be distinguished from each other. In the middle range of the scale most people can distinguish tones four vibrations apart.

What apparatus in the ear will account for the experience of pitch? The answer given by Helmholtz is the basilar membrane. If you will step up to your piano and sing out a note, and then listen, you will hear, beside the protests of your neighbors, a sound of the same pitch coming from the piano. You will discover that the string of the same frequency as the note you emitted has started to vibrate sympathetically with you. This phenomenon is known as sympathetic vibration or resonance. According to Helmholtz, the resonators in the ear are the fibers of the basilar membrane. There are about 18,000 to 20,000 fibers on the membrane, differing in length.

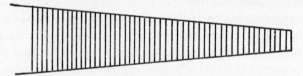

Illustrating the principle of the arrangement of the fibers of the basilar membrane.

Each fiber is tuned to a specific rate of vibration. When the ossicles impart a certain vibration to the perilymph of the cochlea, the basilar fiber of that particular frequency resonates, transmitting the vibration to the hair cells, which in turn start the impulse along the auditory nerve to the brain—when this final stage has been reached, a sound of a specific pitch is heard. In playing a stringed instrument, you shorten the vibrating portion of the string to produce a high note. By the same principle, a short basilar fiber picks up a rapid vibration, a long fiber, a slow vibration.[1]

Suppose a chord is sounded on a piano. The listener not only gets the total pattern, the blend of the notes, but he can detect the separate notes which compose the chord. It is the resonance of the fibers of the basilar membrane that makes the analysis of complex sounds possible.

The resonance theory of Helmholtz has been supported by an ingenious experiment on guinea pigs. It is a well-known fact that exposure to intense noise results in auditory disturbances—witness boiler-makers' deafness. Upton was interested in seeing whether prolonged exposure (70 days) to an intense tone of a specific frequency would decrease the sensitivity to that particular vibration rate without affecting the sensitivity to tones of other frequencies. How could he tell whether the guinea pig heard the tone or not? The guinea pigs were conditioned so that they would invariably respond by a change in the respiratory rhythm when tones of a particular pitch were sounded. After the seventy-day exposure to an intense tone the animal could not be reconditioned to manifest a specific change in breathing rhythm in response to the specific tone to which he had been listening for so extended a period. Upton's conclusion is that a specific section of the basilar membrane had degenerated under the continuous influence of the particular frequency to which it was resonating. Sensitivity to other frequencies, after the exposure period, indicated that other portions of the membrane had not been

---

[1]There are objections to the Helmholtz theory of resonance but we shall not go into them.

A wave of a particular frequency actually causes more than one basilar fibre to vibrate. The above description is an oversimplification. It serves, however, to illustrate the principle involved.

affected. The experiment, therefore, supports Helmholtz's theory of sympathetic vibration.[1]

b. Loudness. Air waves not only differ in frequency but in amplitude of vibration. Amplitude of vibration is the prin-

The two vibrations represented have the same frequency, but differ in amplitude.

cipal factor in determining the loudness or intensity of the auditory experience. The physiological correlate for loudness is still in considerable doubt.[2]

c. Timbre. Tones of the same pitch emanating from different musical instruments have a characteristic distinguishing mark which enables the listener to tell whether the note is being played, for example, by a piano or a violin. This distinguishing characteristic of tones is known as timbre. It is the awareness of timbre which permits the blind to ascertain what person is speaking, as individual voices differ in this respect. Timbre depends upon the number, the pitch, and the relative intensity of the overtones. When a string vibrates, it not only vibrates as a whole but in sections. The string as a whole produces the fundamental; the sections, the overtones (partials). If you play a note on the piano, you will hear the

---

[1] Morgan Upton: "The Auditory Sensitivity of Guinea Pigs," *The American Journal of Psychology*, 1929, 41, 412–421.

"Functional Disturbances of Hearing in Guinea Pigs after Long Exposure to an Intense Tone," *The Journal of General Psychology*, 1929, 2, 397–412.

Bray, Wever, and Horton have conducted similar experiments and come to the opposite conclusion: the impairment of hearing is general and not specific. Report at the 43rd Annual Meeting of the American Psychological Association, 1935.

[2] For an exhaustive account of modern views on hearing, see E. G. Boring: "Auditory Theory with Special Reference to Intensity, Volume, and Localization," *The American Journal of Psychology*, 1926, 37, 157–188.

fundamental, and, after practice, you can detect the overtones in addition. It is the nature of the overtones which determines the timbre.

This diagram represents a string vibrating as a whole and in sections.

d. Consonance. Another auditory experience is that of consonance or harmony. The harmonizing notes constitute a melodious blend pleasing in its effects, while a note off key shatters the nerves brutally. Consonance, of course, is a *Gestalt*, a total pattern, which comes as a unitary experience. Harmony depends not only on the way the fundamental tones fit together, but also on the teamwork of the various overtones.

e. Tonal Islands. Corresponding to color blindness in vision is the phenomenon of tonal islands in hearing. Some persons are deaf to certain portions of the scale while they remain sensitive to notes in the other regions. The range of hearing is greatly reduced in approaching senescence, causing deafness at both extremes of the auditory scale.

2. The Hard of Hearing. Many children with defective hearing are kept in the same grade year after year because their teachers, not realizing their condition, think they are dull, according to 7500 tests of hearing given to the children of the Holyoke, Massachusetts, schools.[1]

Defective audition may have its compensations. Thomas Edison, for example, found his deficiency a distinct advantage as far as his work was concerned, since he was free from auditory distractions when he wanted to concentrate his attention upon the task in hand.

[1] The Boston *Sunday Herald*, June 30, 1935.

Deafness has very serious effects upon the psyche, as may be seen in this letter written to Dr. S. Parkes Cadman:

> I am as deaf as a post, lonely, sad, with a lot of things I would like to say, but few care to talk to me, and they are not always near when I need them. I am getting disheartened, and at times I know I am cranky. What shall I do to avoid being sour and repellent?

Social intercourse is subject to friction where a deaf person is involved. When you talk to an individual who is hard of hearing, you begin in a normal tone because you do not want to embarrass him. He does not "let on" that he is missing most of what you are saying, but his irrelevant reply to your statement makes it evident that he is at sea. So you shout at him. Whenever you are angry, you express your temper by raising your voice. In reverse, when you shout you find yourself growing angry, in spite of any effort to maintain your mental poise. Your irritation is contagious, producing a state of annoyance in the listener.

Furthermore, you cannot impart a secret where you have to bellow each word, unless you have retired to the wide-open spaces. Hence no intimacy can be cultivated at social functions. It is embarrassing to converse with a deaf person at a public gathering because your stentorian tones inevitably evoke the attention of all those present. It is no wonder that a person whose hearing is defective finds himself a social nuisance. Beethoven was forced to endure an ostracism that afflicted him very deeply. He wrote to a friend:

> I am living in misery. For two years I have been avoiding people almost entirely, because it is not possible for me to tell them that I am deaf . . . In whatever way possible I will defy my fate, but there will be moments in my life when I will be the most unhappy of God's creatures.[1]

---

[1] Emil Ludwig: "Beethoven," *Hearst's International-Cosmopolitan*, December, 1928.

A common trait in the deaf is suspiciousness. Since a voice of normal tone sounds like a whisper to the individual who is hard of hearing, he comes to believe that people are plotting against him—otherwise, why should they lower their voices? Consequently, he is inclined to develop delusions of persecution.

3. The World of the Deaf. The person with normal hearing does not realize to what extent audition is dependent upon the other senses. Lip reading by sight, for example, facilitates the auditory process. This fact may be realized if you notice how much more difficult it is to catch sounds accurately over the telephone, where the visual clues are lacking. The deaf person merely takes advantage, to an extraordinary degree, of the sensory cues employed by all of us.

Gault is conducting a research to determine how far the sense of touch can be employed to detect the tactual qualities of objects that are in vibration. Both hearing and touch are receptors for vibratory stimuli. Where the auditory mechanism is defective, therefore, the logical sense to train is touch. Gault has found the tactual capacities surprisingly acute. He defines the aims of his program to be:

(1) to find what characteristics of speech can be detected through the skin—through the sense of touch; (2) to find to what extent these felt characteristics of speech can be made use of to aid the deaf—in receiving and interpreting speech—and in improving their own art of vocal expression, or spoken language.[1]

The acquisition of speech is dependent upon hearing. We learn to speak by hearing ourselves talk. Place a pair of ear phones on your ears and listen to the radio. While the program is coming to you, converse with somebody and then ask him if you have been speaking in your normal tone of voice. He will inform you that you have been shouting. The ex-

[1]R. H. Gault: "Studies on the Psychology of Touch," *Carnegie Institution Year Book.* No. 27, 1927-1928, pp. 401-407.

planation is that you govern your voice by hearing it, and
with the noise from the radio pounding on the ear drums, the
voice must be increased in volume in order to make an impression on the speaker himself.

"MAKING THE DEAF TO HEAR"

Dr. Robert H. Gault of Northwestern University, Evanston, Ill., testing his
"teletactor." He speaks through the microphone while Miss Helen May
Martin, 34 years a blind deaf mute, listens through her finger tips by means of
vibrations.   She has learned to play the piano.[1]

The use of gesture is widely resorted to by the deaf for the
communication of thought. A child of deaf-mute parents,
Lon Chaney trained his face and fingers and his whole body
to tell stories to his mother when she became afflicted with
rheumatism. "All his life afterward he was more talkative
with his muscles than with his voice. . . . Today people

[1]By permission of the Keystone View Company of New York, Inc.

remark on the expressive hands of Lon Chaney; they marvel at the delicate shades of meaning the great pantomimist can put into subtle little gestures; but few realize that the genesis of this uncanny art was the bedside of that sick mother."[1]

4. *Psychological Effects of Sounds*. Music has an extraordinary capacity for stirring the soul, for arousing the emotions, for swaying the moods. A military march can carry patriotic fervor to a high pitch.

While music has its charms, too much of it can upset the mental balance. Continuous assault upon the ears is a trying punishment which a human being can hardly be expected to endure. A murder is committed now and then under the stress of the unabating pandemonium which the invention of the phonograph and the radio has made possible. A man in Watertown, South Dakota, became so enraged when one of his two stepsons persisted in tuning in the radio, disobeying his orders to turn it off, that he arose from bed, took his shotgun, and slew the offender. Of course the radio may merely have offered him an excuse for an act he had long contemplated, but the circumstances in the case do not make that supposition likely. A fifteen-year-old boy was killed by his stepfather in New York for playing the phonograph against the parental will.

Sound, too long continued, is torture—more especially if the sound takes the form, not of music, but of noise. In our day, the two may be easily confused, but none the less we endure more noise than we should. The noises of civilization levy their toll on the nervous system. It has been estimated that we expend forty per cent of our energy in resisting the clatter of city life. If we were more intelligent, we would refuse to tolerate it. Our capacity to adapt ourselves betrays us. We do not realize how the incessant racket saps our vitality. Campaigns are under way in London and other cities to insure

---

[1]*The Literary Digest*, September 13, 1930.

silence during the night hours.   There are still those who feel like Schopenhauer when he wrote that "the superabundant display of vitality, which takes the form of knocking, hammering, and tumbling things about, has proved a torment to me all my life long."[1]

C. Touch.   The skin is the organic basis for the sense of touch.   It would be difficult to estimate the importance of tactual sensations in the process of knowledge.   It is through the sense of touch that we become most intimately acquainted with the objects in our environment.   Sight and hearing convey impressions from stimuli at a distance; touch requires contact.   "The skin you love to touch" may determine your destiny.

The average person thinks that his skin is sensitive over its whole surface but careful experiment indicates that it is sensitive only in spots—the distribution is punctiform.   By applying the appropriate stimuli four different kinds of cutaneous sensations may be evoked: pressure, cold, warmth, and pain. All other tactual experiences, such as wetness, smoothness, itch, and tickle, are variations or combinations of these elementary sensations.

1. Pressure.   If you apply a boar's bristle to the skin, you will discover that the stimulus is not perceived at all points of the surface but only at some.   These spots where a sensation of pressure is aroused are known as pressure spots.   That the distribution of sensitivity is punctiform may be confirmed by employing an æsthesiometer, an instrument resembling a compass, having two sharp points which may be adjusted to various distances apart.   Applying the æsthesiometer with the points very close together, the sensation is of one point and not two.   Investigation will show that the points must be a certain distance apart before they will be felt as two. This distance is known as the two-point limen, and it differs

---

[1]Arthur Schopenhauer: *Essays*, p. 447.   Home Library.

on various parts of the bodily surface. Find the limen for the finger tip, using a hairpin if no æsthesiometer is available, and apply the points to the back of the neck. The finger tip will give the sensation of "two," the neck, the sensation of "one."

It should be noted that the skin itself is not the receptor for touch; the receptors are specialized organs in the skin. The pressure spots on the hairy surface of the body are located to the windward of the hairs. The nerve endings around the hair bulb pick up the mechanical effects communicated to the hair by the stimulus. The usual stimulus in experimenting on pressure sensations is a boar's bristle.

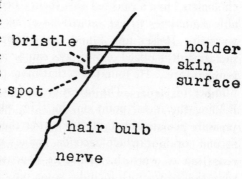

The number of pressure spots tends to increase toward the extremes of the limbs. The finger tips are particularly sensitive.

Adaptation to pressure is a familiar phenomenon—the professor looking for his glasses which are on his forehead is a proverbial illustration.

2. Temperature. Temperature is perceived through two distinct sets of receptors which render possible the experience of cold and the experience of warmth respectively. The cold spots may be located by applying a rod dipped in cold water, the warm by a rod dipped in warm water. The exact receptors for cold, as for warmth also, have not as yet been definitely ascertained. The accepted theory of skin sensation, which holds that each of the warm, cold, pressure, and pain spots is capable of feeling only its own kind of sensation, must be revised in the light of experiments performed by Heiser, reported in 1932.[1]

Heiser's work seems to show that first of all there is not such a definite location of the spots as has been supposed, because when he varies the temperature of the metal point touching a spot, or its pressure, the positions of the spots change. Under the usual theory the feeling of warmth is due to the actual raising of temperature of the hot spots on the skin. But psychologists have suspected this theory because they have been able sometimes to get sensations of heat without the use of warmth. Heiser first found that if the temperature of the metal point is raised, more spots can be found than with lower temperature. He found also that more pressure increased the number of spots. The latest work is changing the time of holding the metal point on the skin, while temperature and pressure remain constant. Whether the contact lasts a half-second, or four whole seconds, makes no differences in the sensation of warmth. This, he concludes, means that the sensation of warmth includes something besides heat, for half a second with the point he employed is too brief a time to deliver heat. With hypodermic needles under the skin he discovered that in the half-second there was actually no rise in the skin temperature even though the sensation of warmth was felt. He said these experiments indicate the possibility of some other organization of nerve receptors than hot, cold, pain, and touch spots. Heiser's data indicate that the present knowledge of tactual sensation is still very limited.

Although the bodily temperature remains very constant in normal health, the temperature of the skin varies more widely. The psychological zero above which a stimulus will be felt as warm and below which a stimulus will be perceived as cold shifts with the temperature of the skin. Berkeley's famous

[1]F. Heiser: "Stimulus, Temperature, and Thermal Sensation," *Archives of Psychology*, 138, 1932.

experiment in temperature adaptation will serve as an illustration. Fill three basins with water as follows:

Hot   Neutral   Cold

Place your left hand in the hot and your right hand in the cold for a minute, then plunge them both into the water of neutral temperature. The water will feel cold to the left hand and warm to the right. Berkeley's question is worth speculating on—if the water feels cold to one hand and warm to the other, which is the water, actually, cold or warm?

3. Pain. Pain, an elementary cutaneous quality like pressure, warmth, and cold, is mediated by the free nerve endings in the skin. The pain receptors are near the surface since it is their function to protect the organism from harmful stimuli. The pain spots may be located by pressing a sharp point against the skin—or by going to a dentist.

D. Taste. The sense of taste acts as a custodian for the stomach by inspecting all food upon its entrance into the alimentary canal. To make the process of selection doubly sure, the sense of smell coöperates as a further check. Few persons realize how much of the gustatory experience is really olfactory. When you have a cold, food tastes flat, partly because you cannot smell it. Stuff your nostrils with cotton and blindfold yourself and you won't be able to tell whether you are eating a piece of apple or a piece of onion. If you do not enjoy cod-liver oil, hold your nose and you will not notice the taste. The elementary taste qualities are sweet, salt, sour, and bitter. More complex gustatory experiences are combinations of some of these four qualities.

The organs of taste are the buds found in the papillæ of the tongue chiefly. In children the papillæ are also in abundance in the mucous membrane of the cheek as well, explaining why children like to take big bites. Adults sometimes take big bites, but not with the same physiological excuse.

There are several buds in a papilla, each taking care of its appropriate quality.

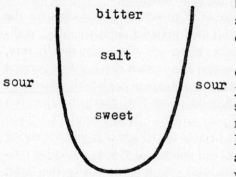

A substance must be soluble to taste at all. The solution descends into the depressions in the surface of the tongue, where the hairs detect the stimulus and transmit the impression to the bud in the papilla.

Taste is distributed on the tongue as shown in the diagram below. You like to lap lollipops and ice-cream cones because the buds for sweet are situated at the forward end of the tongue.

Adaptation may occur in taste. A subject carried a strong solution of brine in his mouth all morning. His lunch tasted flat, as well it might. If you become adapted to sweet, the sour components will stand out by contrast.

The sense of taste has possibilities that are not capitalized by the usual human being because it is considered shameful to glory in the pleasures of the stomach. The Epicure cultivates the gustatory consciousness so that food not only provides sustenance for his physical survival, but nourishment also for his spiritual welfare.

How much taste can be relied upon as a guide to diet is a

big question. "Eat what you like because if you like it, it's good for you" may or may not be wise counsel. Certainly a child would feel that this was a more rationally governed universe if spinach and cod-liver oil tasted as pleasant to him as candy or ice cream. Indeed, we are apt to follow our whims in regard to food—reactions which are conditioned in various ways—by the manner of service, remarks of others at the table, or the state of the stomach at the moment. Habit is such a powerful factor that if we have eaten food a certain way several times we must always have it prepared that way or we are annoyed beyond endurance.

E. Smell. In these days of B.O. (bodily odor) and halitosis the sense of smell is assuming a new importance in human behavior. Perfume, it has long been known, is not conducive to Platonic friendship. The large rôle of olfactory sensations is not usually realized because, for one thing, talk about smell is taboo in polite society. You can tell a friend that he does not look well, but you cannot inform him, without the risk of alienation, that he smells bad. Even as his best friend, you cannot tell him. On social occasions it is not the thing to do to mention candidly the disagreeable odor belonging to one of a lower caste—instead the nose is turned up in the act of snubbing—it means the same thing, "I don't like your odor," but it is recognized as the proper way of putting the point across. Though we do not live so much in the world of odors as do dogs and primitive man, still odor does exert a subtle influence upon our attitudes.

It has been found that a house is more salable if it is permeated with the odors of varnish and fresh paint. Silk stockings attract the purchaser more readily if they are slightly perfumed.[1] The sales of glues, raincoats, and oilcloths have

---

[1] See D. A. Laird: "How the Consumer Estimates Quality by Subconscious Sensory Impressions. With Special Reference to the Rôle of Smell," *Journal of Applied Psychology*, 1932, 16, 241–246.

been increased by the inclusion of a little perfume in the manufacturing process. A fire insurance company promoted its sales program by using stationery emitting a smell of wet, burned wood.[1]

The nostrils provide a channel for the air currents involved in respiration, steering them into contact with the sense receptors. The stimulus for smell must be gaseous, just as the stimulus for taste must be soluble. If you were so careless as to empty a bottle of eau de Cologne down your nostrils, you would not smell it.

The olfactory fissure is above the direct respiratory tract, thus protecting the receptors from foreign substances by ex-

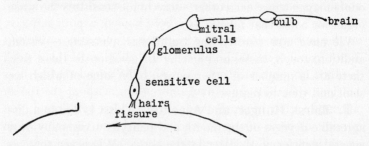

posing the sensitive cells only to eddies of air inspired and expired. The glomerulus, mitral cells, and bulb serve to "step up" the stimulus, to increase the sensitivity for odors.

Odors are aroused by chemical stimuli. It is difficult to investigate smell for various reasons. Adaptation to smell is very rapid so that the stimulus is no longer sensed after a minute or so. Extraneous odors must be eliminated. Language is woefully inadequate for describing olfactory experiences, since reference to smell is barred from ordinary conversation.

Henning took a few trained observers on smell excursions

[1]See M. T. Bogert: "Your Nose Knows," *Scientific Monthly*, 1934, 39, 345-353.

through the zoos and other resorts.   On the basis of his experiments he finds six elementary smell qualities:

Fragrant	Ethereal
Spicy	Putrid
Resinous	Burned

All other olfactory experiences are complexes of these.

Synthetic perfumes are made on the principle that two stimuli may fuse to form a new quality.   Two different odors may exist simultaneously.   Odors can be analyzed from a pattern as notes from a musical chord.   Two odors may act antagonistically to weaken each other—Listerine and halitosis.   Two odors may enhance each other—strychnine sensitizes the sense organ for odors that follow.

We have now covered the traditional five senses—vision, audition, touch, taste, and smell.   In addition to these five, there are a number of other senses, only some of which we shall find time to discuss.

F. Thirst, Hunger, and Appetite.   Thirst is due to a disagreeable dryness of the mouth and pharynx accompanying a general deficiency of water in the body.   Whenever there is a shortage of water, the percentage in the blood remains fairly constant at the expense of the salivary glands.   When the salivary glands are artificially stimulated by means of pilocarpine, rabbits refuse water entirely or barely touch it even after they have been deprived of it for seven days.   Thirst is a local sensation of dryness caused by a deficient flow of saliva.

The sensation of hunger is due to rhythmical contractions of the stomach walls.   These contractions are aroused locally and are not due to a deficiency of food in the blood.   The contractions have been registered by sinking a balloon in the stomach, with an attachment to the outside for recording the alternating pressures.   Hunger is experienced when the diminished bulk in the stomach causes the walls to contract.   It is not due to distress over lack of nourishment for the tissues. The contractions occur, in part, as a conditioned response. When the customary meal hour arrives, starvation is experienced because the contractions are conditioned to occur at that time of day. If the meal is postponed for a few hours, the hunger will ultimately disappear.

Appetite is another matter. Appetite is a desire for a repetition of a previously experienced pleasantness. You start a meal because of hunger. You eat enough to satisfy your hunger before you get to the dessert, but you do not stop. You eat the dessert because you know it will taste good. If a dog's œsophagus is cut and a tube inserted, diverting the food from going to the stomach, the dog will eat for hours. If the Romans had known of this procedure, it would have spared them the disagreeable necessity of regurgitation. Cafeteria owners capitalize the urge of appetite by displaying the desserts first in order, because the customer will be certain to buy a dessert at that stage, while he might ascetically leave it off a full tray at the further end of the march. "Johnnie's eyes are bigger than his stomach" is the reason for much of Johnnie's overeating. We might avoid the surfeited feeling of being stuffed if we ate our desserts first. Then we would be more likely to stop eating when we had consumed enough. We could still save Thanksgiving as a day for appetitious dissipation.

G. The Kinæsthetic Sense. It is by means of kinæsthetic sensations that the movements of our own members are appreciated, involving the muscles, tendons, joints, and skin. The muscle spindles and corpuscles of Golgi are the chief sense organ structures, being classified as proprioceptors. When you go into a dark room and reach for the light chain, you guide yourself by kinæsthetic cues. In learning any game of skill the kinæsthetic sense is highly important for getting "the feel" of the correct motion. In golf or tennis it is difficult for the beginner to master the proper swing. Showing the pupil how you do it is of limited value. It is far more effective to let him make the swing while you guide it through the right arc. Such a procedure gives him the "feel." The expert is one who notices how it "feels" to make a good stroke and then on the basis of that "feeling" can produce another stroke of the same kind. A short pitch to the green in golf requires a mastery of kinæsthetic cues—to swing through the correct arc and with just the right amount of momentum. To put a ball in a cup four hundred yards away in four strokes is a tribute to human skill, and to the marvel of the kinæsthetic sense. When you stop to think of it, you cannot help but wonder— wonder if you will ever do it again.

H. The Sense of Equilibrium. In the internal portion of the ear are located the semi-circular canals, the utricule, and the saccule. These structures have nothing to do with hearing but are the sensory structures which enable a person to judge the position of the body in various planes. Lymph is contained in each of these organs with openings communicating from the utricule to the saccule and from the saccule to the cochlea. (See diagrams on page 150.)

If you are rotated on a piano stool, you sense the direction in which you are spinning. If you suddenly stop rotating, you get the sensation of whirling in the opposite direction from which you have been turning. As you start to rotate, the side of the canal moves before the lymph has gained momentum. The lymph deflects the crista and the impulse is imparted to the nerve. The sensation of rotating to the right, we shall say, is experienced. As the canal continues to rotate, the lymph catches up to it and moves at the same speed. The sense of spinning is no longer present. Were it not for the eyes you would not be conscious of rotating. Now as you come to a stop, the canal comes to rest but the lymph keeps on going. The crista is now deflected in the opposite direction

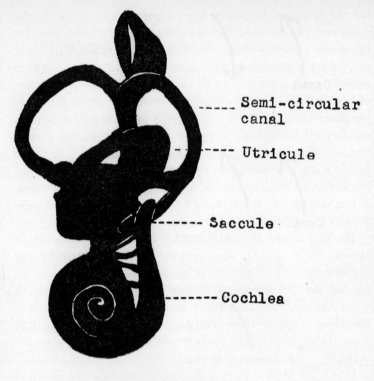

Semi-circular canal

Utricule

Saccule

Cochlea

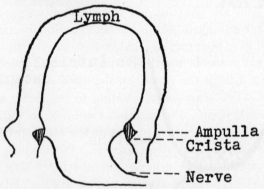

Lymph

Ampulla
Crista

Nerve

A semi-circular canal.

150

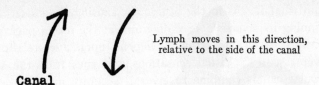

Canal

Lymph moves in this direction, relative to the side of the canal

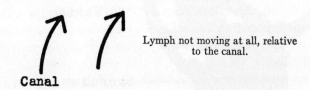

Canal

Lymph not moving at all, relative to the canal.

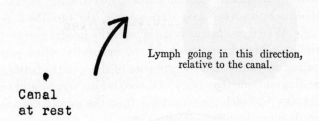

Canal at rest

Lymph going in this direction, relative to the canal.

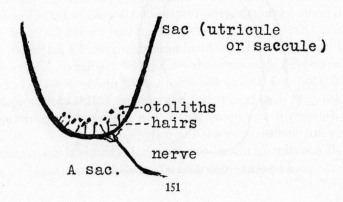

sac (utricule or saccule)

otoliths

---hairs

nerve

A sac.

from what it was in the beginning, causing the sensation of spinning in reverse.[1] (See diagrams at the top of page 151.)

Many of our adjustments depend upon a correlation of several senses. Visual sensations and cues from the semi-circular canals combine to give an accurate maintenance of equilibrium. The rôle of the eyes may be discovered by trying to walk on a line on the floor, watching the feet through the wrong end of a pair of opera glasses. The feet should be planted in a direct line, one in front of the other, in walking. The distortion of the visual cues by the opera glasses, causing the floor to look farther away than it really is, upsets the equilibrium.

Non-rotatory movement is sensed by the utricle and saccule. When a train comes to a stop, you have the experience of moving backward. When you start suddenly forward, the otoliths (particles of calcium carbonate), through inertia, are left behind and when you stop quickly, the otoliths keep on going. When you are at rest the otoliths inform you of your upright position by pressing on the hair cells; when you are standing on your head, the pressure of the otoliths is released. (See diagram on page 151.) Of course kinæsthetic and visual cues coöperate with the sensations from the sacs to keep us informed on our bodily position.

When a crayfish sheds his shell, sand particles get into his otocysts, serving the same function as the otoliths in the human sacs. Kreidl inserted iron filings and then waited for the shell to form. After the shell had formed, he placed a magnet over the crayfish, drawing the iron filings off the hairs. The crayfish sensing it was upside down turned upside down to bring itself right side up, so that it was really right side up even when it thought it was upside down. In reading this description you are confused—so was the crayfish.

If a section of a semi-circular canal is removed in a pigeon,

[1]The canals do not spin inside the head but rotate as the head rotates.

his balance is seriously disturbed. The alcoholic gait is due to the effect of the narcotic upon the canals—as well as to the effect upon the nerves which control the muscular coördinations in accordance with the cues received from the canals and the eyes. Deaf mutes are frequently defective in the sense of equlibrium because their sensory apparatus is impaired. A deaf mute on a merry-go-round is as apt to lean outward as inward in rounding the curve—with disastrous results.

III. SUMMARY

Protoplasm possesses a characteristic irritability which leads it to respond to a variety of stimuli, whether it be the protoplasm of a unicellular or a multicellular organism. As bodily organization increases in complexity, irritability becomes more specific, being delegated to special sense organs. We have reviewed the kinds of experience to which we, as human beings, are subject by virtue of our various receptors.

CHAPTER V

THE NERVOUS SYSTEM

THE link between the stimulus and the response is furnished by the nervous system. We have noted how stimuli are picked up by the sensory mechanisms. Impulses are conducted from the receptors by afferent nerves to the brain, which is itself a complicated system of nervous connections. From the cerebrum the impulse is conducted by efferent nerves to the effectors which carry out the appropriate responses. The nervous system makes possible an effective coördination through which organized behavior can secure exact adjustment of the needs of the organism to internal and external stimuli. An understanding of human nature, its experiences and reactions, necessitates a careful investigation of the structure and functions of the nervous system.

I. NERVES

Nerves are made up of neurons arranged in series. Each neuron consists of:

        a. cell body
        b. axon
        c. dendrites

The nerve fibre resembles an insulated cable, the neurons being enclosed in one or more sheaths.

There are three types of fibres in the nervous system:

1. Projection fibres—which conduct impulses to and from the cord and cortex.

154

2. Commissural fibres—which connect the right and left cerebral hemispheres.

3. Association fibres—which connect areas on the same hemisphere.

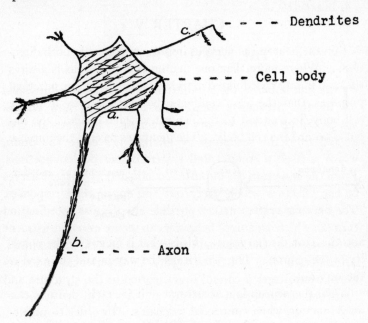

Dendrites

Cell body

Axon

II. SOME ELEMENTARY FACTS ABOUT NERVOUS FUNCTIONS

A. The Polarity of the Neuron.   The dendrites are short stubby structures which spread out into numerous branching processes. The branches pick up impulses which are conducted by the dendrite toward the cell body.

The axon is a slender outgrowth from the cell body.   There is usually only one axon to a cell body. The axon is to be distinguished from the dendrites by its straighter course, its uniform diameter, and its smooth outline. The axon on ending usually splits up into a terminal brush. These brushes always end:

    a. around the dendrite of another neuron or
    b. in a muscle or
    c. in a gland.

Within the neuron the nervous impulse may pass in both directions. Where more than one neuron is involved, as is always the case in any coördinated activity, we may say, for practical purposes, that the axon conducts the impulse away from the cell body, in contrast to the dendrites which conduct the impulse toward the cell body. The dendrites receive the impulse

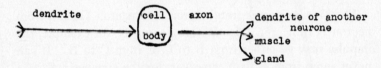

and the axon discharges it—this is what is meant by the polarity of the neuron. The dendrite is the way in and the axon is the way out.

While the neuron is a structural unit in itself, neurons can only function when connected in chains. In order to understand why the impulse travels only in one direction through the chain we must examine the synapse.

B. The Synapse. The synapse is the connection between two neurons, *i.e.*, the place where the axon of one neuron comes into physiological relation with the dendrites of another neuron. Physiologists have found that the threshold for large fibres is lower than the threshold for small fibres, or, in other words, that the large fibres can be more readily stimulated than the small fibres. The terminations of the axon are always smaller than the dendrite with which it makes a synaptic connection. Consequently, the axon may stimulate the dendrite, but never the reverse. This produces the one-way effect.

C. The Law of Forward Conduction. The synapse acts as a valve, allowing the impulse to travel only from axon to dendrite across the gap. The nervous impulse can never pass in the reverse direction from the dendrite to axon across the synapse.

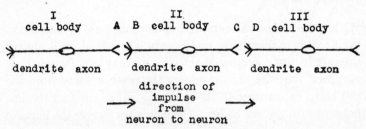

The impulse passes from neuron I to neuron II, and from neuron II to neuron III. Within neuron II, for example, the impulse may go either from B to C or from C to B. It can never jump from B to A, however, for the synapse acts as a valve so that the impulse cannot pass from dendrite to axon across the gap. The impulse can pass from C to D, from axon to dendrite. Whereas the impulse thus moves in both directions within the neuron, interneuron conduction or synaptic conduction, as it is called, can only be in the forward direction.

D. The Reflex Arc. The lowest level of coördinated activity in the nervous system is the reflex arc. The reflex arc, reduced to the simplest terms, takes care of the stimulus which has been received by a sense organ, conducting the impulse to the spinal cord and then out again to a muscle or gland, thus leading to a response appropriate to the stimulus. It may be summarized in this way:

The reflex arc is the simplest unit of action. The reflex arc as

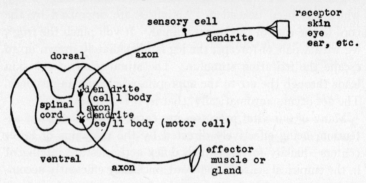

pictured above is merely schematic. The reflex arc consists of five mechanisms:

a. A sensitive receiving organ (receptor or sense organ);

b. A conductor (afferent or sensory nerve) transmitting the nervous impulse inward from the receptor;

c. A correlation center or adjustor, generally located within the central nervous system;

d. A second conductor (efferent or motor nerve) transmitting the nervous impulse outward from the center to

e. the effector apparatus, consisting of organs of response (muscles, glands) and the terminals of efferent nerves upon them.

Note that the sensory cell lies outside the cord, the motor cell within the cord. The impulse must always come in the dorsal (back) side of the cord and come out the ventral (front) side, in accordance with the law of forward conduction. One of the functions of the spinal cord is the distribution of efferent impulses. The reflex arc in actuality is a very complex affair, involving the selection of proper channels from a number of possible pathways. Organized acts would be impossible if the distribution of the outgoing impulses were haphazard. As a matter of fact, the distribution is selective, that is, only the pathways are traversed which lead to the effectors appropriate for carrying out an effective response to the stimulus.

The reflex arc may be illustrated with a spinal frog—a frog which has been beheaded. Activities are organized by the cord in the case of the spinal animal. If you pinch the frog's leg with a pair of forceps, the leg is immediately drawn up to escape the irritating stimulus. The stimulation of the skin leads through the arc to the appropriate behavior in response. The act occurs automatically, that is, it is a reflex.

Many of our vital processes are carried on without our attention, being effectively directed by the thalamus or lower centers—luckily for us. Such reflex activities are intelligent in the empirical sense of the word since they efficiently accomplish ends of real biological value. Since the decerebrate animal responds to stimuli in a sensible fashion, for example, moves to avoid a disagreeable object, one is forced to admit that the thalamus and lower centers exhibit the same organizing genius as the brain, only to a less degree.[1]

A number of human reactions belong to the reflex category. A well-known reflex is the knee jerk (patellar reflex). A physical examination usually includes a blow from the doctor, just below the knee cap while the patient is in a sitting position with his legs crossed. The foot kicks up if the nervous system is sound. Other reflexes include:

Hiccoughing
Sneezing
Snoring ⎬ under the control of the medulla
Yawning
Vomiting
Shivering—under the control of the thalamus

Some reflexes lie outside the realm of conscious control, others are sometimes controllable. If somebody threatens your eyes, it is well nigh impossible to avoid blinking. Hiccoughing is so difficult to stop of your own volition, except by the supple-

[1] For an interesting passage on this question, see Morton Prince: The Unconscious, pp. 240–245. 1914.

mentary aid of drinking, that it sometimes precipitates a panicky feeling, especially as you recall the case of the man you read about in the newspaper, who hiccoughed steadily for weeks. Sneezing is also hard to control.

We shall examine the fundamental kinds of reflex arc.

1. The Simple Reflex.

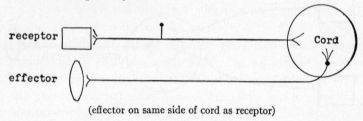

(effector on same side of cord as receptor)

For purposes of simplification we shall represent the simple reflex as follows: If your finger touches a hot stove, you with-

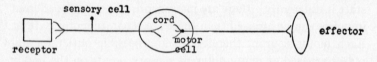

draw your hand immediately. This is a simple reflex, that is, relatively simple.

2. The Chain Reflex. The response of the first reflex serves as a stimulus to the second reflex and so through the series:

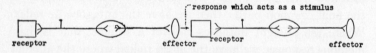

Deglutition (swallowing) and digestion make up a long chain reflex. The stimulus of the food in the pharynx starts the swallowing process, and the particles are carried down the œsophagus, where the activity of one segment acts as a stimulus for the next segment—which in turn becomes a stimulus for the next. Thus the food is carried along, without the necessity of our turning our attention to the passage of the food. Each response becomes a stimulus for the next response in the chain until the chain is completed.

3. Allied and Antagonistic Reflexes. There are about five afferent paths to every one efferent path in the nervous system.

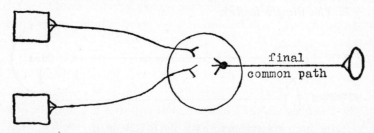

This means that several paths carry impulses in from the receptors to the cord where only one path is available for carrying the impulse out from the cord to the effector. To state it differently—there are many more points where afferent impulses can be aroused than there are separate motor outlets. Each motor neuron, therefore, is the possible outlet for impulses aroused at many different sensory points on the bodily surfaces. The single efferent path is known as the final common path. Sometimes afferent impulses will reënforce each other in their excitation of the final common path—then we have the allied reflex; at other times afferent impulses will interfere with each other—will struggle for the monopoly of the final common path—then we have the antagonistic reflex. Where the afferent impulses call for a similar, that is, harmonious response, we have the allied reflex; where the afferent impulses evoke responses which cannot both occur at once on account of mutual interference, we have the antagonistic reflex. The distinction will become clear with a few illustrations.

a. The Allied Reflex. Certain reflexes combine harmoniously, being mutually reënforcing reactions. Take the scratch reflex in the dog, as demonstrated by Sherrington. "If while the scratch reflex is being elicited from a skin point at the shoulder, a second point distant, *e.g.*, ten centimeters from the other point but also in the receptive field of the skin, be stimulated, the stimulation at this second point favors the reaction from the first point."[1] The greater the similarity in the type of action which each stimulus separately applied would evoke, the greater the reënforcement when both stimuli are applied simultaneously.

The allied reflex may be illustrated in the summation of inadequate stimuli. To understand this phenomenon I shall remind you of what is meant by the limen of consciousness. The limen means the threshold, and any stimulus must be of a certain intensity (higher than the threshold) to be felt, that is, to arouse a sensation. Let us picture this mathematically:

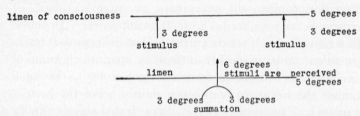

Suppose a sound must be as loud as 5 (an arbitrary amount of loudness) to be heard. Then a sound of 3 units of loudness is not loud enough to be heard. Now if two sounds of 3 units each occur, they will combine (add together) to make 6 units which is loud enough to be heard. A girl is left at home to take care of a baby and she falls asleep. The parents ring the doorbell upon their return, but there is no effect upon the slumbering caretaker. Then the baby cries—still with no effect. Finally the doorbell rings, the baby cries, and the telephone rings, all simultaneously, and the guardian is aroused. In other words, the three sounds ally themselves to

[1] C. S. Sherrington: *The Integrative Action of the Nervous System*, p. 120. By permission of the Yale University Press.

break over the threshold. Each stimulus in itself is inadequate, but all three summated reach the intensity adequate to
arouse consciousness.

Now let us return to the scratch reflex in the dog. He is
being scratched at the same points as above, but at each point
the stimulus is of subliminal (below the threshold) intensity.
What happens? "The two stimuli, though each unable separately to invoke the reflex, yet do so when applied both at the
same time."[1] This phenomenon is known as the summation
of inadequate stimuli.

b. The Antagonistic Reflex. As you know from experience,
you cannot extend your arm and flex it at the same time. If
two stimuli occur simultaneously, one calling for flexion of
the right arm and the other for extension of the right arm,
either flexion alone will take place, or extension alone, or
neither—never both, for both would be impossible. In actual
life, a host of stimuli act concurrently, but the organism reacts
now to one, now to another, depending upon which group of
stimuli becomes prepotent (gets the right of way). We shall
examine the factors in prepotency shortly. For the present
let us see how antagonism can be demonstrated experimentally
—by applying stimuli which evoke reflexes which inevitably
interfere with each other.

Suppose you stimulate a dog on the right shoulder so that
he flexes his right foot (scratch reflex). Now while this reflex
is in progress, stimulate the left shoulder. If he flexes his left
foot for purposes of scratching, he finds that he has no leg left
to stand on. So he stops scratching with the right foot, and
stands on it instead. Where two reflex activities are incompatible, one of them must be suspended in favor of the
other. What is it that determines which stimulus will succeed in evoking its reflex to the exclusion of the other? In
other words, what kind of stimuli are prepotent?

[1] C. S. Sherrington: *loc. cit.*

D. Prepotency. We shall note three factors which determine prepotency:

1. Fatigue. A reflex may dispossess the rival reflex from a common path when that rival is fatigued. Thus the too prolonged continuous use of a common path by any one receptor is prevented and serial variety of reaction is insured.

2. Nociceptors. Stimuli exciting pain are apt to be prepotent. It is clear that this fact is related to the function of self-preservation, for an animal must give special heed to dangerous stimuli. A hornet will usually have the right of way.

3. Intensity. Intense stimuli enjoy precedence in gaining the final common path. A strong stimulus will inhibit a reflex in progress.

E. Coördination. Reflex activity is not a general convulsion but an orderly affair. How is such organized behavior made possible? There are three principal means by which this end is attained—the final common path, reciprocal innervation, and synaptic conduction.

1. The Final Common Path. The final common path is a very important instrument of organization. The cord distributes the impulses selectively and they converge on the final common path where the prepotent impulse monopolizes the path to the exclusion of less urgent impulses. Allied and antagonistic reflexes are produced in an ordered manner, since unlike reflexes have successive but not simultaneous use of the common path, while like reflexes mutually reinforce each other on their common path. The common path, adapted to serve but one purpose at a time, thus effects singleness of action.

2. Reciprocal Innervation. Reciprocal innervation is the principle underlying the crossed-extension reflex. If the right foot of a spinal cat is stimulated vigorously, the right leg is flexed and the left leg simultaneously extended. Thus the endangered foot is removed from the source of injury, and the unharmed leg is engaged for support. Excitation and inhibition work reciprocally. In the right leg the flexion reflex is excited while the extension reflex is inhibited; in the left leg, just the reverse (reciprocal) reflexes occur—the extension reflex is excited while the flexion reflex is inhibited. Wherever you have excitation, there is a reciprocal inhibition.

3. Synaptic Conduction. Any act, no matter how simple, involves more than one neuron. The impulse, therefore, crosses one or more synapses. The synapse is a significant factor in the organization of nervous functions. The synapse, for one thing, is the basis for the law of forward conduction. The direction of the impulse through the arc is irreversible, since the synapse acts as a valve. It is obvious that irreversible conduction promotes orderly activity. The synapse is responsible in other ways for coördination but we shall elaborate no further. Through these means coördinated activity is secured.

F. Facilitation, Summation, and Inhibition. *1. Facilitation.* When two acts are allied, one of them may facilitate the other, that is, cause it to be increased or exaggerated. This phenomenon may be illustrated with the patellar reflex (knee jerk). Let the subject be seated, strike the tendon just below the knee with a sharp blow while the leg is hanging limply with the knee bent, and the leg will be seen to swing upward slightly. If a dynamometer (an instrument for measuring the gripping strength of the hand) be squeezed at the moment the tendon is struck, the extent of the jerk is augmented.

2. Summation. The summation of inadequate stimuli has already been mentioned in the description of the allied reflex. Adequate stimuli, of course, may also be summated. With respect to the temporal factor, summation may be simultaneous or successive. Simultaneous summation is illustrated by the girl who awakened to the combination of doorbell, telephone, and crying baby; successive summation, by the salesman who bombards the prospective customer with selling-arguments until sales resistance is overcome, by the police court judge who makes an example of the last of several persons who come before him on the same day for the same misdemeanor, and by the child who obtains a bicycle through persistent teasing.

3. Inhibition. The process of checking an activity is called inhibition. To inhibit a movement is to stop it. It is fairly easy to see how a muscle may be excited to action, but how are you going to "excite" it so that it will stop contracting. Inhibition is no less significant than excitation as a means of securing harmonious activity. Let us take a simple example. When flexion of the arm takes place, there must be reciprocal inhibition of the extensor muscles—that is, when a particular movement such as flexion occurs, there must be a synchronous inhibition of the antagonistic movement, extension.

G. The Nature of the Nerve Impulse. The excitation of a nerve initiates definite electrical disturbances which can be detected by a galvanometer. The disturbance is probably propagated by a progressive redistribution of hydrogen and carbonate ions about the semi-permeable nerve membrane.[1]

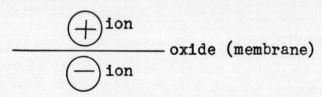

Lillie illustrates this theory with a piano (iron) wire and nitric acid. The acid produces a film of oxide around the wire. An electrical potential is established by polarization. Scrape a little of the oxide off one end of the wire and you can see bubbles travel down the wire, due to the progressive re-

---

[1] For a more detailed account of the nature of the nerve impulse, see L. T. Troland: *The Mystery of Mind*, Chapter XII, 1926.

moval of the film, which is analogous to the increased permeability of the nervous membrane under excitation.

H. Specific Energies. Each sensory nerve has its peculiar or specific energy—each sensory nerve gives rise to its own quality of sensation and to no other, regardless of the nature of the stimulus. No matter how it is stimulated the auditory nerve never gives the sensation of touch—but always the sensation of hearing.

Consider vision. Stimulation of the optic nerve invariably produces visual sensations. Light rays affect the optic nerve through the retina to evoke the experience of light. A blow on the eyeball causes you to *see* stars. If the optic nerve is stimulated electrically or is mechanically injured, a flash of light is perceived.

Consider sound. Drugs affecting the auditory nerve produce ringing sensations—much like the experience you get after you have been swimming and acquired an ear full of water.

Consider touch. Tactual fibres inevitably bear sensations of touch whether the stimulus be mechanical, thermal, electrical, or chemical.

Where does the specificity lie? What is peculiar about the optic nerve which restricts it to visual experience? There are three possibilities:

1. The Nerve Itself. Johannes Müller, the discoverer of the law, believed that each sensory fibre was constructed peculiarly. Research, however, has revealed no histological or physiological difference between an optic nerve and an auditory nerve, for example.

2. The Sense Organ. Visual sensations are due to the peculiar receptor, the eye; auditory sensations to the ear, etc. This possibility is eliminated by the fact that direct stimulation of the nerve gives the peculiar sensation—the impulse, in this case, not entering the sense organ.

3. The Sensorium. The third possibility is the sensorium —the area in the cerebral cortex in which the nerve finally ends—the optic nerve ending in the occipital lobe, the auditory nerve in the temporal lobe, etc. The specificity of any sensation, there fore, is determined by the particular part of the brain where the particular nerve fibre reaches its destination.

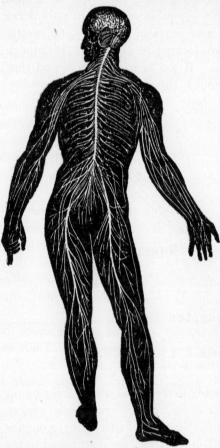

Diagram illustrating the general arrangement of the nervous system.[1]

III. ORGANIZATION OF THE NERVOUS SYSTEM

The nervous system is divided into (A) the central nervous system, (B) the peripheral nervous system, and (C) the autonomic nervous system. *The central nervous system* (cerebrospinal) consists of the brain and the spinal cord. The brain is encased in the skull where it is protected from injurious stimuli in the outside world. The cord is an extension of the brain passing down through a tube in the backbone.

[1]From H. N. Martin: *The Human Body*, p. 120. 1912. By permission of Henry Holt and Company.

Nerves ramify to all parts of the body from the central system which secures the integration necessary to unified behavior. With a possible exception or two, the only nerve connection between any two parts of the body, no matter how closely these parts are located to each other, is through the cerebro-spinal system. If the hand is pricked and then withdrawn from the stimulus, the path of nervous conduction may be represented thus:

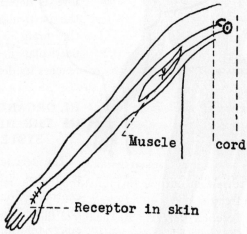

Muscle   cord

Receptor in skin

Diagram adapted from R. S. Woodworth's *Psychology*, p. 510.[1]

The sensory nerves running to the spinal cord and the motor nerves leaving the cord make up *the peripheral nervous system.*

The nerves of *the autonomic system,* a chain of ganglia outside the cord, exclusively motor in function, are distributed to the organs of digestion and circulation.

A. The Central Nervous System. The nervous system is a hierarchy, with the cerebral cortex in supreme control. The governing mechanisms between the cortex and the cord are principally the thalamus, the cerebellum, and the medulla

[1]By permission of Henry Holt and Company.

oblongata.   If the layers of the brain are removed the general
locations are as follows:

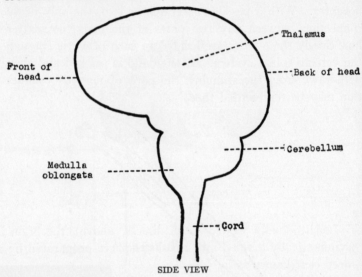

SIDE VIEW

We shall review in outline the functions of the main levels
of the hierarchy.

1. The Cerebral Cortex.   At the top of the central nervous
system is the cerebral cortex which, from the psychological
standpoint, is the most important part of the brain.   It is
the cortex which is most intimately related to consciousness,
and which takes care of the higher mental processes such as
perception, imagination, and reasoning.

In order that as much surface as possible may be packed
into a small container, the brain is folded over and over into
convolutions.   The surface area is thus increased without a
corresponding increase in the bulk of the hemispheres.   It is
the surface area of the cortical tissue rather than the size of the
skull which constitutes the physical basic of intelligence.

The brain is well protected by three layers—the pia mater,
the arachnoid layer (containing the cerebro-spinal fluid),

and the dura mater. These three layers serve as a sort of wrapping within the bony packing case.

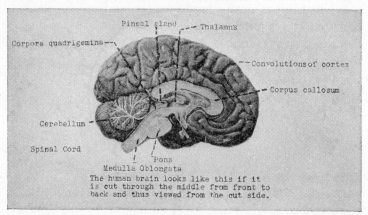

Pineal gland — Thalamus

Corpora quadrigemina —

— Convolutions of cortex

— Corpus callosum

Cerebellum —

Spinal Cord

Pons
Medulla Oblongata
The human brain looks like this if it is cut through the middle from front to back and thus viewed from the cut side.

Longitudinally viewed (from directly above), the brain is symmetrically divided into two hemispheres, separated by a deep cleft known as the longitudinal fissure. The two hemispheres are joined by a large band of transverse fibres known as the corpus callosum. See the illustration above. As you look at the page, the fibres run in the plane to and from the eyes. The fibres of the corpus callosum are called commissural fibres. Their function, as I have stated, is to link the right and left hemispheres.

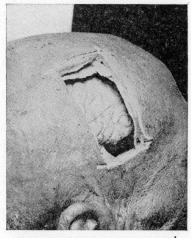

BRAIN IN POSITION INSIDE SKULL[1]

a. Cephalization. As we proceed upward in the animal

[1]Reproduced by permission of D. A. Laird.

scale, we discover that one end of the organism becomes the most important portion of the body. Wormlike forms have a definite habit of moving head first, the head and tail ends are functionally separate, and the leading segments are highly dominant over the rest of the body. It was natural that the chief sense organs should develop at the front end—which is the first to come into contact with objects—and that the brain should develop at that extremity too. The progressive elaboration of the head, with its assumption of supreme control, is known as cephalization. The upright posture of man has brought the front end to the top, where the bodily leadership is still centralized. Cephalization has made possible the marvelously coördinated activity of the higher organisms. If you cut a worm in two, you have two worms; if you cut a human being in two, you have nothing. That is the price we pay for the advantages of cephalization.[1]

b. Localization of Functions. The cerebral cortex is such a very complicated system that it deserves special attention, for in its intricate organization is to be found the physiological explanation for the mental activities which constitute the superiority of man. Specialization of functions in the cerebral cortex is an indisputable fact. Different areas have different functions.

(1) Phrenology. The serious study of the cerebrum goes back to the early nineteenth century when Gall introduced the pseudo-science of phrenology. Gall believed that there are certain bumps on the skull which are indices of special abilities. Thus one bump would indicate mathematical ability and another wit. The picture[2] of Andy Gump's faculties (page 173) caricatures Gall's general conception. Phrenology took hold of the popular mind and it became the rage for people to go about feeling each other's heads.

---

[1] See C. J. Herrick: *Neurological Foundations of Animal Behavior*, p. 96. 1924.
[2] From a drawing by Sidney Smith in the comic sheet of the Boston *Herald*.

External configurations of the skull do not furnish a sound basis at all for estimating the sizes of different areas of the brain. There are neither psychological nor neurological grounds for departmentalizing the mind into distinct faculties, each operating in a special area of the brain, yet phrenology is still practiced by quacks who pose as scientists.

Valuable data accumulated by Gall eventually inspired investigation which led to the discovery of a localization, not of faculties, but of functions. During the Franco-Prussian War, an army surgeon named Fritsch made a remarkable observation. While operating on a wounded soldier, he applied the galvanic (electric) current to the exposed surface of the brain—and noted that certain muscles of the body twitched. By means of various methods which we shall examine soon, the areas of the cortex have been mapped.

The sensory areas are:

Sight—*occipital lobe*
Hearing—*temporal lobe*
Touch and kinæsthesis—the
   somesthetic senses—
     parietal lobe
Smell—*hippocampal lobe*
Taste—*hippocampal lobe*

The somesthetic area of the cortex is in the region behind the fissure of Rolando; the motor area of the cortex is in the region in front of the fissure of Rolando. Each localization on the sensory side has a corresponding localization on the motor side of the fissure. Suppose we stimulate the region to which impulses from the lips are conducted. When a stimulus is applied to the sensory area, the impulse is transmitted to the motor area and thence to the part concerned—

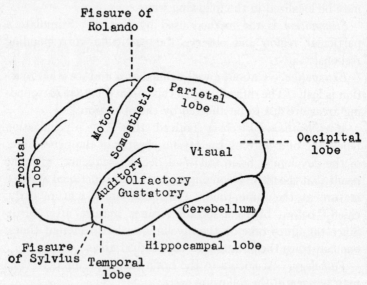

and the lips move. This was the phenomenon which Fritsch discovered. If a cat's brain is exposed, stimulation of one sensory region will cause the legs to move, another the head, etc.

In addition to the sensory and motor areas are the association areas which link together the various cerebral areas. The association areas are undeveloped at birth. It is upon these areas, therefore, that experience has the most effect. The difference between an intelligent person and a stupid person would be largely a matter of the development of the association regions of the cortex. The infinitely complex human mind is based on the vast system of nervous connections in the association areas. The conditioned reflex is not so simple an affair when these cortical areas are taken into account, as they must be, to explain the associative basis of the conditioning process.

(2) *Methods of Studying Localization*. Cerebral functions may be localized in the following ways:

Stimulation is the method used by Fritsch. Stimulate a particular region and observe the particular corresponding response.

Extirpation. Cut out a well-defined area and see what function is lost. The difficulty with this method is that surrounding areas are apt to be affected by the operation.

Myelinization. Flechsig noticed that the myelinization (enclosing of a fibre by the myelin sheath) of the nerve fibres of the developing brain follows a definite sequence, with the result that the fibres belonging to particular functional systems mature at the same time. Projection fibres mature early, chiefly before birth; association fibres mature after birth. Since the fibres take on the myelin sheath at different times, one can trace their courses to the cortical areas.

Pathology. Accidents to the brain leave specific defects as may be seen in the following cases:

Alfonso Debra, 10-year-old Chicago boy, lost five ounces of his brain in an accident. He suffered a cut in his head when struck by an automobile and lost part of his brains from the occipital region. Examination revealed that he was above the average mentally in spite of the injury. The youth's only difficulty was his inability to see when he looked to the right because of an injury to the left occipital lobe of the brain.[1]

Harry Cowan murdered his sweetheart, Miss Edith Burton, in an alleged suicide pact in 1925. Cowan is totally blind, partially deaf,

[1]The Boston *Herald*, January 3, 1927.

and has lost the sense of taste as the result of the bullet he fired into his own head after Miss Burton was fatally wounded.[1]

In 1848, Phineas P. Gage, a foreman in a quarry, was engaged in tamping a blast when the charge exploded prematurely, driving a crowbar through the left side of his jaw and out through the top of his head in the frontal region. He lived for twelve and a half years after the accident. He was able to perform practically all his somatic functions, such as voluntary muscular movements, hearing, and seeing. His judgment and reasoning power, however, were seriously impaired. His disposition suffered considerably as he became prone to unprovoked fits of rage. He grew dishonest and irregular in his work habits. For most of his faults he may, I think, be forgiven!

The pathological approach to the study of the localization of cerebral functions can well be illustrated by an examination of aphasias. Aphasia is the total or partial loss of the use or understanding of language, the vocal organs and the sense organs remaining intact. Any of the qualities or varieties of speech may be affected, both spoken and written. Since speech is so intimate a part of many mental operations, the aphasia may involve widespread consequences.

In motor aphasia, of the partial sort, the individual can utter articulate words correctly, but he cannot combine them into grammatical sentences. Words are thrown together in random fashion so that a "word-salad" results. Motor aphasia is due to an injury in the frontal lobe.

Sensory aphasia may take the form of word-deafness in which the person hears what is said but derives no meaning from the utterance, or it may take the form of word-blindness in which the individual can see the printed words (written speech) but cannot make any sense out of them. In word-deafness the association areas about the temporal lobe are injured; in word-blindness, the association areas about the

-----

[1]The Boston *Post*, March 18, 1927.

occipital lobe. The experience of listening to or reading an unfamiliar foreign language is comparable, since the lack of comprehension is due to a paucity of connections in the associative areas requisite to an adequate understanding of that language.

It is important to point out that the lesion which produces aphasia affects the association centers rather than the projection centers, since there is no primary sensory deficiency—the word-blind person, for example, is not blind. The words are seen but not understood because the associative connections with the occipital lobe are impaired. With the correlations lacking, experience remains a jumble.

(3) *The Present View of Localization.* Through these four methods, data have been gathered which indicate that:

There is a specific localization of function in the cerebral cortex, in the sense that particular systems of sensory projection fibres terminate in special regions (the sensory projection centers), that from other special regions (the motor projection centers) particular systems of efferent fibres arise for connection with the lower motor centers related to groups of muscles concerned with the bodily movements, and that between these projection centers there are association centers, each of which has fibrous connections of a more or less definite pattern with all other parts of the cortex. . . . All conscious processes probably require the discharge of nervous energy throughout extensive regions of the cortex.[1]

Recent experiments by Lashley on the maze-learning abilities of rats whose cerebral cortices have been subjected to various degrees of extirpation offer evidence pointing toward less emphasis on the specific localization of cerebral functions. Rats may learn a maze after extensive cerebral lesions, though the learning process takes longer. Retardation is proportional to the amount of cerebral tissue injured, or to put it conversely, the rate of learning depends upon the amount

---

[1] C. J. Herrick: *Introduction to Neurology,* pp. 334–335. Third edition, 1922. By permission of the W. P. Saunders Company.

of cerebral tissue which remains intact and capable of functioning. Reëducation after cerebral lesion offered no certain evidence that the reacquired functions are carried out vicariously by any specific loci. It seems probable that the reacquired functions were to be attributed to a reorganization of the entire neural mass rather than to an action of specific areas. For the learning of the mazes, no part of the cortex is more important than any other.

"In spite of the greater specialization of cerebral areas in the higher forms, the problems of cerebral function are not greatly different from those raised by experiments with the rat,"[1] says Lashley. Consequently he feels justified in drawing the following conclusions applicable to human beings:

In one phase or another the results with every habit indicate the importance of the total mass of tissue, and a certain lack of specificity in cerebral function. . . . The most surprising outcome of the work has been the number of lines of evidence pointing to the equivalence of function of all parts of the cerebral cortex for learning. . . .
The more complicated and difficult the activity, the less the evidence for its limitation to any single part of the nervous system. . . .
The mechanisms of integration are to be sought in the dynamic relations among the parts of the nervous system rather than in details of structural differentiation.[2]

2. The Thalamus. The thalamus, located in about the center of the brain, is the vestibule through which all sensory impulses, except smell, must pass on the way to the cortex.

The thalamus is also the seat of affective experience (the emotions).[3] Head, Sherrington, Bard, and others have demonstrated that decorticate animals express rage in a manner very

---

[1] K. S. Lashley: *Brain Mechanisms and Intelligence*, p. 176, 1929.

[2] *Ibid.*, pp. 122, 156, 176. By permission of the University of Chicago Press.

[3] The seat of emotions is in the diencephalic region (the midbrain), probably more specifically in the thalamus.

similar to that of normal animals. The sham rage of the decerebrate animal is elicited by trifling disturbances of any kind, is astonishingly intense, and possesses a width and energy of expression that make it unmistakably the counterpart of intense fury in the normal animal. Bard points out that the behavior attending the major emotions, fear and rage, is evoked by the urgency of certain definite circumstances, and that it is plainly directed toward the preservation of the individual. It constitutes a reaction that is primitive, energetically purposive, and common to the divergent members of the vertebrate series. Bard removed the cerebrum of an animal and found emotional behavior of an integrated sort still persisted, indicating that the organizing center for such reactions is below the cortical level. From the evolutionary point of view it is significant that such important adaptive reactions should be under the control of a subcortical center.[1] We shall note that this is in keeping with the general principle that the more fundamental activities essential to the continuance of life are delegated to the lower levels of the nervous system.

3. The Cerebellum. The cerebellum is situated at the base of the brain, to the rear. See diagram on page 170. The cerebellum, the functions of which are imperfectly known, probably coördinates the postural components of voluntary movements initiated by the cerebral motor cortex. The two lobes of the cerebellum are connected by a transverse band of fibres called the pons.

4. The Medulla Oblongata. The medulla oblongata is located forward and just above the juncture of the brain stem and the spinal cord. See diagram on page 170. The medulla oblongata contains the nerve centers which control circulation

---

[1] See P. Bard: "A Diencephalic Mechanism for the Expression of Rage with Special Reference to the Sympathetic Nervous System," *American Journal of Physiology*, 1928, 84, 490–515.

and respiration.   Again it is pertinent to remark that in view
of our ignorance of the principles of breathing and blood circulation, it is to our advantage that these processes are not
ordinarily[1] under our conscious regulation, but rather are
taken care of by a lower nervous center.

   5. The Spinal Cord.   The spinal cord is an extension of
the brain.   The spinal cord is the coördinating agency of the
lowest level, organizing some of the reflexes which constitute
the basic units of all behavior.

   The cord serves to gather in the sensory impulses destined
for the higher levels, and to distribute the motor impulses

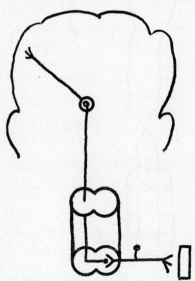

descending from the higher
centers to the muscles and
glands. We shall trace, first,
the path of a typical sensory
impulse, and second, the
path of a typical outlet over
the motor tracts.

   We shall take first the
path of conduction for a sensory impulse.

   The diagram represents
the typical path of an impulse from the skin (receptor) on the left side of the
body to the opposite side of
the cord, up through the
medulla and thalamus to the

cerebral cortex (right hemisphere).   No portion of the cortex
is directly connected with sense organs.   All sensory impulses,
except smell, pass through the thalamus on the way to the
cortex.

_____

   [1] I say "ordinarily" because when we are sick with a head cold, breathing often
becomes a conscious process, much to our discomfort and fatigue.

The motor impulse is transmitted over the pyramidal tracts.

Note that the impulse leaves the right hemisphere (cortex) and comes down the left-hand side of the cord, thus bringing the impulse back to the region of stimulation. It is natural that the response be made in the region of stimulation.

The motor tracts are made up of pyramidal neurons — neurons which are comparatively long. Therefore, there are fewer synapses to be crossed, and the time required for reaction is reduced to a minimum.

In a right-handed person, the left cerebral hemisphere is dominant—that is, the left hemisphere is more developed. On account of the decussation (crossing), the left hemisphere takes care

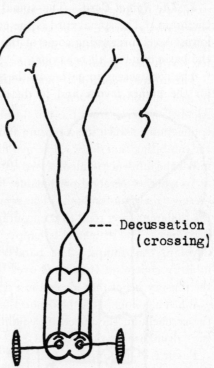

--- Decussation (crossing)

of the right-hand side of the body, while the right hemisphere governs the left-hand side of the body.

The graduated importance of the levels of the nervous hierarchy may be appreciated by a study of the effects of alcohol on the human system. Alcohol is a narcotic, not a stimulant. It impedes nervous conduction.

Alcohol begins at the top of the nervous hierarchy and works downward. Thinking cannot proceed at its maximum efficiency because the nervous connections in the cerebrum have been narcotized. A drunkard's wit can only be appreciated by another drunkard, whose cortex has likewise been drugged, and whose critical faculties have been paralyzed. Alcohol seems to be a stimulant because it removes the inhibiting effects of the cortex. The cortex normally controls the lower levels through inhibition and reënforcement. Alcohol interferes with the regulatory functions of the cerebrum.

The ultimate control of our emotional experience is effected by the inhibitory influence of the cortex upon the thalamus. Alcohol, working from the top downward, affects the nervous connection between the cerebrum and the thalamus, paralyzing the inhibiting functions. The real man underneath comes out under the influence of alcohol, we say, but it may be questioned as to whether cerebral or thalamic behavior is the expression of the "real" individual. The removal of inhibition allows the thalamus freer rein, thus encouraging exaggerated affective reactions. The drunkard is happy, hic, oh so happy, or way down in the dumps. The paralyzing influence on the inhibitory control of the cortex over the thalamus accounts for the illusory belief that alcohol is a stimulant.

When alcohol affects the connections between the cortex and the cerebellum, the uncertain equilibrium so characteristic of the "drunkard's gait" results.

Further consumption of alcohol, by affecting still lower levels, may endanger the vital functions of respiration and circulation, thus suspending animation.

B. The Peripheral Nervous System. In addition to the central nervous system there is the peripheral nervous system, made up of the nerves outside the brain and cord. The peripheral nerves are classified in two groups, the spinal and the cranial, according to the portion of the skeleton from which they emerge.

1. The Cranial Nerves. Some of the cranial nerves are motor in function, some are sensory, and some are mixed. In man there are twelve pairs of cranial nerves, all of which find exit through holes in or between the bones forming the base of the skull. The first and second pairs differ from all the other peripheral nerves in that, developmentally, they are really outgrowths of the brain substance. The cranial nerves are:

I. Olfactory (sensory)—connected with the organ of smell.
II. Optic (sensory)—connected with the organ of sight.
III. Oculo-motor (motor)—to certain muscles of the eyeball.
IV. Trochlear (motor)—to a muscle of the eyeball.
V. Trigeminal—sensory to face and tongue, motor to muscles of mastication.
VI. Abducent (motor)—to a muscle of the eyeball.
VII. Facial—sensory to tongue, motor to all muscles of facial expression.
VIII. Auditory (sensory)—connected with the organ of hearing.
IX. Glossopharyngeal—sensory and motor to tongue and pharynx.
X. Pneumogastric or vagus—sensory and motor to viscera.
XI. Spinal accessory (motor)—a portion joins the vagus; the other portion supplies two muscles of the neck.
XII. Hypoglossal (motor)—to muscles of the tongue.

2. The Spinal Nerves. The spinal nerves pass out from the sides of the vertebral column between adjacent vertebræ. In man there are thirty-one pairs of spinal nerves named from the regions of the vertebral column where they emerge:

8 Cervical—neck region
12 Thoracic—region of chest
5 Lumbar—region of loins
5 Sacral   } —terminal portion of the spinal column.
1 Coccygeal }

C. The Autonomic System. Outside the spinal cord is a chain of nerve fibres which make up the autonomic nervous system. The function of the autonomic system is motor only (not sensory). It controls the vegetative processes such as digestion and blood circulation, by regulating the glands and the smooth muscles of the viscera. The whole autonomic system is under the control of the central nervous system by means of the pre-ganglionic neuron.

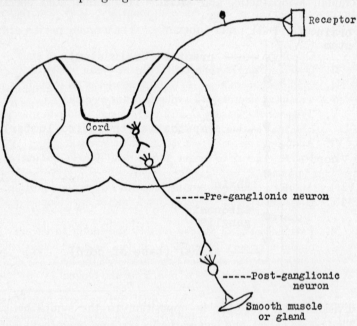

What is the purpose of the relay—of the extra neuron that is interposed? The post-ganglionic neuron is non-medullated. Lacking the medullary sheath this neuron slows up the rhythm of the impulse. The slower rhythm is more suited to the smooth muscles which are called into action by the autonomic system. There is no need for the quick, rapid movements which are characteristic of the activity of the skeletal muscles. The smooth muscles around the digestive tract and the blood vessels function slowly but surely. The impulse to the skeletal (striped) muscles is direct; the impulse to the smooth muscles is relayed through the outlying (autonomic) neuron. The vegetative processes, which are activated by the autonomic system, are not under direct voluntary control.

The autonomic system is organized in three sections—cranial, sympathetic, and sacral. The cranial and sacral

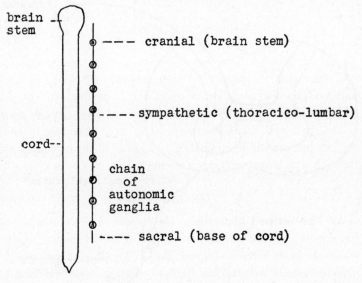

divisions work together in opposition to the sympathetic. The cranio-sacral and sympathetic systems operate in the same organs, but with antagonistic reactions. The sympathetic dilates the pupil, the cranial contracts it; the sympathetic inhibits digestive and sexual activities, the cranio-sacral augments them; the sympathetic accelerates the heartbeat, the cranial retards it, and so on. Either the cranial and the sympathetic or the sacral and the sympathetic divisions innervate all organs where there is smooth muscle or gland.

CHAPTER VI

MOTOR EQUIPMENT

THE receptors inform the organism of the environment in order that the proper adjustments may be made by the motor equipment. Adaptive behavior is carried out by effectors which consist of the striped and unstriped muscles and of the duct and ductless glands. Our understanding of the way we behave will be improved by a study of the mechanisms through which our reactions are effected.

I. THE MUSCLES

A. The Striped Muscles.   The human skeleton is a bony framework, consisting of about two hundred bones, upon which the body is hung and stretched.   The skeletal or striped muscles usually are attached to the contiguous ends of adjacent bones.   As the muscle crosses a joint, a lever is created which adds to the effectiveness of muscular exertion.   In most activities such as lifting, running, and jumping, the muscles work with the coöperation of the skeleton.

A striped muscle with which everybody is familiar is the biceps muscle of the upper arm.   It is this muscle which bulges on the professional strong man who flexes his arm for the benefit of magazine readers.   A husky biceps is somehow accepted as the symbol for robust health, although the truth is that Herculean muscles are often acquired at the expense of physical vitality.   Of what possible use can a powerful biceps be to a bookkeeper?

1. Contractility.   The striped muscle, as has been stated, is attached to the contiguous ends of bones by means of terminal cords which are called tendons.   The belly of the muscle can shorten under certain conditions, thus exerting a pull upon the passive tendons which transmit the movement to the bones, just as a tug on a rope will pull a sled.   The shortening of the muscular tissue causes it to thicken in diameter, and to become

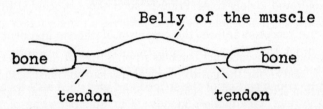

hard and rigid.   When the young athlete asks you to feel his muscle, he contracts it so that you are impressed with the properties just described.   The fundamental characteristic of a muscle is this contractility, the capacity to change from a long and narrow shape while at rest to a shorter and thicker form in activity, thus exerting a forceful pull on the bones.

Under the microscope the skeletal muscle is seen to be striated—hence the term "striped."   The muscle is composed

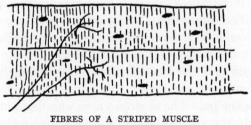

FIBRES OF A STRIPED MUSCLE
(Highly magnified)

of tiny fibres which are living cells specialized for the function of contraction.   When hundreds of these small fibres shorten the total force of the whole muscle is considerable.

2. Nervous Control. Muscular contraction may be evoked by mechanical, chemical, or electrical stimuli, etc., but the usual excitation for the shortening of the fibres is an impulse imparted by the motor nerve, the electro-chemical processes of the nerve inducing chemical changes in the muscle. The phasic contraction of a muscle begins with a latent period during which the muscle remains unexcited, followed by a slow, a rapid, and a slow contraction in succession, concluded by a relaxation. The whole operation involves a mere fraction of a second.

A simple muscular act, such as tipping the hat, involves the whole body—for the entire physical mechanism must assume a certain set or attitude before the act can ensue. The organization of the reaction of course is taken care of by the nervous system through its coördinating functions.

3. Tonus. When the belly of a resting muscle is dissected, the two ends of the muscle draw away from each other. This evidence indicates that even the resting muscle is kept in a slight tension continuously, probably by a constant stream of impulses from the brain and cord. The steady tension of muscular tissue is known as its *tonus*. In everyday parlance we speak of people being "toned up," or vigorous. The exact nature of tonus is not known. Functionally speaking, tonus is a condition of alertness, making for rapid response. The tonus is maintained by the cerebellum. In a spinal frog, whose cerebellum has been removed, the muscles become lax and sluggish. If the foot is pulled down, the leg will hang limp—the tonus is gone.

4. Antagonism. The muscles are arranged in antagonistic groups. In the arm, for example, there is one set of muscles to bend the arm (the flexors), and another set to straighten the arm (the extensors). The direction of the force depends upon the ratio between the two tensions. When the flexors contract, the extensors relax, and vice versa. The antagonistic tensions promote the smooth functioning of the musculature so that movements of delicate skill can be executed.

5. The Erect Posture. You may have noticed how fatiguing it is to stand still. The human body was never designed to remain upright. It was originally constructed to be used "on all fours." The internal organs were designed to hang freely from a horizontal backbone, like clothes from a line. The legs and arms were designed to serve as supports at the corners of a four-legged body, like a table. The spine was intended to be a girder, not a column. The upright position imposes a strain which involves a large proportion of the striped musculature. It is easy to understand, therefore, why standing still is very tiring—the muscles are under a constant strain with little relief through variation.

6. Muscular Work. Muscular activity is work which means that fuel must be utilized and converted into energy

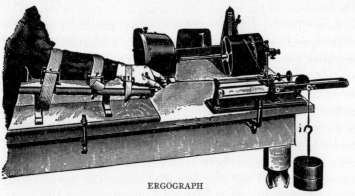

ERGOGRAPH
(Reproduced by courtesy of the C. H. Stoelting Company.)

(metabolism). The food for the muscles is furnished by the sugar distributed to the muscles by the blood. Reserve sugar is stored in the muscles themselves, and is also stored in the liver in the form of glycogen. The reserve supplies in the liver are tapped by the ductless glands which transfer the fuel to the bloodstream, and then direct the supply of blood to the muscles. As the sugar is burned, fatigue products are created, the chief of which are carbon dioxide and lactic acid. These products are gradually carried off by the blood—the ductless glands coöperating, as we shall see later, to minimize the conditions of fatigue. Experimentally muscular work is studied by using an ergograph, an instrument which calls for the lifting of a weight by a finger, the contractions being timed to the beats of a metronome.

The ergograph test was given to three runners while they were training for their respective events. Each record reads from right to left (page 191). First is Fuque, a sprinter; second is Hornbostel, a middle-distance runner; and third is Brocksmith, a long-distance runner. The interpretation of their performances may yield light on the effects of specialized training on physical condition. Psychological factors may also be involved.

7. Exercise. Exercise is absolutely essential for the maintenance of healthy muscles. A muscle which remains unused atrophies, as may be seen in cases of paralysis where the nerve has been seriously impaired or destroyed. The muscular tissues wither away until little is left. A person who has been confined to bed for several weeks, experiences considerable difficulty in walking. Athletic training hardens the muscles so that their power is increased. For the ordinary routine of life, however, no such force is required. Rest and exercise should alternate, else softness and exhaustion will ensue, as the case may be. Too frequently athletes train themselves to the point of exhaustion for the sake of Alma Mater, and to their own permanent harm.

B. The Smooth Muscles. The smooth or unstriped muscles are found chiefly in the viscera—the "insides"— involving such organs as the stomach, intestines, heart, lungs, and sex organs. The viscera are hollow organs mostly, the

contents of which are constantly changing—the stomach
(food), lungs (air), and heart, arteries, and blood vessels
(blood). During the process of handling these metabolic
ingredients the visceral organs are reacting and thereby supplying stimuli that may impel the whole body to action. The
contraction of the smooth muscles in the stomach walls may
provide the stimulus for the striped muscles to propel the
organism to a restaurant. Visceral reactions may call the
striped musculature into action in order to carry an urge
through to its fruition.

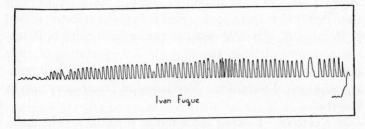

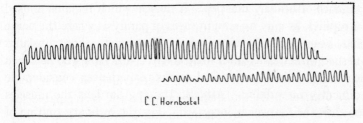

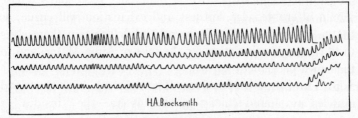

ERGOGRAPHIC RECORDS OF RUNNERS
(Reproduced by courtesy of J. M. Harmon.)

Smooth muscles are also found in other parts of the organism—around the hairs on the skin, making it possible for the hair to stand on end; in the eye, adjusting the size of the pupil.

Two typical forms of smooth muscle are the longitudinal and the circular. The longitudinal unstriped muscle is found,

among other places, in the intestine where it serves to change the local length of the canal. The circular type of unstriped muscle functions to regulate, among other organs, the size of the blood vessels, thus determining the distribution of the excess blood supply.

SMOOTH MUSCLE EN-
CIRCLING AN ARTERY

1. Slow Contractions. Smooth muscles are less prompt in their response than skeletal muscles, and more independent. By voluntary effort a person may contract his striped muscles, but he is unable directly to contract or dilate his blood vessels through the operation of the unstriped musculature. The smooth muscles go about their business in a slow and steady manner; they discharge their functions with a reliability that insures the efficiency of the body as a whole. The postganglionic neuron of the autonomic system, you recall, slows up the rhythm of the impulse to suit the smooth muscles which take their time.

2. Control. The unstriped musculature is regulated by two sorts of control—by the autonomic nervous system and by the glandular secretions.

3. Internal Stimuli. It is easy to fall into the fallacy of thinking that the stimuli which provoke our responses come solely from the external environment. It is important to note that many of the stimuli which excite us to activity are furnished by our internal processes and that there are receptors inside us to detect these stimuli just as the eye, for example, picks up the goings-on of the external world. Our "environment"—our world of stimuli—is not only one of external objects, sights, sounds, and smells; it is one of internal objects as well—hunger contractions, bladder distensions, palpitating heart, rapid breathing, and muscular changes.

II. THE GLANDS

The glands complete the motor equipment. Behavior consists not only of muscular responses, but also of glandular responses. Glands are organs with which we behave. Secretion responses are aroused by the stimulation of the sense organs. Tears may flow as a reaction to the presence of onions, to intense pain, or to sad news.

There are two types of glands: the duct and the ductless glands. The duct glands have an outlet (duct) through which they secrete externally (sweat glands) or into the alimentary canal (salivary glands). The ductless (endocrine) glands which, as you may have suspected, have no duct, man-

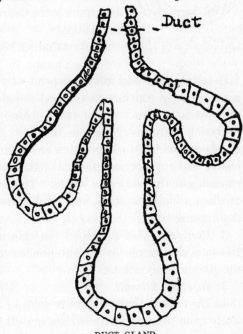

DUCT GLAND

ufacture powerful chemical bodies which are absorbed into the blood stream, as the blood bathes the cells of the gland.

A. The Duct Glands. The duct glands pour their secretions through an opening.

1. Some of the Glands. *a. The Sweat Glands.* In the deep tissues of the skin lie the sweat glands. There are about two million in the entire cutaneous surface. The duct is composed of smooth muscle cells, and makes its outlet through the pores of the skin. The sweat glands play an important part in hot weather in the maintenance of a constant bodily temperature, and also in the release of impurities injurious to health.

b. The Salivary Glands. The salivary glands are located in the mouth cavity. As we noted in Pavlov's experiments on the dog, saliva is secreted when food is presented or anticipated. The secretion facilitates the process of mastication and lubricates the alimentary canal for the downward passage of the food.

In the stomach and intestines are a number of glands secreting substances which serve to break down the food into chemical products that can be readily absorbed by the bodily tissues—the gastric glands in the walls of the stomach, the glands in the walls of the intestines which secrete intestinal juices, and in addition, the pancreas and the liver. These various glands lubricate the alimentary canal, supply the enzymes which digest the food, and eliminate waste products from the blood.

c. Other Duct Glands. Other duct glands are the lachrymal glands which secrete tears, the kidneys which secrete urine, and the sex glands (gonads) which secrete the substances necessary to reproduction.

2. The Duct Glands in Emotion. Cannon has demonstrated that during emotional excitement the glands involved in digestion stop secreting.[1] When a person is experiencing anger or fear, for example, the digestive process comes to a halt, due to the cessation of secretion. If a meal is fed to a dog and he is then intensely frightened, hours afterward the meal

---

[1] W. B. Cannon: *Bodily Changes in Pain, Hunger, Fear, and Rage.* 1923.

may be found in his stomach, still undigested. Nature stops the digestive process in an emergency. Emotional excitement occurs when vital adjustments must be made for self-preservation. At such a time there are other activities more important for the moment than digestion. If you find yourself suddenly in a dangerous situation, it does not make much difference whether your meal is being taken care of—the important thing is to act to survive—for digestion means little to a dead man. The organism, therefore, in an emergency, concentrates upon external action and neglects momentarily the contents of the alimentary canal.

It is poor psychology to quarrel at mealtime because it retards digestion. Bad temper is conducive to indigestion and indigestion aggravates bad temper—it is a vicious circle. Although the modern parent may see his offspring only at mealtime, unless he makes an appointment, he should refrain from scolding, if he respects the child's health. Children would undertake the study of psychology at an early age, if they realized how guilefully they might evade a scolding by reminding Dad that the duct glands must continue to secrete until the enzymes have completed their preparation of the food for absorption.

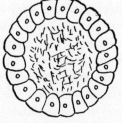

B. The Ductless Glands. The ductless or endocrine glands exert an influence upon the body and mind, the importance of which was not suspected until comparatively recent times. The history of the experimental discoveries which have gradually enlightened the world in regard to the endocrine functions is a fascinating story.[1]

CROSS SECTION OF A PART OF A DUCTLESS GLAND

The cells of the ductless gland secrete into the closed sacs

[1] See Louis Berman: *The Glands Regulating Personality*, Chapter I, "How the Glands of Internal Secretion Were Discovered." 1921.

which they surround. The secretion then passes out between the cells into the lymph spaces of the connective tissue.

The locations of the principal endocrine glands can best be illustrated by the following diagram:

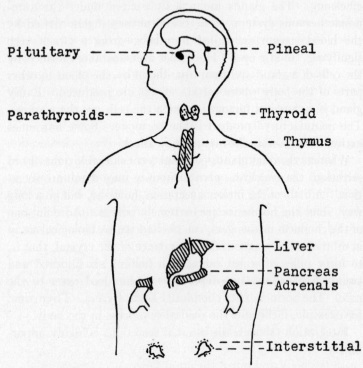

Pituitary --------- Pineal

Parathyroids -------- Thyroid

--------- Thymus

--------- Liver

--------- Pancreas

--------- Adrenals

--------- Interstitial

(From a sketch in Dashiell's *Fundamentals of Objective Psychology*.[1])

1. Integration. The endocrine glands are the chemical regulators of the body, effecting an integration of the organism similar to the coördination secured by the nervous system. The nerves connect every part of the body with every other part—and the blood, as a transportation system for carrying substances, discharges the same coördinating function. The

[1]By permission of and arrangement with Houghton Mifflin Company.

endocrine system produces a chemical integration of the total organism. The neural mode of inter-connection, of course, is much faster than the glandular. The two systems, each with its peculiar advantages, coöperate to insure adaptive efficiency. The glands are reflexly excited under the autonomic nervous system. The chemical messengers carried by the blood stream are called hormones—from a Greek verb signifying "to stir up." Hormones are substances formed by the cells of a gland and then distributed by the blood to other parts of the body where certain effects are produced. Every gland is a chemical factory in which the cells are the workers. The manufactured product is the hormone. Some hormones excite, some inhibit the organs they affect.

Whereas the duct glands pour out a considerable quantity of secretion, the endocrine glands produce only a minute secretion. A little of the internal secretion, however, will go a long way, since the hormones are extremely potent. Adrenin, one of the chemical messengers, can be detected by biological assay in dilution of $1:300,000,000$—one ounce of the crystal, that is, to forty miles of water carts, each holding six hundred and twenty-five gallons and deployed two hundred carts to the mile. The hormones act chemically as catalyzers. Thyroxine, for example, facilitates the oxidation process in the body.

Integration through the internal secretions is highly important.

There is good reason for the belief that this is the primitive method of control by which the various parts of the body are kept working in harmony. The chief lines of evidence are: chemical control is found in the lowest forms of animals and even in man; the so-called vegetative functions such as digestion or growth are preëminently under chemical control; reproduction, likewise, with its numerous bodily and psychic adaptations, is strikingly dependent upon hormone factors. It is perhaps significant in this connection that hormones seem to be completely interchangeable from one species to another. . . . This would seem to indicate that the hormones have been common factors from a remote ancestral period.[1]

Arthur Keith, conservator of the Museum of the Royal College of Surgeons of England, believes that evolution has to a con-

(By permission of Keystone View Company.)

siderable extent worked primarily through hereditary variations in the endocrine glands.

The fact that the hormones of different species are inter-changeable, is significant, since it makes possible the administration of animal hormones in the treatment of human glandular disorders.

Our knowledge of the specific functions of the various ductless glands has been seriously impeded by the intimate inter-dependence of the glands. Disturbances in one gland involve changes, too, in other glands, so that it is difficult to determine the exact properties of any particular gland.

The endocrine system, in which the various secretions balance or supplement each other, presides, in general, over four bodily functions:

1. growth   2. nutrition   3. sex
4. the vegetative process of gland secretion and involuntary muscle control.

---

[1]Julius Stieglitz (Editor): *Chemistry in Medicine*, p. 192.   1928.   By permission of the Chemical Foundation, Inc.

Endocrine disturbances produce serious deformities which may be observed in the freaks both in and out of the circus— the giant, the fat lady, the bearded lady, and the living skeleton.

2. Glandular Influence on the Psyche. The effects of the endocrine glands on the psychic functions are no less remark-

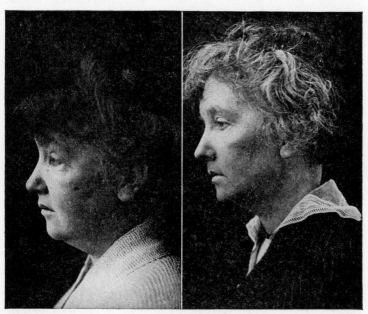

EFFECT OF THYROXINE ON AN ADULT SUFFERING FROM A DEFICIENCY IN THYROID SECRETION[1]

able than on the physical. When thyroxine is administered for cretinism, the benefits that follow are expressed in improved mentality as well as in physical rehabilitation. The implicit responses which may be confined to the muscular and glandular systems inside the body exert a profound influence upon the mental life, all the more profound since it is so subtle.

[1]Reproduced by courtesy of the Chemical Foundation, Inc., and Dr. E. C. Kendall.

The stream of feeling which underlies our psychic states originates, not in the brain itself, but in the viscera, muscles, blood vessels, and glands. The vegetative apparatus is the physiological correlate of that phase of mental life so loosely described as the subconscious. The term "subconscious" becomes more meaningful if we think of it in terms of the implicit responses which affect our moods and behavior in ways of which we are little aware. The glands may determine to a large extent the whole attitude toward life—whether life is worth living, as the familiar saying runs, depends on the liver. Psychology must look to the glands for an account of a large share of experience.

3. Some of the Glands. The various glands have specific functions which have gradually been discovered by the painstaking research of the physiologists.

a. The Pituitary[1] Gland. The pituitary gland, located beneath the brain just over the back part of the roof of the mouth, has been described as Nature's Darling Treasure since it is so safely located in the interior of the head. There are two divisions to the gland, the posterior and the anterior, which must be differentiated since they secrete separate hormones.

Only recently, in 1929, Oliver Kamm succeeded in isolating two hormones in the posterior lobe which are known as the pituitary twins, alpha and beta. The alpha hormone is important as a tonic for the uterine muscles in childbirth, while the beta hormone acts to raise the blood pressure, to quicken the respiratory rate, and to control the retention of water in the cells of the body. The beta hormone is important in the treatment of burns. The difficulties in glandular experiment may be grasped by remarking that a single laboratory experiment of Kamm's required the posterior pituitary glands of fifty thousand cattle.

The hormone of the anterior pituitary gland controls bodily

[1]For locations of the glands, see diagram on p. 196.

growth. A deficiency of this secretion will stunt growth so that a dwarf results. The midget Adams sisters, natives of Martha's Vineyard, were victims of such a glandular disturbance. Miss Lucy grew to a height of 43 inches and Miss Sarah to a height of 40 inches. As babies, they were of normal size, but it soon became apparent that they were not growing normally. The first shoes they had were made at home, for none small enough could be purchased. Their mother often measured their height to see if they were growing. When Miss Sarah was 19, she weighed just 40 pounds, and it had long since been accepted that both young women were destined to be midgets. For several years they appeared with the troupe of Mr. and Mrs. Tom Thumb, world-famous dwarfs.[1]

Early overactivity of the anterior lobe of the pituitary gland results in gigantism. If the hypersecretion commences later in life, the bones of the face, hands, and feet become enlarged, producing a misshapen gorilla type (acromegaly). A middle-aged English clergyman suddenly found his gloves no longer fitted him. Each time he bought a new pair he was obliged to take a size larger. With his hats it was the same way. He was outgrowing his shoes too. He hied himself to a physician who informed him he was suffering from acromegaly.

Research on the pituitary gland may be illustrated by a description of an experiment performed at the Harvard Medical School. Two pedigreed thoroughbred English bulldogs, female littermates, aged four weeks, were received on March 1, 1927. They were observed in the laboratory, and were found to grow and behave as normal puppies should. On April 7, the animals weighed 4.87 and 5 Kg. respectively. Beginning on this date, daily intraperitoneal injections of sterile anterior lobe extract from the pituitary glands of cattle were given to the smaller of the two dogs. The heavier puppy was reserved as a control. By May 1, it became apparent that the dog

---

[1] The Boston *Herald*, October 24, 1930.

which received the injections was growing faster than the control. From that time on, there was an increasing difference between their respective weights. By June 1928 the dog given the extract was almost double the weight of her littermate. On June 14, a very warm day, the oversized dog succumbed to the heat and died. The heart and lungs could not stand the strain imposed by the artificially enlarged body.[1]

b. *The Thyroid Gland.* Growth is not under the sole dominance of the pituitary gland. The thyroid gland, near the windpipe, also influences growth through its effect upon the rate of basic metabolism. The hormone, thyroxine, contains about 65% iodine. The activity of the gland depends upon the amount of iodine present. The thyroid through its hormone provides a means for maintaining a higher rate of metabolism than would otherwise obtain, and it also provides a means for varying the rate of metabolism to meet changing physiological needs.

Thyroid deficiency means a slow heat production (metabolism). A baby born with an inadequate thyroid develops into a stunted bandylegged imbecile, with protruding abdomen and drooling tongue. His thinking and behavior are sluggish. Emotional depression, lack of interest in things, and retarded thinking are characteristic symptoms.

Hyperthyroidism or oversecretion of thyroxine occurs in exophthalmic goitre, with rapid heartbeat, high blood pressure, elongation of the skeleton, and nervous excitability. A person with excessive thyroid secretion is feverishly active, nervous, and is apt to suffer from insomnia.

c. *The Parathyroid Glands.* Anatomically associated with the thyroid are two pairs of glands known as the parathyroids, minute in structure. Removal of the parathyroids causes tetany (muscular convulsions) which issues in death. Early workers attributed tetany to removal of the thyroid. The

[1] The Boston *Sunday Herald*, April 14, 1929.

mistake was easily made since in extirpating the thyroid they unknowingly took out the parathyroids too. The tetany is due to a blood deficiency in calcium which renders the muscles overexcitable. Oversecretion of the parathyroids lowers muscular activity to a subnormal level. Rapid decay of teeth in childhood indicates a parathyroid deficiency. The teeth often suffer decay in the pregnant mother as pregnancy provokes glandular disturbances. The iodine content of the thyroid hormone stimulates metabolism; the calcium content of the parathyroid hormone prevents overexcitability. A proper balance between iodine and calcium in the blood is necessary to bodily efficiency.

d. The Puberty Gland. The sex glands not only furnish an external secretion for reproductive purposes but also an endocrine secretion. The external secretion is supplied by the gonads (true sex cells). Situated among the gonads are the interstitial cells which constitute the puberty gland. During embryonic development the hormone from the puberty gland regulates the formation and growth of the primary internal and external genital organs. A special hormone produced in the active uterus during pregnancy stimulates the development of the mammary glands in the mother, at the same time inhibiting the formation of milk, and at birth it is the cessation of this hormone which permits lactation to start. Sexual vigor is dependent upon the interstitial cells rather than upon the gonads as most investigators had earlier supposed. The castrated animal lacks pugnacity, his whole personality is altered, because his organism has been deprived of the hormone from the puberty gland. When the secretion ceases at the menopause, bodily functions suffer a disturbance which expresses itself in symptoms of nervous tension. The rhythmical occurrence of ovulation in the female is associated with rhythmical changes in the secretions from the interstitial cells. The appearance of the secondary sexual characters at puberty is due to this same secretion—affecting the physical differentiations between male and female in respect to bodily shape, beard, breasts, height and weight, voice, and temperament. It has long been recognized that the eunuch differs in appearance and personality from the normal male.

e. The Pineal Gland. The pineal gland is a very small structure located in the brain itself. It develops until about the seventh year and then atrophies. The secretion of the pineal gland serves to hold sex development in check until puberty.

f. The Thymus Gland. The thymus gland, in the lower neck, like the pineal gland, acts to inhibit the premature growth of the sex glands and the premature appearance of the secondary sex characters. It is largest at puberty and then undergoes involution.

g. The Pancreas. The pancreas, located next to the small intestine, was considered solely as a duct gland until Langerhans discovered a collection of cells which differ in their microscopic structure from those cells known to be responsible for the secretion of the digestive juices. These cells were named the Islets of Langerhans and their hormone was designated "insulin." An insufficiency of the hormone insulin disorganizes metabolism with such resulting symptoms as increased sugar in the blood and sugar in the urine, symptoms of the disease known as diabetes. Metabolism in a diabetic may be compared to the retarded combustion of wet coal.

The treatment of diabetes includes the reduction of sugar-producing foodstuffs in the diet, and the injection of insulin to supplement the inadequate endocrine secretion. Early workers injected too much insulin, reducing the blood sugar so low as to produce convulsions and often death. The antidote for an overdose of insulin is an injection of adrenalin (adrenal gland hormone) which liberates sugar (glycogen) from the liver into the circulation. Normally the pancreas and the adrenal glands counterbalance each other to maintain the proper sugar content in the blood. The discovery of insulin as a cure for diabetes has been a great boon to humanity.

h. The Adrenal Glands. The adrenal glands are two small structures shaped like a cocked hat and fitting snugly on top of each kidney. Each gland is composed of two parts, cortex and medulla, which have distinct functions. The secretion of the adrenal cortex acts as a detoxicating agent for certain poisons. Overactivity of the cortex leads to a marked accentuation of the masculine sex traits in either male or female. The adrenal medulla secretes a hormone which has been isolated and is known as adrenin, epinephrine, or adrenaline.

Adrenin evokes the same internal responses as are induced by the excitation of the sympathetic portion of the autonomic nervous system. All the reactions of adrenin may be duplicated by the electrical stimulation of the appropriate sympathetic nerve. Emotional excitement provokes the secretion of adrenin which acts as a mobilizer of energy for a physical exertion which may be a matter of life or death. The organism is set for the emergency by means of the following processes initiated by adrenin:

1. The secretion of digestive juices is halted.
2. The heart beats faster.

George H. Austin, 46, an employee of the Eastman Kodak Company, was brought back to life by an injection of adrenalin. Respiration and heart action had stopped, the reflexes of the pupils had ceased, and the face had taken on the ashen color of death, when he was found collapsed on the floor by Dr. Benjamin J. Salter, chief of the company's medical staff. Under the influence of the adrenalin Austin's heart started beating again, and his life was restored.[1]

3. The glycogen in the liver is converted into sugar and released into the blood stream. Anger sweetens the blood, but not the disposition.
4. The major part of the blood supply is transferred from the

---

[1] The Boston *Herald*, December 4, 1929.

vegetative organs to the skeletal muscles so that there is less blood in the stomach and more in the arms and legs. Sugar is thus pumped to the muscles to provide the additional fuel for heavy exertion. Sugar not burned by the muscles may appear in the urine as Cannon noted in his investigation of spectators who had just undergone the emotional excitement of a football contest. A riot after a game is an apt method of burning up the excess sugar.

5. Fatigue products are neutralized or carried off by the increased blood supply. Adrenin will restore a fatigued muscle to a normal condition in five minutes where a rest of one hour would be necessary to produce an equivalent change.[1]

6. The pupils are dilated to improve the clarity of vision.

7. The blood clots faster, thus preventing death in case of wounds.

Emotional excitement, involving, as it does, the adrenal glands with their preparatory measures for exertion, is a detriment to the adaptive activities of modern man.[2] Civilized competition is carried on in terms of intelligent manœuvres and not in terms of mere physical strife. Where the social code forbids assault and battery as a means of expressing antipathy, it is of no avail that the blood is pumped to the skeletal muscles. Being full of sugar is not conducive to that clear, quick thinking which is necessary to success in the struggle for existence as carried on under the present rules. It is most distressing to get "all riled up" and to have no adequate vent. The glands behave as if we were still primitive men fighting it out with our brute strength to determine survival. Instead of facilitating adjustment, our visceral tensions befuddle our wits and leave us emotionally distraught, feeling the urge to do something, yet hemmed in by inhibitions which

---

[1] See H. M. Johnson: "The Real Meaning of Fatigue," *Harper's Magazine*, January, 1929.

[2] W. B. Cannon: *op. cit.*, especially Chapters XI and XII.

shut off our natural outlets. We laugh, sometimes, at a terrible tempered person because he does the violent things to people we all would like to do at times. Pent-up emotions can only result in nervous disorder and unhappiness. Education must see to it that the viscera are trained as well as the brain.

4. The Endocrine System. The ductless glands are intimately interrelated in their chemical regulation of the various bodily processes. They supplement and counterbalance each other to maintain a delicate equilibrium between the hormones. Through the endocrine glands, as well as through the nervous system, effective integration of sensory and motor equipments is secured.

PART IV

DETERMINING TENDENCIES

There are in human nature certain tendencies and habits which determine experience. In Chapter VII we shall note how bias inclines the mind in definite directions. In Chapters VIII and IX we shall study the sources of bias in certain urges and the habits built around them. Thus the groundwork will be laid for an understanding of the mental adjustments described in Part V.

CHAPTER VII

THE IMPORTANCE OF BIAS

To the naïve person it is not apparent, though it is none the less true, that the nature of experience is determined by bias. By virtue of characteristic dominant urges and ingrained attitudes we are predisposed to observe the environment through subjective lenses, and to adjust ourselves in accordance with deep-seated prejudices. Since our motivating interests and propensities set us for various modes of experience, the study of attitude is fundamental to an understanding of the mind. Interpreting personality is a matter of discovering attitudes. Is a man conceited or depreciatory as he views himself? Is he interested or bored as he discharges the duties of his job? Is he coöperative or individualistic in his social relations? Is he obedient or rebellious toward those in authority? Is he optimistic or pessimistic as he faces the future? The answers to such questions tell the story of the real man.

I. THE DETERMINING OF EXPERIENCE

A. Definition. A bias is a slant or bent, a pointing of the mental life toward certain views and reactions. Consciously, a bias is a point of view; behavioristically, it is a posture, a set, a preparedness for acting, thinking, or judging, in a definite manner. A bias is an attitude—an anticipation—a prejudice which may manifest itself in overt behavior or in thoughts and feelings about behavior. Very often the determining tendency operates unconsciously, that is, without the individual's being

211

aware of the motive fundamentally responsible for his thinking
or action.

B. *Aufgabe.*   Suppose, for example, you are presented with
the following stimulus pattern:

$$\frac{5}{2}$$

What do you get?   Perhaps you get 7.   Why?   You were not
instructed to add the figures.   Why, then, did you add, when
there was no plus sign?   You added because you were set by
your past experience in arithmetical situations to do what you
usually have done when a similar pattern was given.   Perhaps,
instead of adding, you subtracted to get 3, or multiplied to
get 10.   The character analyst might discover in your reaction
a manifestation of your character—if you obtained 7, you are
generous; if 3, you are stingy; if 10, you are inclined to exaggeration or fertility.

Now, instead of leaving it to you to express your natural
bent, suppose I determine your set for you by supplying the
sign.

$$\frac{5}{-2}$$

The only thing you can do in compliance with the instruction
is to subtract.   The Germans have a word for this kind of set—
Aufgabe.   *Aufgabe* is the problem or task which determines
your set for you.

Münsterberg tried some class experiments to demonstrate
the influence of attitude.   He talked about university life and
then exposed for an instant the word "courage"—a number of
students read it as "college"; then he discussed the subject of
colonial policy and suddenly flashed the word "Philistines"—
the audience, as you would expect, saw "Philippines."[1]

C. Expectation.   Four men called on a sick friend in
Szegedin, Hungary.   They were informed by the patient that

[1] Hugo Münsterberg: *On the Witness Stand*, p. 34.   1908.

his illness was due to the visits of a witch who cast a spell over him.   While the sick man was speaking, an old woman entered his room, begging for alms.   The four men hacked her to death.   They were tried for murder and convicted.   The judgment was appealed on the ground that their belief in witches prompted their sudden action and they were acquitted of murder.

In summing up, the judge of the superior court said: "The murderers acted under an irresistible impulse.   Moreover, not only these statements, but all attendant circumstances, pointed to the presence of a witch.[1]

In early 1934, two taxi-drivers, Berrett and Molway, were indicted for a murder committed in a hold-up of the Lynn Paramount Theater.   They were identified by a large number of witnesses.   The trial was about to end in their conviction and probable electrocution when the real culprits confessed to the crime.   In a situation calling for the recognition of a criminal, the positive identification of the suspect by one witness establishes a tendency in other witnesses to fall into line, lest they appear stupid.   Thus expectation facilitates identification.

A puzzle, once solved, becomes surprisingly simple, since you know exactly what to look for.   The novice in the use of the microscope experiences difficulty in observing the appearance described by his instructor because his amateurish conception of the object to be seen is lacking in precision.   He can become more adept in the use of the microscope by consulting the illustrations in the textbook, for they enable his mental eye to realize the pictures which it should entertain.   He may be altogether too much influenced by the pictures thus suggested to his mental vision, however, and draw what is really not under the microscope at all.   Training in correct and

---

[1] The Boston *Herald*, January 20, 1928.

accurate vision involves the acquisition of an alert mental eye, which observes all that is objectively visible, but does not permit the subjective to add to or modify what is really present.

The strategy of football coaching illustrates how a team may build up expectation in its opponents, and then thwart the established set by the sudden shift of tactics. Lou Little, the Columbia coach, prepared his team in such strategy for the Columbia-Stanford game of 1933. A series of plays was run off in which the quarterback faked passing the ball to Barabas, one of their star back-field players, and Barabas pretended to conceal the ball as he circled the opposing end. The Stanford tacklers on that side of the line chased him the first few times and then, as they decided to ignore him because they were led to expect the fake, Barabas was given the ball. He ran unmolested for the touchdown that won the game.

D. The Operation of Set: *1. Perception.* The naïve person thinks of perception as a passive process in which the environment impresses itself upon the mind, much as a signet ring leaves its impression upon sealing wax. To him the mind is a tablet upon which experience inscribes its record. Deeper analysis of perception, however, reveals the fact that the mind through its activity contributes an important part to the total awareness of the world in which we live. We create the world in which we live in accordance with our predispositions. In every perception two factors contribute to the result. The one is the nature of the object perceived, the other that of the percipient. The latter factor is the one that is apt to be overlooked and it is, therefore, the one upon which we are concentrating our interest at the moment. Literally, what you perceive depends upon your point of view. The mental set of the spectator is as important as the event which is witnessed. Both must be taken into account in an adequate description of any given situation.

It is proverbial that appearances are deceptive. Adjusted as we are to the most probable event, what seems to be is readily mistaken for what is. In our anticipatory attitude we unconsciously insert items to round out the picture we had ex-

IT DEPENDS ON YOUR POINT OF VIEW
—Doyle in the Philadelphia *Record*

pected to get, not realizing, in doing so, our easy liability to error. The mind's eye perceives what it is prepared to experience.

Alexander Kerensky was slapped in the face by a young woman on the stage of the Century Theater in New York. The reporters present differed considerably in their descriptions of the manner in which the young woman struck the blow.

World: "Slashed him viciously across the cheek with her gloves."
News: "Struck him on the left cheek with the bouquet."
American: "Dropped her flowers and slapped him in the face with her gloves."
Times: "Slapped his face vigorously with her glove three times."

Herald-Tribune: "Beat him on the face and head . . . a half-dozen blows."

Evening World: "Struck him across the face several times."

Mirror: "Struck him a single time."

Post: "Vigorously and accurately slapped him."

And this is what happened next:

American: "Kerensky reeled back."

Evening World: "He stood unmoved."

News: "He stepped back, maintaining a calm pose."

World: "He stood still, but used his arms to wave back his friends."

Herald-Tribune: "He stood still, with his arms thrown back."

Journal: "He reeled."

Post: "He remained unmoved."

Mirror: "He reeled from the blow. His supporters were stemmed by a handful of royalists. Fists flew; noses ran red; shirts and collars were torn."

These accounts come from trained reporters who were set to witness what transpired. Casual witnesses would be even more inaccurate in their descriptions of the scene.

The determining tendencies which constitute the mental set distort the perceptual process just as the reporter and editor juggle the news before it reaches the reader. Our preconceptions serve as stereotypes to which we fit what we behold. The eyewitness does not get a naïve picture of a scene, for he brings something to the scene which results in a transfiguration of the event. His experience is not merely given, it is partly made. The rôle of the observer is always selective and usually creative. We imagine most things before we experience them, and our preconceptions affect deeply the entire process of perceiving. In most of our observations we do not notice all the details, but pick recognizable signs here and there which suggest ways of filling in the gaps in accordance with our stereotypes.

The following stereotypes will serve to crystallize definitely the preconceptions with which we are all equipped. How closely do they approximate your own mental pictures of these representative characters?

Clergyman   Farmer   Professor

(Drawn by Warren Sillen.)

It must be kept in mind that our stereotypes, in general, do not conform accurately to reality but, rather, are caricatures, subject to gross exaggeration.   The stereotype of the reformer, for example, does not do justice to many of the noble persons who have devoted themselves to the amelioration of conditions in our society.   The lack of personal charm in the stereotype of the reformer is the product, in part, of the hatred felt by the ignorant for those individuals who dream of a better order of things and who are willing to sacrifice any superficial popularity in order to bring their aims to fruition.

A similar stereotype, equally distorted in its conception, is that of the missionary, who is represented as a cadaverous individual clad in a frock coat too short in the sleeves, carrying a very bulging umbrella in one hand and a hymn book in the other.

This picture of a missionary . . . has made its impression and forms part of the strange mental furniture stored at the back of the head of the simple souls who today spend their evenings at the movies and their Sundays in reading comic supplements.

Then came the novel and the drama wherein the missionary was shown to be essentially a hypocrite and coward, in marked contrast to the lady of fortune or the gentleman adventurer, who might be a dope addict and a fugitive from justice but who was still one of nature's noblemen.[1]

MISSIONARY
(Drawn by R. Wilson Hammell)

The college professor, as a stereotype, is a simpleton who dashes with his net through fields of daisies in pursuit of butterflies. His large glasses fairly conceal his emaciated countenance. When he speaks, it is only in words of five syllables, consciously articulated with stilted precision. Under one arm is a bulky volume into which he peers at every opportunity. He does not watch where he is going—in fact, the poor

[1]Henry A. Perkins: "The Case for Foreign Missions," *The American Mercury*, February, 1931.

absent-minded fellow does not know where he is going. He is the perfect fool.

The artist, according to the popular conception, is a picturesque, effeminate person, with long hair, a black hat, a flowing tie, and a flabby physique. He is eccentric, indolent, and lax in his morals.

Babbitt is the stereotype of the American business man. The intellectuals know that the business man is an inferior order of human animal, full of bromides and platitudes, whose mental operations are fully contained in "yours received and contents noted." He is a Rotarian, a Babbitt, a 100-per cent American, a go-getter, able to handle dollars—an operation which seems to be attached to hopeless imbecility—but otherwise juvenile. The intellectuals can find something to respect in proletarian thought. They would have more use for a convention of piano-movers than piano-makers. A business man's gathering is rated as something which enables the men to pin red ribbons on themselves, laugh fatuously, call out "Come up to room 410, Bill. We have everything," and try out new golf courses. . . . If the business man enters politics, he is a sinister influence. It is orthodox pink doctrine that no business man could be interested in politics except to try to corrupt government for his own gain. In this he is always Big Business. Then the public should climb telegraph poles or hide out in the brush while the reformers go gunning and bring in the hide for the barn door. In his family life the business man is an old fogy to his children and a check book to his wife. He is something that fusses when the kids have the cars out all night, knocking down the concrete traffic posts, fusses when daughter comes home at 3 A.M., and fusses again when a basket of empties is cleaned out of Reginald's dresser. He is something that eats breakfast by himself to get to the office by 8:30, and makes the servants sore by getting them up.... If he with other business men try to arrange sports for the public, they are brutes, and the women tell them so.

Such are the fictions by which we organize our observations of reality. Inevitably, our accounts of what we notice are often more revealing of ourselves than of the event under observation.

If what we are looking at corresponds successfully with what we anticipated, the stereotype is reinforced for the future, as it is in a man who knows in advance that the Japanese are cunning and has had the bad luck to run across two dishonest Japanese. . . . If the experience contradicts the stereotype, one of two things happens. If the man is no longer plastic, or if some powerful interest makes it highly inconvenient to rearrange his stereotypes, he pooh-poohs the contradiction as an exception that proves the rule. . . . But if he is still curious and open-minded, the novelty is taken into the picture, and allowed to modify it.[1]

Thus do our prejudices evolve as stereotypes.

2. Attention. Attention is a matter of interest. We notice what we are interested in. A man may never bother to read the stock-market page in the newspaper until he entrusts his funds to Wall Street. A person who travels brings back those impressions which particularly struck his fancy during his tour.

The Romance of the Sea

"Sailor," said I, to the sun-browned lad
  With the mariner's rolling gait,
"What glorious cruises you must have had
  From Oporto to Bering Strait!
You have seen the flying fish skim the foam
  Where the Gulf Stream rippled blue,
And the cachelots spout in the darkling gloam
  (As I've read that they often do.)
Tell me of every thrilling cruise,
  Talk of the life you've led—"

---

[1]From Walter Lippmann: *Public Opinion*, pp. 99–100. 1922. By permission of The Macmillan Company, publishers.
See also L. W. Doob: *Propaganda; Its Psychology and Technique*, p. 35 ff. 1935.

"The movies was good down to Newport News—
  None better," the sailor said.

"But, sailor," I cried, "you have seen whole fleets
  Of the Portuguese men-o'-war,
You have heard the whine of the brine-wet sheets
  As you beat off a leeward shore;
You have cleft a track through the green sea moss
  While it clung to your rusty prow;
You have glimpsed the gleam of the Southern Cross
  As it rose on the starboard bow.
From Pe Chi Li to Matanzas Bay
  You have breasted the rolling tide—"
"There's plenty o' hooch down Havana way—
  Swell licker," the tar replied.

"But what of the equatorial sun
  To the sou'-sou'-west of Spain,
And the desperate time when the spindrift spun
  In the terrible hurricane?
What of the calms, when you tossed for days,
  With never a breath of breeze,
And nothing at all to attract the gaze
  But a desert of empty seas?
You have dropped your anchor in bights and sounds
  From Brest to Van Dieman's Land—"
"I seen Babe Ruth at the Polo Grounds,"
  Said the sailor; "the blighter fanned."[1]

3. Memory. The importance of intention or set for learning has been widely recognized. A person has a poor memory, often, because he does not desire to remember what he is assimilating. A student, in preparing for an examination, is often annoyed by the irksomeness of his task to such a degree that there is generated, if it is not already present, an aversion for the subject, which renders facile recall unlikely. The student hopes to forget it all as soon as the test is over, but alas, too frequently he does not time his forgetting accurately

[1] James J. Montague, in the Boston *Globe*, June 28, 1921.

and his memory fades too soon.   What he needs is an interest
which will give him an incentive.

If the student of psychology could appreciate the value of
the subject to the degree depicted in the following cartoon,
his learning would be considerably facilitated.

First Hobo: Remember your selling argument when you
tackle that prospect up there, Bill.   It's psychology that
counts.
Second Hobo: Check![1]

For the best results observation must be carried on with the
deliberate intention of grasping the impressions not merely
for the moment, but of retaining them permanently.   If we
make a special effort to imprint the observations upon memory
in order to reproduce them subsequently, we actually retain
them more readily.   When we want to remember, we assume
a certain attitude toward the observation.   In the first place,

---

[1]Drawn by G. B. Inwood.

we dwell upon the impressions longer than is necessary for mere apprehension; we notice the impressions exactly. Secondly, we make a stronger effort to bring them into relation with one another. The will to remember what is observed involves a characteristic attitude especially favorable to the formation of associations among the various aspects of experience, and these connections facilitate remembering.

Interest is an important factor in memory, as Bartlett discovered in his study of the Swazi natives of Africa. He found that the Swazis displayed remarkable powers of remembering only when the experimental tests concerned cattle, for their whole life centers in the possession and care of cattle. One herdsman gave him a minute description of all the cattle purchased by his owner a year previous, with an accurate account of all the prices involved in the transaction. The herdsman was present when the cattle were bought, he drove them to the farm, and he had seen no more of them. There were only two trivial errors in his entire description. Herds and all dealings concerning them are of tremendous social importance among the Swazis.[1]

It should be noted, in connection with memory, that prior experience is very important in determining how and what we perceive now. Examples of this significant relationship have already been offered.

4. Judgment. In looking for a psychological process which would characterize judgment as such, Watt discovered that the *Aufgabe* is all-important. A person judges when he is set to pass judgment. Furthermore, the nature of the judgment will be dependent upon the determining tendencies involved in the particular context of the situation. When a man whose wife was a shrew, was haled into court on a charge of desertion, he pleaded that he was not a deserter, that he was a refugee.

---

[1]See F. C. Bartlett: *Remembering. A Study in Experimental and Social Psychology*, pp. 248–251. 1932.

Considering the nature of his experiential predisposition, his judgment of the rôle he was playing is perfectly comprehensible. Ella Wheeler Wilcox, in discussing the relations between the sexes, describes the reactions provoked by a young man making amorous advances to an alluring maiden: "If the man be not especially pleasing to her she at least suspects that he is attempting liberties, and repels them. If he is attractive to her she calls them gallantries, usually, and forgives them."[1]

5. Choice. Ach worked on the problem of choice by experimenting with the influence of set upon reaction time. He asked his subjects to move the right finger when the letter E was shown and the left when the letter O was exposed. The times required for each movement were measured. Then he instructed the subject to move either finger to either stimulus. The reaction times were longer since, under the conditions, choice was involved. Under the first instruction the experimenter prescribed the reaction and thereby determined a definite set; under the second instruction the subject was left free to react in accordance with his own choice in the matter. Ach's experiments show how important are the instructions of the experimenter in determining the attitudes and associations of the subject.

Geissler demonstrated that under certain conditions, positive instructions make for unity and clearness, while negative instructions tend to produce interference of associations. "A simple positive instruction sets up only one determining tendency . . . ; while a negative instruction sets up at least two determining tendencies"[2]—do and don't, we might say. Only in the latter instance, of course, where more than one determining tendency is evoked, would choice be involved. And the choice itself, in that case, would be dictated by a bias.

---

[1]Ella Wheeler Wilcox: *Men, Women, and Emotions,* pp. 108–109. 1893.

[2]L. R. Geissler: "Analysis of Consciousness Under Negative Instruction," *American Journal of Psychology,* 1912, 23, 183–213.

6. Belief. It is often asserted that people believe only what they want to believe—which is only another way of saying that our beliefs are determined by our underlying inclinations. The nature of the process through which belief is generated may best be illustrated by reference to delusions which are false beliefs. A person who entertains delusions appears rational enough when the grounds for his strange fancies are discovered. If his premise is accepted, that is, if his attitude is understood, then his ideas become readily comprehensible. The paranoiac believes strangely because his complexes are strange. We shall not pause to analyze here "how he gets that way" but shall simply note how the nature of the bias determines the character of the belief.

Clifford Beers, who has told the story of his madness in *A Mind That Found Itself*, describes his fears, upon being incarcerated in an asylum, lest he be brought to trial for certain imaginary misdemeanors which he considered serious enough to condemn him to death, if his case ever came before a tribunal. He lived in constant dread of the talons of the law. When we appreciate this background, we can realize how an innocent remark of his brother's precipitated a state of genuine alarm. "You are looking better," his brother told him, "and getting stronger. We shall straighten you out yet." Straighten him out—ah, that meant he was soon to be hanged or electrocuted for his crime—thus to be straightened out, in the horizontal posture, to eternity. No wonder he became excited.[1]

Delusions of jealousy are very common. Here is a typical case:

A man suspected his wife of infidelity because, when he rushed into the house unexpectedly one day, she looked surprised and startled; when he called her on the phone, the line was busy; when he announced he was going away on a trip, she seemed delighted at the prospect.

[1]Clifford Beers: *A Mind That Found Itself*, p. 72. 1923.

False beliefs, of course, are not limited to the inmates of lunatic asylums. There are persons at large who entertain delusions on a grand scale. Commander William A. Allen occupied the pulpit of a Los Angeles church where he instilled terror into the hearts of the congregation by describing what Einstein's visit to California really meant. His speech is described by one of the audience in these words:

> The things he told were enough to . . . prove, among other things, that Einstein is here in the interest of communism, and that he has facts to prove that within the past few weeks he said exactly what he was told to say about pacifism by Joe Stalin and his bunch. He told things like this—that a large ranch was being gotten in shape in Riverside County as one of the communist centers for arms and ammunition, and that special basements are being constructed so thick and strong that they can only be gotten into by dynamiting, and a lot of it at that. Also, that a lot of canned goods, labeled as being made in Argentine, is coming from Russia; that two societies, the Women's International League for Peace and the American Association for Outlawing War, are the direct tools of the Russian communists. He claims they are thoroughly organized all over the world and preparing for "Der Tag"—which will be a terrible revolution, and that American business men are so blinded by their pursuit of the dollar, that they are blind to the menace. Well, the Lord help us if it's true.[1]

A suspicious attitude predisposes an individual to misunderstand his fellows, through inclining him toward the misinterpretation of their behavior. It is true indeed that sometimes there are adequate grounds for suspicion but in many instances slight evidence is accepted as damning proof. Innocent remarks may be converted into malicious insults. I recall a situation where a young man was the first to arrive at a party given in a neighbor's home. The charming hostess ushered him into the living room where they engaged in conversation. The next guest to appear was an attractive young lady. The

---

[1] A letter quoted to the editor, in the *Christian Century*, February 18, 1931.

hostess, anxious for a chance to supervise the servants in their final touches on the refreshments for the evening, asked the young man if he would be willing to entertain the charming lady for a while. He replied, "I shall be delighted." The hostess took the conventional remark to mean that he was glad to get rid of her for somebody with more appeal, and, consequently, she brooded over her injured feelings. Thus suspicion manufactures its own provocation and reinforces itself through its own beguiling distortions.

II. SOME DETERMINING TENDENCIES

A. Mood and Temperament. Temperament has been defined as the predisposition to pleasant or unpleasant emotions. We speak of a sanguine temperament or a melancholy temperament. The optimist is set to see the silver lining in the cloud while the pessimist can see only the cloud; the optimist is inclined to see the doughnut, the pessimist, the hole. Suppose it was sunny one day and rainy the next for a number of weeks. The sanguine individual would say the sun shone every other day, while the melancholy person would say it rained every other day. Temperament is an enduring bias.

Moods, on the other hand, are more passing. A mood is an emotional hang-over. Repressed or thwarted anger leaves a dynamic set for rage which may be touched off on the slightest provocation. A person who only awaits the opportunity to explode is in an ugly mood—ready to take out his feelings on the first victim who turns up. When a person is suffering from the blues, every stimulus becomes the occasion for further gloom. Everything seems to go wrong. Similarly, an individual in a suspicious mood finds adequate grounds in the most innocent remarks to confirm his feelings of distrust.

Bias, as we have just noted, is a readiness to feel or behave in a certain manner with reference to approaching situations.

Further light will be thrown upon the subtle influence of bias by considering the meaning of the term, complex, which has found a wide use in late years.

B. Complex. A complex is a system of emotionally toned ideas which functions as a tendency to produce actions of a certain definite character. When a person with a party bias on political matters considers a proposed measure, the attitude he adopts is apt to be independent of the merits of the issue. He naïvely imagines that his opinion is derived from a cool weighing of the pros and cons of the situation, for it pleases him to believe that he is rational in his thought and conduct. In reality, his party complex predisposes him to accept the arguments advanced by his colleagues, and to discredit the arguments offered by his opponents. The complex operates the more effectively because the individual is unconscious of its important rôle in his actions. A person in such a situation invents reasons to account for his convictions, reasons which are insufficient and illusory. This process of self-deception, through which the individual conceals the real grounds of his decisions by a system of adventitious props, is termed "rationalization."[1]

What is now technically known as a complex used to be called a "bug." The vegetarian bug has become the anti-meat-eating complex. Each of us is a "nut" about some special interest or hobby.

Every "red-blooded" person can be set in a furor of excitement over some issue which strikes "close home to him." We all have our favorite loves and pet aversions which determine our thinking and our behavior. Our complexes become the very core of our being, calling insistently for promotion and defence.

Partisan leanings are well exposed in the impressions of Gene Tunney and Jack Dempsey which follow.

[1]Bernard Hart: *The Psychology of Insanity*, Chapter V, "Complexes." 1929.

Gentleman Gene—For he is a gentleman, courteous, considerate, with irreproachable manners and with no affectations. I have played golf with Gene Tunney. I have been out on the sea with him. I have lunched with him. I have had long and intimate talks. He is a reader of good books, and has taste and intelligence. . . . Good reading and good music have been an immense resource to him all his life. . . . His knowledge of modern poetry and modern fiction is good; he makes no pretenses, never tries to show off, but talks about literature in a natural, unaffected and interesting manner. . . . A newspaper reporter called me up by telephone to ask if Tunney really did know something about literature, or whether that was just press-agent stuff. I assured him that Gene Tunney's culture is genuine, that he loves books for their own sake. . . . If he and I should exchange our professional jobs, he would be more effective at lecturing on literature than I should be in the ring. (Professor Phelps.)

In the first place, it is not Mr. Tunney's intellectual attainments one objects to, but his intellectual pretensions. No wonder men like Heywood Broun, Louis Bromfield, Sinclair Lewis, and H. L. Mencken have expressed a preference for Dempsey. One has only to contrast the interviews given by these two men, Dempsey and Tunney; one simple and profound, the other "a mixture of bombast and cant." Tunney should be forced to fight, but should be forbidden to talk. Both his Chicago and New York orations fell flat. (A Dempsey admirer, probably.)

The only way, of course, to settle an issue of this nature is to get at the facts. But how are the facts to be ascertained when complexes are coloring, in a subtle manner, every observation? The rôle of bias may be compared to that of the newspaper in reporting events—both distort the view through the interposition of a viewpoint. It is pathetic the way the average person naïvely accepts the word of an expert or an authority for fact. Experts, too, have their prejudices. Representative Dempsey of New York, returning from Europe, announced that there was no feeling there against the United States because of the new (higher) tariff, and that, as a matter of fact,

Americans were more popular there than ever. Representative LaGuardia of New York, returning from Europe, reported that all the nations there were angry over the tariff and were preparing to pass retaliatory measures. One of the Congressmen, of course, favors a high tariff and the other does not. Each found exactly what he wanted to find. What is the perplexed bystander to believe? Probably, what suits him.

The denouncer, wherever he storms, betrays a strong affective attitude toward the ideas in question. "His vitriolic language serves to illumine, not the issues under discussion, but the character of his mental reaction to the opposition."[1] Wherever discussion of a topic degenerates into a denunciation of personalities, wherever feelings are expressed which are all out of proportion to the apparent triviality of the occasion, whenever a sense of humor seems totally absent, you may be sure that a complex is operating. Thomas Paine, author of *The Age of Reason*, used to be called a "filthy little atheist," an injustice undoubtedly provoked by a deep-seated bigotry in some believer who was only too willing to convert his difference in dogmatism into an attack upon the infidel's character.

Partisanship often seeks religious sanctions. God has been identified, at one time or another, with slavery, war, and the Republican party. One lady wrote to the Boston *Herald Traveler* just before the presidential election of 1928 that she was voting for Hoover because, as she stated, "God is with Hoover."[2] The Lord even has a hand in the weather, though New Englanders might hesitate to believe it. Dr. Gray, President of the Moody Bible Institute, is convinced that the Deity, realizing the shortcomings of the Republican administration in handling the farmers' plight of 1930, solved the agricultural question over night by means of the drought,

[1] A. H. Kamiat: "The Subjectivity of the Believer," *Social Science*, 1929, 4, 217–221.

[2] See W. F. Vaughan: "An Experimental Study of Political Prejudice." *Journal of Abnormal and Social Psychology*, 1930, 15, 268–274.

which increased the price of corn and disposed of the wheat surplus.[1]

The tendency to take sides under the prompting of complexes precipitates the mind into embracing conclusions even before the facts are ascertained. When C. E. Bechhofer Roberts's picture of Dickens in *This Side Idolatry* was published, buckets of wrath were emptied upon him by critics who were later forced to admit that they had not read his book before denouncing it. "Big Bill" Thompson, when he was Mayor of Chicago, found time to anathematize Rupert Hughes for his biography of Washington:

> "Hughes is a damned liar," declared "Big Bill." "He is a cheap skate trying to get some personal publicity. . . . He lied about Washington's personal habits. In any other country they would put him where he belongs." A reporter asked the Mayor if he had read the book. "No, I haven't," he shouted. "I wouldn't read any part of it. He's just a muckraker for profit."

It requires the long discipline of a high intelligence to preserve an open mind. Only the ignorant can be dead sure of themselves. Where adequate rational grounds are absent, the mind skids joyously to convictions that are none the less binding because they precede a search for the facts. Indeed, the search will probably never take place.

We have indicated briefly the general nature and function of the complex. It will now be of interest to look into some specific complexes which are common in our everyday life.

1. The Inferiority Complex. The inferiority complex is essentially an attitude an individual takes toward himself. It is a self-evaluation in which the person finds himself, in some respects, wanting.

The sense of inferiority may be engendered by a real defect, such as a crippled limb or weak eyes, a low intelligence, or a

---

[1] *The Literary Digest*, September 27, 1930.

weak character.[1] The feeling of inadequacy may be due to a peculiarity which lays the person open to ridicule, such as red hair, though the idiosyncrasy is not in any sense a real deficiency. The feeling of insecurity may be due primarily to the attitudes of others who instill a sense of incompleteness upon grounds of social expediency, for example, the contempt that is displayed toward the immigrant. The immigrant may come to feel he is inferior whereas, in truth, he may actually be a superior personality. Inferiority and superiority are relative terms, dependent in the large upon social relationships. A deep sense of sinfulness may be felt by a person who has made an inventory of his moral life only to discover the balance on the debit side, or by an individual who catches the conviction of sin by contagious exposure.

There are many situations in college life which breed a sense of inferiority, such as academic shortcomings, defeat in class elections, exclusion from fraternities, or failure to make an athletic team. A big man from the small high school who finds himself lost in the stiffer competition of the collegiate race is likely to come to the realization that he had been just "a big frog in a small pond" before. Lower-classmen are duly impressed by upper-classmen whose superiority is made manifest by means of ceremonies of chastisement and traditions of privilege, in which the lower-classmen are discouraged from assuming any sense of importance in the distinction of becoming "college men."[2]

The inferiority complex often undermines poise and self-confidence. It may encourage self-pity and self-depreciation, both of which are detrimental to mental health. It may lead to excessive daydreaming where imaginary attainments reap praise and glory. But sometimes the inferiority complex in-

---

[1]See W. F. Vaughan: *The Lure of Superiority*, Chapter III, "The Genesis of Inferiority." 1928.

[2]See G. E. Gardner and Helen D. Pierce: "The Inferiority Feelings of College Students," *Journal of Abnormal and Social Psychology*, 1929, 24, 8–13.

spires a person to real achievements through which he may gain distinction and enhance his self-esteem. Such a compensatory reaction may not only have social value, but it may also serve to diminish the sense of inferiority in the individual.

2. The Nicotine Complex. Some people are fanatically opposed to the use of tobacco in any form by anybody. Smoking is made a moral issue. People who are anti-this are often anti-that, too. At one of the meetings of a church assembly, the group first assailed the "wet press" and then went on record as "showing its strong disapproval of the boldness of the tobacco interests in advertising their wares over the radio, in newspapers, magazines, and on billboards." It was voted to protest to the radio companies. Regardless of the "cause," most people do not become emotionally excited over tobacco. Alarm, exaggerated statements, vehement opposition indicate the presence of a complex. One medium for giving expression to anti-nicotine sentiments is to write an editor. Here is a sample:

To the Editor:

Whereas: There has been an increase in the use of cigarettes amongst the youth and the ladies of our communities, and

Whereas: This increase has been due to the advertising in our magazines and on our billboards and other pernicious publicity to a large extent, and

Whereas: We believe this to be contrary to the best moral and Christian principles of our age, therefore

Be it resolved: That We, the Ladies' Class of the Perkins Grove Church, LaMoille, Illinois, go on record as being opposed to your methods of allowing such advertising to appear in your magazine, and

Be it further resolved: That unless this ceases immediately, we as a congregation shall cease to support your publication by refraining from subscribing to it and also discourage its circulation amongst our friends and acquaintances, and

Be it further resolved: That a copy of the above resolution be sent to all magazines of your standing which permit such advertising. LaMoille, Ill.[1]   —Secretary   —President

---

[1]*The Forum,* February, 1930.

3. The Barleycorn Complex. Should the consumption of liquor be prohibited? Any open-minded person, if there is any, would like to be in possession of facts upon the basis of which he could reach a sane judgment of the issue. When a "wet" conducts an experiment, he discovers one set of "facts"; when a "dry" goes in for research, he finds another set of "facts." Raymond Pearl in his laboratory notes the beneficent effects of alcohol under certain conditions.[1] Leonardo Bianchi of the University of Naples seems to differ:

The demonstration of the poisonous effect of alcohol on the nervous system is no longer disputable. The proof is direct and immediate. . . . Idiocy, imbecility, criminality and hysteria major are followed in a descending order by lack of spirit, indifference, idleness, vagabondage, tendency to gamble, malice, coldness for every noble enthusiasm, irascibility.[2]

Even when the same facts are ascertained, different conclusions are drawn from the evidence, depending upon the nature of the complex. If alcohol is physically harmful, some "wets" ingeniously argue, it will weed out the weak and unstable and thus improve the racial stock. It might be well to pause, at times, and examine the nature of our reasoning as it determines our conclusions. We shall do this very thing at more length when we analyze the thinking process. But let me here just raise these questions: Is the consumption of alcohol a cause or an effect, or both? Do the unstable take a drink or does drinking produce instability? Is alcoholism merely a symptom of psychopathological tendencies?

Certainly there are few people who can keep a clear head in considering the demon rum. We are intolerant—we go to extremes—we let the complex run us. A newspaper editor remarks: "We have always admired a man who could quit

----

[1] R. Pearl: *Alcohol and Longevity.* 1926.
[2] Leonardo Bianchi: *Foundations of Mental Health.* 1930. By permission of D. Appleton-Century Company, Inc.

drinking without becoming an evangelist." And he might have added his tribute to the man who can like his liquor without becoming an evangelist. The alcoholic complex, either way you look at it, raises havoc with reason.

4. The Monkey Complex. "Monkey men," declares Dr. Straton, "make monkey morals."[1] In opening his *drive* on evolution, the eminent divine pointed out that the educational authorities in America by teaching the "Godless and materialistic" Darwinian doctrine were responsible for the waywardness of our young people as expressed in "commercialized amusements, sensuous dances, best sellers, and the ever-present downward drag on stage and screen, which are enough to debauch any generation." It is no wonder, then, in view of all these calamities which have followed the teaching of evolution, that a Tennessee legislature passed a law in 1925:

Be it enacted—that it shall be unlawful for any teacher in any of the universities, normals, and all other public schools of the State which are supported in whole or in part by the public school funds of the State, to teach any theory that denies the story of the Divine Creation of man as taught in the Bible, and to teach instead that man has descended from a lower order of animals.

5. The Aphrodite Complex.[2] Sexual hunger has caused men and women any amount of trouble and worry ever since Adam and Eve first bit into the forbidden fruit. Love is dangerous because it is so desirable. Tending to extremes, the libertine gives free rein to his lust while he ignores the perils of his course; while, on the other side, the ascetic is so scared of his own longings that he dares not seek satisfaction even in lawful ways. The number of conventions evolved by society to restrict the satisfactions of the sexual urge is evidence that the power of the love motive has long been recognized, with its attendant threats to the security of the social order.

[1] The Boston *Herald*, April 16, 1928.
[2] Aphrodite was the goddess of love and beauty.

Any attempt to improve upon the solution of the sexual problem is mistaken as a plea for free love by the conservative element in society, which element seems, in spite of the maladjustments evidenced in neuroses, divorces, and sash-weight murders, to be convinced that the *status quo* is the ideal.

Consider, for a moment, the question of birth control. To Margaret Sanger the modern practice of birth control is a blessing which should be legalized and disseminated; to the Pope contraception is a violation of the divine will. One side sees the issue in terms of human suffering—homes where unwanted children overtax the mother's strength and the family budget—traceable to the ignorance of birth control among the poorer uneducated classes; the other side likewise sees the misfortune, not, however, as the consequence of ignorance, but as the punishment for lack of self-control. To the one contraception is the solution; to the other, continence. The difference lies in the premise—to the former, sexual experience, within the marriage bond, is a delight which should be wisely cultivated since it contributes to the beauty of life; to the latter, connubial relations savor of carnal lust and, therefore, should be resisted as evil, except, of course, on occasions when the desire for propagation offers an adequate justification.

No attempt has been made to evaluate the issues involved in the controversies mentioned, since our interest is solely to see how complexes lead to extreme arguments to support extreme positions, in either direction.

C. Two Important Attitudes. *1. The Scientific Attitude.* As scientists who are interested in psychology, it is important that we take, as far as is possible, the objective attitude which characterizes psychology as a science. Personal bias is out of place in science. An open-minded attitude is the only adequate preparation for the achievement of sound knowledge.

2. The Æsthetic Attitude. An experience is æsthetic when the individual assumes the æsthetic attitude, that is, when he is set to perceive beauty in the environment. One may contemplate the stars in the heavens with the purely scientific interest of an astronomer, or with the reverent gaze of admiration for the beauty of the vast patterns of light.[1]

A censor sometimes cannot appreciate the loveliness of a work of art because he is taking the ethical attitude rather than the æsthetic attitude. Both values cannot dominate the mental outlook simultaneously.

The genesis of the æsthetic attitude serves to demonstrate the fact that our biases or determining tendencies are to be traced to the fundamental urges of human nature, and the habitual complexes into which they are built by the experiences of life. A charming woman is generally regarded as exquisitely beautiful because the sexual urge predisposes us to such an appraisal; the particular type of feminine beauty which a given individual will prize most highly will depend upon his training.

The next two chapters will be devoted to a description of the urges in human nature and their incorporation into habits. Thus we shall discover how the distinctive character of the individual human being is evolved.

---

[1]See H. S. Langfeld: *The Æsthetic Attitude*, pp. 39–40. 1920.

CHAPTER VIII

THE FUNDAMENTAL URGES

For a long time man tried to convince himself that his behavior was dictated by reason, but the obvious follies of his everyday conduct compelled him to give due heed to the impulsive side of his nature.

I. GENERAL ASPECTS OF THE EMOTIONS

A. Prime Movers. The true story of our motivation is to be found in the emotions, for the emotions are the prime movers, determining our wants and impelling us to seek satisfaction. Reason usually functions in the service of desire by selecting the most effective means for gaining the ends set by affective nature. Man is fundamentally a creature with urgent needs, the satisfaction of which brings a momentary cessation of desire. There is a will to live that keeps us going in search of the means of appeasing our hungers, thus making both for self-preservation and the preservation of the race.

What do human beings want? What do they desire? What do they crave? What do they need? An understanding of motivation is necessary for making a successful appeal to others, whether it be the minister endeavoring to arouse in his parishioners an enthusiasm for a better life, or the advertiser seeking to inculcate in the buying public a longing for a particular brand of soap.

B. Feeling. The main business of living is to adjust ourselves to our physical and social environment. In making our adjustments we behave in typical ways. These modes of be-

238

havior are in part instinctive (unlearned) and in part acquired through experience (learned). What are the urges that drive us to seek satisfaction in characteristic activities and what is their nature? The answer lies in a study of the affective aspects of the mind—in the feelings and emotions which stir (*e-moveo*) us to action.

1. Pleasantness and Unpleasantness. The primitive aspect of our affective life lies in the experiences of pleasantness and unpleasantness. In terms of behavior, pleasantness means attraction and approach (positive behavior), while unpleasantness means aversion and withdrawal (negative behavior). It may clarify our thesis if we refer briefly to tropisms.

2. Tropisms as Prototypes of Human Behavior. A tropism is an innate tendency of an organism (usually referring to plants and lower animals) to respond in a definite manner to external stimuli. A positive tropism is the tendency to approach a stimulus, and a negative tropism is the tendency to withdraw from a stimulus—the first being analogous to the pleasantness, the second to the unpleasantness of human experience. In other words, we have a tendency to approach stimuli that are pleasant to us, and to avert stimuli that are unpleasant.

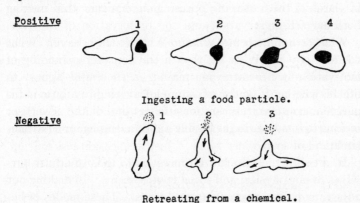

Ingesting a food particle.

Retreating from a chemical.

A tropism is a response to stimulation involving a change in orientation of the body in reference to a stimulus. As lowly an animal as the amoeba (one cell), a shapeless bit of jelly-like protoplasm, exhibits positive reactions toward solid bodies, particularly in the process of obtaining food, and displays negative reactions toward certain chemicals, heat, and strong light, in the presence of which it retreats as rapidly as its limited locomotive capacities permit.[1] The mental life of an amoeba is obviously a most simple one, yet in its behavior it exhibits the prototypes for the pleasant and unpleasant experiences of the human animal.

3. Attraction and Aversion. The same sort of behavior is exhibited in the classic example of the child and the flame. The child is attracted to the flame (analogous to positive tropism), and extends his hand to touch it. The fingers are burned and automatically, by a reflex, the hand is withdrawn (analogous to negative tropism). Since the painful burn is unpleasant, the natural reaction is withdrawal. The child does not have to learn that the pain is unpleasant—the connection is a part of his native equipment. After a number of such experiences, he will in the future avoid what was unpleasant in the past (retro-hedonism).[2] A person who brushes his teeth in the dark with shaving cream manifests the same sort of avoidance reaction.

4. Differentiation into Emotions. Human behavior can be treated very neatly in terms of attraction and aversion, but the whole story is not exhausted on such a simple basis. As life became more and more complex through evolution, the affective consciousness became differentiated into a variety of emotions which make possible a nicer adjustment to specific situations over a wider range. Just as pleasantness and unpleasantness guide the lower organisms in their efforts to pre-

---

[1]See H. S. Jennings: *Behavior of the Lower Organisms.* 1915.
[2]See L. T. Troland: *Fundamentals of Human Motivation.* 1928.

serve themselves, so the emotions have a survival value for the higher animals, as we noted in Chapter VI. Activities which promote biological ends are on the whole pleasant. Those individuals who find pleasantness in harmful ways are eliminated in the struggle for existence, so that by a process of selection, feelings become a proximate guide to sound biological behavior. Emotional experiences, on a higher level, render possible even finer discriminations in adjustment.

Emotion only became possible through an increasing complexity of the mental life. Cognition on a complex level discharges an important function in the arousal of emotion, and complicated effector mechanisms are necessary to an adequate expression of the emotive experience. The bodily commotions involved in the emotional life are complex, on a much more advanced level than that of the elementary feelings.

C. Theories of Motivation. The mere indices of pleasantness and unpleasantness are an uncertain guide for conduct. Regarding motivation superficially, it often seems that man is activated in his behavior by a desire for the pleasant and an aversion for the unpleasant. The problem, however, deserves more profound analysis. We shall turn to a consideration of the Hedonistic and Hormic theories of motivation for our answer.

1. Hedonism. Hedonism is the theory that human conduct is motivated by the desire for pleasure—or to state it more accurately, the desire for pleasantness and the aversion for unpleasantness. In a given situation a person will do the pleasant thing. If he aids a friend in need, it is because the spirit of helpfulness affords him pleasure. It would make him unhappy to ignore his friend's plight or to refuse his request for succor. Many people object to the Hedonistic theory, because it interprets altruistic behavior in terms of selfish ends. The martyr gives his life for a principle because that is the thing he *wants* to do—it is his way of realizing the utmost pleasure. It seems cynical to think of the kindly deed as a selfish act done for the satisfaction the doer derives from his benefaction. Yet we may be misled by a misunderstanding of the word "selfish" which has such emotional connotations as to obfuscate the situation.

I may do you a favor because I like you, because I feel it is my duty, or because I expect to get something out of you in return. In the first case, my motive would be admirable; in the second and third cases, my motive would be open to censure. Yet in all three cases, I do what makes me feel good. It is obvious that the doer himself reacts to his own behavior—and in that sense all behavior is "selfish." As far as others may judge, my conduct as a thoroughgoing Hedonist may be beyond reproach, though I do good only because it brings a glow of satisfaction.

Hedonism is sometimes rejected because the word "pleasure" is taken to mean carnal indulgence. "Eat, drink, and be merry, for tomorrow we die," is supposed to represent the Hedonistic program of the Epicureans. Because pleasure often has this connotation, I prefer the terms "pleasant" and "unpleasant" for describing behavior. Epicurus, himself, realized that intelligence must be used in the selection of pleasures if life is going to yield the utmost happiness. Momentary pleasures must be subordinated to the pleasures of the long run. The weakness of Hedonism is revealed, it seems to me, in that it does not provide the principles upon which we are to select our pleasures wisely. Those principles are only to be ascertained by studying the needs of human nature. The satisfaction of these wants brings pleasure—as we shall see in the Hormic theory.

One more comment on the Hedonistic theory is necessary before we pass on. The crux of the Hedonistic doctrine lies in the answer to this question: is the individual thinking of the pleasant results of his action when he plans his behavior?

That question can only be solved by a resort to introspection. Analyze your own behavior; see what you find.

There seems to be something about Hedonism that savors of the professional. The amateur spirit, in contrast, means engaging in an activity without giving a thought to the rewards, either financial or psychological.[1] When an athlete gives his last ounce of strength for Alma Mater, is he thinking of the pleasure of the glory that is going to be his in victory, or is he impelled unconsciously by a will to win that spurs him on no matter what the cost? When an inventor works day and night to realize an idea, denying himself the ordinary recreations of life and impairing his health, is his mind occupied with dreams of the pleasure that success is going to bring or is his mind kindled with a consuming desire to solve the problem confronting him? To put the question succinctly, is man's interest in a pursuit extrinsic or intrinsic? Of course, there are differences between individuals and between situations, and perhaps, therefore, a theory of motivation is misleading that seeks to pronounce judgment in a generalizing fashion on human conduct. There may be some value, nevertheless, in seeking to reduce behavior to its common denominator in terms of fundamental motivation. Further light may be shed on this issue of the intrinsic or extrinsic nature of interests by a consideration of the Hormic theory.

2. Hormism. According to the Hormic[2] theory there are certain fundamental urges inherent in human nature which function, under proper stimulus conditions, as wants impelling us to certain activities for their satisfaction. When these basic needs are gratified, a feeling of pleasantness follows as a by-product. Pleasure and unpleasure, as one writer states it, depend on the successful functioning of the instincts.[3] If we

---

[1]See John R. Tunis: "Are You an Amateur?" *Harper's Magazine*, April, 1931.

[2]Refer back to Chapter III, to the exposition of Hormism.

[3]A. H. Burlton Allen: *Pleasure and Instinct: A Study in the Psychology of Human Action.* 1930.

feel hungry and eat enough of the kinds of food that satisfy our hunger, we experience pleasure. We do not eat because we wish to secure pleasantness, but because we are hungry. Pleasantness and unpleasantness are psychic indicators which assure us when we are headed in the right direction, and which warn us when we are headed in the wrong direction for the satisfaction of our dominant urges. Whether a given experience will be pleasant or unpleasant, depends on the urge. Music may be pleasant when we are resting and unpleasant when we are trying to study.

There are certain basic needs in human nature, hereditary in their origin and developed through experience, which supply the interests of life. To follow these interests in an integrated way is to find happiness. Sometimes our interests work at cross-purposes so that the satisfaction of one want may defeat another. Coveting another man's property, for example, may involve the loss of social approval. Native urges must thus be organized to accord with social experience. To win happiness you must satisfy your urges, and, further, you must learn to satisfy them in ways which are socially approved. All of our interests must be considered in a given situation. No single craving constitutes the one end in life.

The Hormic theory assumes there are certain urges which motivate our behavior. We shall describe these urges as emotions. Emotions are the sorts of experience which we know as fear, anger, hunger, love, vanity, avarice, hatred, embarrassment, and awe. The only sensible way to define emotion is in terms of experience. We all know how it feels to be aroused, to be stirred up, to be eager to do something about it. Different situations evoke different emotional responses. We find a uniformity in emotional behavior which makes it possible to describe affective life in a classificatory way, giving a name to a particular mode of response. I know how it feels to be angry, and I can guess with some assurance that your anger is an experience very similar to my own—you feel hot under the collar, your heart thumps, you breathe in snorts, you clench your fists, you tighten your jaws, you gnash your teeth, and you have an impulse to hit, scratch, or take it out in some other way on your victim according to your own favorite manner.

Emotion, we may say, is the experience of being aroused in such way as to feel the urge to do something. Widespread and profound organic changes (implicit behavior) and expressive movements (explicit behavior) are involved in emotion—but they are not the emotion. The consciousness of these physical processes constitutes the emotion. It is true that you can read my emotions only through my behavior. My emotion means behavior to you but to me it means something more than that—I feel as I behave.

D. The James-Lange Theory. James and Lange called attention to the importance of organic changes in the emotional experience. James' exposition is well known:

Our natural way of thinking about the . . . emotions is that the mental perception of some fact excites the mental affection called the emotion, and . . . this latter state of mind gives rise to the bodily expression. My theory, on the contrary, is that the bodily changes follow directly the perception of the exciting fact, and that our feeling of the same changes as they occur *is* the emotion. Common sense says, we lose our fortune, are sorry and weep; we meet a bear, are frightened and run; we are insulted by a rival, are angry and strike. The hypothesis here to be defended says that this order of sequence is incorrect, that the one mental state is not immediately induced by the other, that the bodily manifestations must first be interposed between, and that the more rational statement is that we feel sorry because we cry, angry because we strike, afraid because we tremble and not that we cry, strike, or tremble, because we are sorry, angry, fearful, as the case may be. Without the bodily states following on the perception, the latter would be purely cognitive in form, pale, colorless, destitute of emotional warmth. We might then see the bear, and judge it best to run, receive the insult and deem it right to strike, but we should not actually *feel* afraid or angry.

Objects do excite bodily changes by a preorganized mechanism . . . the changes are so definitely numerous and subtle that the entire organism may be called a sounding-board, which every change of consciousness, however slight, may make reverberate. The various permutations and combinations of which these organic activities are susceptible make it abstractly possible that no shade of emotion, however slight, should be without a bodily reverberation as unique, when taken in its totality, as is the mental mood itself . . . Every one of the bodily changes, whatsoever it be, is felt, acutely or obscurely, the moment it occurs . . .[1]

The James-Lange theory excited a great deal of controversy, prompting Cannon, Sherrington, Head, Bard, and others to investigate the rôle of organic sensations in emotions. Nervous connections, for example, were severed in an animal so that the visceral reactions would not reach the brain and yet the animal seemed to express in his behavior what were apparently emotional responses. Evidence from experiments by extirpation, from the effects of anæsthetics, and from pathological cases indicates that emotive responses are dependent upon a subcortical center, probably the thalamus. Thalamic centers are ready for instant and vigorous discharge when they are released from cortical restraint, and are properly stimulated. The quality of the emotion is added to simple sensation when the thalamic processes are roused, as the latter not only innervate muscles and viscera, but also excite afferent paths to the cortex.[2] This theory fits all the facts: the presence of bodily changes in emotion; the short latent period; the emotional effects of assumed postures; the impulsive character of emotion; the conditioning of emotional responses through intimate connections between the thalamus and the association

---

[1]William James: *Principles of Psychology*, II, p. 449ff. By permission of Henry Holt and Company.

[2]W. B. Cannon: "The James-Lange Theory," *American Journal of Psychology*, 1927 39, 106–124. Refer back to Chapter VI.

areas of the cortex. Thus the James-Lange theory has been considerably modified. The important point for our discussion is that bodily changes constitute the physical basis for the conscious state we call emotion.

E. Power. Physiologically, emotion means energy for physical exertion, as we noted in the description of the work

TO THE STORE

TO FIRST BASE

(Reproduced by courtesy of the George Matthew Adams Service.)

done by the glands. Psychologically, if we assume the Hormic position, emotion means force, power, energy. The Vitalist postulates a life force—to him life is energy. For our purpose, let us assume that this life force expresses itself through the channels of the various emotions, inciting us to actions conducive to survival. Emotion, in its derivation, means *to move.* Emotions move us to behavior. They are *motives,* impelling us to activity. Energy comes to those who get emotionally aroused.[1] Will power is a matter of interest. Provided you are normally healthy, if you want the drive that gets things done, all you need is incentive.

F. Objections to the Term "Instinct." The term "instinct" is being avoided in this discussion of motivation because it has so many implications which only serve to obscure the understanding of behavior. Instinct involves an emphasis on genetics, a field of which we are much in ignorance. Furthermore, the word has lost its exact technical meaning at the hands of writers who abuse it. A sales manager for a life insurance company was engaged in a search for the motives that lead people to invest in insurance. One of the impelling urges, he found, as he ruminated on the subject, is the "savings instinct." The research was thus completed by the invention of a term.

Instinct is often confused with habit by popular writers. "The child," says one author, "at 7:30 instinctively goes to a certain spot, takes down a tooth brush in a certain manner. . . ."[2] Who ever heard of a tooth-brushing instinct? The author means "habitually," not "instinctively."

The fundamental objection to the use of the term "instinct" is that it is mistaken for an adequate explanation of an occurrence, thus precluding investigation.[3] Instinct-psychology explains "human nature in terms of the fact that it is human nature."[4] Why do we fight? Because of the instinct of pugnacity. A social worker stated that "children who run away without reason and adults who do the same thing, are

---

[1] See W. F. Vaughan: *The Lure of Superiority,* Chapter V, "The Sources of Power."

[2] James Langdon-Davies: "Education: Savage and Civilized," in *The New Generation,* p. 38. 1930.

[3] See "What Is Instinct?" *The Forum,* November, 1927.

[4] E. S. Robinson: *Practical Psychology,* p. 58.

sufferers from *habitual nomadism*." Since *nomadism* means running away, the startling disclosure reveals the fact that people run away because they run away. A student once explained that crullers are doughnuts which cannot resist the pretzel instinct. It sounds all right, but it has nothing to do with reality. The same criticism applies to many situations where an instinct is arbitrarily invented to account for behavior. Explanations in terms of instinct are often either fantastic or tautological. The latter case was well illustrated in the diagnosis reached by a board of psychiatrists who examined a workman in Düsseldorf, Germany, who had confessed to eleven murders. "These symptoms," decided the psychiatrists, "betray a lust to kill."[1]

The term *emotion* will be used instead of *instinct* for the above reasons, and *emotion* is to be understood merely as a descriptive term. To call behavior "angry" is not to explain it, but merely to describe it by classifying it under a characteristic category of experience.

G. Emotions and Goals. Emotions may be specified in terms of the way they feel, or in terms of the way they are expressed in behavior. In the latter sense, as I have just pointed out, there is a danger of misinterpretation unless the total situation is adequately understood.

Introspectively, each emotion is characteristically unique. The person who is experiencing the emotions is fairly clear in his own mind as to how anger, for example, feels differently from fear. Where the emotional state is complex, of course, self-observation is much more difficult. However, we can delineate the more elementary emotions with fair accuracy by a study of our own experiences.

Emotions can also be characterized by their expressions, with the reservations I have already indicated. For example, you would not mistake the following exhibition as a manifestation

---

[1] *Time*, May 4, 1931.

of deep affection on the part of the human participants:[1]

The obstacle in the way of reading the emotions of adults is the fact that we learn through experience to conceal our feel-

[1]Reprinted by permission of the Des Moines *Register and Tribune.*

ings.   It is often wise for a person to hide his anger lest he provoke the ire of a stronger antagonist. It is essential to our pride
that we disguise fear and jealousy.   Love is a game in which
much feigning precedes the ultimate surrender.   Thus we
pose and bluff—and often succeed in deceiving the observer.

The truth of the matter is, however, that adults are hopelessly inaccurate in observing the behavior of infants who have
not yet learned the wisdom of hypocrisy, as is shown in some
experiments conducted by the Shermans, in which expert observers, after witnessing the emotional behavior of an infant,
were requested to name the emotion.   The conclusion is stated
thus:

Most persons judge the emotional behavior of an individual in
terms of the stimuli which have produced the reactions.   They have
learned the names of a number of emotions, and have learned to
evaluate various emotional responses in terms of the stimulating
conditions which have aroused them.   If the situation confronting
an individual is estimated to be one which arouses an aggressive
reaction, the resulting response is named "anger," but if it is considered dangerous to his welfare, the response will be called "fear."
In this way the differentiation of emotions is based upon a knowledge of the character of the stimulating circumstances rather than
upon differences in overt behavior.[1]

Since Darwin advanced his theory of evolution, there has
been a disposition to interpret activities in the light of their
usefulness.[2]   Our emotional reactions have survival value,
preserving both the organism and the ego.   "Back of living
things there is an energic drive to accomplish certain ends,
which brings about a state of tension within the individual until
its gratification is achieved."[3]

---

[1]Mandel Sherman and Irene C. Sherman: *The Process of Human Behavior*,
Chapter V, "The Observation of the Emotions."   1929.   By permission of
W. W. Norton and Company.

[2]Charles Darwin: *The Expression of the Emotions in Man and Animals*.   1920.

[3]Karl Menninger: *The Human Mind*, p. 266.

Emotion supplies an impulse which requires for its satisfaction the doing of something by way of bringing a release of tension.   The stirred-up state of the organism must find some outlet.   Its purpose is realized when the goal of the behavior is reached.   Activity is purposeful or at least purposive—it is directed toward ends.[1]   Behavior can only be understood in terms of its goal.[2]   A man may be stingy because he is greedy, or because he is caring for an aged mother, or because he has found "the girl" and has a love nest in view.   A given act must be interpreted in reference to the purpose it serves in the individual's emotional life.[3]

An urge is to be defined not by a specific pattern of behavior, but by the nature of the goal.   The same end may be achieved by different modes of behavior, as in the case of two young men who want to be promoted: one of them gets to work on time, the other marries the boss's daughter.   On the other hand, the same pattern of behavior may be directed toward very different goals—running down the street may mean "going to a fire," "training for the marathon," or "catching a train."

II.   SOME FUNDAMENTAL URGES

For purposes of convenience, human interests may be classified.   These interests, propensities, or urges are not to be conceived as behavioral units but rather as tendencies toward seeking satisfactions for certain characteristic needs.   From the vast conglomeration of human interests we may select a few of the propensities that are commonly thought of as being fundamental to human nature, such as the following:

---

[1] "Purposeful" implies that the individual is conscious of the purpose which his behavior is realizing.

[2] Alfred Adler: *The Neurotic Constitution.*   1921.

[3] C. Macfie Campbell: "Mental Hygiene and Education," *Social Aspects of Mental Hygiene.*   1925.

Self-enhancement	Creativeness	Love
Acquisitiveness	Gregariousness	Fear
Curiosity	Hunger	Anger

This list is not intended to be exhaustive.

A. Self-Enhancement. There is no use disguising the fact that every human being wants to achieve some sort of glory to nourish his own ego. We all want to be noticed for some distinction whether it be erudition, sex appeal, or notorious crime. There is a will-to-power which keeps us everlastingly on the go in search of some unique superiority which will set us apart from the ordinary run of human beings.

Vanity, vanity, all is vanity. I do not intend to be unduly cynical when I assert that modesty is only a pose. When the famous dancer, Pavlova, was in Africa, a guide introduced her to a native chieftain as "the greatest dancer in the world." The chief stepped forward, bowed, and politely informed those present, "I beg pardon, but I am the greatest dancer in the world." The chief was amusing because he had the effrontery to voice the sort of conviction each one of us feels in regard to his own worth.

At times, of course, we feel the recurring desire "to go out in the garden and eat worms," but it is only a temporary respite from the pursuit of self-esteem. The reason we are occasionally sensible of our own unworthiness is that we are measuring ourselves against our ideal of what we think we should be. An inferiority complex is merely a symptom of the persistent struggle for superiority. We may suffer the agony of obscurity, but sooner or later we come back like the man who advertised in the column of a Boston newspaper for a large plot of ground in one of the exclusive suburban sections where he proposed to erect a home as an additional ornament to the community. "The person who is anxious for an ideal neighbor without children," said he, "will not regret making some small concession in price when every other advantage is on his side."

Envy and jealousy are prompted by the urge toward self-enhancement.[1] If we experience discomfort at the success of others, it is because we covet that glory for ourselves. We can respond to the situation by emulating their endeavors, or by minimizing their importance. The easiest way to elevate ourselves is to run down the other fellow.

People who fail to achieve glory in reality sometimes develop delusions of grandeur, mistaking themselves for kings, plutocrats, or other prominent persons.

The drive to attract the spotlight is sometimes referred to as the impulse of self-assertion. The will to dominate, to be a big frog even in only a small pond, is a constant spur to aggressive industry. To be important, to maximize the ego, and to occupy high places and associate with only the best people, are desiderata which motivate not only the social climb but self-advancement in general. The will to power prods us to win success by hard work or cunning ingenuity. "The quest of ego-adequacy is the unremitting business of our life."[2]

B. Acquisitiveness. Closely allied to the urge for self-enhancement is the acquisitive impulse, for part of the drive for accumulating worldly goods is the craving for the distinction that comes with the possession of more treasures than competitors. We not only want to keep up with the Joneses but we are eager to surpass them. The conspicuous consumption of wealth is a means of impressing upon the less fortunate the fact of superiority.[3]

Avarice and greed are expressions of the drive for acquisition. A child will appropriate any desirable objects until he is taught

---

[1]Envy and jealousy are sometimes called secondary emotions because they are aroused in the pursuit of a primary emotional satisfaction.

[2]Samuel Schmalhausen: "Family Life," in *The New Generation*, p. 284. 1930.

[3]T. B. Veblen: *The Theory of the Leisure Class.* 1915.

to respect the property of others. A small girl accompanied her father into a drug store while he purchased some medicine, and when they had made their exit to the street, he discovered a magazine under her arm. Even adults are known to collect umbrellas. It is common for a person to borrow a fountain pen and then to deposit it in his own pocket—adults, excusably enough, have learned to perform such acts unconsciously.

When the impulse to appropriate property becomes irresistible, kleptomania results. The kleptomaniac may be a shoplifter who steals articles which are of no use whatever to him and which he merely hides for safe-keeping. Sometimes a wealthy person who can afford to pay for anything he desires, prefers to acquire them by the more adventurous method of shoplifting. Such a kleptomaniac was Doris Trounson, the village belle of Southport, a British summer resort. She was arrested one June morning in 1914, much to the amazement of the townfolk, for shoplifting. Reared in luxury by an indulgent and wealthy father, pampered by an idolizing mother, twice married to men of means, the tall, lithe, hazel-eyed beauty could not resist the temptation to take goods belonging to others. In the twelve short years since the day Doris walked into a china shop in St. Anne's Square, Manchester, and surreptitiously and expertly swept three pieces of Crown Derby chinaware into her spacious muff, until she was caught redhanded rifling a safe-deposit box in St. Albans Place, London, she led an exciting life, both within and without the law. She entertained lavishly and moved in the best social circles. At no time, so far as Scotland Yard has been able to ascertain, was she forced by necessity to steal.

Another exaggeration of the acquisitive propensity is found in the business magnate who keeps on accumulating property long after he has appropriated enough to insure him of an adequate income. The investor on the stock market often fails to take a small profit because he is playing for bigger stakes. His greediness often spells disaster. When the gambling "bug" gets us, it is hard to resist. Getting something for nothing is an urgent desire in most of us.

Collecting is a phase of acquisitiveness. The desired objects may be postage stamps, bugs, or the coin of the realm. When money is acquired just for the sake of hoarding it, we have the miser, who has forgotten that money is merely a medium of exchange. Jacob Frankel, 65, for years a pitiable figure in New York's Ghetto, was buried by the Hebrew Free Burial Society. For fifteen years he lived free of rent in the tenement house of sympathetic Abraham Sirotes. Frankel died of pneumonia and malnutrition. The next day police found in his room six bank books showing savings of $28,000.[1]

Whether we collect marbles, badges, books, art treasures, or the pictures of popular athletes, actresses, opera singers, prizefighters, or race horses, it is all the expression of the same acquisitive mania.

C. Curiosity. Curiosity is the beginning of wisdom. When the child gets to the stage where he begins to ask "why," his education begins and his parents' education starts over again. What makes the kettle boil? How many legs has a grasshopper? Why does a bee sting?

There are so many wonders in the universe to stir our curiosity and to challenge our dumbfounded ignorance. Investigation of the nature of things goes back to the earliest speculations of man, and finds its highest fruits in the pure science of our day where the motive is merely the ascertainment of the truth with indifference to its utilitarian results. Applied science, too, begins with a curiosity actuated by the needs of specific problems in the work-a-day world. Invention is stimulated and research encouraged because we want to know. Philosophy grows out of an eagerness to penetrate the ultimate nature and significance of the world in which we live.

---

[1] The Boston *Herald*, March 10, 1930.

Unfortunately, in the lives of the majority, the consuming curiosity of childhood is lost in the process of growing up. Education helps, in many cases, to anæsthetize curiosity. As Bertrand Russell has pointed out, the child likes to think— the function of education is to cure him of this habit. If only the average college undergraduate could revive the spirit of inquiry which beset his childhood, he would compel a new pedagogy which not only would be more stimulating, but which also might even resuscitate his teachers.

In too many of us, curiosity has degenerated into a mere penchant for gossip. It has been degraded into a search for scandal. Prying eyes no longer peep through microscopes but through windows. Now that we are on the subject, did you hear about So-and-So? The meanest "cuss" in the world is the individual who hints that he has heard something, that he is sorry, but that for reasons he cannot reveal, he is prevented from telling.

D. Creativeness. The creative urge finds its satisfaction in workmanship which serves as an expression of individuality. The impulse may find its outlet in the construction of a piece of pottery, in the production of a drama, in the painting of a picture, or in the evolution of an idea. The desire to objectify himself through some symbol of his own creation spurs a man to externalize an inspiring idea. We are all artists at heart.

Recent education has focused its attention upon providing adequate opportunities for the encouragement of creativeness, especially in children. Manual training, drawing, painting, and æsthetic dancing develop the personalities of the individuals who express themselves through the realization of the beautiful.[1] Hinkle has found in her psychiatric practice the necessity for creative activity in the attainment of happiness, for contentment depends upon the effective exercise of the individual's capacities and the adequate employment of his

---

[1]Florence Cane: "The Creative Impulse in Children," in *The New Generation.*

unique talents. The personality is recreated through the realization of its creative potentialities.[1]

The Industrial Revolution which culminated in the mechanized industry of our own day has deprived a vast number of people of any adequate opportunity for the satisfaction of their creative urge. It was one thing to make articles with one's own hands; it is quite another to fasten nut number sixty-five on bolt number sixty-five in the assembling room of a modern factory. Being a mere cog in an overwhelming machine has cramped the creative impulse. Having lost the chance to express himself through his work, man must depend upon the wise use of his leisure time to compensate him for this deprivation. But even leisure time has become mechanized in an age when we play the piano with our feet, or press a button to release a voice announcing the benefits of some tasty food product turned out by machines. Furthermore, the sane utilization of spare moments depends upon the cultivation of our artistic interests, and in our impatience to master the mechanical routine of our bustling industries we neglect our creative nature until it is lost sight of, except for the symptoms of restlessness and ennui which rise so perniciously to haunt our waking and even our sleeping hours. We have slain ourselves with our own weapons. We are civilizing ourselves too thoroughly for our own good.

E. Gregariousness. As gregarious beings we like to be with people, particularly people with interests common to our own, since "birds of a feather flock together."

Take the case of a large number of people who have formed themselves into a league for the purpose of carrying out some practical object; if there be two rascals among them, they will recognize each other as readily as if they wore a similar badge, and will at once conspire for some misfeasance or treachery. In the same way, if you can imagine—*per impossible*—a large company of very intelli-

---

[1] B. M. Hinkle: *The Recreating of the Individual.* 1923.

gent and clever people, among whom there are only two block-
heads, these two will be sure to be drawn together by a feeling of
sympathy, and each of them will very soon rejoice at having found
at least one intelligent person in the whole company.[1]

Just to be with a kindred soul is a source of satisfaction.
Carlyle and Emerson are said to have passed an evening together in silence, smoking their pipes, and enjoying themselves
thoroughly. Fellowship and friendship answer a profound
need of human nature.

According to Trotter, man is above all things a herd animal,
as indicated by a number of characteristic traits. First, the
human being is intolerant and fearful of solitude, either physical or mental. Even Crusoe had his man Friday. In 1821
officials conducted an experiment in Auburn Prison where they
kept a number of men in solitary confinement over a period of
time. The prisoners became raving maniacs. It was as a
result of this experiment that New York State established the
Auburn system. Under this plan, which has always been used
at Sing Sing, the prisoners are locked in solitary cells at night,
but work together in groups, or companies, during the day.
Formerly, the prisoners were not allowed to speak to each
other, but the "silent system" has not been in effect in Sing
Sing for over fifteen years.

Secondly, man is more sensitive to the voice of the herd than
to any other influence. The herd is the source of his moral
codes and his philosophy.

Thirdly, man is subject to the passions of the pack in his
mob violence and the passions of the herd in his panics.
Witness, lynching bees and the crashes of the stock market.

Fourthly, man is remarkably susceptible to leadership.
Fluency of speech seems to be the most important requisite in
a leader. "The successful shepherd thinks like his sheep, and

---

[1]Arthur Schopenhauer: *Essays*, p. 143.

can lead his flock only if he keeps no more than the shortest distance in advance."[1]

Finally, man's relations with his fellows are dependent upon their recognition of him as a member of the herd. Possibly the necessity of distinguishing friend from foe was one of the conditions which favored the development of articulate speech.

F. Hunger. Love and hunger are supposed to be the most potent drives in human nature. The satisfaction of hunger is conducive, obviously, to the preservation of the individual; the fruition of love, to the preservation of the race.

Seldom do most of us experience really intense hunger. Eating becomes a conditioned reaction so that instead of hunger we actually get only the bare experience, it's-time-to-eat-again. A meal becomes a matter of habit. Ravishing hunger is an unknown experience to many of us. To go for days without a meal on account of poverty or the inaccessibility of food, and not on account of illness, is to know the painfulness of starvation. In sympathy with the needy, a prominent business executive made the remark, which was widely circulated by the press, that if he were out of work and hungry, he would rather steal than starve—a dilemma which is no mere academic problem for many of the unemployed.

The pleasures of eating have become a dominant goal in the glutton. It is curious how people insist on eating when they get together, whether it be ladies at an afternoon tea munching between a perfectly good lunch and a hearty dinner, or men assembled at a banquet who feel they must gorge themselves before submitting to the dull oratory of the after-dinner speakers.

G. Love. It is love that makes the world go 'round. The observer has only to look at our songs, our movies, our literature to behold how much mankind is preoccupied with love.

Our popular songs chant incessantly of "taking sugar to

---

[1] W. Trotter: *Instincts of the Herd in Peace and War*, p. 116. 1919.

tea," "being crazy about Baby and Baby's being crazy about me" (not to be confused with the parent's doting on his child), "feeling woozy over Susie," and a host of soul-stirring ballads dealing with the woes of shattered romance. The predominant sexual theme betrays more than a passing interest in wonderful men and still more marvelous women.

The movies are devoted almost exclusively to dramas that are "saucy, sparkling, snappy, and sophisticated," featuring petting parties in the purple dawn. Thus are our appetites exploited.

Our literature likewise is preoccupied with the erotic theme, with D. H. Lawrence, Hemingway, Aldous Huxley, and others leading the way, or perhaps trailing others who excel them in libidinous portrayals. When Haldeman-Julius put Balzac's "The Fleece of Gold" on his five-cent book list he sold only 4,000 copies the first year. He changed the title to "In Quest of a Blonde Mistress," and sold 16,000 copies the next year. In 1926 Hugo's play was translated and sold under the title, "The King Enjoys Himself," 8,000 copies. In 1927 the title was changed to "The Lustful King Enjoys Himself" and 38,000 copies were sold. Pornographic periodicals abound with an increasing circulation of monthlies of the "Hot Dog," "Red Pepper," "Whiz Bang" type, which add to the suggestiveness of the French magazines a coarseness and vulgarity that are entirely American. In one small city in Ohio, of approximately 25,000 inhabitants, out of 110 weekly and monthly periodicals on sale, 68 were either out and out devoted to "sex stuff," or were so close to the borderline as to be almost over it. In another city of the same relative size, 1,800 copies of a single monthly, devoted exclusively to sex experiences, are sold of each issue. It is the biggest single seller of them all, and says the dealer, "mostly to women."

Nature has conspired through the medium of the powerful sexual urge to insure the perpetuation of the species. The biological goal of love is reproduction. There are observers who assert that parenthood is psychologically tied up with sexual satisfactions in such an intimate way that the indulgence of sex merely for momentary pleasure results inevitably in a sense of frustration. Parental love, supplementing mate love, yields a more lasting satisfaction.

The continuance of the race has been facilitated by the mutual attractiveness of the two sexes. Nature, however, in her zest to turn out feminine charm on a large scale slipped up here and there and consequently, to minimize the seriousness of her errors, conspired further by making love blind. "What can he see in her?" It is a foolish question, since love does something to the vision of the one who is doing the seeing. There is a song to this effect: "You have a funny face, I like your face. . . . You're not much, but you're mine." What could be more irrational?

The sexual emotion has played such a prominent part in modern psychology because mental conflict centers mostly around the adjustment of individual desire to the taboos laid down by the social order. These taboos in regard to love have always been strict because the sexual urge is so potent as to necessitate severe restrictions. Proposals intended to change the conventions of the sexual life are hailed by those who are set "in the good old ways" as mere encouragements for free love, whether disguised as trial marriage, companionate marriage, or what have you. All the commotion over the sex problem indicates that "something is wrong somewhere." Perhaps our institutions are not suited to human nature; perhaps individuals should be more willing to sacrifice their immediate satisfactions for the welfare of society as a whole. Certainly, adjustment of craving to taboo is a difficult task under the most favorable circumstances. Economic conditions which are conducive to late marriage have served to aggravate the problem.

According to Freudian psychoanalysis, the sex impulse is complicated by two pairs of interests, to show and to look, masochism and sadism.

1. Show and Look. The desire to show oneself, particularly to expose the body, is known as exhibitionism. The chorus girl is one case, Walt Whitman working in his garden in the nude is another, the Dukhobor is still another. The evening gown is a medium of display. With many of us, exhibitionism gets a chance only in dreams when we find ourselves standing scantily clad in a hotel lobby, or on a prominent street corner.

Looking is technically known as voyeurism and is most characteristically seen in a Tom the Peeper who climbs a roof to peer through a bedroom window. More refined peepers go to musical comedies and burlesque shows. Rufus Choate, in his description of the nude bathing in the Moscow River, stated that some Americans never leave the river bank. Many casualties have resulted, he wrote, when observers have fallen off the bridges or street cars while witnessing, for the first time, the public ablutions.

2. Masochism and Sadism. Masochism is taking delight in being tortured. The girl who likes to be manhandled by a cave man is a masochist. Religious fanatics who scourge themselves, ascetics who deny themselves this or that, dancing marathons, martyrs to illness, and football players belong in the same category. (See cartoon on page 264.)

Sadism is deriving satisfaction through inflicting cruelty. The practical joker, the he-man lover, the boy who pulls the wings off a fly, parents who punish their children violently, Dante describing the torments of the Inferno, Loeb and Leopold committing an atrocious murder, Jonathan Edwards preaching on hell, persons who enjoy bull fights or prize fights, individuals who are enthusiastically insistent that the criminal be duly castigated, are all sadists.

In 1930, a retired banker was arrested in St. Louis where he had established a dental practice. He was practicing dentistry, he said, in an unprofessional way. He had been pulling women's teeth for ten years in St. Louis, New York, Kansas City, and Joplin, Missouri. "I guess I get a thrill out of it," he explained.

"Cheer up, Ed; there's another game next Saturday!"

(Reproduced by permission of *Judge*.)

The romantic ideal of love so well symbolized in the impetuous, self-dramatizing courtship of Romeo and Juliet has contributed in a large way to sexual maladjustment, for romantic love is most evanescent. It comes and presently it is gone. You cannot tell much about a girl's disposition, tastes, intellect, or sense of values by climbing her balcony in the moonlight.

Lovers who have nothing to do but love each other are not really to be envied; love and nothing else very soon is nothing else. The emotion of love, in spite of the romantics, is not self-sustaining; it endures only when the lovers love many things together, and not merely each other. It is this understanding that love cannot successfully be isolated from the business of living which is the enduring wisdom of the institution of marriage.[1]

---

[1]From W. Lippmann: *A Preface to Morals*, pp. 308–309. 1929. By permission of The Macmillan Company, publishers.

According to the romanticists there is one fated romance in store for each of us which comes to pass when by some coincidence affinities meet. Love is not something that a man does, it is something that happens to him. Love may come and just as mysteriously it may go. In its presence he is helpless. Marriages are made in heaven, compatibility is instinctive, happy unions are just lucky accidents. When true love exists, nothing need be added; when it does not exist, no substitute will take its place. When the dream girl and the prince meet, they marry and live happily ever after.

Married life cannot be one continuous thrill, one prolonged glamorous ecstasy. The romanticists take too much for granted in assuming that, with the right person, things will take care of themselves. They see habit formation as an evil to be resisted instead of welcoming it as an opportunity to be used. Compatibility is a process and not an accident. It depends upon the maturing of instinctive desire through a process of mutual adaptation. Marriage is a venture calling for the development of a system of coördinated habits by husband and wife. If meals are always on time, this is a family habit; if they are never on time, this is still another habit, and one to which the members of the family must adjust themselves. Quarreling, nagging, sulking, and weeping grow, by episodes, into established habits. With the passing of the years there is more and more of the life of the home that can be taken for granted, since the modes of living have matured into recognized customs. When this process of habit-building is effected through forethought and self-discipline, the psychological foundations are laid for the creation of those patterns of coöperation which constitute a happy marriage.[1]

It would be folly to disparage the value of romance. There is, however, a tendency for the romantic cult to rely too much

[1] See Robert C. Binkley and Frances W. Binkley: "Should We Leave Romance out of Marriage?" *The Forum*, February, 1930.

upon the magic of destiny and too little upon the advantages of individual effort. Passion transmutes an ordinary attachment into a thing of beauty, but persistent adjustment is necessary to sustain its continuity.

The technique of love is an art for which there should be thorough preparation. Instinct is an insufficient guide for the solution of problems so vital to the achievement of happiness. Young people contemplating marriage should have access to competent instruction in matters affecting their emotional natures so that their union may be psychologically complete. Such a suggestion may seem plain heresy to purists, but the widespread failure of marriage would seem to indicate that something more than the conventional mode of unpreparedness is needed.

Marriage, at best, is a gamble. To minimize the rôle of chance, the young man might give a test to his prospective mate and then take the evidence to a psychologist for consultation. Ask her these questions:

1. Do you dream of a time when you'll be in a better position than friends who look down on you?
2. Do you smoulder and sulk a long time when you are angry?
3. Are you undisturbed by rainy weather?
4. Can you be happy without a bath-tub?
5. Would you go "dutch-treat" to a theater with a poor young man?
6. Do you hope your husband will always want to take you with him on his good-time trips?
7. Do you prefer a dog that likes you alone to one that likes everyone?
8. Is perfection your aim?
9. Do you wish people wouldn't give you presents?
10. Do you always come out at the little end of the horn?

The perfect wife must feed her husband's ego, adapt her life to his schedule, and never forget that he is the most important man in the world.

Parenthood, as I said before, is the psychological as well as the biological outcome of mate love. The family is needed to give the sex relation its greatest emotional value, to rear children in an atmosphere of intelligent affection, to socialize the individual, and to prepare the child for satisfactory mating in the future.[1] The ideal marriage provides the opportunity for a satisfaction of the sexual craving, for a fulfillment of biological destiny, for the enrichment of personality, and for guiding the children to happy maturity.[2]

H. Fear. What are we afraid of? In general people fear anything that threatens their security. Watson tells us that infants can be frightened by a sudden loud noise or the sudden removal of support. The unexpected character of both of these stimulating situations is the essential provocative of fear. A noise in the dark conditions the fear of the dark, while a noise in the daylight does not condition a fear of the daylight. The difference is the distinction between the unexpected, the strange, the unknown, and the expected, the familiar, and the known. Any stimulus which makes us feel insecure arouses fear. The longing for security is a deep-seated desire in our nature.[3]

In our modern life, one of the most important elements in providing a sense of security is a job. In families dependent upon the pay envelope from week to week for their livelihood the possibility of unemployment is a constant source of worry. Worry is a chronic state of fear which renders the attainment of happiness impossible. In the daily lives of most men and women, fear plays a greater part than hope. The most insidious worry of all the vast working population is due to the insecurity of employment.[4]

---

[1]E. Sapir: "What Is the Family Still Good For?" *The American Mercury*, 1930, 19, 145–151.

[2]B. Glueck: "Psychoanalysis and Child Guidance," *Mental Hygiene*, 1930, 14, 813–827.

[3]See Alfred Adler: *The Neurotic Constitution.* 1921.

[4]Whiting Williams: *What's on the Worker's Mind?* 1921.

Convention is based upon respect for public opinion which at bottom is largely a fear of the insecurity that would ensue were nonconformity to provoke the wrath of the community. There is a time and a place for any given mode of conduct, and woe be to him who thinks and does otherwise. It takes more than ordinary courage to flout convention, since rebellion against the accepted ways of doing things upsets a lot of people, and in their eagerness to regain their traditional security they will not hesitate to avenge themselves upon the disturbing culprit, by gossip, social ostracism, or even physical punishment. If workingmen think freely about property, the rich are endangered; if young men and women think freely about sex, morality is undermined; if soldiers think freely about war, military discipline is weakened. It is fear that keeps us chained to the conventional; it is fear that impels us to goose-step for our security.

Primitively, the fear of physical danger was most important, as wild animals and the unruly elements were constantly threatening life. Civilization has minimized many dangers, only to introduce new possibilities for injury. No savage ever had to worry about the harmfulness of steam heat. But the vendor of devices for moistening the air in our homes assures us that dry air sucks the humidity from our bodies, injures the tender mucous membranes of the throat and nose, dries the skin and scalp, and exposes the lungs to dust, so that people are rendered susceptible to colds, catarrh, constipation, headaches, sleeplessness, grippe, pneumonia, tuberculosis, and bronchitis. We can depend upon the advertisers to keep us informed of impending disasters.

When it comes to preying on our anxiety, the insurance men are not far behind the advertisers. A letter from an insurance company warns home-owners that their houses will be especially attractive to burglars during the summer vacation period, and that an accident on the premises will make the owner liable to an expensive lawsuit. In addition, an airplane may descend through the roof at any moment, and during the excitement the household jewelry may be stolen. In the midst of these alarming possibilities the suggestion is dropped that it might be wise to buy the insurance to cover such losses in full.

Far more upsetting than physical harm is the host of threats to the esteem in which one is held by one's fellows. Job may have had boils, but he escaped athlete's foot, pyorrhea, halitosis, and cachexia. Costly advertising campaigns magnify the ills to which the flesh is heir so that readers are induced to purchase the magic remedies guaranteed to bring quick relief. Thus some disease may be avoided that might leave a tragic aftermath of broken hearts, engagements, and business careers, for no one can succeed who has "eructosis."

The fear "I won't make good" is the greatest and most common fear of all, according to David Mitchell, a clinical psychologist. We all have had a normal and healthy fear at times that we might not make good in certain situations, such as dealing with the boss, or making a speech, or meeting a customer, and the like; but with some people it has become so chronic that it crushes the heart out of them, saps their nerve, and militates against their succeeding. This fear grows out of the demands made upon people to try things which are beyond their physical, mental, and temperamental capacities. Our schools are the worst offenders in requiring children to attempt tasks which a large share of them are unable to accomplish. In setting up such foolish demands and false standards, the schools actually drill into the children the habit of fear and the feeling of failure.[1]

Stagefright in the presence of an audience is occasioned principally by the self-conscious query, "I wonder what kind

---

[1] See Albert E. Wiggam: "What Are You Afraid Of?" *The American Magazine*, October, 1927.

of an impression I am making." Many students fear to recite lest the exposure of their ignorance classify them among the stupid. Heine was reciting a poem at school exercises when he suddenly caught sight of a little girl in the audience, of whom he was secretly fond. He fainted. Many a person has been thrown into a panic by the mere thought of having to face an audience. Sarah Bernhardt never overcame her stage-fright. Disraeli's first speech in Parliament was a complete failure. Russell Conwell forgot his speech when he arose to debate as a member of the team at Wilbraham Academy, vowed he would never try again, and then in later years became internationally famous as a lecturer. With most of us it is the fear that we may not do ourselves credit, that we may even disgrace ourselves beyond redemption, that makes a public speech such an ordeal—for both the speaker and his audience. The malady is not really the fear of the audience but the fear for ourselves, lest we fail to please. As soon as we begin to worry about what the audience is thinking of us, we are lost. The love of esteem exaggerates the dread of humiliation.

Assuming that fear has been aroused, what are the characteristic reactions? The most typical behavior patterns are paralysis, fleeing, or fighting.

Being rooted to the spot in terror or lying motionless in bed at the sound of intruding footsteps are forms of the paralytic response. It is a common experience in nightmares to be unable to move as the pursuer approaches. Speculating in an evolutionary manner, such paralysis probably is related to the death-feigning proclivities of certain animals who escaped the attention of attacking beasts by remaining stationary against the background, or who evaded further onslaught by assuming the appearance of death. "Playing 'possum" is a familiar example of this adaptive response. Death-feigning has its limitations in the modern world where standing paralyzed in the middle of the street is hardly the most effective way of convincing the automobile driver that it is no use hitting us— even though his insurance may permit him to run down his quota for the year. Similarly, standing speechless on a lecture platform does not enable us to fit so perfectly into the background as to elude the peering eyes of the audience, nor does it help our cause to feign death even though our imposture be most convincing.

The only thing to do in such a predicament is to flee—literally or figuratively. We can make a graceful exit and beat a hasty retreat, or we can say that we're not much as a public speaker and then go on to demonstrate our apology. Or we can flee by refusing ever to speak again—for which everybody will be thankful. Or we can make our flight into daydreams of stirring oratory in which we hold our listeners spellbound.

In the physical sense, fear may precipitate a headlong rush for cover. The soldier who was passed by a bullet and who later passed the bullet is a case in point. The story is told of a boy clad in a red sweater who found himself in an enclosure with a charging bull. He, the boy, took to his heels and jumped the high fence, clearing it by a wide margin.

Even a bedridden invalid has been known to discover revived power in his limbs when danger threatens. A New Jersey man who had been partially paralyzed for six years surprised his friends by declaring that he felt fine as he walked without crutches. It appears that an escaped maniac had leaped upon him in bed and attempted to strangle him. The invalid forgot about being paralyzed, jumped from his bed, and sprinted up a stairway where he made his escape. His paralysis was apparently psychic, and he was the victim of his own fears.

Another typical reaction of fear is fighting. A person who is scared will become pugnacious, particularly if he discovers

that he can overcome his intimidator.   Anger frequently issues
from fear, for we tend to hate what we fear, since our personal
security is threatened.   Tyranny in the state leads to bloody
revolution, in the prison to violent riots, in business to vicious
strikes.   The employer, therefore, who resorts to intimidation
to get the most out of his employees is courting disaster, notwithstanding the gospel of Judge Gary who wrote:

> Fear of losing his job is making the man in the shop toe the line.
> At first glance the average individual will say that there is some-
> thing very ugly and inhuman in that statement.   It isn't ugly and
> it isn't inhuman.   It is the sane and reasonable answer to the in-
> dustrial tangle.   It is its only solution.   Fear is the word I used.
> I might, with equal truth, have said competition.   They mean the
> same thing in industry.[1]

It is to be hoped that the new economic order which is in process of emergence will appeal to higher motives, for industry
as a coöperative enterprise must elicit good will.

A phobia is a morbid fear, morbid in the sense that repression
of an earlier experience has minimized or even eliminated
awareness of the sources of the dread.   Claustrophobia is a
well-known phobia, the fear of closed places.   Such a fear may
go back to a forgotten incident of childhood when, for example,
the father shut the child up in a closet as a punishment.   The
sense of terror might carry over to affect the person in later
life, so that he would be frightened at being in a room with the
doors closed, without being able to account for his acute un-
easiness.   In one case, a young man could not be induced to
enter a subway.   Investigation revealed that some years before his drunken father had locked him in a closet to punish
him, and had then forgotten all about him until the next day
when he sobered up enough to think of releasing him.   When
Floyd Collins was trapped in his living tomb in Sand Cave,
the fear of closed places was probably encouraged in the minds

---

[1] Elbert H. Gary, in the New York *Times*, January 9, 1921.

of many news readers.[1] The dread of being buried alive is another expression of this same phobia.

Some overenthusiastic individuals have advocated the elimination of fear from human life. Such a goal seems to me not only unattainable, but even undesirable. Fear has its functions in promoting caution, providence, foresight, and wisdom. Further, fear often adds a zest to life, whether it be a ride on a roller coaster or an expedition to the South Pole.

Ignorance may be bliss, but, as a general rule, it is unwise to undertake a hazardous venture by ignoring danger.

It is often helpful in controlling fear to become enveloped in another emotion such as anger or love. When a person gets mad enough, his adversary no longer terrifies him. Peril is forgotten in the enthusiasm for conquest. Similarly, "perfect love casteth out fear." We can afford to live dangerously if we have the confidence that comes with religious faith, with the sense that there is a Power higher than ourselves lending us support. Faith, of any sort, is a potent means of controlling fear.

Another method for overcoming fear which is sometimes effective is to do the thing of which we are afraid. If an individual is afraid to make a speech, he should force himself to make one; if he is afraid of staying in the house alone over night, he should compel himself to do it. Hal Winkler, famous goaltender, took up goaltending in hockey when his brothers called him a "sissy." It is one of the rules of flying psychology to go up in a plane immediately after an accident. When Lindbergh and Miss Morrow experienced a mishap on one of their early flights, they made it a point to fly again the next day. Thus they gave fear no chance to dim their courage.

I. Anger. Anger is provoked by the thwarting of some desire. When an urge is blocked, an incentive is supplied for

---

[1]John E. Pember: "Cave Reactions of Collins Case as Seen by a Professor," The Boston *Sunday Herald*, February 22, 1925.

overcoming the obstacle. Rage may be evoked in an infant by hampering his movements. The same method often produces a similar result in the adult. Hampering of any sort will produce anger, whether the restrictions are physically or psychologically imposed.

To call a person by an insulting name is to interfere with the good opinion he holds of himself. Rage will be likely to ensue. Like the London fishwife who "blew up" when she was called a parallelopipedon, a person is most incensed when he is called something he does not understand. A shoemaker's wife was brought into court for calling the saloonkeeper next door an albatross. Answering an inquiry from the bench, the plaintiff admitted that he did not know what an albatross was, "but it was something highly improper or she would not have used the word." He had gathered that much from the tone of the lady when she uttered it. Inquiring further the court was astonished to find that the lady herself, when she called her neighbor an albatross, was a little at sea. "Your honor," said she, "it is a striped horse."

The characteristic behavior pattern in anger is pugnacious attack. When a person "sees red," he strikes out in the hope that he will hit his adversary—or a bystander—or somebody. The urge to violence must vent itself before a return to a peaceful state of mind is accomplished. When the path to the fulfillment of desire is blocked, something must be done about it. War, either nationalistic, private, or family, is a wholesale outlet for the emotion of anger. Less harm is done when an individual stops to break the barrel stave that has risen to smite him on the shin bone. One man was so infuriated by his automobile which stalled that he seized the crank and beat in the hood and radiator of the car, deriving a vicious satisfaction from his violence until he was arrested for disorderly conduct.

There are people who are foolish enough to say that we shall always have war because human nature is what it is.

Human nature can be directed if an intelligent effort is made. Dueling has vanished in most countries in spite of the prediction that the practice would be permanent since human nature was built that way. In a public debate in 1858 the Reverend W. G. Brownlow maintained "that slavery having existed ever since the first organization of society, it will exist to the end of time." Yet slavery has been abolished in many countries. In spite of the cynics we have traveled a long way from the caveman. Our civilization itself is a demonstration, however feeble it may be, of man's effort to curb his turbulent emotions for his own good as well as for the good of the whole.

Anger can be controlled if the proper means are taken. It can be restrained, in the first place, in respect to the stimulus. One person will get mad at a slighting remark while another will make a joke of it. The difference is a matter of attitude. A man is no bigger than the things that make him mad. Our reactions reveal our weaknesses. If a person places a proper estimate on his own worth, he is less likely to be tormented by a deprecatory remark. Nine times in ten, the woman too easily insulted flatters herself. If an individual is puffed up with pride, his pomposity is more easily punctured.

A man wrote to Dr. Cadman: "I am ashamed to say I am called 'touchy,' and some one recently told me when I resented the omission of my name from the speakers' list of our club social that I had an inferiority complex. How can that be, when I don't feel inferior?" Dr. Cadman's reply was: "But you do, and you confessed the feeling in your resentment. . . . Knowing the bait to which you rise, don't bite. Forewarned is forearmed. . . . A complete diagnosis by yourself of yourself will result in your being less liable to anger when others pass you by. Instead of sleepless nights over slights which may be imaginary, you can indulge a quiet chuckle over your own eccentricities."

A large share of the occasion for anger, just as Santayana said of love, lies in our own minds. We are set to interpret the stimulus in a certain way, we draw our own inferences, and we get mad. Suppose I make a statement of fact and you contradict me. I can respond in a common way by inquiring, "Do you mean to call me a liar?" Now, of course, that may not have been your full intention at all. You may merely have considered me misinformed on the matter—which in itself, indeed, might make me mad, too—especially if I pride myself on my superior wealth of information. You may really think I am a liar but your remark did not carry that implication, unless I cared to draw the inference.

A sense of humor is a most vital factor in self-control. The ability to "laugh it off" is an efficient protective device. Humor will relieve the tension even after ire is aroused. An angry division in the British Parliament, which bade fair to end in personal conflicts, ended in shouts of laughter. A bareheaded, redheaded Conservative rose to a point of order. Etiquette required that a member in such a situation must be seated and wearing a hat. A hundred voices pointed out his error, and the questioner borrowed hastily from his neighbor a silk hat many sizes too small and put it on his head. The sight of the silk "topper," balanced precariously, was too much for the dignity of the House. The members burst into roars of laughter, the questioner never succeeded in raising his point of order, and the House adjourned shortly afterward without further incident.[1]

It is interesting, in connection with the control of anger on the stimulus side, to study the rôle of propaganda in the promotion of modern warfare. The fact that propaganda is so necessary to arouse the citizens to a pitch where they will be not only willing but eager to slaughter fellow beings, is an indication that we are not fundamentally as warlike as we are supposed to be. That the fighting instinct is not primarily responsible for war between nations is indicated by the fact

[1] The Boston *Herald*, June 11, 1931.

that the fears and hatreds of the masses have to be stimulated artificially before they will go to war. Propaganda of falsehood and distortion is indispensable to the waging of modern war. In addition, governments must resort to conscription. Voluntary enlistment failed to produce the required number of soldiers in all belligerent countries during the recent war.

Whereas cities and states live in peace with one another, nations frequently go to war. The explanation of the difference is to be found in the dogmas and emotions of nationalism. It may not be possible to make radical changes in human nature, but it is possible to transform the doctrines of national interest, national sovereignty, national honor, and national patriotism, and to bring them into conformity with the economic and political realities of the modern world.

It is plain that in the past very little sincere effort has been made to educate for peace. History has been taught in terms of wars. Generals have been the chief persons glorified. Patriotism has been conceived in terms of "bearing arms" and of military service. Dr. Rugg of Columbia is making a noteworthy contribution to education, in a series of textbooks the design of which is to condition the minds of school children of a whole nation to tolerance, peace, and understanding of the world's peoples and problems. Emphasis is placed on an economic and industrial interpretation of the world in place of the age-old story of strife and bloodshed. Wars are given brief mention. The story of the World War is told in five pages, and then not in terms of battles, but in terms of organization of resources, of tremendous costs, and wholesale loss of life. It will be by means of such efforts that peace will be secured, and not by increased armament.[1]

Anger may also be controlled on the side of the response. It may be curbed by a direct method or by a change of outlet. A direct means for restraining the temper is to count ten

[1] *The Rugg Social-Science Course.* Edited by Harold Rugg. 1930.

before you strike your victim—and then, if you must, count ten over him afterward.

A shift of outlet is known as displacement. Instead of swearing at his wife, a man may go out and chop up the woodpile. Since violent rage is taboo in polite society, more acceptable forms of expression must be found, such as venting one's anger through making more money than one's adversary, and then gloating over his inferiority. Anger can be put to work for constructive ends.[1]

An understanding of emotional displacement is very helpful in the process of personal adjustment. The cartoons of the man who starts the day wrong when his toast burns at breakfast, and who then "takes it out" on the stenographer illustrate the point. It is important to realize that a particular misdemeanor may merely offer the occasion rather than the sole provocation for an emotional outburst. A series of annoying mishaps may accumulate a charge of anger which needs only to be ignited to reach the explosive stage. When his wife has had a trying day at home, with the baby sick and the department store sending out the wrong dress, a man comes home from work and forgets to wipe his shoes on the door mat. His wife may "go up in the air" and repent that she ever married such a careless man who doesn't care how much work he makes for her. He should not take her complaints too seriously. He should offer himself as the scapegoat upon whom she can lay her accumulated wrath. An understanding of this bit of psychology would aid in the avoidance of the ill feeling which is often nourished by trivial grievances. The only danger in my advice is that the "innocent" husband may fail to assume the responsibility for faults of his own which may legitimately provoke an outburst of considerable proportions. It must be clearly understood that this situation of husband and wife is reversible.

[1] R. F. Richardson: *The Psychology and Pedagogy of Anger.* 1918.

Displacement, too, offers a valuable solution for war on a larger scale, the conflicts of nations.   William James suggested that there were moral equivalents for war.[1]   Fighting moral and social evils is one outlet.   Through the newspapers, pugnacious citizens may take part vicariously in the chase, prosecution, and punishment of criminals.   That righteous indignation may be satisfied through battling the liquor traffic is obvious in this letter written to the *Literary Digest* by a doctor who was disturbed by a news report of the prevalence of drinking among college undergraduates.   He calls for a revival of the dry fighting spirit in these terms:

Is there a remnant left in this country who stand for righteousness and honor?

If so, let us rally as did Joffre's men at the Banks of the Marne, and declare again as they did on that immortal day, "They shall not pass."

This is a matter greater than even Prohibition enforcement.   It is a question of maintaining the foundations of our American institutions.

I wish that every man and woman in the United States who believes in the enforcement of the Prohibition Law would wear some insignia—to encourage each other.

I have faith to believe that we shall yet rally and drive the forces of evil back to the Hindenburg line.[2]

Another moral equivalent is to combat the forces of nature. Have you ever pushed a boulder up an incline?   When you succeed in reaching your destination and get the better of the thing, you derive the same sort of satisfaction as comes to the engineer who builds a great canal against heavy obstacles, or to the chemist who wars on disease germs, or to the doctor who conquers a tropical fever.

Another equivalent, amusing in its paradoxical nature, is

---

[1] William James: *Memories and Studies.*   1917.

[2] The *Literary Digest*, May 3, 1930.

arguing about war. No discussion can be carried on with more feeling than a debate on war between belligerent pacifists. Ford's Peace Ship enjoyed a voyage bellicose enough to release considerable tension.

The realm of sport is another substitute for war, providing an excellent vent for pugnacity among both the players and the spectators. Indeed, prizefighting used to be called "the manly art of modified murder" by the noted sports writer, W. O. McGeehan.

Most important of the equivalents, as far as social values are concerned, is the fight against the forces of evil, whether it be Livingstone fighting slavery in Africa, Lincoln fighting the traffic in America, or Parkhurst fighting political corruption in New York City. The wicked flee when no man pursueth, according to Parkhurst, but they make better time when the righteous are after them. Surely the struggle for a better society provides plenty of opportunity for the expression of human pugnacity without the need of periodic wars to relieve the tension.

III. HEREDITY AND TRAINING

There has been a long controversy among psychologists as to whether heredity is everything or whether environment is everything. Both groups are probably wrong in their insistence upon an exaggerated one-sided view of human nature. It is an issue that can never be settled since it is impossible to determine how much of a person's development is an unfolding of latent capacities, merely evoked upon the occasion of an adequate stimulus. A living creature grows from within. Education or training merely draws forth what there is in a person.

The process of growth from within is known as maturation. For a considerable period, while the instinct theory was particularly under fire, the influence of organic development upon

The Photographic Recording and Observation Dome. The dome is located in the laboratory of the Yale Clinic of Child Development. The interior of the dome is illuminated. The surrounding laboratory is darkened. The infant is examined in the clinical crib in the center of the dome. The dome is encased in a one-way vision screen which permits complete visibility for the observers outside but conceals the observers from the infant. A motion-picture camera enclosed in a sound-quieted box attached to the curved track of the dome makes a cinema record of the infant's behavior. Reproduced by permission of Arnold Gesell.

behavior was ignored, and there was a tendency to attribute all increments in learning to environmental training.[1] Maturation fell under the general suspicion directed against native factors in behavior. More recently, the importance of maturation has been realized, through the studies of Gesell and others who have been making careful observations of growth in infancy and childhood. If a certain behavior

[1] See P. A. Witty and H. C. Lehman: "The Instinct Versus the Maturation Hypothesis," *Psychological Review*, 1933, 40, 33–59.

pattern appears at about the same stage in a number of children despite the differences in their experiences, it seems clear that maturation is responsible. Problems have been planned to determine the various ages at which these specific tasks can be performed, and there is a striking uniformity in the manner in which progress gradually unfolds.

Gesell has made a motion-picture record of the progressive behavior of some of the infants in the Yale Psycho-Clinic, demonstrating beautifully his developmental examination procedures.

The course of behavior development has been charted in a graphic manner. The infant is seated in a diminutive Morris chair at a table. A small sugar pellet is placed upon the table, within the infant's arm length.

He is sixteen weeks, or four lunar months of age. He fixates upon the examiner's hand as the pellet is placed in position. Rarely he fixates upon the pellet. At twenty weeks he may regard the pellet and advance upon it with the crude inward approach of one or both hands. At twenty-four weeks he scratches with pronate paw-like hand in the vicinity of the pellet. At twenty-eight weeks he may rake it up with simultaneous flexion of the fingers against the palm. At thirty-two weeks the thumb and forefinger begin to display a preëminence in the prehensory act. This preëminence becomes progressively perfected so that at forty weeks the infant plucks the pellet with pincer-like utilization of the index finger and thumb. At fifty-two weeks he plucks the pellet yet more adeptly and may deposit it in the mouth of a bottle, though his own mouth remains a strongly competing destination. . . . Behavior grows. Every lunar month witnesses distinguishable changes in the patterning of the behavior manifestations. . . . So swift and continuous are these changes that in the first six years of life the individual traverses far more development ground than he will ever again compass in a similar period.[1]

---

[1] Arnold Gesell: "The Study and Guidance of Infant Behavior," in *Psychology at Work*, Paul S. Achilles, Editor. By permission of McGraw-Hill Book Co., Inc.

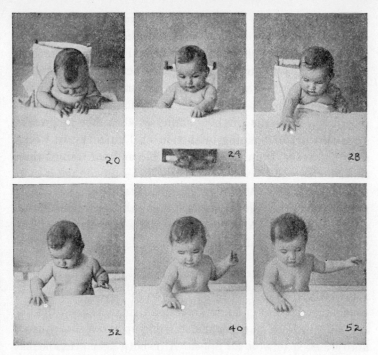

PATTERNS OF PELLET PREHENSION AT 20, 24, 28, 32, 40, 52 WEEKS[1]

The influence of maturation has been studied by the method of co-twin control.   Identical twins have practically the same heredity.   One twin is trained in a given task, the other is reserved as a control.   Twin T is trained for ten minutes daily over a period of six weeks in stair climbing, beginning at the age of forty-six weeks.   At forty-eight weeks she scales the stairs for the first time with slight assistance.   At the conclusion of the six weeks' training period (age, one year) she is a relatively expert climber.   At the age of one year, her un-trained co-twin C cannot yet scale the staircase, even with

[1]With the permission of Dr. Arnold Gesell.   From Volume 18, No. 2, Pro-ceedings of the National Academy of Sciences, and from an educational picture, "Life Begins."

assistance. At the age of fifty-three weeks, however, C climbs to the top of the staircase without any assistance, and without any previous specific training whatsoever. The pattern of C's climbing is purely a function of maturation. Then C is given two weeks' training and at the age of fifty-five weeks she approaches the skill of Twin T. A motion-picture record compares the climbing ability of C at fifty-five weeks, after two weeks' training, with that of T at fifty-two weeks, after six weeks' training. Although T has been trained three times as long and seven weeks earlier, this advantage is more than overcome by the three weeks of C's added age. The influence of maturation upon the climbing skill of infants is thus clearly revealed.[1] A similar study of the acquisition of language in the same pair of twins likewise discloses the effects of maturation.[2]

McGraw gave one identical twin elaborate training in motor skills while the other twin was allowed to mature without any coaching. Her investigation revealed that some activities like reaching for toys, crawling and standing up alone, sitting erect, and grasping objects all appeared in both youngsters at the same time without regard to training, whereas climbing, roller skating, and leaping from elevated positions were definitely developed by training alone. The control twin, however, was able to benefit to such an extent from coaching when it was finally given to him as to indicate that maturation had functioned to increase his learning facilities.[3]

It is apparent from these studies that the infant develops in response to his environmental influences, but that basically his progress is an unfolding of his native capacities. He is a

[1] A. Gesell and H. Thompson: "Learning and Growth in Identical Infant Twins: An Experimental Study by the Method of Co-Twin Control," *Genetic Psychology Monographs*, 1929, 6, 1–123.

[2] L. C. Strayer: "Language and Growth. The Relative Efficacy of Early and Deferred Language Training by the Method of Co-Twin Control," *Genetic Psychology Monographs*, 1930, 8, 209–319.

[3] Myrtle McGraw: *Growth; a Study of Johnny and Jimmy.* 1935.

product of both environment and endowment. In the total picture his growth potencies play an important rôle. Improvement in the performance of any task is not wholly due to practice, but, in part, to organic maturation.

Jennings sums up the matter by stating that identical twins, when reared separately, reveal marked differences as the result of their distinct environments, but they disclose more likenesses than can be accounted for on any basis except their identity in genetic constitution. Effects produced in one case by genetic constitution may be produced in another case by environment.[1]

There is something in heredity. A study of animal breeding is convincing evidence that heredity counts heavily. Witness, for example, the sons of the remarkable race horse, Man O' War: Mars, Scapa Flow, Dress Parade, American Flag, By Hisself, and Crusader—all of whom were winners in many of the outstanding race events in which they were entered. This is no indication that heredity is the whole story either for animals or human beings. It does, however, seem to show that blood will tell, as it has in the Darwins, Edwardses, Beechers, Lowells, and Adamses.

Some psychologists went to the extreme in their assertions that instinct and intelligence were set by inheritance, and that nothing could be done about them. Such a dogma offered a remarkable alibi for failure. If a student did not do well in school, he could shift the blame on his parents. While the excuse was consoling, yet, at the same time, it was discouraging to believe that the "die had been cast," the limitations set down, and nothing further could be done.

It was not so long, therefore, before some other psychologists

[1]See H. S. Jennings: *The Biological Basis of Human Nature*, pp. 166–169. 1930. See also H. J. Muller: "Mental Traits and Heredity: The Extent to Which Mental Traits Are Independent of Heredity, as Tested in a Case of Identical Twins Reared Apart," *Journal Of Heredity*, 1925, 16, 433–449, and H. H. Newman: "Mental Traits of Identical Twins Reared Apart," *Journal of Heredity*, 1929, 20, 49–64; 97–104; 153–166.

went to the other extreme and asserted that all babies are alike at birth, and that the individual discrepancies which appeared later were merely the results of training.[1] Watson, Dorsey, and Adler insisted that a person could make anything out of anybody with the proper methods of training.[2] It is a very encouraging doctrine. The story of the two frogs who fell in their separate pails of milk is a parable of such optimism. The first frog said to himself, "This is a strange situation. I am not equipped to solve it. My personal resources are inadequate. I might as well sink and get it over with." So he drowned. The second frog cogitated thus, "Here I am in a challenging predicament. How intriguing! Now is my chance to show what I can do in a trying situation. I'll fight it out to the finish." He "trod milk," as it were, through the long night and as dawn drew nigh, he found himself astride a mound of butter safe and sound. Excelsior!

Such a sunny view of life is apt to degenerate into superficial optimism. We should try to solve the problems of life, but with a recognition of the limitations within which we must work out our salvations. We may not know exactly what our limits are, yet that does not appear to be sufficient reason for assuming there are no limits. One cannot make a genius out of an idiot, even through creative education. It is wise to recognize our limitations, but it is foolish to lay all the emphasis on them. If a boy is awkward in his muscular coördinations, he would show more insight if he tried to become a scholar, given a modicum of intelligence, instead of straining after athletic glory. The truth probably resides in the middle path—between the two extreme emphases—heredity, on the one hand, and training, on the other.

---

[1]The behavioristic view that children can be taught anything has not been borne out by the observations of Dr. Arnold Gesell in his studies at the Yale Clinic, some of which have been recorded for the talking pictures.

[2]See especially Alfred Adler: "Character and Talent," *Harper's Magazine*, June, 1927.

That human nature can be modified has already been maintained in the discussions of love, fear, anger. The process of modification through experience is a matter of conditioning or habit formation, which will be analyzed at some length in the next chapter.

CHAPTER IX

THE FORMATION OF HABITS

IN THE days when Darwin's evolutionary theory was a center of scientific interest, instinct was the rage in psychology. McDougall's *Introduction to Social Psychology*, published in 1908, awakened a widespread interest in man's instinctive nature. For a while every sort of behavior was explained in terms of some one instinct or a combination of instincts.

But many psychologists were soon convinced that the instinct-psychology was fruitless. There was too much theory and not enough scientific observation. Ignorance of genetics encouraged the formulation of hypotheses without experimental bases. As a result of such convictions, there came a shift to *habit* as the explanation of human conduct. Heredity, nowadays, is discounted in psychology. Everything is training.

I. THE NEW OPTIMISM

There is, indeed, an advantage to this new emphasis. The formation of habits can be observed and controlled. There has developed an optimism which no longer capitulates to the limitations of heredity. With the proper training, assert the new enthusiasts, anybody can become anything. Men are built, not born. Watson says,

I can take the squirmings of the throat muscles, and weave them into those highly organized acts we call talking and singing (and, yes, even thinking). I can take the infantile squirmings of the gut—the unstriped muscular tissue of the alimentary tract, diaphragm, heart, respiration, etc.—and actually organize them into complicated emotional responses we call fears, loves, and rages.

The behaviorist asks for nothing to start with in building a human being but the squirmings everyone can see in the newborn infant.[1]

Alfred Adler says,

Talent is not inherited, and . . . the possibilities and potentialities of any individual for performance are not fixed. . . .

The development of a personality cannot be foretold from the phenomena of physical inheritance. The inherited instruments with which we fight the battle of life are very varied. *How we use these instruments*, is the important thing.

We can never tell what actions will characterize a man if we know only whence he comes. But if we know whither he is going we can prophesy his movements toward his objective. . . .

The great accomplishments, the really worthwhile achievements, have been made by individuals whose equipment was poor.[2]

The attitude of many contemporary psychologists toward the relative importance of heredity and environment is that people do not do what they do, because they are urged from within, but because they are driven from without. In other words, one's environmental situations are more impelling than one's inborn drives. Knowledge about the world in which a given individual lives sheds more light on an understanding of his personality than any citation of hypothetical instincts.

The new optimism in psychology, with its whole stress upon habit building, seems very superficial. It is true that none of us ever realizes his full potentialities. It is true that life situations are an important factor in our development. It is true that training can produce startling results. It is true that an optimistic outlook encourages successful achievement. But it is not true that heredity is totally insignificant.

[1] John B. Watson: "The Behaviorist Looks at Instincts," *Harper's Magazine*, July, 1927.

[2] Alfred Adler: "Character and Talent," *Harper's Magazine*, June, 1927.

As applied to characteristics, heredity and environment are not mutually exclusive categories. Bow-legs may result from hormone and (not *or*) vitamin deficiency. Hereditary and environmental factors may be distinguished, however, where differences between particular specified individuals are concerned. For example, one man may have a dark complexion because of his genes, and another man may have a dark complexion because of exposure to sunlight. No distinction between nurture and nature is generally valid. The particular facts of each specific case must be taken into consideration. It is a common fallacy to assume that if a characteristic is affected by the environment, it cannot be hereditary; that if it is hereditary, it cannot be influenced by the environment; in other words, that characteristics fall into two mutually exclusive groups in respect to these matters.[1]

When Watson asserts that he can make any *normal* child into a doctor, lawyer, merchant, or chief, he excludes by definition all genetic classes with insufficient capabilities for adjustment. His claim is true only as a positive statement. The negative conclusion is untrue: that heredity has nothing to do with the diverse aptitudes, temperaments, and fates of individuals.

There is danger in drawing negative conclusions from positive observations. It is definitely fallacious to hold that the discovery of one cause requires the exclusion of another.[2] The significant point in Watson's assertions is that it would require different treatment to train different individuals to be lawyers. As Jennings says, it is no news that unfit persons may be made into lawyers, but it should be realized that good merchants may be spoiled in the process.[3]

The most important contribution of genetics is denied by

----

[1] H. S. Jennings: *The Biological Basis of Human Nature*, p. 147.
[2] *Ibid.*, p. 217.
[3] *Ibid.*, p. 179.

the Behaviorism of Watson, namely, that human beings are endowed with diverse tastes, temperaments, aptitudes, and diverse ways of responding to the same conditions.[1] Respect for the individual involves the recognition of hereditary differences. This is a fundamental axiom of the psychology of individual differences.

An adequate account of the human being must include both nurture and nature.   Training is important—but what is going to be trained? Stimuli are effective—but what is going to be stimulated? Environment exerts a potent influence on the inherent nature of the individual.

II. NATURE AND NURTURE

In our present ignorance it is useless to draw a sharp line between heredity and environment. We can, however, be sure that experience does modify nature. Habits are built from the stuff of heredity.

Emotions, for example, are soon developed into habits. Habits are activities which have been repeated so often as to become automatic. Habitual behavior becomes second nature.   There must, of course, be some motive for repeating an act.   The fundamental urges impel us to the repetition which establishes habit.   Habits are quickly acquired where interest is involved. Pleasant, that is, satisfying consequences encourage the recurrence of a given activity.

A. Conditioning.   Repetition may ingrain a mode of behavior so that it becomes an integral part of the individual. The process of habit formation is fundamentally that of conditioning responses. Repeated association of stimuli and responses builds in conditioned behavior.

How are bears, for example, trained to dance?   The bears are stationed on a heated surface while music is played.   When this situation has been repeated a number of times, the bears

[1]H. S. Jennings, *op. cit.*, p. 222.

will dance on an unheated surface when they hear music, because an association has been established between *music* and *hot surface*. The bears, therefore, when they hear music, dance as if they were still bothered with hot feet.

Human beings acquire their habits in a similar fashion. A child may be given medicine, the disagreeable taste of which is alleviated with grape juice. Later, the sight or smell of grape juice is enough to provoke a spell of nausea.

1. Substitution. Conditioning is effected through substitution. It may be a substitution of one stimulus for another, or a substitution of one response for another.

a. Substitution of a Stimulus. Suppose a young man is in love with a girl who resembles her mother. Other factors being equal, he will feel (response) toward the mother (stimulus) as he does toward the girl (stimulus).

b. Substitution of a Response. Suppose some night the mother is so disagreeable as to inform him that he is not good enough for her daughter. He will then have a grudge (response) instead of a feeling of adoration (response) toward the daughter (stimulus) as well as toward the mother (stimulus).[1]

2. "Belongingness" and the Time Factor. The readiness with which conditioning occurs depends, to some extent, upon the "belongingness" of the two stimulus-response patterns, and, to some extent, upon the temporal relationship between the conditioned (substitute) and unconditioned (original) stimuli.

Conditioning is effected rapidly when the belongingness is highly natural, as in a situation when a child "gets the connection" between his misdemeanor and the appropriate punishment.

In considering the time factor, there are three possibilities to be taken into account: the substitute stimulus may appear

---

[1] See J. B. Watson: *Behaviorism*, Chapter II. Revised edition.

before the original stimulus (the bell rings, then the food appears), or the two stimuli may be simultaneous, or the substitute stimulus may follow the original stimulus (the food appears, then the bell rings).   Pavlov reports that the maximum conditioning occurs when the (substitute) stimulus is given from .2 to 2 seconds before the original stimulus, that is, when the food follows the bell.[1]   Griffith, however, states that the most favorable rate of learning obtains when the substitute stimulus follows the original stimulus, that is, when the bell follows the food.[2]   The two stimuli may be separated by a considerable interval and association will still result.   Pavlov has reported such separation effective for intervals as long as thirty minutes.   The ability to appreciate the belongingness of objects and events will, of course, determine the possible length of the interval.   If the substitute stimulus is repeatedly given without reinforcement from the original stimulus, temporary extinction takes place, that is, the substitute stimulus no longer evokes the conditioned response.   For example, if the bell is rung repeatedly and no food appears, the salivary reflex is no longer elicited by the sound of the bell.   Temporary extinction may disappear after a period of rest.   When extinction is carried out repeatedly, recovery is progressively diminished until it no longer takes place.

B. Learning.   Learning is a matter of habit formation. Learning is pointed toward the novel, while habit is pointed toward the old and familiar.   Habit is established as the novel becomes increasingly familiar.

C. Thought and Action.   Habits are usually conceived as explicit actions, but of course there are habits of thought as well as habits of an explicit nature.   Table manners are habits of action.   Prejudices are primarily habits of thought.   The

---

[1] See E. R. Guthrie: *The Psychology of Learning*, Chapter IV, "Time Factors in Conditioning." 1935.

[2] See C. R. Griffith: *Introduction to Educational Psychology*, p. 398. 1935.

"crapehanger" has the habit of seeing the gloomy side of a situation. The person with a dirty mind sees the bad in everything. Any technique is a habit of thought. Some people go at a problem slowly and surely; some just slowly; some fast and unsurely; and some fast and surely.

D. The Education of the Emotions. In the past, education has been primarily intellectualistic, though it has long been recognized that successful living is fundamentally an emotional matter. Most of the emphasis has been placed upon the inculcation of information and knowledge. Yet a cultivated intellect is not nearly so important for happiness as well-trained emotions. The education of the future, if it aims, as I assume it will, at producing happier human beings, will give more and more heed to the emotional aspects of human nature. An article written by a graduate for one of the Vassar publications shows a profound appreciation of this vital need in college:

Among my friends there are a few who are geniuses in the field of business, literature, music, and engineering. And yet I have looked behind the curtains of their homes, and the things I see there freeze my marrow with pity. Here is an engineer, master of the principles that control the natural world about him, who cannot control the devils that ride him, and who has wrecked three lives through his jealous passion. Here is a rich business executive, who directs the destiny of a corporation, and yet cannot guide his own sottish son, or level the barricade of hatred between him and his wife. And here, there, and everywhere are friends and relatives ruining themselves with bigotry and egotism, wearing out their lives in loneliness because of timidity, or else consumed by the worm of satiety and ennui. . . .

What can Vassar do about it? that is, if she considers such a superficial problem worth troubling about? If it is possible for a faculty, largely unmarried, to show girls how to get along in their own homes, do so, I pray, in the name of many wearied families. . . . More than fifty per cent of Vassar students are going to be called upon to exert, not so much their intellects as their ability to get along with people, including perverse husbands and eccentric cooks. Somehow or other I wish that sympathy might be fostered, and unselfishness and tact and a desire to help. And, above all, a sense of humor.[1]

Just as a person's intelligence is supposed to mature at a normal rate, so his emotional growth should proceed from lower to higher levels with the approach to adulthood. The normal person, as he grows up, matures in his emotional patterns. Childish modes of reaction are outgrown. The adult "acts his age."

1. Fixation. Progress toward maturity is often checked by influences which arrest development. Whether a person will grow up emotionally depends very largely on the training he gets at the hands of his elders. Pampering, coddling, and babying tend to retard emotional development. When a person remains too long at a certain level of emotional evolution, he is said to be fixated.

Negativism, the technical term for what used to be called "pure cussedness," is characteristic of the emotional behavior of a child between the ages of two and four. The negativistic person does the opposite of what he is told to do. "Keep off the grass" is merely a challenge to get on the grass. Such rebellious self-assertion is to be expected of a child, but in an adult, it is regarded as "childish," that is, out of keeping with his age. Some people are adults only in the chronological sense. Emotionally, they are still just "kids." Individuals who drink spiritous liquors as a protest against prohibitions belong in the negativistic category. They are cases of arrested emotional development.

Sulking is a childish reaction. Adults are expected to work out their mutual adjustments at a higher level. Once in a while a man and wife live together in glum silence, nursing their separate grievances, and refraining doggedly from addressing

---

[1]Margaret M. Miner, in the *Vassar Quarterly*.

each other by word of mouth. Usually such a hostile silence is the aftermath of a quarrel.

Fixations are apt to occur in the love life, especially when parents spoil a child with such an overindulgence of affection as to render the severance of the apron strings impossible. At maturity a person should be in a position to assert his emotional independence, break the family bonds, seek a mate, and establish a home of his own. When John Ruskin was twenty-nine, his mother decided that perhaps it would be best for him to marry, so she selected a wife for him from among the daughters of her own few friends. This girl, Euphemia Chalmers Gray, was beautiful, vivacious, charming, and ten years Ruskin's junior, and he was casually interested in her; so he married her April 10, 1848, and he was joined on a belated wedding tour by his father and mother.

An adult is entitled to a life of his own, with the assumption of responsibilities outside the narrow circle of his ancestral fireside. Fixated persons may be so imbued with nesting habits that they cannot spread their wings and fly. Parental tenderness which promotes a crippling dependence is short-sighted and essentially selfish, however noble it may seem to the sentimentalist.

2. Regression. In Chapter III, in the section on Jung, a description of the relation between fixation and regression was given. Growth proceeds against obstacles. If the difficulties prove insurmountable, fixation occurs. Further struggle may result in renewed progress. When the new tasks prove discouraging, there is a tendency to regress, to go back, to an earlier stage of development, to the point of fixation. The stronger the fixation in the past, the more likely is regression in the present.

The girl who at last finds a man who remotely approximates the perfection of her daddy, may be induced under pressure to enter the holy bonds of matrimony, but when the first serious quarrel arises, she packs her suitcase and flees for moral support back to the family hearth where she knows she can count on protection and consolation. At least, that is the way it is told in story books. If the description is not literally true to life, it at least symbolizes the drama of regression. Advance and retreat are the campaigns of war, international or domestic.

When difficult problems face the adult, calling for the use of all his resources, the temptation is strong to fall back on the earlier reactions of childhood. Unable to face the grown-up situation in a grown-up way, the timid flee, the lazy shirk, the incompetent wonder what to do, and the irresponsible kick up their heels and have a good time. Regression to the infantile is not just a return to the childish; it is a return to the childish for the sake of accomplishing something by infantile means when the situation obviously demands adult intelligence.

If you want to ascertain your emotional age, turn back to the questionnaire on pages 89–91.

KEY TO TEST

1. Yes—11 No—21	10. Yes—7 No—26
2. Yes—7 No—20	11. Yes—6 No—25
3. Yes—26 No—7	12. Yes—11 No—29
4. Yes—12 No—30	13. Yes—13 No—26
5. Yes—40 No—8	14. Yes—7 No—25
6. Yes—10 No—20	15. Yes—5 No—30
7. Yes—31 No—9	16. Yes—11 No—28
8. Yes—11 No—20	17. Yes—7 No—25
9. Yes—26 No—10	18. Yes—12 No—30

19. Yes—5	22. Yes—11
No—20	No—21
20. Yes—7	23. Yes—22
No—24	No—7
21. Yes—7	24. Yes—10
No—21	No—20

25. Yes—5
No—20

All those who answered question 1 *Yes*, put down 11. All those who answered it *No*, put down 21. And so on down to the 25th question.

Add the resulting column of twenty-five figures. Divide the total by 25 and you have your emotional age.

      25 is the Perfect Emotional Man or Woman

      22 to 25 is Normal Maturity

      20 to 22 is Very Human

      18 to 20 is Average

      16 to 18 is Skidding toward the Infantile

      14 to 16 is Not Grown Up

      12 to 14 is Adolescent

      10 to 12 is Childish

      Below 10 is Infantile[1]

A more scientific test of emotional maturity is the Willoughby EM Scale.[2] The rater may check the items as they apply to others or to himself. The reliability is slightly lower for self-rating. The scoring of the scale represents the pooled judgments of 100 expert students of personality. EM is conceived as "freedom from egoistic or other infantile attachments."

III. IMPRESSIONABILITY OF MATTER

The basis of habit—and memory—is the impressionability of matter. Matter has the capacity to take impressions. Furthermore, the impressions are retained for a period of time.

---

[1] J. G. Frederick: *What Is Your Emotional Age?*
[2] See R. R. Willoughby: *Willoughby EM Scale.* 1931.

Fold a piece of paper and it will fold more readily along the same crease thereafter.   Once a suit has wrinkled, it tends to fall into the same folds from then on.   A sprained ankle is more apt to sprain again.

A. Perseveration.   The tendency of an impression to persist is the basis of perseveration.   On his day off the postman takes a hike and the sailor heads for a gondola in the public garden.   Once a catchy tune takes hold it is hard to shake. The refrain keeps "running through the head" with annoying persistence.   When a teacher gives a pupil a certain grade at the beginning of the semester, a momentum involving inertia impels him to continue the same mark through the final examination.

B. Positive Adaptation.   The threshold for a stimulus may be lowered by practice, or, in other words, impressionability may increase with training.   "Because of practice, the lookout on board ship is able to signal the approach of a vessel more readily than the landsman who stands beside him.   If the situation is such that we always get up when the alarm clock rings, the clock may be moved farther and farther from the bed on successive nights, until we are finally aroused by a sound much too faint to have gotten us out of bed on the first morning.   A physician may develop a positive adaptation to the telephone at night, while his wife sleeps through the disturbance."[1]   We can train ourselves to notice the events in which we are especially interested, as in positive adaptation, or we can train ourselves not to notice events which may detract from our dominant purposes, as in negative adaptation. The determining tendencies may, in some cases, operate unconsciously to turn the effects of repetition toward higher impressionability (positive adaptation) or lower impressionability (negative adaptation).

---

[1] S. Smith and E. R. Guthrie: *General Psychology in Terms of Behavior*, pp. 76–77.   By permission of D. Appleton-Century Company, Inc.

C. Negative Adaptation. If a subliminal stimulus is repeated with gradually increasing intensity, at intervals too long apart to induce summation, the response may not occur when the stimulus reaches or even passes the usual threshold point. Thus the impressionability may be decreased by adaptation, especially when fatigue is involved. If the temperature of a room falls gradually, we fail to notice it. The physician, through continued contact with sickness, becomes inured to the manifestations of suffering. If taxes rise by slow degrees, the increase in burden upon the citizen is imperceptible.

Experimentally, negative adaptation is brought about by so controlling the situation that the undesired response is absent, and the cue which has been responsible for it is present. There are three chief methods for securing such an end. First, the stimulus may be subliminal. Thus a person may lose his fear of cats by handling a kitten. Second, fatigue may be employed. Thus a rider may "break" a horse by sticking it out on the saddle until the animal is too exhausted to rebel any longer. Third, the undesired response may be inhibited by evoking a response incompatible with it. Thus an individual may get used to studying under noisy conditions by starting with a novel that is so exciting as to rule out the distracting effects of the environment.[1]

Habitual risk-taking breeds careless contempt. Figures gathered by the Bureau of Labor Statistics confirm the popular belief that structural steel erectors have a perilous job. There can be no doubt that erecting a skyscraper is dangerous work even with every possible precaution observed. The margin between life and death is small. A slip of the foot, a slight miscalculation of distance, a blow from a beam, and a man is plunging downward to destruction. But even with the haz-

---

[1] See E. R. Guthrie: *The Psychology of Learning*, Chapter V, "Inhibitory Conditioning."

ards inseparably connected with the job, there is an outside factor making for accidents which increases the danger materially. It is the familiarity which breeds, if not contempt, a deadening of the sense of caution. Doing a dangerous thing as a matter of everyday routine soon causes the peril to fade into the background of the mind. It is simply impossible for any one to concentrate his thoughts for hour after hour, day after day, on the same manual task, let it be as dangerous as it will.

Habituation makes it possible for man to endure some of the persistent annoyances of modern urban life. We get used to noises, smoky air, interruptions, bustling crowds, and bill collectors. As one views the monstrous conditions under which human beings live, one marvels at man's meekness and complacency. A salesman for air conditioning informs his prospective clients:

Every day we eat three pounds of food, drink four pounds of liquids and breathe 34 pounds of air. Perhaps some of us eat more than we should and drink things we shouldn't. The point is, we spend thousands of dollars and give a lot of thought to what we eat and drink. But to the one thing we consume the most of, we give never a thought.

The air we breathe in cities is heavy with soot and other foreign matter. In St. Louis, 600 tons of soot per square mile falls every month, and in Chicago 1430 tons. Boston air is relatively clean, but our monthly deposit must be at least 300 tons. This together with other impurities seeps into our homes and offices. All the air we breathe is charged with it. We wouldn't dream of eating bad food or drinking impure water, but we complacently breathe dirty air. Air conditioning corrects that situation. . . .

The argument sounds convincing, but it is likely to lose its efficacy in so far as the client has become negatively adapted to the horrible conditions described. The air is filthy, but what do we care?

A young man had a job in a factory where heavy machinery

jarred the whole building. He was not very robust, and he did not like the jar of the machinery—which is to say, he could not or did not care to work out for himself a negative adaptation. Instead, one day he brought a rubber mat to the factory, and stood on it. At once he found relief. The jar did not annoy him when he stood on the mat. After several days, somebody stole his mat. So he got two pieces of rubber and nailed them on his heels. This idea gave him two little rubber mats that nobody could steal. The name of the young man was O'Sullivan. If he had been more inclined to negative adaptation, he would not be heading the largest firm for the manufacture of rubber heels in the world today.[1]

Even the appeal of intriguing pleasure tends to fade under continued repetition, until ennui sets in.

There is in debauchery something so intrinsically dull, something so absolutely and hopelessly dismal, that it is only the rarest beings, gifted with much less than the usual amount of intelligence and much more than the usual intensity of appetite, who can go on actively enjoying a regular course of vice or continue actively to believe in its wickedness.

Most habitual debauchees are debauchees, not because they enjoy debauchery, but because they are uncomfortable when deprived of it. Habit converts luxurious enjoyments into dull and daily necessities. The man who has formed a habit of women or gin, of pipe-smoking or flagellation, finds it as difficult to live without his vices as to live without bread and water, even though the actual practice of the vice may have become in itself as unexciting as eating a crust or drinking a glass from the kitchen tap. Habit is as fatal to a sense of wrong-doing as to active enjoyment. . . . It is difficult for a routine to seem wicked.[2]

D. The Learning Curve. The decreasing effectiveness of persistent repetition in the learning process indicates that the most efficient method for acquiring any skill involves the wise

---

[1] Adapted from H. N. Casson: *Will-power in Business*. 1931.

[2] Aldous Huxley: *Point Counter Point*, p. 217. Doubleday, Doran & Company, Inc., 1928.

distribution of practice periods.   If the beginner goes at his task too rapidly, he soon becomes stale.   The rate of acquiring a skill may be represented by a learning curve.

At certain stages in the learning process no further improvement is made. This stage is known as a plateau. The retarded progress may be partly due to fatigue and partly due to the limit of the method of procedure. A change in method, indeed, may mean slow progress for

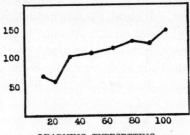

LEARNING TYPESETTING

The vertical axis represents the amount of type set per hour. The horizontal axis represents the number of hours of practice.[1]

a while, during the time the person is mastering the new technique.   In learning to typewrite, for example, the beginner first learns the keys for the separate letters.   The next step is to type, not in letters, but in words.   Then a further stage is typing in phrases.   And so on.   Practice in each stage may show a rapid improvement at the beginning, known as positive initial acceleration, but later a limit is reached.   Then a period of no progress or slow progress may set in during which a new stage in execution is being mastered.   As practice perfects the new mode of skill, a further improvement is achieved.

The acquisition of any habit may be represented by a curve which furnishes graphic evidence that practice must be distributed and new modes of procedure acquired, if the maximum proficiency is to be achieved.

IV. CHILD TRAINING

The modern emphasis on habit has aroused a widespread interest in child training as a part of the general program of

[1]C. M. Celley and H. A. Carr: "Curve of Learning in Typesetting," *Journal of Experimental Psychology*, 1924, 7, 447–455.

mental hygiene. The nurture of a healthy personality in the child is the responsibility of those who mould the characters of the young through the technique they use in handling them. The personality of the child may be loaded with neurotic traits, such as whining, rebelling, and flying into tantrums, or it may be blessed with healthy traits, such as thoughtfulness, kindness, and self-control, according to the wisdom of the guardians. The child must be socialized. He must learn to be responsive to the interests of others. Socialization is the main task of education.

Parents often do not take the bad habits of a child seriously, because they think the unfortunate modes of behavior will be laid aside as he grows older. Nothing could be more illusory. Children do not usually outgrow habits. The tendency is to grow into them. Life is not divided into a series of independent eras. The child is, indeed, father to the man. The career of an individual is a total pattern, every incident in every stage of life contributing its bit to the mosaic of personality. Great care should be taken, therefore, to start the child wisely, and to direct the course of his development with a view to its ultimate completion.

The idea of a career as a total pattern is an important one to keep in mind in the education of the new generation. Take, for example, the problem of obedience. Parental authority, to be effective, must be relentlessly insistent. Once rebellion is tolerated, the cause of discipline is lost. Yet the obedient child who is easy to manage may grow into the timid and obsequious sort of adult who is a social liability rather than an asset. Rigid authority must gradually give way to the maturing intelligence and initiative of the child. The child, too, deserves respect. His search for the independence of maturity should be wisely encouraged.

Another general principle in child guidance is to regard unfortunate habits as symptoms, the cure for which must be found in the underlying sources of the disorder. Thumb-sucking, for example, is a symptom of emotional malad-justment. If the feeding experience is incomplete in its satisfactions, either because of faulty physical equipment of the mother, inadequate milk supply, too rapid flow of milk, or, as in many cases, the more intangible negatives furnished the child by the mother's attitudes of unresponsiveness and rejec-tion, a whole series of feeling tones of a more unsatisfying kind are prone to develop. In children who are deprived on either the physical or the emotional level, substitute pleasures de-velop. One of the most common is thumb-sucking. This behavior response is due to the child's need for finding a means of completing his cravings for pleasure, which are not being met in a more natural way.

Thumb-sucking treated by threats, punishment, or artificial restraint, is not cured. The parent who attacks the problem in this way is failing. The punishment or restraint to which the child is exposed only augments the negative values already established and the consequent emotional damage that in-evitably follows. In the nursing situation the mother satisfies the child's need for love as well as his hunger cravings. A denial of the breast before the child is ready to wean himself is liable to evoke unhappy reactions. There are satisfying ways of preparing the child for this next step in growing up. Since the sudden withdrawal of the breast is sometimes necessitated due to illness or sometimes to insufficient nutritive value of the milk or to loss of the supply, it is advisable to introduce the use of a bottle at least once a day from the beginning. In this way, the bottle is identified as a source of satisfaction at the same time as the breast, and, if the mother holds the child in the same relative position during the bottle feeding as at breast feeding, little negative value seems to be produced. The in-troduction of new and pleasing foods such as orange or prune juice by spoon feeding facilitates the further transition to more mature food habits. The pleasurable element of the taste would seem to offset the displeasure of the new reality. Taking the last few drops from the cup, if made an adventure by the mother's enthusiasm, helps to make the passage to the more grown-up levels with a minimum of dissatisfaction and conflict.[1]

Habit clinics have been established in many of our towns and cities to advise parents in regard to the problems of child training. An expert staff, well versed in psychiatry, psychology, and social work, lends its counsel to fathers and mothers who are baffled by the problems involved in the rearing of their children. The *Parents' Magazine* has been developed to impart the wisdom of mental hygiene to puzzled elders. Dr. Karl Menninger runs a column in The *Ladies' Home Journal* where he answers questions concerning problems of emotional adjustment. The entire program of guidance is a recognition of the vital importance of correct habit formation.

Certainly the mental health of the child is just as important as his physical health. Parents have long been interested in the problems of physical hygiene, but it is only recently that due attention has been directed toward mental hygiene. Parents, somehow, resented advice as to how to bring up their children. Once at the close of a lecture before parents by Watson, a dear old lady arose and said, "Thank God, my children are grown—and that I had a chance to enjoy them before I met you."[2] The older attitude of antipathy toward mental hygiene, however, is changing to one of enthusiastic acceptance. As the awareness of problems becomes more vivid, an eagerness for scientific advice is growing, a good omen for the future.

How are habits formed? This question can best be answered by considering specific habits.

---

[1] See Marion E. Kenworthy: "Social Maladjustments (Emotional) in the Intellectually Normal," *Mental Hygiene*, 1930, 14, 837–852.

[2] J. B. Watson: *Psychological Care of Infant and Child*, p. 69.

A. Some Specific Habits. *1. Eating.* The obvious purpose of eating is to supply the fuel necessary for the bodily metabolism. The consumption of a meal is attended by many rituals which may engender bad habits. The fundamental mistake committed by parents is the assumption that a certain amount of food must be consumed at every meal if health is to be maintained. Feeling it is the child's duty to eat, they coax and threaten him until an issue is made out of the situation. The child uses the opportunity to become the center of attention. Where the meal should be a matter of course, it becomes a drama. Parental indifference is essential to impress upon the child the routine nature of eating. He should not be scolded for failing to eat or praised for consuming the provender.

A child should be given every encouragement to form the proper eating habits. He should have his meals served in the dining room, if possible, or in the kitchen if there is not too much bustle or confusion around him. He should not eat in the playroom. He should not be allowed to bring his toys to the table. Furthermore, he should eat alone, instead of dining with adults who are privileged to indulge in items of diet denied to the younger members of the family.

Idling over the meal should not be tolerated. The child should be given a generous amount of time to finish his meal and then it should be removed without any words of reproach. No ill effects will be suffered from missing most of the meal or all of it. After being deprived of a meal or two, and being denied any sustenance between meals, hunger will become intense enough to insure the consumption of the following repast without protest.

Dawdling over the food may be a means of postponing a disagreeable task. Idling over the breakfast, for example, may be due to a distaste for school. Dawdling is a symptom, and the cause is to be found in a study of the child's whole routine.

Wherever possible, therefore, mealtime should be followed by pleasant diversions which will furnish an incentive to eat without unnecessary "stalling."

Whims are readily developed in regard to certain foods, particularly vegetables. To cure the child of such caprices, the vegetables may be served first with the understanding that nothing else will be available until they are entirely consumed. If the child refuses to eat the vegetables, remove them and dismiss him from the table.

It is wise to serve the meal in courses, so that the child is not compelled to face a task that seems overwhelming. Eating a little at a time, he does not become aware of how much he is storing away.

Warning should be given in advance of an approaching meal so that the child is given a fair opportunity to adjust his play activities accordingly. It is not fair to the child to issue an immediate call and to expect him to drop everything at once in response to the summons. His legitimate rights deserve respect.

2. Sleeping. Another important bit of child training is the formation of proper sleeping habits. As in the establishment of any habits, regularity is essential. The bedtime of the child should not be adjusted to the convenience of adults who may find that he interferes with their social life.

A child deserves a bedroom of his own where he can rest undisturbed. He should sleep alone. Parents are unwise who take their children into bed with them, as such a procedure encourages unhealthy fixations. Once a child refuses to go to sleep without the comforting presence of an adult and succeeds in getting his way, difficulties are in store for the parents. Elders must learn to steel themselves to the plaintive appeals of crying offspring who will use any excuse to summon aid.

Relaxation is a necessary preliminary to sleep. Coercion may make sleep impossible. The importance of the child's going to sleep is often overemphasized by adults. The afternoon nap may become a real problem, on this account. Since the important thing is rest, relaxation should be stressed. Before the child knows it, he will have dropped off into slumber. A person cannot make himself go to sleep and he cannot force sleep upon anybody else, either. Sleep is more apt to steal over one when one least suspects it. When the proper conditions are set, that is, when a regular time is unequivocally insisted upon, when comparative quiet is assured, and when a peaceful state of mind is encouraged, drowsiness soon ebbs into sleep.

3. Elimination. Control of the excretory functions is important not only for sanitary reasons, but also for its influence upon character. Discipline in these matters is one of the first lessons in self-control. The socializing of these functions is absolutely vital. The poor training given in this field is many times the cause of much trouble during not only the first five or even ten years of childhood, but also often in later life.

Regularity, again, is essential. Elimination can be conditioned by training to occur at definite intervals. The child should be left alone in the room so that no disturbances may interfere with the processes of excretion. A time limit should be followed.

Enuresis of a nocturnal order is often a serious problem. Bedwetting may be due to a number of factors. A very vital one is excitement. Playing strenuously after supper is likely to produce a state of tension conducive to enuresis.

The parental attitude is highly important. Too great a sense of shame is sometimes inculcated in the child. Wetting garments may become the basis of a profound inferiority complex, affecting the total personality. The shame attached to faulty elimination may lead to unfortunate psychological consequences more serious than any material damage that may be done. Training a child should proceed as objectively as house-breaking a dog. The principles of conditioning are the same in both cases. Clinical consultation may be very helpful to parents who face the problem of establishing proper habits of elimination in their children.

4. Sex. According to Watson, the love response is elicited by stroking the erogenous zones, such as the lips and the breasts. The infant child loves anyone who strokes and feeds it. There is no "instinctive" love of a child for its parents. The child sees the mother's face when she pets him. Soon, the mere sight of her face, by conditioning, calls out the love response.

It is a harsh statement to assert that parental love is often very selfish. It is easy, for the sake of one's own pleasure, to love the child more than is good for him. Affection often interferes with the development of healthy habits in the young by preventing the objective attitude which is essential to sound training. A bachelor, therefore, may be the wisest counselor in matters of bringing up a child. At least, he has not been humbled by wayward offspring. Parents often love their children, not wisely, but too well. A nursery-school training may be necessary to offset the faults inculcated in the young by doting parents and relatives.

Parents fondle their children too much.[1] Let the parent kiss the child once on the forehead at night, if he must lose control of himself, and shake hands with him in the morning. It sounds absurd—it is certainly unsentimental—but many bad habits would be avoided if such a program were conscientiously followed. A caress is often an encouragement to the child to take advantage of the doting elder.

Parental love is dangerous because it fosters those nest habits of invalidism. "Bless its little heart" is the kind of babying that is not conducive to growing up. Marital rela-

---

[1] John B. Watson: "Should a Child Have More Than One Mother?" *Liberty*, June 29, 1929.

tions, in later years, may suffer from such childhood nest habits, as mother's boy demands the petting Mother gave him, and his wife demands the coddling Father gave her, neither of them being able to effect an adjustment on a mature level.

Another important aspect of sex training is the inculcation of a healthy attitude toward the sexual life.   By evasions and lies, parents impress the child that love is something shameful. The untruthfulness of the stork story is soon discovered.   Indeed, in later years, he will learn that the only truth in the story is the big bill.   Children's curiosity and implicit faith should be met with frankness and truthfulness.   No more need be told than is asked for, but what is revealed should be honest. Thus truthfulness will be encouraged in the child, and also an attitude toward sex that will make possible a happy love life when the mating period arrives.   So much of our happiness depends on successful love that it does seem as if parents should give more attention to wise training in this direction.

5. Anger.   Anger is evoked by hampering the infant's movements.   Dressing the infant with modern clothes gives us almost a laboratory set up for building in rage behavior. Temper is called out almost every time the infant is dressed, undressed, or changed.

Temper tantrums are often encouraged in a child by the poor example of a raging parent.   Discipline should be imposed calmly but firmly.   The parent who loses his temper and spanks a child viciously is liable to establish the same habits of rage in his victim.   A youngster should in no case be granted a favor which he has sought by means of a tantrum.   "Giving in" to appease him is merely building in a bad habit more firmly.   See to it that he gains no ends through the tantrum. Make his rage highly unpleasant for him.

6. Fear.   Fear is evoked in an infant by a loud noise or the sudden loss of support.   If Watson is correct in asserting that these are the only two stimuli occasioning fear in an infant, and if one pauses to consider the variety of stimuli of which adults are afraid, one will appreciate how much training has done to make people fearful. Children's fears are home grown. The parents do the emotional planting and the cultivating. There is good evidence to show that such early built-in fears last throughout the lifetime of the individual.

A child is not instinctively afraid of the dark. A loud noise in the dark, caused by a falling screen or a flying shade, will build-in such a fear. Playing "bogey man" or frightening the child with stories of goblins will produce a fear of darkness. A trembling mother picking up a child during a thunderstorm and huddling in a corner in a terror-stricken attitude will cultivate a fear which may last throughout life.

The stimulation of fear is useful in securing discipline. The method, however, is grossly abused. To train a child in the avoidance of an undesirable activity, a painful stimulus should be objectively applied immediately upon the commission of the deed, if the conditioning is to be effective. Waiting until Father gets home to inflict the punishment is poor psychology. It is practically impossible to condition a negative response where the painful stimulus is postponed. It would be ideal if tabooed objects could supply the punishment themselves. If a precious vase could provide an electric shock, thus rendering parental discipline unnecessary, the problem of training a child would be vastly simplified.

"Don't touch" is a frequent admonition directed at the child. Unfortunately a youngster is often warned to leave a harmful object alone, not because the object itself is dangerous, but merely because Mother or Father says so. Thus a child may avoid fire in order to please Mother whereas it would be wiser if he learned to avoid fire in order to escape physical harm. This point in the technique of training is stressed because adults often guide their conduct by what their parents once told them when they were children, instead of directing their activities in reference to the actual consequences of their deeds as observed from their own study of their own personal experiences.

B. General Principles. On the basis of our study of training we can formulate some general principles in accordance with which habits may be effectively formed or broken.

1. Forming Habits. a. Get started immediately on the formation of the habit. A person must seize the first opportunity to act on every resolution he makes and to capitalize on every emotional prompting he may experience in the direction of the habits he aspires to gain. The individual must not put off until tomorrow what he knows he should be doing today, as the habit of procrastination grows with practice, too. Evasion of a disagreeable task is paralyzing.

b. Fortify each resolution with as many efficient motives as possible. Training should begin with a strong initiative. All the possible circumstances should be organized to reënforce the right motives; such as making engagements incompatible with the old, or taking a public pledge, if the case allows. Thus the new beginning will be given such a momentum that the temptation to break down will not be likely to occur. Every moment of success contributes its increment to the establishment of the desirable habit.

Utilizing the technique of reward and punishment, the individual should concentrate on the pleasant consequences of his habit, fit it into the scheme of his interests, and remind himself constantly of the rewards of success.

An author found that he stalled in the morning to avoid writing. He would sit down after breakfast, light his pipe, and read the newspaper for several hours. Realizing that his tendency toward procrastination was becoming seriously detrimental to his professional success, he decided to deny himself his pipe until he started work in the morning. His longing for a smoke encouraged him to begin his labors as soon as breakfast was over.

c. Never allow an exception to occur. Continuity of training is absolutely essential. If a parent wants his child to obey, he must see to it that the first command is heeded. Calling a child until the fifth time without getting a response establishes the habit of disobedience four times as firmly as the habit of obedience.

d. Distribute practice wisely. Repetition imbeds a habit most effectively if it is not carried out so continuously as to produce fatigue and staleness. Diversion by means of other compatible interests, in easing the grind, encourages the formation of the habit.

2. Breaking Habits. Breaking a habit is a difficult task because it involves not only learning a new habit, but also unlearning an old one. For this reason, athletic coaches often prefer a greenhorn. A football star in high school acquired the habit of running back when he was circling an end. He was so fast that he could elude tacklers and make substantial gains. When he entered college, a brilliant football career was predicted for him. In faster circles, however, his old habit could not succeed; since he had run backward in carrying the ball for so many years, his coaches did not consider it worth their while to use him in the line-up, lest he score for the opposing team.

It is wise to learn a thing correctly in the first place. Then it will be as difficult to do it wrong as it is for a person who has learned it wrong to do it right. If a parent makes it a practice of leaving a child's bedroom door open when he puts the youngster to bed, it will cause a disturbance if the door is closed some night. In reverse, if the child is trained to have the door closed, it is impossible to leave it open without incurring displeasure.

Attention should be directed upon the new habit. The less

heed given the old habit, the better.   A change in surroundings and a cultivation of new interests may prove effective in reducing one's thoughts about the old habit.

As a general policy in breaking an undesirable habit, it is wise to attack the problem with a definite suddenness.   According to Confucius, "one conquers a bad habit more easily today than tomorrow."   By plunging into the new program of conduct, a protracted struggle may be avoided.   Success at the outset is imperative.   It is well, therefore, to give the new habit every possible advantage.   Abrupt acquisition of the new habit is the best way, if there be a real possibility of carrying it out; but we must be careful not to give the will so stiff a task as to insure its defeat at the very outset.

Several definite methods have been devised for breaking habits.   One is repeating the habit itself.   Dunlap has conducted some experiments to test the hypothesis that repetition may be employed in the dissolving of habits as well as in the formation of habits.[1]   For example, he broke himself of typing "hte" by typing "hte" voluntarily throughout several practice periods, reminding himself meanwhile that this was a "word" that he would not write in the future unless he wrote it deliberately.

Another method is unconditioning, which may be carried out by the gradual reduction of the stimulus or by the association of a pleasurable stimulus with the unpleasant one.   If a child has been accustomed to sleep with a light on, he may be unconditioned by dimming the light slightly each night.   Done gradually, the habit is broken without creating a disturbance. A child may be relieved of the fear of an object if the object is repeatedly presented in a pleasant situation.   A girl lost her fear of her bedroom, where she had experienced terrifying dreams, by working out a program with the guidance of a

[1]See Knight Dunlap: *Habits: Their Making and Unmaking*, Chapter X, "The Breaking of Specific Bad Habits."   1932.

psychologist. She repainted her bedroom furniture and invited her chum to tea in the room. The association of pleasant times with the room removed the fear.

Other methods of breaking a habit may be illustrated by the curing of fears.

Discussion may be used. Assure the child he has nothing to fear. Reason it all out with him. If he fears rabbits, read *Peter Rabbit* and talk the story over with him. This method is not very effective.

Disuse is another method which is not very efficient. Shield the child from the feared object for a time.

Ridicule may be resorted to, but it is not very effective.

Social example is helpful in many cases. A little girl who was afraid to submit to a physical examination became reassured when another girl "showed her the way."

Repetition, in some instances, works successfully. By frequent exposure the child gets used to the object, that is, becomes negatively adapted.

3. Reëducation. The replacement of bad habits with good habits, or the formation of new habits to replace habits which have been lost, is known as reëducation.

New habits must sometimes be developed to replace habits which have been lost. If a soldier has lost his right arm and he has been right-handed in his motor habits, he must be trained to perform with his left hand. Try stirring your coffee with your right hand, if you are right-handed, and notice how skillfully and readily you carry out the action. Then shift the spoon to the left hand and try to duplicate the graceful movements of the right hand. Unless you are ambidextrous, you will discover an awkwardness you would hardly believe possible. The degree of difficulty you experience is a proximate measure of the problem you would face if you had to make your adjustments with your left hand. With the establishment of a proper mental attitude, the utilization of effective incentives, and the employment of a definite technique, many persons with handicaps, either physical or mental, are being reëducated to adapt themselves adequately to the tasks of daily life.[1]

Frequently new habits must be established to replace faulty habits. Reëducation would be unnecessary, many times, if education had been wise in the beginning. Unfortunately, however, many of us acquire habits in our childhood which prevent successful adjustments in the adult stage. The adult may be unable to meet his problems happily without knowing the sources of his failure since they go back to forgotten experiences of childhood. The task of the psychiatrist is to unravel the career of his patient, to discover faulty conditionings in the early training, and then to recondition through the formation of healthy habits to supplant the old. Leaning too much upon others may have to be superseded by the development of independence and self-reliance. Reëducation reveals the situations out of which the unwholesome attitude originated, and then proceeds to build in a normal pattern of adult behavior.

One project in reëducation is the cure of the alcoholic habit. While alcoholism is an adult disorder, the basis for its genesis may go back to faulty habit training in childhood.

Alcoholism is a disease of immaturity, regardless of the actual age of the individual suffering from it. The drunkard is not only a child, but a spoiled child. He has far too keen a sensibility for likes and dislikes, chiefly the latter. By trying to avoid everything unpleasant, and to make what he cannot avoid artificially enjoyable, he reaches a state wherein he likes nothing when sober. He must be reëducated in a manner that will show him that, while a diversity of interests is desirable, it is not necessary to like everything, nor is it possible to escape entirely from unpleasant duties.[2]

---

[1] See S. I. Franz: *Nervous and Mental Reëducation*. 1924. See especially Chapter III, "Mental Attitude and Incentive."
[2] Richard R. Peabody: *The Common Sense of Drinking*. 1931. Reprinted by permission of Little, Brown & Co.

The alcoholic must want to be cured for his own good. He must avoid occasions where wine, women, and song encourage drinking. He must avoid daydreaming about the joys of by-gone parties, and, instead, concentrate his thoughts on the unhappy hangovers, the days of inefficiency at the office, and the sorrow that his indulgence has brought his family. The crux of the reëducation lies in the emphasis on positive thoughts of the benefits to be derived from abstinence. This general method applies to reëducation for any sort of habit.

V. THE RELATIONSHIPS BETWEEN HABITS

Habits sometimes interfere with each other. A bad habit in golf, for example, will interfere with the acquisition of the correct habit. Lunging at the ball makes it difficult to execute a well-balanced swing.

Sometimes habits reinforce each other. The habit of violating one law may breed a disrespect for all laws.

Will a habit established in one line of activity carry over to some other line of endeavor? This problem is the problem of transfer of training. The answer to it is not so simple as most persons believe, for it is very generally assumed that transfer is the usual thing. The question deserves a close examination. Will the person who develops a habit of carelessness in translating his Latin assignment find that this habit will carry over to his Mathematics where he may, for some reason, desire to be accurate? Educational policies have been based on the assumption that transfer invariably takes place. Football, for example, is advocated on the ground that the hard bodily contacts and the spirit of "do or die" teach the players lessons that are invaluable for enduring the hard knocks of life in the world of affairs. But will the athlete who gives himself unflinchingly to the game on the playing field, devote himself with the same unsparing enthusiasm to his studies in the classroom? Probably, no!

Whether transfer will occur in any particular situation may be somewhat determined in the light of what we now know about the specificity of habits. It is customary to speak of a person as an honest or a dishonest man, implying that he is honest or dishonest, as the case may be, in all situations. We are all familiar with the fact, however, that a man who is scrupulously honest in his business may kick his ball out of a bad lie on a golf course. A child may cheat on the playground who would not think of cheating in the schoolroom. A person may eat with a foreigner in the school lunchroom, but will draw the line on drinking a soda with him at the drugstore.

An investigation has been made of character organization which has shown that habits are specifically established to meet specific situations.

In proportion as situations are alike, conduct is correlated. In proportion as situations are unlike, conduct is uncorrelated. . . . Deception, helpfulness, coöperation, persistence, and inhibition were groups of specific habits rather than general traits. We found that, when situations involving the possibility of deception were almost identical, the behavior did not greatly vary from occasion to occasion. But when the situations permitting dishonesty were altered, as when one moves from a classroom to a party or an athletic contest or has the opportunity to steal money rather than to copy the answers of a test from an answer sheet, then there was considerable alteration in the practice of deception. As the situations became less and less alike there was found greater and greater diversity of behavior, so that one could not predict from what a person did in one situation what he would do in a different situation. . . . A child does not have a uniform generalized code of morals but varies his opinions to suit the situations in which he finds himself. . . . Knowledge of right and wrong is a specific matter to be applied to specific situations which the child encounters in his daily living. . . . There seem to be different codes for different situations, that is, a home code, a school code, a Sunday-school code, a club code.[1]

[1]From H. Hartshorne, M. A. May, and Frank K. Shuttleworth: *Studies in the Organization of Character*, pp. 373, 1, 108, 105. 1930. By permission of The Macmillan Company, publishers.

A specific habit is developed to meet a specific situation. An individual personality may be made up of unintegrated habits where the element of transfer is negligible, as is so well illustrated in the insane person who may talk intelligently on some topics and rant on others. Habits are specific. The child who brings home a report card with an A in deportment may be an unmanageable rascal in the family group. The gasoline station attendant who demonstrates remarkable courtesy in asking after the oil may be very rude to the grocer at the store. A man may exercise critical judgment in matters scientific and be gullible in matters religious.

Habits are specific. Transfer occurs in some instances because there are identical elements present to encourage an integration. Long before Ann Harding became an actress she aspired to be a business woman, and her first job was as typist and file clerk for a life insurance company at $12.50 a week. Her zeal and ability soon raised her to a responsible position, where, instead of taking dictation, she dictated her own letters into a dictaphone. It was not long before she found that her letters were coming back to her badly typed— obviously the work of inexperienced girls. She found out that the best typists claimed the best dictaphone records, and that hers did not rank in that category. At once she set to work to perfect her voice and enunciation—to space her words correctly, to accent the important syllables, and to speak with distinctness. What she learned from this has been of inestimable value to her in her stage and talking-picture career.

The appreciation of general principles may facilitate transfer from one illustrative case to another. A student manager of a college hockey team was outstanding in the efficiency with which he discharged his managerial functions. In fact, he was so thorough as to lead the observer to wonder if there were not some peculiar reason to account for his untiring industry. When he was asked to account for the enthusiasm about his work, he explained that he looked upon his managership as a real opportunity to prepare himself for business. Indeed, training as a student manager will undoubtedly benefit him in business, because he saw the relationship between his college activity and his prospective business career. Through such organization of experience, one habit may reinforce another to good effect. Without integration, habits that are in the least incompatible are liable to interfere with each other. Since, as we have noted, habits are specific, transfer is not likely to occur unless there is a recognition of a common principle, or unless there is an effort made toward integration. Further discussion of transfer will follow in the chapter on intelligence where we shall consider, among other questions, whether school success is a presage of success in later life.

VI. CHARACTERISTICS OF HABITUAL ACTION

There are four characteristics of habitual action which are worthy of mention: propensity, facility, automaticity, and inertia.

A. Propensity. In a specific situation a person is prone to do what he has done in that specific situation before.

The propensity of habitual action may be described more exactly in terms of the principle of partial identity: "Any part of a situation which causes a definite act may later call forth the same response either in whole or in part."[1] For example, a person may go to his bedroom to dress for dinner, take off his clothes, and retire, only to wonder, suddenly, how he was going to get to sleep in broad daylight.

B. Facility. Habit simplifies the movements required to achieve a given result, makes them more accurate, and diminishes fatigue. The practiced adept proceeds surely and

---

[1] J. R. Butler: *Human Nature: A Guide to Its Understanding*, p. 16. 1933.
See also the principle of redintegration as expounded by H. L. Hollingworth: *Psychology: Its Facts and Principles.* 1928.

rapidly, while the learner continually takes false steps which he must retrace in a bungling manner.   Practice makes perfect sometimes.

The beginner on a piano is very unsure of himself, even when he plays with one hand.   He can never be certain he will strike the key he is aiming at.   When it comes to playing with both hands, he is as a man confronted with a dilemma, not knowing what to do.   After years of practice, the same person may play over the keys readily and accurately with little or no effort.   Language habits follow the same principle.   A person who has been reared in an English-speaking country, finds it very difficult to understand spoken German, no matter how thoroughly he has mastered the vocabulary.

Applying the principle of partial identity, it is clear that a uniform manner of performing an act facilitates the execution of that act, for when the conditions recur in the customary fashion, the response regularly called out by that particular situation is the more readily evoked.

Writing is performed with more facility if it is always carried out according to standard conditions.   A newspaperman, at a rickety typewriter in the tobacco-stained corner of a hurly-burly newspaper office, turned out copy that made his name famous among editors.   At the request of a magazine he wrote a story, working it out after hours on the same old typewriter in the same old corner.   The story was such a success that it made him wealthy.   His affluence gave him a chance to realize his life's dream, an elegant office, beautifully decorated and luxuriously outfitted, where bay windows afforded him a restful view.   When the office was finished and a gleaming new typewriter shone upon a magnificent desk, he sat down to write.   He sat, and he sat some more.   His mind remained barren of ideas.   After more fruitless attempts to create something literary, he gave up in desperation, locked the place up, and returned to his old folksy corner in the newspaper office, where he dropped into the old chair, and where, in the midst of the old bustling confusion, he recovered the old inspiration. Things were all right again.

"GOLFER WILL TRY ANYTHING"
(Drawn by Fontaine Fox)

C. Automaticity. An habitual action tends to become automatic, that is, to take place independently of attention.

Few people can tell which shoe is put on first in the morning because the act is so habitual as to require no attention. Skill in any activity depends upon practice that is continued until the exact movements can be executed unconsciously. When consciousness is applied to an activity which has become automatic, the interference is disastrous.

> The centipede was happy quite,
> Until the frog for fun,
> Said "Pray, which leg comes after which?"
> Which wrought his mind to such a pitch,
> He lay distracted in a ditch,
> Considering how to run.

When a person pauses to wonder how a familiar word is spelled, he plunges himself into confusion. Is it b-e-l-i-e-v-e, or is it b-e-l-e-i-v-e? A person who knows the Lord's Prayer by heart may not even remember how it begins if he is suddenly called upon to lead in prayer, and is thereby compelled to think hard on the initial phrase.

Sleep and digestion are habits which proceed most efficiently when least thought is given to them. Insomnia and dyspepsia may be the consequences of unwanted attention.

Habits are performed unconsciously. Biting the nails, coughing, or putting the hands in the pockets may develop without the person's being aware at all that he is doing such things. A nervous chuckle may become so automatic as to entirely escape the chuckler.

The unconscious nature of habit is a significant psychological fact. It means that much of our behavior is motivated by factors of which we are unaware. The training of infancy has produced its effects upon our habit systems without leaving any explicit memories.

A large part of our world is never described in words. No names are given to many of our responses which, therefore, remain unverbalized. Many people cannot describe how they do certain things—their word-world does not correspond to their object-world. The activities of the unstriped muscles and glands, the goings-on in our bodies, are unverbalized. The world of infancy is

totally unverbalized for the first year and remains practically unverbalized until the end of the second year.   This is the period when many thousands of reactions are built in, both manual and emotional.   . . .

May we not say that the *unverbalized* of the behaviorist is a scientific substitute for the unconscious of the psychoanalyst.[1]

The automaticity of habit is an important feature in mental economy.   By relegating much of our activity to unconscious direction, the mind is left free to concentrate on the improvement of its adjustments and on the extension of experience into new fields.   "We must make automatic and habitual, as early as possible, as many useful actions as we can.   . . . The more of the details of our daily life we can hand over to the effortless custody of automatism, the more our higher powers of mind will be set free for their own proper work. There is no more miserable human being than one in whom nothing is habitual but indecision, and for whom the lighting of every cigar, the drinking of every cup, the time of rising and going to bed every day, and the beginning of every bit of work, are subjects of express volitional deliberation.   Full half the time of such a man goes to the deciding, or regretting, of matters which ought to be so ingrained in him as practically not to exist for his consciousness at all."[2]   Unfortunately, habit works against us as well as for us, since bad habits can become second nature as readily as good ones.

D. Inertia.   Once an action has been thoroughly ingrained by long practice, it tends to persist in the same form, even though the environment which first evoked the response may have changed radically in the meantime.   Habit is the basis

[1]J. B. Watson: "The Myth of the Unconscious," *Harper's Magazine*, September, 1927.

[2]William James: *Principles of Psychology*, I, p. 122.   By permission of Henry Holt and Company.

of custom, the inertia of which is notorious. People in modern times cling to the modes of action established by their ancestors ages ago. Thus the American policy of isolation which prevailed in pioneer America at a period when the United States was comparatively cut off from the rest of the world is still advocated by patriotic citizens who are apparently unaware that the situation has undergone a revolutionary transformation since the days of George Washington. It is highly absurd to insist that our country remain aloof from the affairs of other nations, when, economically and otherwise, our own welfare is intimately dependent upon the prosperity of foreign lands. Yet isolationism dies hard, so strong is the pull of custom. Many customs, of course, are still useful in our day. We tend, however, to retain the customary ways of doing things, whether or not they fit our present needs.

Similarly, the habits formed in childhood persist into adulthood, often causing serious maladjustment. The inertia of habit is thus responsible for the arrest of development technically referred to as fixation. A child who is trained in the habit of obedience may become a docile, spineless adult who "has no mind of his own." The intelligent person takes an inventory of his habits at various stages of his growth and discards those which interfere with mature adjustments. Overcoming the inertia involved in reëducation requires considerable effort, and most people prefer to cling to the good old ways, no matter what the cost, rather than to go through the painful process of thinking things through for themselves. Social pressure, indeed, is very powerful in "keeping us in line." Conformity is usually the easiest way out. The desire for approval and the fear of disapproval combine, with a host of other factors, to encourage the inertia which comes so naturally to us. Habit, said James, is the flywheel of society. It insures the standardization which seems so necessary for social stability.

VII. HABIT AND CHARACTER

Character is a system of habits. Our characters are determined by the kinds of habits we form. "We are spinning our own fates, good or evil, and never to be undone. . . . As we become drunkards by so many separate drinks, so we become saints in the moral, and authorities and experts in the practical and scientific spheres, by so many separate acts and hours of work."[1] A sound character is a matter of sound habits. To say that a man has "lots of character" is only to state that he has many habits. Such an ambiguity in language indicates that the relation of habit and character is little understood by "the man in the street."

Weakness of character results from the habitual avoidance of the distasteful tasks of life and the habitual shirking of responsibility. A strong habit is built up against the performance of duty. A student once remarked that his college teachers were softening his fibre and unfitting him for his business career by excusing him from this and from that assignment on the slightest grounds, instead of imposing a stern discipline. The college student can shirk his duties and often get away with it by playing upon the sympathy of his teacher. He gets lazy and lax without paying the penalty. In spite of all the hullabaloo about the importance of character, educators frequently do not make an effort to discover the small ways in which big issues are gradually determined. A coach would never tolerate in his charges the shirking habits that are encouraged day after day in the classroom. That same student confided, "I wish you Profs would be just as hard on us as our boss is going to be later on. Otherwise, we're going to find the going hard."

In one of his speeches, President Frank of the University of Wisconsin said: "I do not covet for my sons any brilliance,

---

[1] William James, *op. cit.*, p. 127.

any magnetism, any striking personal attributes that will open all doors to them at a touch. I covet for them hard jaws and firm muscles, the capacity to stay with their work an hour longer than the other fellow, and to hold on when more brilliant men have decided the thing is too slow and have quit." A strong character, such as Frank covets for his sons, is achieved only by the cultivation of a tenacity of purpose in the small assignments of everyday life. A firm character is the outgrowth of an arduous training in which habits of firmness are resolutely developed.

Will is character in action. The will is a man's total personality as it is represented in his conduct. If a person continually acts against the dictates of his better judgment, and then continually regrets his actions, he will be cursed with a weak will. If a person persistently acts in accordance with his ideals (what he considers valuable), and refuses to swerve from the path of resolution, he will be blessed with a strong will. Will is not something which operates independently of our habitual modes of conduct. Aristotle pointed out, long ago, that a man is not really moral until he is good without having to think about it.

There used to be a lot of discussion about the freedom of the will. Probably there is very little freedom exercised in the lives of most of us because we are, so much, creatures of habit. Once in a while a choice is made, but then the individual must take the consequences. We are free only within the bounds of law. You may be free, let us say, to board or not to board a train. After you have boarded it, the train will take you. So it is with habit. Lay hold of a habit by way of deliberation, practice it, and soon it will have a hold on you.

Freedom used to be conceived merely as a native endowment, a gift from the Lord. It is probably nearer the truth to think of whatever freedom we do possess as an individual achievement. Freedom may be won, and it may be lost.

Many of our habits involve a craving. The formation of such habits often imposes such limitations upon freedom as to reduce the individual to virtual slavery. The appetite for alcohol drives men at times to drink the anti-freeze solutions from automobile radiators. Occasionally, confirmed drunkards beg the police to arrest them and to put them where they cannot "get the stuff." Recidivists have been known to request a sentence to the electric chair because they have come to realize their helplessness in situations tempting them to crime.

It is said that there are a million drug addicts in this country —that virtually one person in every hundred takes drugs regularly. If we think of these people as wilful abusers of their physical and mental health, it is one thing, but if we realize that these people are not "fiends" but sick men and women, our attitudes must change.

It is just as true that the formation of wise habits makes it impossible for a person to act unwisely. If an upright citizen were asked to help rob a bank, he would refuse in no uncertain terms. "I can't do it," he would insist. A violation of his long-established habits would be virtually out of the question.

As the twig is bent, the tree is inclined. Our habits make or break us. A study of their significance is the key to the wisdom of a full and joyous life.

PART V

EFFECTIVE ADAPTATION

In Part V we shall see how the mind functions in securing successful adaptation to environmental and personal demands. Chapter X will describe how the individual ascertains exactly what is going on about him, through *Attending and Perceiving*. Chapter XI will explain how the past is used in the anticipation of the future, through *Remembering and Anticipating*. Chapter XII will reveal the various means by which mental conflicts are solved, in *Mental Conflict*. Chapter XIII will analyze the *Thinking* process through which the individual reasons his way to the beliefs that eventuate in action. Chapter XIV will seek to discover what is meant by intelligence, by an investigation of *Intelligent Adjustment*.

CHAPTER X

ATTENDING AND PERCEIVING

W<small>E NOTED</small> in Chapter IV the rôle of the receptors in the accurate detection of stimuli. In the present chapter the processes through which the individual becomes aware of events will be studied with more emphasis upon their psychological nature. Briefly, something is vaguely sensed, it is attended to, it is clearly perceived, and overt movements are executed in response to the stimulation.

I. ACCURATE ADJUSTMENT

Attending is an activity making for clearer perception. Where you attend determines what you will perceive, and how well you attend determines how clearly you will perceive.

Experience is characterized by varying degrees of clearness.[1] As you are reading this passage, a man may be whistling on the street outside, or your clock may be ticking on your mantelpiece. If you are attending to this page, the experience of its contents will be more distinct to you than the waves propagated by the whistler or the clock. If the musical passerby should fire a gun, you would immediately cease to give heed to this discussion.

The phenomenon just mentioned may be described in various ways. One is to state that your experience varies in its degrees of clearness. The page may be clearer than the whistling or vice versa. Another is to explain it in terms of

[1]E. B. Titchener: *Lectures on the Elementary Psychology of Feeling and Attention.* 1908.

levels of consciousness, one stimulus being perceived on the conscious level, the other on the subconscious level. Another mode of description is in terms of focus and margin, in which

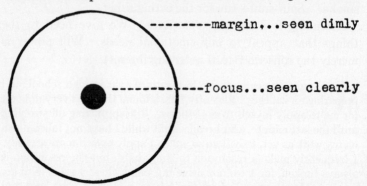

the field of consciousness is conceived on the analogy of the visual field. You see clearly what you are looking at directly, and less clearly the stimuli on the periphery. Experience is comparable to a flashlight which illumines most brilliantly the object at which it points, fading on the fringes into darkness. Still another way to describe the same experience is by figure and ground. Holding the illustration at arm's length, what do you see?[1] You may see two profiles or a vase, depending on whether you take the

black as the figure and the white as the ground (background), or vice versa. The figure is clearer than the ground.

[1] From E. Rubin: *Visuell wahrgenommene Figuren.* 1921.

Viewed behavioristically, attending consists in wrinkling the brows, squinting the eyes, inhibiting movement, checking respiration, and executing an adequate motor response. Smell smoke? Sniff-sniff—run for the extinguisher.

Attending is a matter of interest. We give heed to the things that appeal to our emotional needs. Will power is merely the consequence of a driving interest.

I am a girl 16 years of age, in my third year in high school, and preparing for college. Recently I have found that it is very difficult for me to apply myself to my studies. I keep putting off studying until the last minute, and I realize that while I have not fallen down on my work as yet, I shall do so unless I apply myself more steadily. I frequently make a resolution to study hard, but the resolution is always broken, for I cannot drive my mind where I want it to go. . . . My question is how can I force myself to work first and play afterward.[1]

She cannot drive her mind, she says, where she wants it to go. The explanation for her failure is that she does not want her mind to go to her studies, though she is trying hard to persuade herself that she does. If she were interested in her studies, the problem would readily be solved. If, for example, she were wholly dependent upon her own efforts for her livelihood, and if she were studying law with the success of her legal career hanging upon her school record, the motivation would be strong enough to overcome her inertia. Probably she would be wise to give up pining for a college education which she does not really crave.

"I cannot pay attention" is a frequent complaint. It is, however, psychologically fallacious, since the individual actually can pay attention—to the wrong things. Attention is pointed in the direction of our interests. To achieve a full understanding of the nature of attention, we must turn again to the topic of Chapter VII, the rôle of bias or set.

---

[1] From a question asked of Dr. Cadman.

II. SET

Below is a diagram.[1] Study the locations of the numbers on the chart for thirty seconds.

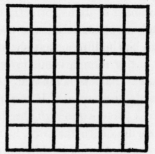

Cover the chart. Fill in the numbers on the chart below in their proper locations. Now fill in anything else on the chart

which you can remember. Uncover the original chart, and check your performance. How many numbers did you locate correctly?

Did you notice the words?

```
    B       N
    O   O
      SD
      NT
    O   O
    L       N
```

---

[1]Borrowed, with modifications, from an experiment by Külpe.

If you carried out the initial instructions, you should have located the numbers more accurately than the letters or miscellaneous figures on the chart. If you did not do what you were told, your behavior is a reflection on your intelligence.

A. Selectivity. The superior accuracy in locating the numbers on the chart indicates that we perceive more clearly the stimuli to which we attend. The experiment also demonstrates that the set determines the direction of attention. The bias, attitude, or interest is the determining tendency. We report best on what we are set for.

Cancellation tests may be used to measure attentive capacity. The subject is instructed to mark out, with maximum speed and accuracy, certain designated recurring items on a page of material. If the time-limit method is employed, the score will be the number of items correctly crossed out within a given time, usually two minutes; if the work-limit method is used, the score will be the time necessary to complete the list plus a penalty of one or more seconds for each item omitted. Various kinds of material are available. One form of cancellation test consists of a series of letters printed in random sequence. The task is to cross out the letter "a." Other tests consist of digits or geometrical forms. Münsterberg used a newspaper page in testing telephone operators, requiring them to cross out a certain letter. Perception and speed of movement are involved in the process of selecting the specified items and cancelling them.

Another measure of attention is card sorting. Link devised such a test in which forty-nine cards were employed, each card bearing from seven to twelve letters. Twenty of the forty-nine cards contained the letter "O." The subject was instructed to sort the cards into two piles, placing in one pile the cards containing the letter "O" and in the other pile the cards not containing the letter "O." His test results correlated .55

with skill in inspecting shells, a vocation demanding quick movement and rapid hand-eye coördination.[1]

Since the range of attention is limited, attending must inevitably be selective, like the magnet which picks the nails out of the sawdust. Attending to one thing means diverting attention from another. In looking at a jigsaw puzzle the design of the cutting is not apparent when the puzzle is picture side up; indeed, it is practically impossible to select out the cutting design. If the puzzle is turned over on the reverse side, the clear prominence of the cutting design is very striking.

Selection is in accordance with the dominant interests. On a cold day during the war, a soldier lay down under a booming cannon for a nap. He slept soundly, undisturbed by the explosions. His major happened along. "Jones, get up. What's the matter with you?" he ordered in a firm but quiet tone. Jones immediately awoke. Thus a mother will sleep through the noise of traffic but will be awakened instantly by her infant's cry—while Daddy sleeps on and on. The prospective bride notices chinaware, mops, garbage pails, and ice boxes in the store windows she had often passed before without heed. Go through a book you read two years ago, and see how you discover statements you had not even noted in a previous perusal. New interests acquired during the interval set you to notice with a new selectivity.

Concentration requires a set for concentration. This set is a matter of interest. Voluntary attention[2] is often painful because distracting stimuli have more appeal. The passing fire-engine is more enticing than the psychology lesson. "Taking pains" requires a strong interest for its sustenance. Every motive should be utilized to intensify the interest in concentrating, and habit will facilitate the process of concentrating

---

[1] See H. C. Link: *Employment Psychology*, p. 39. 1920.

[2] Attention is sometimes involuntary. A loud clap of thunder catches your attention even though you prefer to ignore it.

if the individual is interested enough to keep at the struggle without weakening. It is easy to become scatterbrained, because the mind has a mischievous tendency to wander at the slightest provocation.

B. Catching Attention. Certain sorts of stimuli or situations catch the attention because they appeal to fundamental human interests. It is important for us to adjust ourselves to such situations. A study of the means of attracting attention is of vital importance for advertisers and public speakers. What sorts of things get the attention?

1. Intensity. A very bright light or a hard slap on a sunburned shoulder catch the attention. A deeper analysis of the situation reveals the fact that it is a change in intensity which has attentional value. A man who works in a boiler factory gets so used to the noise that he no longer notices it. If the clatter should suddenly subside, he would immediately give heed, just as a person does not notice the ticking of the clock until it stops ticking, or as the sleeper wakes up when the parson stops preaching. There is a baffling of expectation. In his story *Silence*, Leonid Andreyev writes:

There is a difference between silence and stillness. Stillness is the absence of sound; silence is that quietness in which it seems as though someone should speak but will not. . . . He caught himself listening to the silence of the house . . . it almost seemed that he heard silence.

Employing the change of intensity, electrical advertising is most effective if bright and dim lighting are alternated, or if the lights go on and off.

2. Duration. A stimulus which is not noticed at first will catch the attention if it lasts for a while. A faint sound continued will eventually be heard.

Adaptation cancels the effects of protracted duration. If a stimulus does not at first get the attention, it continues until it succeeds in attracting notice, and then adaptation sets in, so that after a while no further heed is given to it.

3. Repetition. Repetition is intermittent duration. A stimulus which escapes attention at first ultimately is attended to if it is repeated. For this reason, the doorbell is rung and rung until something happens. An effective teacher repeats his remarks until the student "comes to" enough to listen. Advertisers must consider the frequency of the appearance of their advertisements as it bears upon the efficiency of the influence upon the prospective buyer. Too frequent repetition is negated in its effects by adaptation. "By special permission of the copyright owners" aims to protect a song from being "killed" by superfluous radio broadcasting.

4. Suddenness. An abrupt change removes the effects of adaptation. Suddenness is particularly effective when there is a shift from one sense organ to another. I was watching a movie thriller, years ago, on the day before the Fourth of July. The hero was chasing the villain, brandishing a revolver, and waiting for a chance to aim and fire. Just as the hero rounded a corner and gained an opportunity for a clear shot, the boy in the seat behind me fired his cap pistol. My response was not only auditory, but was also kinæsthetic. The shift from a visual to an auditory stimulus provoked in me a decided kinæsthetic response.

5. Size. Big billboards, large electric signs, and full-page advertisements catch the attention. Again, upon further analysis, we discover that it is a matter of relative size. A skinny man would stand out at a Fat Man's Convention. A small billboard in the midst of big ones would catch the attention.

6. Quality. A pretty girl has attentional value.

Styles have changed, the advertising pages are no longer what they used to be, and the day is gone when the only proper way to announce a new model of a motor car is to print a diagram of the engine and a bill of particulars as to piston displacement and igni-tion.   The modern way to announce a new model of a motor car is to print a picture of it with two bathing beauties climbing into the back seat from the running board.   .   .   .

This is a new day, and the advertising pages have ceased to be a mere album of things which can be purchased—a portfolio of stoves and dishpans, needlework and linen, hardware and upholstery—and have acquired some of the glamour of the Winter Garden. From the sheer emphasis on black chiffon it is difficult to tell, in many instances, whether the young lady who has disrobed before the camera has consented to do so in behalf of stockings, garters, underwear, shoes, the rug on which she stands, the pillow at her feet, the chair on which she leans, the bracelets on her arms, or the grand piano in the background.   Only close examination of the floor beneath the rug may reveal the fact that it is a floor advertise-ment, not a Follies poster, and that the message which this picture carries is the good news of a wax that will not scuff with wear or blister with hot coffee.

One thing is certain.   A new theme is being introduced into the technique of commercial art, and the business of selling shoes and clothes and household goods has acquired a new method.   What is a dye that will not fade without somebody in a bathing suit to test it?   What is a copper pipe that will not leak, a window screen that will not rust, or a laundry soap that will not streak, without some-body fresh from the seashore to admire it?   .   .   .

Call this commercialism, if you like.   Call it an attempt to ap-propriate charm for a soap or a sofa or a sport coupé by associating it with the symmetry of perfect form.   But for years critics of the American system have been bewailing the fact that American utilitarianism is divorced from art.   We have turned a corner.

Business has discovered beauty.[1]

7. Movement.   Moving objects are more apt to catch the attention than stationary ones.   Many electric signs involve motion.   The traffic officer may not be seen until he moves. The surveyor has his assistant wiggle the marker so that it may be more readily sighted through the telescope.   The

---

[1]Charles Merz: *The Great American Band Wagon*, pp. 147–149.   1928.   By permission of the John Day Company.

golfer who dubs his drive lays the blame on a fellow player who moved just as the remarkable shot was about to be demonstrated. Suzanne Lenglen in her book, *The Love Game*, says that it is easier to hit a moving ball than a still one. If she were right, the canny golfer should have a caddy roll a ball across the tee or throw it at him from a pitcher's box in front, while he takes a vicious swing at it in passage; it should be easier to kill a fly in motion.

The truth is, it is not easier to hit a moving ball. The fallacy in the above discussion is the assumption that the player's attention must be attracted. The golfer on the tee is looking at his ball—he is already attending. If a spectator moves, his attention is diverted to the moving person, away from the stationary ball. After the drive has been sliced to the rough, the search begins. The ball is stationary so that it does not attract the player's attention, a very different situation from that on the tee where he already knew where the ball was. If a golf ball could be invented which would jump up and down in the rough until it attracted notice, the attentional value of motion would be usefully capitalized. A moving ball is easier to find but no easier to hit.

8. Novelty. It is no news when the dog bites the man. When the man bites the dog, the incident has news value.

When introduced, a speaker before an Ohio high school assembly walked briskly to the front of the platform, removed his coat, then his tie and collar and even his shirt; but he did not stop then; he removed his trousers! For underwear he wore a gym suit; in the gym suit he gave a talk on the advantages of physical education in high school.[1]

Kenneth Collins, former Director of Publicity for R. H. Macy and Company, created novel advertising of a very effective kind, as may be seen in the following sample.[2]

[1] Howard H. Higgins: *Influencing Behavior Through Speech*, p. 44. 1930.

[2] Jerome Beatty: "How to Become a Millionaire," *American Magazine*, July, 1931.

"--- and you call this a handkerchief?"

The advantage of carrying a respectable handkerchief

Little Timothy Threap on the front row writhing and scuffing his shoes. is paying the penalty of being impetuous. He's gummed up the magician's trick, all right—there'll be no bunnies pulled out of his shred of a hanky. Worse than that, he's made himself the object of everyone's mirth and scorn. Woe indeed is him.

Novelty is dependent upon the setting in which the object is presented, for the new does not hold attention unless it is in part familiar. At home attention is attracted to a strange face; on the street, to a familiar face.

9. Incongruity. If a woman-hater of our acquaintance appears in public with a girl, he attracts notice, much to his own regret. The question immediately is provoked, "What's wrong with this picture?" If an item is so incongruous that we know it is out of order, we will note it readily.

It is said of a celebrated American preacher, who knows well how to arrest attention, and hold it, and generally does so by appropriate means, that on a very warm summer day, when he arose in his pulpit to preach, his first sentence was, "It's d—d hot this morning." That was a sudden surprise, which arrested and astonished every hearer. After a moment's pause, he proceeded, saying, "I heard that shocking expression fall from the lips of a man as I entered the church a minute ago." He then preached a withering sermon against the sin of profane swearing.[1]

[1]William Taylor: *The Model Preacher*, Chapter IV. 1859.

C. Critical Comments. The important thing in attracting attention is to win notice for the particular item that is vital.[1] The pretty girl in the advertisement may be so attractive as to encourage the observer to ignore the product which is being advertised.

A church sometimes makes its appeal to young people through the medium of bowling alleys, basketball, ping pong, movies, dancing, and uproarious evenings in the church basement. The danger is that religion will be lost sight of in the glamour of social excitement.

Advertisers use clever slogans to attract attention to their products. Do you remember the slogan? Do you remember the slogan and forget the product it eulogizes? Test your own reactions.

1. Comfort through flexibility.
2. A skin you love to touch.
3. Not a cough in a carload.
4. His master's voice.
5. Time to retire.
6. 99 44/100% pure.
7. The blade men swear by—not at.
8. Going, going, gone.
9. Good to the last drop.
10. The instrument of the immortals.
11. Make hard roads easy.
12. From contented cows.
13. A clean tooth never decays.
14. When it rains, it pours.
15. Rules the waves.
16. Pure as the pines.
17. A thousand things may happen in the dark.
18. Aged six months.
19. Ask the man who owns one.
20. It's fun to be fooled.

Turn to the end of the chapter for the correct answers.

[1]See H. H. Higgins: *op. cit.*, pp. 44–45.

III. MEANING

The central factor in the perceptual process is meaning. The mind does not soak up facts as a blotter absorbs ink. The mind is active, contributing meaning to the stimuli of which it has become aware. The act of interpretation not only adds meaning to what we seem to get through our senses, but even alters the character of the sense data themselves. "Blindfolded, you know the difference" reads a cigarette advertisement. The truth is, most smokers, in spite of their insistence to the contrary, cannot tell one cigarette from another unless they see the label. A friend who did not like "Luckies" smoked them with unwitting pleasure when they were substituted for his Chesterfields in a Chesterfield package. An experiment conducted at Reed College by a graduate student in psychology demonstrated that blindfolded smokers could not identify popular brands of cigarettes. In fact, their identifications were correct more seldom than chance would allow, which means that the confidence on the part of the observers, plus a prejudgment leaning toward a certain brand, so confused their sensory experience as to produce results lower than those they would have obtained by wild guessing. The moral is: we live by labels—the knowledge that an article is of a certain brand goes a long way toward determining the nature of the sensations aroused by its consumption.[1]

Perception is a complex affair. Take such a simple experience as seeing red. The naïve person thinks of red as being part of the object. But the red is really a mental affair. The experience of a certain wave length, as registered by the sense organs and conducted to the brain, means red. Now red may carry meanings on its own account: "Stop!" (traffic) or "Goal!" (hockey game), depending on the context in which

[1] Stuart Chase: "Blindfolded, You Know the Difference," the *New Republic*, August 8, 1928.

the wave length appears. The sight of red stimulates the mind to supply the meaning.

Meaning, of course, depends upon a person's past experience. Suppose, for example, you hear a whistle. The sound, familiar to all motorists, means "cop" and, more important still, it means "slow down and pull over to the side of the road. What do you think this is, a race track, and so forth?" Such a simple mental process as hearing a sound becomes very complex when past experience is brought to bear upon the present experience. The word "m-a-n" means one thing to a German and another thing to an American. When a person is reading a German passage, the word, of course, should be interpreted in its German context. I was misled by the context in reading the following item on a sporting page:

George Duncan's numerous friends in the United States hope that he was misquoted the other night at a banquet in London when he charged Walter with putting a fast one over on the British professional golfers in the Ryder cup matches at Worcester a year ago last summer.

I was aware of the "golf context" as soon as I saw George Duncan's name and so, when I came to the word "putting," I read it putting (as used in golf) instead of putting (as in "putting over a fast one"). The words are pronounced differently, and as soon as I reached the word "over," I realized it was *putting* and not *putting*.

A. Signs. In perception, we look for signs on the basis of which we give meaning to the stimuli. Victor Hugo once wanted to find out from his publishers whether a certain manuscript of his would be accepted, so he sent them a card which contained this: "?" His publishers replied: "!"

Through the process of interpreting signs, we come by experience to recognize that a wave length of 7,230 means "red." Similarly the angles in the diagram of the table mean that it is to be projected in a certain spatial plane whereby the oblique and acute angles may be translated into right angles. Where is the animal in the picture on p. 348? How do you know?

Certain wave lengths conveyed through the cochlea to the brain signify certain sounds which themselves are signs through which meaning may be comprehended.

"Feel thus Teins Ford ear roll Maine," means visually, nothing in particular. Read it aloud rapidly, however, and the wave lengths through your ears will eventuate in sounds which, in their turn, will convey the meaning—the Stein Song: "Fill the steins for dear old Maine."

> Gnomme attar; Anna lies align!
> Nation mice lender verse says knot
> Fork rip tick poet real Ike mine
> How Aaron weal demeans allot.

Decipher the poem by auditory means and then refer to the footnote below.[1] Visually considered, these examples are nonsensical, but taken via hearing they become auditory sense data from which meaning is derived through the process of interpretation. Thus we see that meaning depends upon the recognition of signs.

The deciphering of signs by translating visual into auditory cues was the procedure followed by a proprietor of a bookstore who received, by mail, requests for the following books by persons who had obviously picked up the titles by hearsay:

1. One Saw One Thief, by Bernard Johnson.
2. Humdrum Book on Acting.

---

[1] No matter, analyze a line.
Nay, shun my slender verses not
For cryptic poetry like mine
How e'er unwieldy means a lot.

3. Firework King, by Justin McCarthy.
4. The Old Pie Bus, by Warwick Deeping.
5. Sheriton's Cricketers.
6. Farmer's Suitable Pocket Book.

(Drawn by Warren Sillen)

7. Jean's Universal Rounders.
8. Last of the Inkers, by Henty.
9. Odipus the Wreck.
10. Says a Man to Lily.
11. Juice of Night, by Lord Ailesbury.
12. The Red Yacht.

Would you know what to send? The books they really wanted were:

1. "One Lord, One Faith," by Vernon Johnson (Father Vernon).
2. "Humdrum," by Harold Acton.
3. "If I Were King," by Justin H. McCarthy.
4. "Old Pybus," by Warwick Deeping.
5. Sheridan's "The Critic."
6. "Pharmaceutical Pocket Book."
7. Sir J. H. Jeans's "The Universe Around Us."
8. "Treasure of the Incas," by G. A. Henty.
9. "Œdipus Rex," by Sophocles.
10. "Sesame and Lilies," by John Ruskin.
11. "Use of Life," by Lord Avebury.
12. "The Rubaiyat."[1]

B. Ambiguous Figures. A given stimulus may give rise to several interpretations. A stimulus which is likely to induce several meanings is called ambiguous. A classic illustration is the reversible staircase.

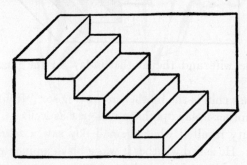

If you gaze at the figure, you will notice that at one moment you are underneath the stairs looking up at them and at another moment you are above the stairs looking down at them. The reversal may be facilitated by shifting the point of fixation. The figure will reverse in spite of all effort to keep

[1] The *Literary Digest*, May, 1930.

it constant.   Shading may accentuate the views, the shaded portion being considered as the nearer surface.

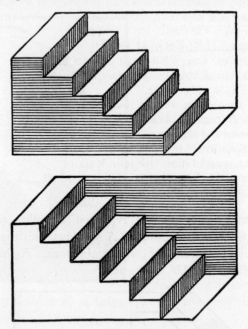

Find the wife and the mother-in-law in the puzzle on p. 351.

The wife's chin is the mother-in-law's nose.[1]   If you cannot find the mother-in-law, perhaps it is just as well.

Ambiguity resulted when a small boy saw a zebra for the first time.   He asked whether it was a black animal with white stripes or a white animal with black stripes.

In the figure on page 351, how many blocks are there, six or seven?

That the meaning of a stimulus may be misconstrued is sometimes capitalized.

[1] E. G. Boring: "A New Ambiguous Figure," *American Journal of Psychology*, 1930, 42, 444.

Lazy Little Lulus

Acquitted of fraud in Budapest last week, Bookseller Bischl triumphantly regaled reporters with the story of how he had sold 2,000 copies of a cookbook to women through the mails by advertising: "This Book Is Guaranteed to Tell What a Girl Ought to Know before Marriage."

That a female was actually aroused to the point of pocketing her dignity and suing Bookseller Bischl for fraud was due, he thought, to the real title (not advertised) of the book, "Lazy Little Lulu Learns to Cook."[1]

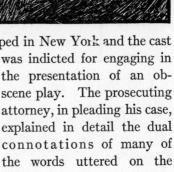

Many a smutty story "gets by"—or nearly does—because some keyword has a double meaning. Recently a dramatic production was stopped in New York and the cast was indicted for engaging in the presentation of an obscene play. The prosecuting attorney, in pleading his case, explained in detail the dual connotations of many of the words uttered on the stage.

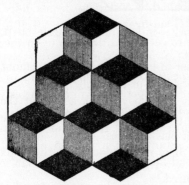

Ambiguity was resorted to by Gladstone when he received a copy of a book from a proud author. He wrote in thanking him: "I shall lose no time in perusing your book."

[1]*Time*, March 2, 1931. By permission of *Time*, Inc.

The crucial thing for experience is not the stimulus, but what the mind does with it. Consider a few horrible puns:

Probably the most promising of all careers is that of a politician.

A skeptic declares that when he attended a seance all he heard was chuckles. He must have struck a very happy medium.

A Philadelphia woman who fired five times at her fleeing spouse now wants him to return home. She misses him so.

There is always a tie between father and son. Probably. And if there is, it's a safe bet that son's wearing it.

An Ohio butcher was recently held up and locked in his ice box by bandits. When released by the police, he was the coolest man in the room.

Mr. Hoover acted after getting a long letter from President Hindenburg. The Hindenburg line must be as good as ever.

That a given stimulus may mean all things to all people is illustrated by an amusing incident which took place in Minneapolis, where citizens listening to a Lenten program were astonished to hear the Courthouse chimes playing "How Dry I Am." Chime-Ringer Auld grew weary answering indignant telephone calls and explaining that he had been playing "O Happy Day," a good old hymn the tune of which had been appropriated for the barroom ballad.[1] A slap on the shoulder may mean "Hello, Buddy," "Good-bye, old pal," or "Tell it to the judge." The meaning, in each case, depends upon the context and the set of the mind.

C. Meaning and Set. Expectation determines ahead of the stimulus what the nature of an experience will be. A test tube in the vest pocket of a Lehigh University student exploded while he was eating in a crowded restaurant. Consternation reigned in the restaurant, and a woman became hysterical, insisting that she had been shot, but a physician's examination proved her uninjured.[2]

---

[1] *Time*, April 13, 1931.
[2] The Boston *Herald*, March 25, 1931.

Every hunting season there are many fatalities resulting from the fact that hunters are mistaken for deer or bears. In one case, a boy climbed a tree to investigate a gum seam. A hunter came along, heard a noise in the tree, looked up, saw a dark brown body there, supposed it to be a bear, and fired. The boy fell, badly wounded.

Reading is performed in snapshots and it is easy for the mind to fall into error through jumping to false conclusions. At times words may be read incorrectly when they are printed correctly. *Persona grata* may be seen as *persona non grata*, the *non* being inserted because it completes the phrase as the reader is more accustomed to seeing it. At other times words may be read correctly when they are misprinted, so that the radio program of "Big Bother" may quite possibly register upon the hasty reader as the program of "Big Brother," according to its usual form. The proofreader's illusion is another case in point. It is easy for an author to overlook errors in his manuscript because the very set which may have predisposed him to make an error may lead him to fail in its detection.

Each of us has the windows of his house built for him by experience, and we can look at life through no other casements. Looking at a bit of landscape, one man sees it as a prospect for a farm, another for a summer home, another as a site for a hotel, another as a subject for painting. "Yet they are all looking at the same scene, each with the same kind of bodily eyes, but very different mental ones. They bring to the scene their dominant interests; and that is what they really see. What you get out of an experience, depends upon what you put in, and you could not change these men's outlooks without first changing their insights."[1]

---

[1] Joseph Jastrow: *Keeping Mentally Fit*, pp. 20–21. 1928. By permission of Greenberg, Publishers.

IV. PERCEIVING SPACE

We tend to think of the perception of space as a passive registration, whereas the truth of it is that the mind makes its judgments of location and distance by means of certain signs which, by virtue of experience, come to convey definite spatial meanings.

A. Tactual Space. Have a trustworthy friend stick a pin in you. Where did he prick you? If your eyes are open, of course, you have visual cues to aid you. But in addition to such cues, you are able merely on the basis of tactual cues to locate the spot with some degree of accuracy. A prick on the arm feels different from one on the foot. That qualitative difference has been called the "local sign." The distinctiveness of the local sign may be due in part to the particular nerve conducting the impulse from the skin. Localization is most accurate where the nerve endings are the most numerous. If a member is amputated, sensations from the stump are still referred to the missing part.

In other situations, reflex movements, executed to protect the threatened spot, aid in the localization.

B. Visual Space. Far more is known about the perception of visual space. It will be sufficient to illustrate the principles of spatial perception if we limit our discussion to judgments of distance.

The naïve person does not pause to realize that the visual field is flat, a single plane of two dimensions. How do we get the experience of the third dimension, giving us spatial depth in the plane extending away from the observer? The most effective way of comprehending the nature of the problem is to consider a picture which is printed on a card of two dimensions, occupying one plane. In spite of the restriction of the view to one plane, we can tell that objects are near or far. Analyze this lake scene and write down the signs you avail yourself of in

determining the relative positions of trees, lake, and mountains. Then check your list with the following discussion.

One of the striking aspects of spatial judgments is the fact that the individual successfully estimates spatial relations without explicit knowledge of how he does it. The individual is unconscious of the factors underlying his judgments. This point will become more apparent as we proceed.

The criteria of visual distance are classified into primary and secondary cues.

1. Primary Criteria. The primary criteria depend directly upon the structure of the eyes.

a. Binocular Parallax. The first of these is binocular parallax. The normal person has two eyes instead of one. Do you realize the importance of this fact?

The images of an object on the two retinas are different. Hold the forefinger of your right hand a foot from your face. Look at it with your right eye, keeping your left eye closed; then look at it with your left eye, keeping your right eye closed. Note the distinction between the two views. Now hold your finger at arm's length and perform the same operations. Note that the two views do not differ so much. The degree of doubleness, the amount of difference between the two views, is a cue to the distance; the less doubleness, the greater the distance away. It is important to note again that this whole process may be completed unconsciously.

The stereoscope applies this principle. An object is photographed from two appropriate angles, giving two distinct views. When the two views are fused, they give an impression of solidity (distance).

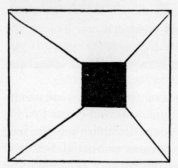 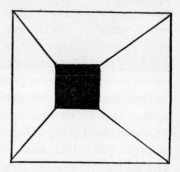

Hold a piece of paper between the two figures in a plane to the nose so that the left-hand figure is seen with the left eye and the right-hand figure with the right. The figures will fuse, producing an impression of solidity. The same experience may be produced by looking way beyond the figures so that they just come into the view.

Take the top off your fountain pen and give your fountain pen to a friend to hold in a horizontal position a yard in front of you, in the right to left plane. Then with one eye closed try to put the top on the pen. Lacking the cue of binocular parallax, you will probably experience some difficulty.

One-eyed persons, though handicapped by the lack of binocular parallax, learn to judge distances on the basis of other cues.

We are all one-eyed, to a certain degree, since the two eyes do not contribute equally to the formation of the single stereo-scopic picture. In a right-eyed person the right eye con-tributes practically all of the picture, in a left-eyed person the left eye. In the former, the left eye merely functions in a subservient fashion to add accessory information to the view afforded by the dominant right eye. Look at a tiny spot in the wall at a distance of a few feet. While still looking at the spot, take a finger-ring and hold it where you will be looking through it. Then close your left eye, and determine whether you still see the spot through the ring. If you are right-eyed, you will. Next close your right eye and look at the spot with your left and you will see it outside the ring. If you are left-eyed, the result will be reversed. Dominancy and subserviency in eyes are peculiar to the human being.

Tests are being developed by Alvah R. Lauer of Iowa State College to examine the fitness of applicants for licenses to drive automobiles. One aim of the tests is to determine the efficiency of depth perception, since those persons who are defective in this particular may fail to gauge the distance or speed of an approaching car and may, therefore, be a menace on the public highway.[1]

b. Accommodation. The second primary criterion is derived from the muscular strains involved in accommodating the lens of the eye so that the image will be focused exactly on the retina. This cue is useful only for distances within a few feet of the eye where the kinæsthetic sensations from the muscular contractions are clearly noticeable. There is more strain when objects are near since the divergent rays from a near object are not as easily focused as the more parallel rays from a distant object.

c. Convergence. The third primary criterion is convergence. When an object is near, muscular strain is experienced as the

[1]A. R. Lauer: *Manual of Tests for Automotive Operators.* Iowa State College, Ames, Iowa. 1934.

eyes are turned in (converged) upon the object.   For a distant object there is less convergence and therefore less muscular strain.

2. Secondary Criteria.   The secondary criteria are more distinctly psychological.

a. Linear Perspective.   First we have linear perspective as a basis for the experience of depth.   The course of contour lines in the field of vision, like the apparent convergence of railroad tracks in the distance, is an important cue.   Everyone knows the tracks do not actually converge.   Their apparent convergence is interpreted in terms of distance, the more converging, the further away the contours.   See illustration on page 359.

b. Aërial Perspective.   In the photograph on page 355 you will notice that you can recognize the distant hills by the indistinctness of their outline.   On a clear day, distant objects look near; in a fog, a ship may be nearer than it appears to be.[1]   Distant mountains may be distinguished by a hazy blueness.

c. Light and Shade.   Light is interpreted as nearer the observer and shade as further away if the source of illumination is

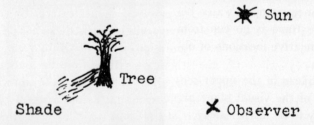

from the direction of the observer.   The effects of light and shade are strikingly brought out in the following illustration.[2]

---

[1]For some excellent illustrations of aërial perspective, see Knight Dunlap: *Elements of Scientific Psychology*, pp. 274–275.   1927.

[2]Courtesy of Mr. J. W. Milford and the General Electric Company.

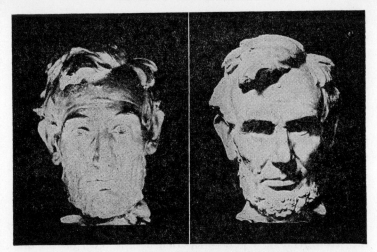

WRONG AND RIGHT WAYS TO LIGHT LINCOLN

Differences in light and shade so alter the distinctions in depth as to give the features a radically different expression.

d. Interposition. Near objects often conceal parts of objects further away. Turn back, for a further illustration, to the animal parking behind a tree on page 348. For this reason it is very difficult to estimate distance on open water because there is no cue from the relative locations of objects.

Objects in the upper section of the visual plane are likely to be further away.

e. Apparent Magnitude. Through experience we become familiar with the size of an object. If the apparent magnitude diminishes, we infer that the object is further and further away. One does not think that a person in the background of the photograph is actually smaller than the person in the foreground but rather that he is more distant.

3. Further Cues. In concluding the discussion of visual distance, it should be stated that the visual cues are supplemented by other cues, notably tactual and kinæsthetic, which increase the accuracy of judgment. The child sees something; he reaches for it; he learns how much muscular work must be performed to attain an object which looks to be a certain distance away. He sees in one plane; he can reach (kinæsthetic) and touch (tactual) in three dimensions.

If you care to determine how much we depend upon a combination of cues, lay out a line on the floor and walk on it, one foot over the other, while looking at the line through the wrong end of a pair of opera glasses. The glasses distort the visual cues enough to disturb the kinæsthetic adjustment.

C. Auditory Space. In these days of the automobile, it is quite important that we localize sounds accurately. It is a surprising fact that we cannot tell by our ears whether a sound comes from the front or from the rear. Fortunately we have eyes to help us in front; in the rear we can only trust to luck. If a witness in court states that the pistol was fired on the road behind him on the dark night of the crime, his testimony is worth nothing.

Test yourself. Station one person directly behind you and another directly in front of you, both to take turns in varying sequence in making identical sounds. Localize them. Your judgments will be subject to grave error.

It is well for us that we have two eyes. It is also an advantage that we have two ears, for it permits us to localize with a fair amount of precision.

One indication by which a sound is localized is the relative intensity in the two ears. The hearer localizes toward the more intense sound, the ear further from the stimulus falling in a shadow. By means of the binaural ratio in intensity, localization can be accurate. When a sound comes from directly in front or behind, the intensity is the same in both ears, thus baffling the judgment.

Another cue for locating a sound is the factor of time. The hearer localizes toward the ear which is prior in picking up the wave. The phase of the wave is liable to differ in the two ears, affording a further basis for judgment. The presence of timbre facilitates accurate localization.

V. PERCEIVING TIME

Aside from the aid of watch or clock, duration may be determined by reference to the experiences occurring during a given interval. When a person is busy, time flies; holidays pass rapidly. Days of illness drag on forever. Filled time is likely to be short while it is passing, and long in retrospect; empty time, long in passing and short in retrospect.

Have you ever dozed off after your alarm had run itself down, only to awake with consternation as you fear you have overslept your train to school or office? It seems as if an hour must have been given over to slumber, and then you look at the clock to see that only five minutes have gone by. The illusion is due to your dreaming, in the course of which events may occur in a brief period which would consume a much more protracted interval in your waking life.

Various sensations, such as hunger or a full bladder, supply cues for the judgment of time. Stomach contractions serve warning that the meal hour approaches.

It is possible, by practice, to determine in advance the hour you wish to awake, and then to do so at the time you have set for yourself. A man whose business it is to set all the clocks in a large office building carries out his work without reference to a watch. He has trained his judgment till he can rely on it perfectly. He is known as "the human alarm clock."

When some persons want to arise early without resorting to a Big Ben, they lie awake all night wondering whether the time has arrived to rise, and then doze off in the early hours of the morning into a sleep that continues indefinitely.

VI. THE RELIABILITY OF OBSERVATION

A. Testimony. A witness mounts the stand and swears before the court to tell "the whole truth and nothing but the truth, so help me God!" With this weighty oath sworn with a hand on the Bible, can the court be justified in relying upon the testimony? Only with many reservations. Assuming the witness is honest and disinterested, he may be describing not facts but illusions. The most obvious course is to lay the blame for misstatements on a faulty memory. The real source of error, however, is usually inaccurate observation. A robbery took place in a railway train. Three diamond merchants were found, gagged and bound, in their drawing room. Five passengers, all of them sitting within a few yards of the door to the drawing room and facing it, asserted that they had seen nobody enter the room since the three merchants had returned, following dinner, and closed the door from the inside. The porter, who had been standing near the door for an hour, stated that he had likewise seen nobody, besides the merchants, enter the room. The detective discounted the testimony of the passengers and the porter, because the evidence of a robbery was too convincing, and because he knew from experience that people do not see what is happening around them. The bandits were captured the next day.[1]

Testimony is unreliable because our sense organs, our sets, and our memories deceive us. Leading questions may mislead. Fictitious facts, it may be said, are usually consistent with facts actually noted. The technique of selecting the

---

[1]Sherman Gwinn: "Unseen Eyes Protect You When You Travel," *American Magazine*, January, 1929.

facts determines their very nature. That rules of evidence are required in law indicates how problematic "factuality" is.

Upon whose testimony can we rely? Can we ever determine the facts? If our senses fool us, if our predispositions trick us, if our recall is subject to subtle perversions, how can we know that we know anything? Philosophers have puzzled over this problem for ages. To give you more material for cogitation on this matter, let us study a few visual illusions, though it should be stated that there are illusions in other sensory fields.

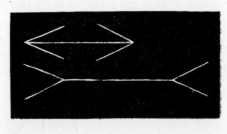

B. Visual Illusions. An illusion is an erroneous perception. A familiar example is the Müller-Lyer illusion. Which is the longer of the two horizontal lines? They are actually equal in length. The observer is fooled, partly because he does not restrict his attention to the specific parts to be compared.

Try this one. Which figure is larger in area?

Then go on to this one.

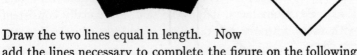

Draw the two lines equal in length. Now add the lines necessary to complete the figure on the following page. Which diagonal now appears the longer?

In all of these cases the items to be compared have been confused with near-by stimuli.

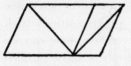

Suppose you were out hunting and a bird flew in the line indicated, where would you aim? If you aimed at A, you would be shooting accurately, but you probably would not aim at A, since, as you will notice, the line of flight, though straight, does not appear to be straight.

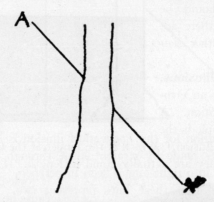

To hit the bird you would have to discount the illusion to an exact degree. This illusion is known as the Poggendorf illusion.

Draw the Poggendorf figure.

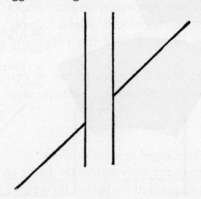

Then complete the figure as follows. Imagine the line is a rope. Tell the men to pull it taut. Watch the line straighten out.

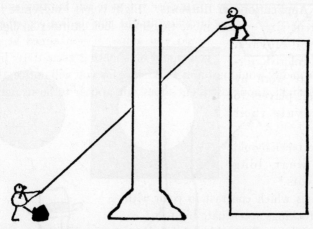

One explanation for the Poggendorf illusion is in terms of angles. Angles made by straight lines, through experience, are translated into right angles seen in perspective. Imagine that these lines represent two roads crossing at right angles. Merely transfer them to a different plane (perspective) to gain this impression. The translation of angles in experience leads us to overestimate acute angles and to underestimate obtuse angles. Apply this fact to the explanation of the Poggendorf illusion.

Habit derived from the repeated use of perspective leads the observer to overestimate the vertical, since the vertical

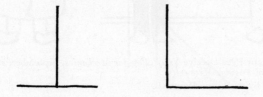

line, in perspective, represents a line continuing into the distant background.

C. Applications of Illusions. Light colors exaggerate the apparent size. Small men, therefore, look sturdier in light-colored clothes. Light-colored jerseys are worn by football players to aggravate their bulk.

Short men should not wear long overcoats.[1]

Shoes which contrast in color with the stockings accentuate big feet.[2]

A plain straight skirt makes large

---

[1]"How Your Eyes Deceive You," *Popular Mechanics*, September, 1926. By permission of *Popular Mechanics*.

[2]Drawing by R. Wilson Hammell.

ankles look larger; a full and rippling skirt gives the ankles a slim appearance.[1]

Camouflage has become a valuable phase of modern warfare.[2]

VII. PROBLEMS OF ATTENTION

A. Range. There are four major problems of attention: range, duration, division, and degree.

Only a certain amount of the objective world can be taken in through one momentary perception. The amount which can be absorbed through a passing notice is known as the span of attention. Under experimental conditions the stimulus is exposed by a tachistoscope, an instrument which makes it possible to control the interval during which the stimulus

---

[1]Drawing by R. Wilson Hammell.

[2]See *Fortification. Camouflage for All Arms.* War Department; Washington, June 15, 1926. Photograph reproduced by permission of Acme Newspictures, Inc.

appears at a slot in a screen and to regulate the intervals between successive exposures.

The span I am going to discuss is sometimes described as the simultaneous span as contrasted with the successive span involved in the experience of recognizing how many times the clock has struck, without actually counting the bells.

PROJECTION TACHISTOSCOPE

This instrument consists essentially of a pair of simple projectors using standard width movie film but arranged for "stills" instead of motion pictures. One of these projects the pre-exposure field, with fixation point; the other projects the exposure material. The two fields are thrown on the same screen area, and are alternated by a magnetically controlled reciprocating shutter. The timing of the exposure period is accomplished by means of a small motor driven timing disk. (Reproduced by courtesy of the Marietta Apparatus Company.)

Turn the page upside down, take one glance at the printed letters, and turn the book right side up again.

H T I V I d T D E V d H

Write on a piece of paper what you saw.

Repeat the operation with the letters printed below.

V I H d E D V T I H d

We learn by experience to group stimuli, thus extending considerably the span of attention.

How many dots do you see in one glance?

A bridge player may be able to tell without counting his cards that he has been dealt fourteen cards instead of the regulation thirteen.

A person may become so completely absorbed in one activity as to be absentminded so far as any other interest is concerned. Absentmindedness is really narrow presentmindedness. Attention may be compared to a lamp—the lamp with a wide illumination will throw its rays over a wide area, or a bull's-eye lantern will narrow its light to a small field. The secret-service man and the hostess must cultivate a wide span—they must see and hear all. The surgeon, on the other hand, trains himself to concentrate on a narrow field.

Speed in reading depends upon the attainment of a wide span, though a wide visual span does not guarantee efficient reading. Some people read by words, others by phrases, others by clauses, others by sentences, and others by paragraphs. Inefficient reading of foreign languages is encouraged by the "word" method when the "meaning" method is so much more advantageous. Speed in any kind of reading depends upon the quick apprehension of meanings. Six words per second, or about four and one-half hours for a standard-size book, is good average reading speed. Interest increases speed in reading, as we notice when we turn from a serious book to an exciting novel. The fast reader eagerly presses forward to get the answers to questions which have risen in his mind. The brain, not the eyes, determines the speed of reading. The eye moves in a series of snapshots with pauses between. These pauses are needed to see the material clearly, but still more to give time for the meaning to be grasped. They take up about 95 per cent of the reader's time, the small remainder being all that the eye requires for its actual motion across the page, once the eye mechanics of reading are mastered. The eye as a machine is able to operate faster than the mind can grasp the sense. Interest, by hastening the grasping process, increases the speed of reading.

B. Duration. Attention can be directed toward a single stimulus for only a brief duration. Attention fluctuates, probably because the threshold for the stimulus varies with changes in blood pressure, respiration, and other physical conditions. There are a multitude of objects to be noticed and adjusted to. A shifting attention, therefore, has some adjustmental value. When the sense organs become adapted to a stimulus, fluctuation is facilitated.

Fluctuation may be studied by the observation of a minimal stimulus, that is, a stimulus so faint as to be barely above the threshold. A physician named Urbantschitsch was the first to discover that a faint stimulus like a watch tick gives rise to fluctuating sensations—the ticks are heard for a few moments, then they are not heard, and then they are heard again. The ticks come and go at intervals.

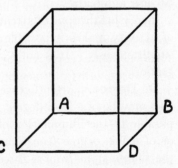

Reversible perspective is likewise good material for studying fluctuation. Look at the cube with the line AB in the foreground and then in the background. Practise on the fluctuation by shifting the fixation of the eyes from AB to CD and back again. Then stare at AB and try to keep the figure steady. Soon it will shift in spite of your efforts to prevent the fluctuation.

C. Division. The term division implies that there can be more than one attention at the same moment. Caesar is supposed to have dictated different material to several different stenographers at once. Such a performance is literally impossible because Caesar only had one tongue to wag.

Attention may be rapidly shifted from one object to another in successive moments. A person who listens to the radio while he attempts to read will find that each stimulus helps him to take his mind off the other.

The problem of division is really one of organization. Just as the span of attention is extended by grouping, so separate acts can be performed at once when they have been integrated into a single pattern of behavior. Playing the piano with both hands is not a task in division but one in coördination. Similarly, two activities may be carried on simultaneously where one of them has become automatic. A woman may knit and talk at the same time, inasmuch as talking, for her, has become automatic.

Increasing the span of attention through skillful organization of activity makes it possible to attend to various objectives simultaneously. It is not a question of division but of integration.

D. Degree. Attention was compared to a lamp. Attention may be of a high degree (consciousness very clear), comparable to the illumination of a hundred candlepower lamp; or of a low degree (consciousness very dim), comparable to the illumination from a three candlepower flashlight. How much attention is a person giving to an object?

One way to ascertain the degree of attention is to measure the reaction time—the more attentive, the quicker the response.

Another method of measuring the degree of attention is in terms of accuracy—the more attentive, the more accurate the response.

Still another mode of determining the degree of attention is to submit the individual to measurable distractions—the more attentive, the less will distraction interfere with performance.

On the face of it, it would seem that distracting stimuli would diminish the speed and accuracy with which a given task were performed. Yet distraction often goads the individual to higher efficiency. He makes such an effort to resist the distraction that he overshoots the mark, and does better than he would have done under circumstances apparently more favorable.

Dr. Geoffrey A. Haylock of London discovered in the course of studies of the amounts of work done by women factory employees that many of the girls actually did more work on days when they had reported headaches than on days when they felt entirely well. Two reasons may account for this paradoxical fact. One is that girls with headaches are less interested than usual in their surroundings and their companions. Accordingly, they do less talking and their attention is less distracted. They are likely to do more work, especially if the work is on a piece-work basis, where each worker can speed up or let down individually without being affected by the others. The second is that mild pain often can be relieved by concentrating the attention on some task. Some of the girl workers apparently concentrate on their work in order to forget their headaches, which results in more work accomplished at the end of the day. Since distraction sometimes facilitates performance, it might be concluded that radio programs should be supplied in the reading room of the public library. The difficulty is that the effort necessary to resist distraction is so fatiguing that it more than counterbalances any advantages to be derived from the superior performance of the task in hand.

The most persistently distracting noises are those carrying meaning. It is harder to work with others talking in the room than with the hum of a machine. It is harder not to try to listen. If persons near by are whispering, it is impossible to resist the impulse to listen—for if they are talking in undertones, they are probably saying something worth hearing. A woman sitting in a theater remarked to her companion, "I wish those pests behind us would talk more distinctly."

An advertisement for a silenced typewriter depicts a man cursing a fellow golf player who has ruined a putt by making a distracting noise at the wrong moment. The next picture shows the same man in his office in conference, trying to put through a big deal. The noise of the typewriters is interfering with his thinking, but he does not seem to care enough to do anything about it.

Most of us have become so adapted to noise that we have attained a state of complete indifference. Little do we realize that our clanging environment often produces shell-shock. Sounds of a more or less intermittent character cause irregularity of the heart rhythm, increase blood pressure, make our muscles more tense for action and our movements more energetic. As a consequence there is a greater wear and tear on the system, resulting in rapid fatigue and nervous exhaustion. Noise interferes very seriously with the efficiency of the worker. At first the worker becomes stimulated, then disturbed, excited, and irritable. His conduct changes and he is subject to loss of temper. Those engaged in brain work are prevented from deep and sustained thinking. In the attempt to overcome the effects of noise, great strain is put on the nervous system, leading to neurasthenia and psychasthenia. Even the digestion does not escape the harmful effects of disturbing noises. Continued loud noises striking the delicate mechanism of the ear cause impairment of hearing. Lesions of the internal ear develop, which manifest themselves as ear noises, dizziness, and headache. The years of profitable activity are shortened in those whose occupation exposes them to persistent loud noises.

Our capacity for adaptation deludes us into believing that surrounding noises do not influence us seriously. Noise causes a fear reaction which includes involuntary bodily changes affecting digestion and blood pressure. In most urban centers man has reached a point in his conscious adaptation to noise resembling the complacent frog which can be boiled alive if only the temperature is raised by very slight degrees. It does not spare the frog's skin that he does not feel the water persistently becoming warmer, and it may not save our sanity that we do not notice noise any more.

KEY TO ADVERTISING SLOGANS ON PAGE 344.

1. Cantilever Shoe.
2. Woodbury's Facial Soap.
3. Old Gold Cigarettes.
4. Victrola.
5. Fisk Tires.
6. Ivory Soap.
7. Durham Duplex Razor.
8. Newbro's Herpicide.
9. Maxwell House Coffee.
10. Steinway Piano.
11. Blue Jay Corn Plaster.
12. Carnation Milk.
13. Prophylactic Tooth Brush.
14. Morton's Salt.
15. Venida Hair Nets.
16. Packer's Tar Soap.
17. Eveready Flashlight.
18. Clicquot Club Ginger Ale.
19. Packard Motor Car.
20. Camel Cigarettes.

CHAPTER XI

REMEMBERING AND ANTICIPATING

WHENEVER we bring back the past through recollection, or "picture" the future through anticipation, we are using our imagination. The phrase "using our imagination" implies that imagination is a thing that lies in readiness, awaiting the call to contribute its bit to the teamwork of mental life. Imagination, however, is not a thing, and we would avoid such a misconception if we used verbs instead of nouns. Thus, by substituting *imagining* for *imagination*, it becomes apparent that recalling and predicting, recognition and precognition, are all forms of *imagining*.

I. IMAGINING

Imagining is the mental activity through which we represent remote objects to ourselves, and thereby liberate the organism from a dependence upon present sensory stimulation. Objects may be thought of, thought about, and reacted to imaginatively (implicitly) before explicit responses are carried out. In planning a house, for example, a person visualizes the structure in all its details, adding here and eliminating there, before the actual erection is begun at all. When the rôle of mind in the process of adjustment is taken as the point of departure, the significance of imagining becomes more and more impressive, for it is through this activity that the experience of the past can be applied in the anticipation of the future, and thus reactions can be planned in advance with reference to situations calling for adaptive responses (intelligence). Behavioristically speaking, imagining is a delayed reaction in the course of which implicit responses are rehearsed before their conversion into overt behavior. Whatever the terminology, the function of imagining is comparable to that of the distance receptors—the organism is spared the necessity of immediate response, and time is gained to prepare for effective adjustment.

We usually think of imagination as having reference to the future. Imagining, however, is just as truly the activity of memory as it is the activity of anticipation. When we recall a past experience, we imagine; when we pause to consider a prospective course of action, we imagine. When imagining has a backward reference in point of time, we call it remembering; when imagining has a forward reference in point of time, we call it anticipating. The individual, of course, is not always conscious of the time reference. He may, for example, recite the alphabet as he remembers it, without any definite awareness of a date in the past when he first learned his ABC's. The time reference exists, however, for descriptive or explanatory purposes, since imagining with reference to the past, even though the element of time may not appear explicitly in the consciousness of the rememberer, may still be properly designated as an act of remembering.

Anticipating proceeds in the light of what is remembered. Imagining which reinstates a past experience is sometimes called reproductive imagination; imagining which transcends the past is sometimes called constructive, or even creative, imagination. Thinking is imagining organized with reference to a project, and may involve both reproductive imagination and constructive imagination.

The rôle of imagining in supplying meaning to experience can be demonstrated by the ink-blot experiment.[1] What does

---

[1]See F. C. Bartlett: *Remembering. A Study in Experimental and Social Psychology.*
Also, S. J. Beck: "Configurational Tendencies in Rorschach Responses," *American Journal of Psychology*, 1933, 45, 433-443.

the following figure mean to you? Can you determine the
sources of your interpretations?

Imagining usually proceeds by the use of signs or symbols

which represent objects
or situations that are remote (absent). The rôle
of symbolism in imaginal
activities may be appre-
ciated by a study of phantasy.

A. Phantasy. Phan-
tasy is the activity of
dreaming, indulged in
while we sleep or while we are awake (daydreams).

1. Dreams in Sleep. A dream is like a cartoon in that a
situation is represented
through meaningful
symbols. Think of this
cartoon as a dream.[1]
What is the meaning of
the symbolism?

The most effective
method of preparation
for the task of inter-
preting dreams is to
make an exhaustive
study of symbolism, in
cartoons, in myths and
folklore, in magic, as-
trology, and supersti-
tion. In analyzing
cartoons, try to get the
meaning without reference to the labels. You will soon dis-

[1]Cartoon by R. Wilson Hammell.

cover typical symbols which can be readily recognized and interpreted.

a. The Freudian Theory. In ancient times, especially, dreams were looked upon as omens of the future. Joseph's interpretation of Pharaoh's dreams of the seven fat kine and the seven lean, for example, prophesied seven years of plenty and seven years of famine in the land, and enabled the ruler to keep the people from starving.

The Freudian interpreter views a dream, not as a portent, but as a revelation of the character of the dreamer. How can the dream be explained in terms of the dreamer's personality?

Dreams were formerly looked upon as chaotic phantasies lying beyond the province of science. Freud insists that dreaming follows very definite mental laws, and that dream-analysis is not guesswork but a scientific technique.

Freud believes that the unconscious mind is seething with suppressed desires which, in the waking life, cannot gain expression because the censor (conscience) blocks their entrance into the conscious mind. The censor represses the primitive wishes, and seeks by a constant vigil to "keep them in their places." The frustrated urges cause a profound unhappiness. The individual is unaware of the sources of his misery because the censor (resistance) conceals from the idealistic self at the conscious level those cravings which are evil according to the conventional code. Freud learned in his therapy that he had to unearth the longings of the Unconscious. But the censor stood in the way. The patient could not reveal the primal urges because they were hidden from his modest gaze. Then Freud discovered that the royal way to the Unconscious lay in dreams. It was through his therapy that he became interested in dream interpretation.

When a person is asleep, the censor, becoming a little groggy, is not careful in the inspection of immigrating wishes. Sleep, like a drug, produces a stupor; but still the censor is enough on guard to recognize undesirables, so that it is necessary for the turpitudinous desire to disguise itself in order to slip by the censor. The disguise it assumes is the symbol.

The dream which we remember upon awakening is the manifest content, made up of symbols. To get at the meaning of the dream, the latent content, the interpreter must translate the symbols. The meaning derived will depend upon the understanding of symbolism. Since Freud takes every symbol to be sexual in its significance, it is obvious that the meaning attributed to the manifest content will be sexual. Every dream becomes a wish fulfillment, affording satisfaction for sexual wishes. Since dreams offer an outlet for suppressed desires, and since the sexual urge is the most suppressed of our desires, due to conflict with the conventional code, according to Freud, it is natural that dreams should be given a sexual meaning.

The translation of the latent content into symbols is known as the dream work, performed in the course of sleep. The work proceeds by means of four characteristic mechanisms:

1. Condensation. One element in the manifest dream content may represent several in the latent. A dream of a statue of Uncle Sam in the style of Venus de Milo would represent the complex fact that the United States was unprepared for war (unarmed).

From the point of view of the analyst the mechanism of condensation is a convenient one, for it permits him to get more out of the dream than anybody would have suspected; indeed, he can derive as many meanings as he assumes there have been condensed.

2. Displacement. Unimportant ideas in the manifest content may be the most important in the latent. The unimportance is a disguise, comparable to that assumed by the spy who appears stupid, or the "overgrown boy" who slouches in order to slip by on half-fare on the railroad train.

3. Dramatization. The dreamer always appears in the dream. If the only creature in your dream is a mule or a cow, that's you!

4. Secondary Elaboration. The waking mind tends to alter the recollection of the dream by filling in the gaps and organizing the chaos into a coherent pattern. In describing the dream, particularly, the dreamer does some elaborating. It is the same propensity which gains expression in the familiar "fish story."

The dream fades rapidly upon the awakening of the dreamer. Freud would explain this phenomenon by stating that the resistance (censor) prevents the recollection of the disreputable incidents of the dream. However the phenomenon is explained, it is true that dreams must be recorded instantly upon awakening. If you wish to study your dreams, keep a pad and pencil at your bedside. To postpone the record until a more convenient moment, say, after breakfast, is to lose the dream forever.

b. Criticism. Some dreams belong to the category of wish fulfillment, such as the child's dream of possessing a toy, or the common adult dream of the death of some enemy, in which the wishes seem definitely non-sexual. But there are other types of dreams. The anxiety dream is typified by dreams of missing trains, of failing in examinations, of climbing interminable mountains, and similar dreams which really are reflections of the dreamer's anxiety that he may fail in tasks which he has undertaken. The teleological dreams are those which suggest courses of action or solutions of difficulties. A masculine woman dreamed of a magic talisman which turned out to be a powder-puff, the idea of the dreaming mind being that more use of the feminine arts might aid this dreamer to relieve dissatisfactions in her life. Self-critical dreams are those in which some dream symbol represents the dreamer's fear of his own faults. A man dreamed of a donkey with weak and wabbly legs, representing the dreamer's recognition and criticism of his own feebleness of character.

The Freudian theory must be supplemented to embrace the various kinds of dreams. Perhaps the following suggestion will answer this need. Emotional experiences persist beyond the immediate situation arousing them, in the form of "a hangover." Anger, for example, can be felt hours after the intense stage has subsided. The effects of the glandular turmoil so stir up the body as to leave residual tensions. In sleep these tensions vent themselves, affording the system a cathartic relief. Imagination sets the stage, prepares the appropriate situation for the drama of a particular emotion. For example, if a person has driven his car home fast at night, involving some fright over a prospective mishap, the hangover of fear will be dramatized in a stereotyped fear situation—a burglar may appear at the window and point a revolver. Any internal stimuli or even external stimuli may be dramatized during sleep. The ring of the alarm clock becomes a fire alarm, or the heartburn of indigestion becomes a bullet wound. A man dreamt that he was trying to cash a check. The teller asked him for identification. He took off his hat. "What else?" queried the teller. He took off his coat. "What else?" He took off his shirt. "What else?" He removed his trousers. "What else?" At this point he awoke to find the bedclothes had fallen on the floor. Imagination had furnished a situation to dramatize the sensations of exposure, and perhaps to fulfill an exhibitionistic wish, tinged with anxiety.

The interpretation of a dream requires an intimate knowledge of the entire career of the dreamer and of the particular emotional situation giving rise to the phantastic drama.

2. Daydreams. Thinking may be directed toward the solution of some problem, in which case it involves work, or it may be on pleasure bent, in which case it is more interested in indulging whims than in honest effort. The former may be labeled reality thinking; the latter, pleasure thinking. When thinking is not interested in reality, when it is not directed toward a constructive end, when it prefers the false to the true, it is sometimes called "autistic," a term coined by Bleuler. Autistic thinking is dominated by pleasure, in that it gives the illusion of aspirations fulfilled, obstacles removed, and impossibilities transformed into realities. Phantasy requires none of the painful effort necessary to actual achievement.

Real love is beset with quarrels and misunderstandings, but such is not the case with the amorous delights of the daydreamer. In a letter to *Picture Play*, a prize fan writes:

It makes me very angry when I hear people say that the movies exert a bad influence. Of course, there are a few exceptions, but for the most part the movies have no trace of immorality and I think they are, on the whole, productive of good taste; indeed, if taken in the right spirit, they can cause their audiences to lead nobler and more virtuous lives.

I will show you what I mean. My hero is Ramon Novarro. To me he is the ideal man. His beautiful bronzed body is like an ancient god's, his charming, cultured manners reminding one of an Old-World grandee's savoir-faire.

When I first saw him it was in silent pictures, when no vehicle given him was worthy of his beautiful presence. Those must have been unhappy days for dear Ramon, when his genius was so vilely cramped by the limitations of his everyday human associates. He could portray the braggart perfectly, and the lover sublimely, but he was not given the chances he deserved. Then came "The Pagan"! Never will I forget the sight of his splendid lithe form. Ah, Ramon, since that beautiful day your clothes have always seemed to hamper you.

I may seem a bit extreme to those who do not feel about Ramon as I do, but one cannot control these things, so one might as well admit them.

Concluding that a great soul like Ramon's must have a beautiful faith, like so many others who love him, I have entered the church to which he belongs, and I am now a Catholic.

I have also, as so many of us have done, taken up the study of Spanish, that I might be in closer communion with him.

You now see what I meant in the beginning of my letter. I feel that my life is more beautiful now and my thoughts run deeper. I have very mystic moods. Ramon, unwittingly, has led me to a higher plane where coarseness is eliminated.[1]

The girl who reads the photoplay magazines is really daydreaming and when she finds no Prince Charming among men with feet of clay, she clings to her "dream men," even as the woman above who went "just mad over Ramon."

The trouble with the truth is that it is mainly uncomfortable and often dull. Building castles in Spain, chasing rainbows, and blowing bubbles offer an escape from harsh reality. Every daydream is more interesting to us than the reality which is contemporaneous with it. Through phantasy the individual forsakes the actual world. There the danger lies, for the individual is apt to lose contact with the life about him—he reaches a state of ecstasy whence he cannot "come down to earth." Phantasy may be so alluring as to diminish interest in real achievement. Fictions tend to dull the sharp edge of reality. It is no use dreaming about the way things ought to be, since the retreat into phantasy makes reality much more awful to bear.

The study of a person's daydreams affords a deep insight into his personality. Phantasies reveal dominant interests which the individual himself may not clearly discern. Adler finds a wealth of material in daydreams which give him a clue to the goal in life around which a person's various activities are organized. Because phantasies are so intimate a part of himself, an individual is usually reticent in regard to them. The egoistic nature of daydreams attaches shame to their exposure. To bare your thoughts, your dreams of fame and fortune, is to expose your soul with shocking immodesty.

---

[1] *Picture Play*, March, 1931. By permission of *Picture Play*.

"A penny for your thoughts" is not enough of an inducement.

Daydreams are a revelation of temperament. There is the "conquering hero" type of dream, in which the individual catches a forward pass and runs for the winning touchdown. Of such is the stuff of fairy tales with the poor little girl coming into glory in the last scene of the drama. The conquering hero, under the influence of his reveries, is as intoxicated as the drunkard who, under the influence of alcohol, "can lick any man in the county."

A person of masochistic temperament prefers the "suffering hero" daydream. His worth unappreciated, he "goes out to the garden to eat worms." He may dream that he is dead, and that people throng the cemetery at his funeral, remorseful for the way they abused him while he was alive. A child is apt to give way to such an orgy of self-pity after he has been spanked for some misdemeanor, especially if he feels that the punishment has been unjust.

B. Imagination and Emotion. It is common knowledge that as a man thinks, he tends to feel, and vice versa. Ideas and emotions are intimately interrelated. It is of vital importance to a man's affective health to guard his mind against those thoughts which are apt to be translated into unhappy emotional consequences.

One of the most potent influences upon imagination in our time is the movie. The vividness of the motion picture makes its appeal particularly effective, but unfortunately that appeal is often seriously unwholesome. The importance of this fact has led to an extensive research. The average weekly attendance at all motion-picture theaters in the country came to 77,000,000 in 1929. Of these 77,000,000, about 28,000,000 were under 21; 11,000,000 were thirteen years old or younger, and 6,000,000 were seven years old or less. The average exposure of the child to the movies is about two hours. That is about twice the exposure of the child to Sunday school—if he goes to Sunday school at all. Many of the younger children sit through the same program two or three times. It may be set down as an established fact that "a movie a week" is impressing itself upon our children's imaginations. Many of the pictures which they absorb deal with the thrills of crime and illicit love. Values are instilled which undermine the training provided in the home, church, and school. Parents may endeavor to teach their children to be unselfish, courageous, honest, hard-working, faithful, and kind, but they cannot compete with the smart, sophisticated, daring, clever, stupendous, passionate, and dazzling ideals emanating from Hollywood. Tests have demonstrated that children retain about 70% of the material portrayed in the movies. More people will probably see the next Norma Shearer release than have seen Shakespeare's "Hamlet" in the three hundred years since "Hamlet" was written. The movies arouse emotions without any particular regard as to whether the consequences will be elevating or degrading. The situation, indeed, is a serious one, meriting careful attention.

Charcot and Janet, the famous French psychiatrists, called attention to the importance of ideas in illness. The nature of a disorder will sometimes be determined by what the person thinks (imagines) is the matter with him. Goldenrod is unjustly blamed by hay-fever sufferers for their ailment. Some hay-fever sufferers aver, "But I start sneezing if I only so much as see a bunch of goldenrod." That is just it. Most cases of that sort are started by just seeing the suspected plant: the sneezes are psychological sneezes. The patient got started by ragweed or some other real troublemaker, mentally associated goldenrod with his trouble, and now he can get a grand sneezing spell just by looking at it and feeling sorry for his poor nose. Try to get some pollen out of a bunch of goldenrod. You will find that you have to shake and thrash the flowers about to get the golden dust to come loose. Then try ragweed. The merest touch will send puffs of its pollen drifting into the wind. In spite of its general innocence, goldenrod may be the guilty plant in a very few cases. But it should be presumed innocent until proved guilty. Many persons believe that fruit juice causes milk to curdle in the stomach, thus producing indigestion. They do not know that there are enzymes in the stomach, anyhow, waiting to curdle the milk as a step in the normal digestive process. The misconception of the bodily functions may produce indigestion, through conscious interference with an habitual process which works best when it works automatically. Wrong ideas encourage inappropriate emotions, which, in turn, mean misdirected energy and lack of harmony within the personality, resulting eventually in maladaptation to the social environment. An extreme case was the boy who refused to exercise because he was afraid of spontaneous combustion. Right thinking bears a vital relation to sound health.

C. Types of Imagery. Francis Galton, the famous British scientist, became interested in the study of mental imagery, particularly of the mode of visual presentation, and he began an inquiry to ascertain the essential differences between the mental operations of different men. The investigation of this problem by Galton and, since his time, by others has revealed the fact that people differ in the kinds of imagery which they employ in thinking of the same situation. One sort of imagery may predominate in a given individual; one sort of imagery is more vivid than others, although correlation, not compensation, being the rule, a person who excels in one kind of imagery is apt, generally speaking, to excel in other kinds as well.

Test yourself. Ideate each of the following experiences and rate them:

1. As vivid as the actual experience.

2. Very clear.

3. Moderately clear.

4. Not clear but recognizable.

5. Vague.

6. So dim as to be hardly discernible.

7. No image at all.

Visual imagery.
   The face of a friend.
   A rose.
   The American flag.
Auditory imagery.
   The tune of the Blue Danube Waltz.
   The chirp of a cricket.
   The voice of your father.
Gustatory imagery.
   The taste of beefsteak.
   Grapefruit.
   Salt.
Olfactory imagery.
   The smell of camphor.
   Old Golds.
   Kerosene.
Cutaneous imagery.
   The feel of wet soap.
   The prick of a thorn.
   A pebble in the shoe.
Kinæsthetic imagery.
   The swing of a golf club.
   Stooping over to pick up an object.
   Threading a needle.
Organic imagery.
   A headache.
   A full stomach.
   A fever.

1. Description. Imagery may be classified, as in the above experiment, according to the various modes, such as visual, auditory, and so forth, or it may be described under the more general categories, concrete and verbal.   In concrete ideation, a person "pictures" the object itself, while in verbal ideation he thinks of the words which symbolize the object.   Thus you may think of a rose by seeing in your mind's eye a pink flower (Concrete Visual), or by visualizing the word r—o—s—e— (Verbal Visual), or by hearing the word as it is spoken (Verbal Auditory), or by speaking it yourself (Verbal Vocal Motor), or by writing it (Verbal Manual Motor).   There are many varieties and combinations of Concrete and Verbal imagery.

Visual images are extremely vivid in some persons.   A painter dismisses his model after half an hour's sitting and then paints her from memory.   Galton tells of a man who habitually worked out sums by aid of an imaginary slide rule, which he set in the desired way and read off mentally.   A statesman assured Galton that a certain hesitation in utterance which he had at times was due to his being plagued by the image of his manuscript speech with its original erasures and corrections.

When imagery is predominantly visual, another mode of presentation must be translated into visual terms before the situation can be grasped adequately.   In listening to the description of a football game over the radio, such a person is likely to convert the verbal auditory images into concrete visual images.   It is most difficult for such an individual to transact business over the telephone since no scope is given his visualization.   He remembers a melody not in terms of tones, since his auditory imagery is deficient, but in visual images of the notes on the music sheet or of the keys to be played on the piano keyboard.   If a foreign tongue is spoken to him, he must go through the same laborious procedure of translating the auditory images into visual ones before he can grasp the meaning, since unfortunately he has probably learned the language in the classroom through reading.   A prominent psychologist ideates the German language in vocal-motor and auditory terms because he learned it by conversation in Germany, whereas he ideates French in visual and manual-motor terms because he learned it in the classroom.

An extraordinary sort of visual imagery has been investigated in recent years—eidetic imagery—which is a special concrete visual imagery.   In a typical experiment, a silhouette picture with a number of items is exposed to the view of the observer who fixates it for 15 seconds.   The picture is presented against a gray mat for a background.   The picture is removed and the observer stares at the gray mat.   If the observer is an eidetic, he will see the picture on the background, and will be able to describe the most minute details of the scene, such as the precise number of buttons on a pedestrian's jacket, or the number of whiskers on a cat's lip.

Eidetic imagery is very rare in adults.   About 60 per cent of children between the ages of 10 and 15 possess the eidetic capacity.   Eidetic imagery enables children to repeat their adaptive responses to the situation represented until satisfactory adjustments are effected.   A child's reaction to the first presentation of a situation is incomplete.   He looks at the same picture book repeatedly, and wants the same stories told over and over.   Eidetic imagery enables the child to review various aspects of a situation until he gradually gains a comprehension of the full meaning of the whole.   By the time he has reached adolescence, he has learned the requisite modes of adjustment, and the eidetic imagery, no longer a necessary aid, declines.[1]

2. Applications.   A boy of thirteen was trying to draw a map of Greece.   Although he had made a thorough study of the map, his outline drawing was very inaccurate.   A psychologist, surmising that the boy belonged to the motor type, had him trace the coast-line with his finger, at first in sections and

---

[1]See G. W. Allport: "Eidetic Imagery," *The British Journal of Psychology,* 1925, 15, 99–120.

then as a whole.   The boy was then able to reproduce the map without difficulty.

A student who is visually minded will learn his lessons most efficiently by reading them.   A well-ordered notebook with ample margins and colored underlining facilitates cramming considerably.   The habit of note-taking, however, is a vicious one.   The notebook becomes a substitute for the understanding.   When the average student attends a lecture, he writes down what is said and then reads his notes to absorb the meaning of the discourse—a most circuitous and cumbersome method.   A college man trained himself to think while he was listening, and to remember what he heard.   He saved himself a lot of dull labor.

If a person has a vivid auditory imagery, he grasps material most easily if it is read to him.   If the verbal motor (kinæsthetic) imagery is superior, he learns best by reading out loud or reciting his lessons out loud.   Some people think best out loud, as the lecturer does whose ideas come with facility when he is speaking.   Such a person would do well to dictate his books, while other individuals can think most effectively while they write.   The wise person will train himself in the various kinds of imagery so that he will be prepared to meet all sorts of situations.   He will not suffer, as some do, from the necessity of translating every mode of imagery into visual images before the meaning can be grasped.

Now that we have made a study of imagery, we are prepared to investigate the two fundamental kinds of imagination, reproductive imagination (memory) which reinstates the past, and constructive or creative imagination (anticipation) which points its interest primarily to the future.

II.   REMEMBERING

It is through remembering our past successes and failures that we are able to profit by experience.   Memory furnishes the data for anticipation. Thus progress is rendered possible.

Some persons think of memory as a storehouse; some persons think of it as a special faculty. The mind, however, is not organized on the department-store plan. The mind works as a whole. When the mind is pointed toward the past, the individual remembers. In the act of remembering, the mind utilizes experiences accumulated through all of its various activities.

There is no general memory. There are only a number of special memories—memories for numbers, names, tones, locations, and so on. A person may excel in some and be deficient in others. To use more exact diction, a person remembers some experiences better than others. "A good memory" means a person remembers many sorts of things well.

An individual learns, retains, recalls, and recognizes by organizing experience according to definite sorts of relations. The student who is preparing for an examination can aid his memory immensely by organizing his notes before he settles down to the grind of memorizing them. The very process of organizing is worth hours of cramming.

A. Dependence of Memory upon Four Tendencies. A good memory depends upon efficient attending, perceiving, and imagining—upon the organization of four fundamental tendencies:

1. Impressional. The strength of the initial impression influences the length of time the experience will be retained. A poor memory may be due to poor attention.

To remember well, a person must first be a good observer. He must know what to look for and note the essentials of the situations by concentrating his attention upon them. A vivid impression is vital. A correct preparation which sets the individual for observation facilitates the perceptual process. Test yourself. Study the picture for 90 seconds. Then, re-

moving the picture from view, answer the following questions:

1. Are the headlights tilted up or down as a result of the accident?
2. Is it a coupé or a sedan?
3. What is the make of the car?
4. Is the hood of the car up or down?
5. What kind of a store is located on the corner?
6. What inscription is on the store awning?
7. Name two products advertised on the signs.
8. Whose ice cream is featured in the drug store?
9. Is the windshield of the car broken?
10. What is the grade of the street to the left of the photograph?
11. Is there a curbstone on the street?
12. How many cars appear in the picture?
13. Is there a mailbox for packages near by?
14. Is there a dent in the left front fender?
15. Is there a woman in the picture?

16. How many people are wearing coats?
17. During what season of the year has the accident occurred?
18. Is it a fair or rainy day?
19. Are the sides of the building made of wood or brick?
20. How many of the bystanders are wearing neckties?[1]

Of course, if you had been a casual observer of the accident and had been called upon for testimony, your answers would have been far more inaccurate.

2. Associative. The linkage between experiences is strengthened by repetition of the association. The cross-examining lawyer instructs the witness to think of one incident in order to bring back, through a connection, the material he wishes the witness to recall. Remembering is facilitated when a person connects what is learned in a meaningful way with his own intimate experiences. Association, as we shall see later, is the real key to memory.

3. Determining. Have a person read a passage with the definite purpose of ascertaining whether he can pronounce every word correctly. When he completes the reading, ask him to repeat the account from memory. He will do poorly because he was not set to remember. One wholesome function of a school examination is that it reinforces the set to learn and to recall by arousing "interest." Interest or set functions as a determining tendency.

An efficient memory depends upon the wise selection of the material worth remembering. Selection is determined by the *Aufgabe*. The brain has been described as an organ of forgetting. The wise person does not attempt to remember everything he sees or hears. Encyclopedic learning may be a burden rather than an advantage. Memory is often a simulator of

---

[1] Reproduced by permission of the Boston *American*, through the kindness of Samuel Stavisky.

intelligence. Under our present educational curriculum the deception is only too often successful. "Believe it or not, William Lyon of Edinburgh can repeat from memory the entire contents of a newspaper after reading it over once." Yes, but who wants to do it?

A person does not remember names because he has no desire (intent) to fix them in his mind. Lacking the intention, he does not even heed the name when he is introduced. Interest is essential to effective remembering.

While the intention to remember is important, it is no guarantee of accurate memory, as any student who is struggling with an examination can bear witness.

The determining tendencies are built up through the learning processes, since education develops new interests. New sets are established which serve to control the course of associations in line with the dominating concerns of the individual.

4. Perseverative. Memory depends upon the fact that impressions "persevere." If a person leaves a problem unfinished to devote himself to another piece of work, thoughts of the uncompleted task will keep intruding. The man who begins thinking of three-letter words that can be derived from Toothpaste will toss all night in his sleep as new words dawn upon him. A tune may persist in running through the head despite all efforts to banish it. The teacher tends to give a pupil the same mark throughout the semester. A phrase will recur time and again. On a certain day, one finds oneself saying "You said it" in response to every remark.

B. Conscious and Unconscious Memory. A clear understanding of the mind necessitates a recognition of the distinction between conscious or psychological memory and unconscious or physiological memory. Though physiological memory shades imperceptibly into psychological memory, nevertheless, accurate description demands the appreciation of some differentiation.

The capacity for retention is found throughout the realm of matter. After a suit has been worn awhile, it becomes deformed in a definite system of wrinkles. Pressing the suit restores the original shape, but it is not long till the garment returns to its characteristic folds. One might say that a suit remembers the wrinkles it is supposed to assume, but the use of the word "remember" destroys the psychological connotation of the term. On a higher level, matter is organized in a living body, with its own memory, as we see in immunity against disease, which is due to the body's having once defended itself against the toxins of a pathogenic organism; its tissues are thereby sensitized against this particular poison, so that should the organism again attempt to enter the body, the defensive mechanisms are immediately mobilized and the organism destroyed before it can multiply in the body.

Conscious memory, in contrast to unconscious memory, is characterized primarily by the experience of "againness" which we designate as recognition. Psychological memory involves meaning. An event is recalled and recognized by its meaning; in other words, by an appreciation of the associative connections between events. The student who understands (the meaning of) his lesson is more apt to recall it than the student who memorizes the material mechanically. Memorizing on a mechanical level is known as rote memory, and it is much inferior to logical memory where meaning is taken into account. Rote memory is more akin to the physical memory exhibited by the egg which remembers how to turn out a complete chick.

C. Rote and Logical Memory. Allow yourself 40 seconds to learn the following list of 20 words. Then close the book and write down the words you can recall, without regard to their order, allowing yourself two minutes to complete the task.

Ball	Pipe
Tree	Trip
House	Song
Fox	Spoon
Book	Wire
Fence	Window
Sieve	Water
Black	Hill
Thin	Study
Sky	Car

Following the same instructions, learn the following list of 20 words:

Ice	Steel
Pond	Thin
Cold	Crack
Skate	Glide
Race	Sharp
Edge	Cut
Snow	Shiver
Smooth	Shore
Stars	Fire
Wind	Heat

Carrying out the same instructions, learn the following list of 20 syllables:

Bew	Sig
Rak	Kor
Doq	Lav
Tih	Wic
Cuv	Dus
Paf	Fod
Huc	Nac
Fip	Mur
Wes	Pib
Rul	Toh

Check up on your lists. Credit yourself 1 for every correct word and subtract 1 for every word you have written down which does not appear in the original list. Compare your scores on the three tests.

In the first list, the words are unrelated, whereas in the second list the words are linked through the medium of meaning. A more obvious case would be the learning of the following list of 20 words:

It
Is
An
Interesting
Observation
That
Learning
A
List
Of
Words
Is
An
Easy
Task
If
The
Meaning
Is
Comprehended.

Such a list stands in marked contrast to the series of nonsense syllables where, undoubtedly, your score was low.

Ebbinghaus invented the nonsense syllable as a medium for testing memory. The nonsense syllable consists of two consonants with a vowel between, meaningful combinations being excluded. Since the syllables are practically meaningless, every subject starts at scratch, as it were, and lists may be constructed which involve a uniform degree of difficulty.

Meaningful words, on the other hand, carry more meaning for some persons than others, thus involving an unfair advantage. The nonsense syllable tests the bare capacity of memory. The method, of course, tends toward artificiality, since in our everyday experience we remember meanings, and the superior memory belongs to the person who can avail himself of a host of associations to facilitate the remembering process. To put it facetiously, we do better to forget nonsense, anyway.

The memorization of a list of words or syllables is tested more scientifically if the words are exposed one at a time, thus preventing the observer from glancing back over the list. With the single exposure it is possible to record the exact number of repetitions necessary for complete learning. If the observer can run back over the list as he wills, there is no way of telling how many repeated observations of the material he makes.

Meaningful experience is much more easily remembered than nonsense. In learning a passage it is very important to grasp the meaning. Mere repetition does not strengthen bonds much. The addition of "belongingness" (meaning) is necessary. "Mere sequence with no fitness or belonging has done little or nothing," says Thorndike in regard to an experiment on learning. "With only a fourth as many repetitions the greater belongingness results in much greater strengthening, producing nearly twice as many correct responses."[1]

Mnemonic devices approximate the nonsense of the nonsense syllable, stressing rote memory.

Many people cannot determine the number of days in a month without running through the jingle, "Thirty days has September." Resort to such mnemonic devices may save time for the moment, but in the long run it is poor economy. Memory experts train themselves to remember names by me-

---

[1] E. L. Thorndike: *Human Learning*, pp. 19, 23. 1931.

chanical links, such as remembering Hicks, the shoe manufacturer, by recalling that "Hicks sells kicks," but they forget
other matters of more importance, as did Robert Nutt of
Greensboro, North Carolina, a memory expert, who failed to
appear for his scheduled speech at the Binghamton, New York,
Rotary Club, because, he explained, the engagement had
simply slipped his mind.[1]

Rote memory may be tested experimentally by the Memory
Span method.　The memory span is the longest series of items
which the subject is able to reproduce correctly after a single
presentation.　Digits are ordinarily used as the material.
The presentation may be visual or auditory.　In the visual
method the experimenter presents a series of cards upon which
the digits are printed, ranging in span from four to twelve
digits.　The upper limit is fifteen if the subjects are college
students.　The experimenter first presents the card with four
digits for four seconds.　The subject is instructed that he will
be required to reproduce the digits in their correct order.
When the card is removed, the subject writes down or gives
orally all of the digits he can remember.　Each card is exposed
for as many seconds as there are digits printed on it.　The
time is controlled by a metronome.　In the auditory method,
the digits are read at a rate of one per second and the subject
is instructed to wait until the digits are all read before he
writes down the items or gives them orally.

Logical memory may be tested experimentally by requiring
the subject to reproduce a narrative which he reads or which is
read to him.　The reproduction may be oral or in writing.
The score is computed in terms of the number of ideas correctly
remembered, the distinct ideas being separated by slanting
lines.　In the Stanford-Binet Intelligence Test there is a test
for logical memory in which the child is given thirty-five seconds to read a passage.　He is to read it with not more than

---

[1]The Boston *Herald*, July 22, 1932.

JASTROW'S MEMORY APPARATUS—USED FOR SERIAL EXPOSURES
(Reproduced by courtesy of the C. H. Stoelting Company)

two mistakes in the reading and to recall at least eight ideas.

New York./ September 5th./ A fire/ last night/ burned/ three houses/ near the center/ of the city./ It took some time/ to put it out./ The loss/ was fifty thousand dollars,/ and seventeen families/ lost their homes./ —In saving/ a girl/ who was asleep/ in bed,/ a fireman/ was burned/ on the hands. [1]

D. The Four Major Aspects of Remembering. *1. Learning.* Learning involves the modification of activity through experience. Learning may be sensori-motor as in the acquisition of a motor skill; it may be perceptual as in the development of observational capacities through which new means of apprehension are achieved; it may be ideational as in the improvement of ability for problem-solving and the cultivation of insight for meanings; or it may be appreciational as in the attainment of a new sense of values. In all its various forms, learning is fundamentally a process of change.

Learning is not remembering, but a preparation for remembering. Since memory depends upon "memorizing," either conscious or unconscious, learning can be studied most conveniently as one aspect of remembering.

a. Trial and Error. According to one group of psychologists, learning proceeds by the trial-and-error method. A person who is faced with a baffling problem is like a man lost in the woods—he darts here, he darts there, until finally, by chance, he finds his way out. Many mistakes are made that will gradually be omitted in repeated trials until the reaction is perfected. In the weeding process, the correct response is "stamped in" because the result is satisfying, while the false step is eliminated because the consequence is annoying.

The method of trial and error may be illustrated by a test of sensori-motor learning, in which the subject is required to trace a star that is visible to him only in a mirror. Due to the

---

[1] Reprinted by permission of, and by special arrangement with, Houghton Mifflin Co.

reversal of his customary movements, the subject in "feeling his way along" must adapt himself by experimenting with a variety of motions until he learns the knack of it.   Learning is measured by the number of trials necessary before the subject is able to keep his pencil on the outline of the star he is tracing.[1]

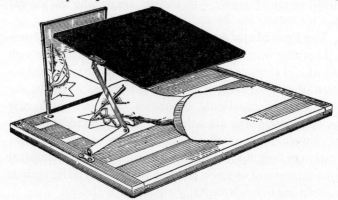

MIRROR DRAWING
(Reproduced by courtesy of the C. H. Stoelting Company)

In a similar manner, an animal is supposed to escape from a cage by making movements blindly until a latch happens to be struck which releases him from captivity.   After a number of repetitions, the correct movement will be made sooner—the animal has learned how to get out of the puzzle box.   The reaction is not deliberative.   The animal learns by doing, not by observing what he's doing.   There is no conscious direction.   The behavior is impulsive rather than reasoning.   Human beings are said to solve their problems in the same fashion.

Thorndike, who is sometimes represented as espousing this view, denies that responses are random in the sense that any one person's response is as likely to occur as any other person's in a given situation.[2]   He definitely abrogates such a view

[1]See H. E. Garrett and M. R. Schneck: *Psychological Tests, Methods, and Results*, Part I, p. 102.
[2]E. L. Thorndike: *Animal Intelligence.*   1911.

when he states that "the great bulk of a child's motor behavior and learning is determined by definite abilities, wants, interests, and the circumstances of his life."[1]

The viewpoint that learning is a fortuitous process by which successful responses emerge through chance selection has no wholehearted advocates. The representation of such a viewpoint has served chiefly as a straw man created for purposes of attack and the joy that comes with the demolition of the enemy.

b. Insight. The trial-and-error method is vigorously opposed by a number of psychologists who maintain that the higher animals, such as cats, apes, and human beings, show some insight in the learning process. Adams put cats in puzzle boxes, just as Thorndike did, and observed their behavior. On the basis of his data, Adams concluded that the cats wanted something, and that they showed foresight in attaining their goal.[2] Adams' hypothesis concurs with that of Köhler, who found that the apes he studied were not fumbling blindly for a chance solution, but were striving intelligently to achieve a goal which had been foreseen. For example:

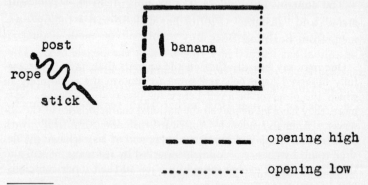

[1]E. L. Thorndike, *et al.*: *The Psychology of Wants, Interests, and Attitudes*, p. 13. 1935. By permission of D. Appleton-Century Company, Inc.

[2]D. K. Adams: "Experimental Studies of Adaptive Behavior in Cats," *Comparative Psychology Monographs*, Vol. 6, No. 1.

The problem could only be solved by pushing the banana across the cage with the stick to the side of the bars and then running around to that side and seizing the banana by the hand. This the ape suddenly did after a period of inactivity, when the solution suddenly dawned on him. Insight was required in that the ape had to anticipate the relationship between a new location of the fruit and its availability at that position. No amount of random movements would have resulted in procuring the banana.[1]

Accordingly, human beings also learn with insight. They know what they are trying to do, at times, and then a sudden insight reveals the way the task can be accomplished. Learning is not a blind mechanical process but a mental activity in which the resources of the mind are brought into play to achieve the goal in view. Trial and error are involved in the struggle for a solution, but the whole story requires the recognition of an additional factor, insight, which guides the activities to a successful completion.[2] The experimental sorting takes place, but it may be intelligently directed.

The controversy between the proponents of the "trial-and-error" and "insight" theories has called forth a telling comment from Bertrand Russell:

One may say broadly that all the animals that have been carefully observed have behaved so as to confirm the philosophy in which the observer believed before his observations began. Nay, more, they have all displayed the national characteristics of the observer. Animals studied by Americans rush about frantically, with an incredible display of hustle and pep, and at last achieve the desired result by chance. Animals observed by Germans sit still and think, and at last evolve the solution out of their inner consciousness.[3]

---

[1] W. Köhler: *The Mentality of Apes*, p. 264. 1925.

[2] K. Koffka: *The Growth of the Mind*.

[3] B. Russell: *Philosophy*, pp. 29–30. 1927. By permission of the Open Court Publishing Company.

The rôle of insight, of course, is clear in experiments involving ideational learning. Substitution Tests require the subject to substitute one set of characters for another according to instructions provided in a key. Writing a paragraph in code is one form of such a test.[1] A Rational Learning Test devised by Peterson sets the subject the task of learning associations between certain numbers and letters as rapidly as possible. Letters A to J are numbered in random order from 1 to 10.

A	B	C	D	E	F	G	H	I	J
6	2	8	5	9	10	4	7	3	1

The number of each letter is unknown to the subject. The experimenter calls out A and tells the subject to guess numbers until he names the right number for A. The experimenter says "right," proceeds to B, and so on through the series. The experiment is continued until the subject gets each number right twice in succession through the series. Performance is judged by the total time consumed, the number of errors committed, and the number of repetitions from A to J required.[2]

c. The Conditioned Reflex. Psychologists with behavioristic leanings are prone to consider the conditioned reflex as the prototype of all learning. Pavlov's description of the conditioning process is a case of oversimplification, since he fails to take into account the manifold associations which constitute meaning. Mere sequence or temporal contiguity may explain the flow of saliva, but it cannot adequately describe the factor of "belongingness" without which human learning is ineffective. Furthermore, much of our learning is a conscious effort to achieve a desirable end, whereas the conditioning of a reflex proceeds without much awareness on the part of the animal as to what is going on, and the secretion of saliva is not a particularly satisfying consequence. Some human learning of

---

[1] See H. E. Garrett and M. R. Schneck: *op. cit.*, Part I, p. 93ff.

[2] J. Peterson: "Experiments in Rational Learning," *Psychological Review*, 1918, 25, 443–467.

course is unconscious and, therefore, simply a matter of mechanical association, but the conditioned reflex is not truly a prototype for conscious learning in which meaning plays a significant rôle.   A little girl was burned by an infra-red lamp; thereafter, she refused to touch it, whether it was hot or not. On the other hand, her father touches it when it is cold and leaves it alone when it is hot, since he understands the mechanism involved in the situation.   There is a world of difference between her learning and his.   The learning of the little girl belongs to the category of response which may be specifically designated as a form of unintentional learning; it is learning without understanding.

Learning involves not only the conditioning of the muscles and glands, but also the interrelated activities of hundreds of millions of associative neurons which can receive and transmit impulses among themselves, thus producing responses involving the subtlest relations known by man and the most elusive intellectual adjustments he can make.

The flow of a person's saliva in response to the noon-day whistle is a simple association compared with his association of the Platonic and Aristotelian attempts to solve metaphysical dualism, a realm of thought never invaded by a hungry dog. Association is the keynote of learning, whether it is called conditioning or not.

d. Efficient Learning.   (1) Learning by Wholes.   It is better in memorizing material to learn by the "whole" method rather than by the "part."   Most people will learn a poem line by line instead of concentrating on the poem as a whole. The usual preference for learning by parts is due to the fact that under such a program the individual is encouraged as he sees his progress advancing step by step.   The part method, however, in spite of its popularity, is uneconomical.

Since the poem is to be recited in the forward direction, associations should be established only in that direction.   In learning by parts, associations are established between the end of the line and the beginning of the line, as the learner goes back to impress the line more thoroughly on his mind. Suppose a person is learning:

> "It is very nice to think
> The world is full of meat and drink,
> With little children saying grace
> In every Christian kind of place."

He proceeds:

> It is very nice to think.
> It is very nice to think.
> The world is full of meat and drink.
> The world is full of meat and drink.
> It is very nice...........

Associations are established:

> think..
> It.............think..
> The...........drink..
> The...........drink..
> It....................

Instead of the desirable links:

> think..
> The...........drink..
> With..........grace..
> In............place..

If each line is learned separately, the problem of mastering the connections between lines still remains to be attacked, whereas, in the "whole" method, the lines are learned in their relationship to the total pattern (forward); consequently, there is no necessity for the double task of mastering both lines and connections separately. Time and energy are saved by achieving both ends simultaneously.

The meaning of the whole must be comprehended if the meaning of each part is to be fully appreciated. The only things which we remember are wholes; and particular things are remembered only as parts of unitary wholes. Memory is a synthesizing activity which combines elements to form wholes. In the light of this fact, it is not surprising that learning is most effective when the "whole" method is employed.

The "whole" method is particularly efficient when material is meaningful, and when the learner is an intelligent person. Since attention tends to flag after prolonged concentration, a pause at intervals will keep attention at a high level throughout the performance. The best method, therefore, is to learn a section, pause for a brief rest, and then continue ahead for another section. The learning is consistently forward, with intervals of rest to maintain attention at a maximum.

(2) *Rate of Learning.* There is an optimal rate of learning for each individual. If a person proceeds slowly, the mind has a tendency to "woolgather," while excessive speed prevents the assimilation of the impressions. The ideal procedure is to start slowly until the "feel" is achieved, and then to accelerate until a maximum speed is reached which still permits an understanding of the material that is being grasped. A person may aim a rifle too short or too long a time. An optimal timing can be discovered through experience. Cramming, while it may be efficient for short retention, may produce more fatigue than knowledge. Speed, with intervals of rest, is efficient.

(3) *Repetition.* According to Thorndike's Law of Exercise, other things being equal, exercise strengthens the bond between a situation and a response.[1] Recent studies, some by Thorndike himself, have indicated, however, that repetition may be effective, but that it is not necessary in the making or

[1] See E. L. Thorndike: *Education*, pp. 95–97. 1914.

breaking of habits. Mere repetition is of little value, particularly if the individual pays slight attention to what is going on. Progress is facilitated if the individual is aware of his goal and of the trend of his efforts.[1] The learner is wise who pays heed to his errors and thereby is enabled to profit by his mistakes. Dunlap's method of negative practice, where the error itself is eliminated by repetition, depends for its success on full cognizance of the folly of the incorrect habit. Practice is more apt to make perfect where the correct responses are the ones that are repeated.

Repetition neither strengthens nor weakens an activity, but it does afford other factors an opportunity to exert their favorable or unfavorable influence. Among the important factors determining the value of practice are interest in the performance and the states of satisfaction or annoyance which result from the successes or failures. Associative connections are established fundamentally because there are urges which are responsible for the continuation of practice. Acts are repeated largely because they bring satisfaction.[2] The affective elements in learning are of basic importance.

Literally speaking, repetition never occurs, for the second appearance of a stimulus is only roughly equivalent to the first; the individual is only approximately the same from one situation to another, and no two responses are exactly alike. Total situations are never repeated.[3] Situations, individuals, and responses may be alike, but they are always alike with a difference. Repetition, therefore, means that one performance is duplicated only in a general way.

Economy is attained by apportioning repetitions over a period of time. If there is no necessity for rushing, a learning today and another tomorrow will be more effective than two

[1]See E. L. Thorndike: *Human Learning*, p. 19.

[2]See E. L. Thorndike, *et al.*: *Fundamentals of Learning*, p. 18. 1932.

[3]See E. R. Guthrie: *The Psychology of Learning*, p. 19.

learnings today. Successive repetitions bring diminishing returns, particularly if they are crowded into a period of continuous work. Repeated reviews of a course during a semester will make for longer retention than will repetitions crammed into the night before an examination, although cramming by the "whole" method has its advantages for immediate retention.

(4) *Reward and Punishment.* In the ideal situation a person carries out a program that sweeps him along by the very force of its appeal. Such an interest is said to be intrinsic. A familiar example would be that of the boy who practises catching a baseball because he wants to become a great ball-player. There are, however, many situations where the learner must engage in activities not because he wants to, but because somebody else wants him to do so. Such would be the case with many children who take music lessons or study arithmetic. Under such conditions, it is necessary to encourage them to recognize their obligations by supplying rewards for compliance and punishment for failure to fall in line with the demands imposed upon them. Interest, thus, is not in the activity itself, but is supplied from without; in other words, the interest is extrinsic.

What can be done with a boy who is not interested in his school work? The obvious answer would be to revise the educational curriculum so that it would fit more readily into the natural interests of the child, but such a solution, many would contend, would rob the school of its disciplinary value. Extrinsic interests may be supplied in terms of half-holidays, trips to the movies, or cash prizes, with the thought, perhaps, that if the pupil be lured into his studies, someday they may come to possess an intrinsic attraction.[1] People may be spurred to industry by the promise of a bonus or by the threat

---

[1] See W. H. Lancelot: *Booklet of Teaching Skills.* Prepared by Department of Vocational Education, Iowa State College. 1926.

of being "fired," they may be inspired with a zeal for goodness by the prospect of Heaven and by the possibility of eternal damnation; and they may be deterred from a life of crime by the fear of social ostracism or a term in prison. We are not fully convinced, you see, that virtue is its own reward.

It is obvious to the careful student of human affairs that the application of reward and punishment is haphazard and unscientific. On the surface it would seem that rewards would "stamp in" a given pattern of behavior and that punishment would "stamp it out," or as Thorndike phrased it in his Law of Effect, other things being equal, the greater the satisfyingness of the state of affairs which accompanies or follows a given response to a certain situation, the more likely that response is to be made to that situation in the future.[1]

However, the situation is more complicated than it appears. The effects of reward and punishment are determined by what they cause the animal or person to do.[2] The consequences of punishment are found to be more problematic than the results of reward. Punishment, to be most effective, must provoke the practice of the correct response, with the immediate award of some sign of approval. Thorndike suggests some definite means for improving the effectiveness of punishment, as he feels that "the influence of customary punishments as actually administered has been inferior to that of customary rewards."[3]

1. Make sure the punishment belongs to the behavior. If you spank a child see to it that he understands just why the rod is being applied. One aid for clarifying the connection is to inflict the punishment at the time of the transgression.

2. Forestall punishment by satisfying the want innocently. Provide sweets in the diet to prevent the stealing of jam.

---

[1] See E. L. Thorndike: *Education*, pp. 95–97.

[2] See E. R. Guthrie: *op. cit.*, Chapter XII, "Reward and Punishment."

[3] E. L. Thorndike, *et al.*: *The Psychology of Wants, Interests, and Attitudes*, p. 151. By permission of D. Appleton-Century Company, Inc.

3. Shift the emphasis from the wages of sin to the comfort and security of right-doing.

4. Use rewards more.

5. Plan punishment scientifically.   The efficient motivation of the learning process depends upon a clear understanding of the incentives to be evoked and the technique for arousing them.[1]

e. Transfer of Training.   Before the findings of scientific psychology arose to controvert them, educators delighted in pointing out the wholesale benefits to be derived from pursuing certain subjects in the curriculum, such as mathematics or Latin, on the assumption that whatever training strengthens one "faculty" will indirectly strengthen all the other "faculties."   Arithmetic, it was alleged, affords a pupil the opportunity to develop habits of mental attention, argumentative sequence, absolute accuracy, and satisfaction in truth as a result.   Such a fond hope has been exploded by the discovery that the effects of educational training, on the contrary, are specific in nature.   "By doubling a boy's reasoning power in arithmetical problems we do not double it for formal grammar or chess or economic history or theories of evolution.   . . . The gain of courage in the game of football is never equaled by the gain in moral courage or resistance to intellectual obstacles."[2]   Transfer of training from one sort of mental endeavor to another occurs only under certain conditions. Transfer is facilitated, for example, by the presence of identical elements, either in the material which is studied or in the procedure which is employed.   Training in addition will facilitate multiplication in so far as both tasks involve the computation of numbers, addition itself being a process in multiplication. Similarly, the study of Latin will help the learning of French

---

[1] Refer back to Chapter VIII, "The Fundamental Urges."
[2] E. L. Thorndike: *Educational Psychology, Briefer Course*, p. 268.   1914.

because many of the words are recognizably similar or identical. Similarities in procedure will explain why a person who trains himself in chemical experimentation may thereby improve his facility for research in physics.

The specificity of habit was mentioned in connection with Hartshorne, May, and Shuttleworth's study of character organization. In all learning, the spread of improvement from one field to another may be facilitated by definite efforts towards correlation, through the appreciation of common aims and the recognition of interrelationships. The student may carry his scientific attitude from the laboratory to his political behavior, if he becomes cognizant of the applicability of science to politics, but more often than not, his scientific training will not affect his vote because he will fail to see any connection or any need for integration.

f. The Age of the Learner. It is an old adage that "you can't teach an old dog new tricks," but a scientific investigation by Thorndike over a period of two years, under a grant from the Carnegie Foundation, reveals the fact that up to the age of 45 there is practically no subject which the average man or woman of intelligence cannot master if he will. People along in years demonstrated that they could learn shorthand, mathematics, or languages with astonishing facility. Thorndike pitted his oldest group—those aged from 35 to 57—against young men and women who averaged 18 years old, in learning Esperanto. The aged group were composed of candidates for the degree of A. M. at Columbia, while the younger group was made up of students in a good private school. The oldsters made twice as much progress as the youngsters, notwithstanding the youngsters had twice as much class study and (provided they did not shirk) twice as much home study as the older people. Thorndike also pitted his older people against children from 9 to 11, who were mostly children of exceptionally high intelligence, and, contrary to the old-fashioned notion, the younger children were the slowest of all in learning the language.

Many a woman of 30 or 40, left without support, has wondered whether she is too old to learn to be a stenographer. Thorndike's investigation demonstrates that the greatest facility for learning shorthand comes between the years of 20 and 24, and that there is only a slight difference in facility at the age of 30.

The traditional belief that childhood is the golden age for learning is untenable in the light of Thorndike's findings. Childhood is not the period in which one learns most readily to read, write, speak, and understand a language, and also the early 'teens are not the next most advantageous period. The gain made by any group of any age from 20 to 40 will be greater than the gain made by a group aged 8, 10, or 12 of equal native capacity.[1]

Older persons appear to be poorer learners for several reasons. When they undertake a new subject of study at 35 or 40, they expect their minds to work just as fast as they did in their 'teens. And of course progress is slow—at first—not because the mentality has declined, but merely because the individuals have interrupted the habit of study for so long a time that they have to build up the habit anew, and sometimes it is a slow process. Often, too, the older people lack the incentive to learn.

According to Thorndike, a person under fifty is never too old to learn. If he wants to get back his old-time facility, he can do so. Adult education is, therefore, justified. Employers must recognize that their older workers can shift to new jobs. All persons who are past the prime of life can keep their intellectual vigor if they will, by continuing to learn the new things that come with the changing times.

[1] See E. L. Thorndike, Elsie O. Bregman, J. Warren Tilton, and Ella Woodyard: *Adult Learning.* 1928.

According to Meumann, adults learn faster than children, but they do not retain material so faithfully.

g. Applications.   In the light of the data on remembering which we have surveyed, valuable applications to school study may be derived:

1. Train your powers of observation.   Traditional education does little to improve perception.

2. Capitalize your special mode of imagery.

3. Develop your several modes of imagery so that you will be equipped to handle all sorts of situations.

4. Discover your optimum speed.

5. Utilize meaning with its numerous associative connections.

6. Realize that mechanical repetition is necessary even where the material is meaningful.   Thorough learning involves some painful drudgery.

7. Be convinced that mnemonic devices are uneconomical, since the mind tends to retain only what is absolutely necessary.

8. Decide at the beginning whether you want to learn to remember for a short or a long time.

9. Improve your technique by taking advantage of the "whole method," and by distributing your practice periods wisely.

2. Retention.   Learning proceeds upon the hope that what is impressed upon the mind will be retained. Material hastily learned tends to be soon forgotten. Rapid learning, therefore, is efficient where the goal is immediate retention.[1] A man who is preparing a speech for a single delivery is practicing economy if he learns it just thoroughly enough to remember it for the occasion.   If the aim is permanent retention, on the other hand, the material should be overlearned, that is, should be repeatedly studied even after it can be completely

---

[1] E. Meumann: *The Psychology of Learning*, p. 171.

remembered. The intention to retain for a short time will call for a procedure different from that employed where the intention is to retain for a long period.

Immediate retention depends more upon the imprinting; permanent retention more upon the development of associations.

People differ in their retentive abilities. A person who excels in immediate retention may be deficient when the goal is permanent retention.

Forgetting is most rapid soon after learning. The curve of forgetting will, of course, depend upon the specific conditions present, such as the nature of the activity, the previous practice of component activities, and what is done in the intervals between practices.

Nonsense material is forgotten more rapidly than meaningful material. Some events may be forgotten because they were unpleasant, some because they made only a faint impression, and some because they are involved in conflicting associations.

There are many persons who think they have forgotten something merely because they are unable to recall it. "I cannot remember the name. Let me see. Smith? No. Jones? No. Well, I give up."

"Was it Adams?"

"Yes, that's it."

The name was gone but not forgotten. Recognition often functions where recall fails. The ability to recognize the forgotten element is evidence that forgetting is not complete.

3. Recall. Recall is the voluntary revival of a past experience, effected when one member of an association enables the mind to trace the other member through a definite connecting link of a meaningful nature. Remembering is not a simple reduplication of a pattern (traces), but a constructive imagining through which past experience is transfigured to meet the present need. Memory transforms ideas. An idea is not a simple revival of a definitely perceived thing, but the product of many perceptions and of their subjective elaboration by the perceiver. It is difficult to draw the line between what is remembered and what is contributed by imagination and judgment, because these parts blend together to form a unitary whole for consciousness. Falsifications of memory are often due to such fusions of habitual associations.

Our thoughts are connected by characteristic links which have been classified under laws of association. Ideas are sometimes related by *similarity*. "That reminds me of a story" gives the after-dinner speaker an excuse to introduce a story, though the possible connection is often hardly appreciable.

"I just thought to tell you of it, my dear. Today I bought the loveliest tea wagon."[1]

Sometimes ideas are related by *contrast*. The fat man in the circus may remind the observer of a thin friend.

Sometimes ideas are related by *contiguity*, either of space or time. "Where have I seen you before?" is a search for spatial contiguity. When you are at a loss for the name of a person you have met before, you may revive it by recalling the time you were introduced to him, through temporal contiguity.

[1] The *New Yorker*. By permission of the *New Yorker* and I. Klein.

Did you ever try to trace your thinking backward to ascertain how you came to a certain idea, or to unearth something that has momentarily slipped your mind? Following a train of thought by means of the connections in either the backward or forward direction is an excellent method for studying the laws of association. A neighbor from back in the old home town dropped into the office of the city columnist and sat down at the end of the desk.

I thought I'd come in and see you, but you don't know me from Adam.

I used to see you when you played baseball in Harrisonville and worked on the *Democrat*. The *Democrat* had a piece about you a while back and that's the way I knew where you were. You're changed some, but not as much as my cousin, John Mellor. I guess you didn't know John. He married one of the Harkness girls. Old man Harkness is dead. He died in '85 or '86. It must have been '86. It was the year Abe King bought the Sample place. Abe couldn't read or write. Ed Spinney saw one of his boys in Florida last winter. It's surprising the way people scatter out. John Trotwood Moore was in Harrisonville not long ago. He married the oldest Daniel girl; I forget her name, I don't suppose you remember it either. I always say I can remember faces but I forget names. I saw Sam Mahaffey in St. Joe in 1896. He came up to me and said, "I guess you don't remember me." I went up to St. Joe to buy a carload of feeders. I never saw a better prospect for corn than there was that year, but we didn't get nothing but nubbins. It seems to me the winters are growing harder. Either that or I notice the cold more.

Women are funny. You wouldn't think to look at me that I'd been married four times. Press Stoneking said to me one day last week, "Newt, you don't look your age by twenty years." I met him in the road below Corriden's pasture. He was driving a new "Lizzie." Well, I've worn out four cars, and I say they're an extravagance. Reck Simlick has run through with everything he had. Women and liquor mostly, and dancing. We had a big row last fall about whether there should be dancing in the school auditorium. We stopped it. I was on the Election Board one year. We didn't get the vote counted till after nine o'clock. John Rothrock was there when I drove in. John went to California. He had a felon on his thumb; he suffered terribly. I had one when my second wife was taken. Her name was Abigail; she was one of the Simpsons that lived down by Buckhorn. You wouldn't know Buckhorn now. You say you never did know it. Well, that's too bad. It's funny. I had an idea you had traveled a good deal.[1]

Plentiful associations facilitate remembering. This fact is made use of in teaching language to children who suffer from some special disability which is often erroneously attributed to deficiency in a special sort of imagery. One boy, for example, was diagnosed as possessing a defective auditory memory. But investigation disclosed that the defect did not extend to all fields, since he could follow and recall with ease a play-by-play description of a ball game announced over the radio. What he needed to remedy his difficulty in school was interest and background. This background may be furnished to the pupil by the word-enrichment technique. If the word "wheel" is unrecognized, it must be enriched by associations, tying the word up with carts, scooters, tricycles, automobiles, wheels in a clock, ferris wheels, and wheelbarrows. With proper training the disability is removed or minimized. The word-enrichment technique exemplifies the general method that underlies the insurance of effective recall, the use of many associations linked especially to personal experiences.

The likelihood of recall depends, in part, upon four factors: vividness, primacy, frequency, and recency. An event which makes a vivid or deep impression is apt to be remembered. First impressions are inclined to be lasting (primacy). Repetition, with qualifications already noted, may facilitate recall (frequency). Recent events are likely to be recalled easily. In terms of conditioning, the influence of recency may be formulated thus: "When two different responses have been

---

[1] Jay E. House: "On Second Thoughts," in the New York *Evening Post*. By permission of Mr. Jay E. House, and the New York *Evening Post*.

attached to the same substitute stimulus or cue, the one attached last has the advantage over the other."[1] The mere lapse of time, however, may not weaken the effects of learning. Weakening occurs when, during the lapse of time, new learning erases the old.   Van Ormer found that less is forgotten during sleep than during waking periods, because in sleep there is no obliteration of the old by the new.[2] Guthrie suggests that grief may subside, not because "time is the great healer," but because other activities become so absorbing that they inhibit the memory of bereavement.

Associations may be studied by Free Association Tests. Such tests may involve *continuous* association where the subject is to think of all the words he can in a certain period of time, say three minutes, or *discrete* association where the subject is instructed to respond with the first word coming to his mind in connection with each of a list of words read one at a time by the experimenter.

Examples of Free Association Tests of the discrete type are the test developed by Jung and the test evolved by Kent and Rosanoff.

A valuable study of the associations underlying recall in particular, and thinking in general, is to be found in Jung's Association Tests for the detection of complexes. A list of words is constructed, with the significant words scattered among the words unrelated to the person's complexes.   The words are read to the observer one at a time and he is instructed to answer as quickly as possible with the first word that occurs to his mind.[3] Words are situations to which the observer reacts and the nature of his response reveals the emotional tones connected with the situation.   If a person has used

---

[1] E. R. Guthrie: *op. cit.*, pp. 114–115.

[2] E. B. Van Ormer: "Retention After Intervals of Sleep and Waking," *Archives of Psychology*, 1932, No. 137, p. 49.

[3] See Carl Jung: *Collected Papers on Analytical Psychology*, Chapter II, "The Association Method."

cyanide to dispose of his neighbor's dog, the word "poison" is apt to evoke immediately the word "cyanide." Such a response would be "a dead give-away." Realizing this fact, the observer casts about in his mind for an innocent word and responds with "rat." In this case, the longer reaction time, among other factors, is tell-tale evidence of his guilt.

The origin of an attitude may be discovered by such an association test. A person may have an aversion for watermelon and be unable to explain his disliking for that particular delicacy. "Watermelon" may evoke "Jones," the name of a farmer whom he knew in his childhood, and the connection may lead to the recall of the punishment meted out to him by his father for stealing one of Jones' watermelons. Thus the source of his "watermelon complex" is unearthed.

Luria has devised an ingenious technique in his experiments at the State Institute of Experimental Psychology in Moscow, where he is studying the manner in which human behavior becomes confused under the stress of intense emotion. Controlled Association Tests were given to students who were about to face the "cleansing" examination determining their fitness for the higher communistic education, and to criminals who had just been arrested for crimes ranging from petty larceny to murder.

Luria takes as an index of confusion (disorganization) the inability of the subject to coördinate his verbal and kinæsthetic behavior when a word connected with the critical situation serves to stir him up emotionally. The subject becomes "rattled" or confused. The cortex is so disorganized by the tense emotion that its inhibitory control over the motor reactions is diminished temporarily.

In the experimental set-up, the subject is seated in a comfortable armchair in front of a table. The right hand lies on the table with the fingers resting on a pneumatic bulb, while the left hand rests passively upon a weight. An electrical key closed by the experimenter registers the moment of stimulation, while a sensitive membrane operated by the subject's voice registers the moment of response. The record is made on a kymographic drum. The subject is instructed to press the pneumatic bulb with his right hand simultaneously with his speech response. The ascent of the curve on the drum represents the pressure of the fingers on the bulb while the descent of the curve represents a decrease of pressure. Involuntary tremors of the left hand due to the excitement (neurodynamic excitation) are also recorded. The combined language and motor reactions constitute a unified motor structure the parts of which must be interpreted with reference to the whole. When a complex is "touched" by the stimulus word, the subject tends to respond with the first word occurring to his mind. This word being a "guilty" one, the subject inhibits the verbal response while he thinks up an "innocent" word to conceal his state of perturbation (affective traces). Meanwhile, however, he has proceeded to press the bulb at the moment when the first or "guilty" word came to him and his motor reaction is a "give-away" of the inhibition and conflict transpiring on the "inside." Due to the set to press the bulb when he gives his verbal response, the subject involuntarily imparts the pressure with his fingers when the initial tendency to speak is experienced. The response word is suppressed but the pressure is registered nevertheless, in a subdued and irregular form. According to Luria the affect upsets the inhibitory functions of the cortex and the unobstructed excitation begins to flow into the motor sphere, distorting and disorganizing the behavior. Control subjects (non-criminals) are used to obtain normal reaction patterns, or reaction formulæ as Luria prefers to call them. The normal patterns are regular, whereas the formulæ observed in criminals under the test conditions are chaotic. Let us consider a sample case.

On the 15th of January, 1926, a body of an unknown man was found in a pile of snow, in a courtyard of a house. The body was lying on its back, in underclothes, with the *valenka* (Russian felt boots) beside it. The head had been split by a heavy instrument, on the body were stab wounds, and the whole body was dirty with coal dust. Tracks in the snow led to a blacksmith shop, and there the instrument of the murder was found—a sledge-hammer bespattered with blood, and the remains of a charred, bloody shirt.

The owner of the blacksmith shop, Sm., 30 years old, was suspected. The murdered man was the porter from a neighboring house, and he and Sm. often drank together. It was found that the day before the murder they were seen together, drinking in a saloon. The preliminary investigation showed that on the morning of the 15th of January, Sm. went to his blacksmith shop by an unusual way which led through the court where the body lay, but by a roundabout path. After arriving there, he then went to church, which was not his custom, and remained some time. It was also brought out that during the night of the 15th of January he was at home and did not sleep, but smoked a great deal.

On being arrested, he denied any participation in the murder. Our experiment was done the 16th of January, 1926, *i.e.*, one day after the crime. Among the 70 word stimuli there were fourteen which had a direct relation to the situation of the crime: porter, quarrel, money, boots, hammer, blow, spot, shirt, body, knife, to cut, to drag, tracks, and blood. The following record reveals the reactions to some of these words.

6. Normal reaction: Hay – 1.8″ – wood (one and 8/10 seconds)
51. Knife – 2.8″ – to cut bread
54. Drunk – 5.6″ – fool
55. To crawl – 3.2″ – to sleep
61. Tracks – 3.5″ – wood
71. Blood – 3.8″ – death
21. Money – 3.4″ – to live
35. Hammer – 3.8″ – to carry

Notice that the first pressure of the right hand is regular, as the stimulus word does not touch the complex. The pressures in response to the key words are irregular.

Sm. confessed his guilt.

Here is the picture of this crime: on the 14th of January, Sm. and his friend, the janitor, were in the saloon, and upon leaving they started to the blacksmith shop, intending to empty another bottle there.   When they had arrived Sm. asked his friend whether he was going to pay him the two-ruble debt which he owed.   When this was answered in the negative, Sm. grabbed the hammer and struck him on the head.   The wounded man fell and began to groan and crawl on the floor.   Sm. became very frightened, and, according to his story, he grew sorry for the struggling man and finished killing him with a knife; after this he removed the outside clothing which was spattered with blood, burned it, and buried the body in the courtyard, where it remained.

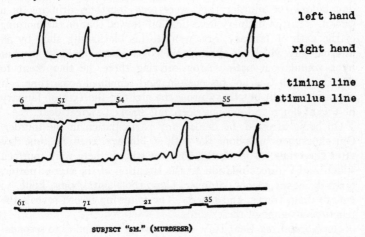

SUBJECT "SM." (MURDERER)

After giving this history of the crime, the disturbances coinciding with such stimuli as money, blow, knife, hammer, drunk, to crawl, tracks, quarrel, etc., are easily understood.

The full meaning of the records obtained by Luria can only be disclosed by a careful study of all the factors in the reaction formulæ characterizing different kinds of persons under varied experimental conditions.[1]

Kent and Rosanoff have developed an association test that reveals common reactions and individual reactions which may

[1]A. R. Luria: *The Nature of Human Conflicts; or Emotion, Conflict, and Will. An Objective Study of Disorganization and Control of Human Behaviour*, especially pp. 102–106.   1932.   By permission of Liveright Publishing Corporation.

shed considerable light, taken as a whole, upon the normality of the subject's personality. Frequency tables have been worked out for one thousand subjects. In response to "table," two hundred and sixty-seven said "chair," four "dining," and two "mahogany." In response to "chair," one hundred and ninety-one said "table," one hundred and seven "seat," one hundred and seven "sit," and one "upholstered." Individual (personal) reactions may indicate abnormal personality trends, whereas common reactions may be evidence of tendencies toward a normally adjusted character.[1]

Associations may be studied also by Controlled Association Tests which measure largely the speed and facility with which certain familiar associations can be reinstated. The subject's response is so restricted by the instructions that only one reply is possible. In an opposites test, for example, there is only one reply to the word "night." Some of the more complicated tests involve the comprehension of relations, and appear, therefore, as a part of intelligence tests.

One of the best Controlled Association Tests is that worked out by Woodworth and Wells, a sample of which follows:[2]

Opposites Test	Part-whole test
high—	elbow—
summer—	hinge—
out—	page—
white—	finger—
slow—	wing—
yes—	morning—
above—	blade—
north—	mattress—

Mixed Relations Test

Eye—see	Ear—
Monday—Tuesday	April—

[1] See A. J. Rosanoff: *Free Association Test.* Sixth edition, 1927.

[2] See R. S. Woodworth and F. L. Wells: "Association Tests," *Psychological Monographs,* 1911, 13, 57. By special permission of F. L. Wells.

Do—did	See—
Bird—sings	Dog—
Hour—minute	Minute—
Straw—hat	Leather—
Cloud—rain	Sun—
Hammer—tool	Dictionary—

Faulty associations account for the errors popularly known as "boners."[1]   Frances Willard was identified as a well-known colored prize fighter, due to a confusion of Frances Willard, Jess Willard, and Jack Johnson, the last a negro pugilist knocked out by Jess Willard in a famous battle some years ago. Similar explanations will reveal the occasions for the following mistakes:

Marconi: a popular Italian dish.
Jane Addams: author of "Pride and Prejudice."
LaFollette: French ambassador to the United States who helped the American Revolution.
Shaw: a former life prisoner now freed.
Barrie: a child movie actor.
Curie: proposer of a peculiar belief—"if you think you are, you are."
Fiume: a delightful peak of nature in the White Mountains.
George A. Gordon: manufacturer of Gordon's fish cakes.
Obregon: an actor in the "Passion Play."
Homer: a type of pigeon.
Lorna Doone: a kind of cookie.
Conan Doyle: a famous detective in employ of English stockyard.
Polonius: a mythical sausage.
Ali Baba: being away when the crime was committed.
Esau: a man who wrote fables.
Senator: half horse, half man.

The Association School of Psychologists, represented by Locke and his successors, based their system upon the associa-

---

[1] See Lowell A. Norris: "Master Mistake Meets Dr. Psychology.   A Review of Dr. W. F. Vaughan's Research into Sources of Student 'Howlers!'" *Psychology Magazine*, September, 1929.

tion of ideas.[1] Ideas were compounded and combined and
associated according to the laws of association. Psychology
was a mental chemistry.

Modern psychology emphasizes the bonds established, not
between ideas, but between impulses or responses and the
stimuli by which they are evoked. The conditioned response
is a case of association. In many conditioned responses, of
course, no ideas are involved. The individual is often unaware
of the manner in which he acquires new reactions. Memory
in such cases is physiological rather than psychological. Advertising succeeds by insidiously planting associations in the
unsuspecting observer. A toothpaste advertisement shows a
beautiful lady in "one of the most expensive hostess gowns in
the world—obviously not for the masses." Unwittingly the
reader comes, through association, to feel in a vague way that
it is something exclusive, and that using it is a mark of cultured
refinement. Thus a response is built in by a conditioning
process which is all the more effective because it is so subtle.

One of the valuable suggestions of the conditioned reflex
formula is the reduced emphasis on learning as a process of
intake, and the increased stress on learning as a process of
output.[2]

The Associationists stressed the factors of primacy, intensity,
frequency, and recency in the process of revival. If the word
"swift" suggests "car" to your mind rather than "arrow,"
or "ham," or "slow," some of the above factors are responsible. Other things being equal, the first or primary association
will prevail; the most intense or vivid association; the most
frequently repeated association; or the most recent association.
These factors determine which similar, contrasting, or con-

---

[1]See H. C. Warren: *A History of the Association Psychology*. 1921.
See also E. S. Robinson: *Association Theory Today*. 1932.
[2]See J. M. Fletcher: *Psychology in Education. With Emphasis on Creative
Thinking*. 1934.

tiguous object will be called to mind by a particular stimulus in a particular situation.

Modern psychology, however, insists that the reproduction of a particular idea in a particular case is due not only to previously acquired associations, but is also due quite as much to factors involved in the present state of consciousness—the determining tendencies in operation at the moment. For example, you may think of a letter which came in the mail because the unpleasant mood engendered by the initial reading of it still persists, predisposing your mind to revive the letter continually as long as the mood lasts. The importance of the present situation in recall is evidenced by the fact that spontaneous testimony is usually very inadequate. Many additional memories may be revived by a skillful cross-examination which provides the mind with a variety of effective sets.

Recall depends, too, upon the intentions uppermost in the mind of the learner during the time when the material was being acquired, since a specific intention in the act of learning has a specific effect upon the result. The likelihood of recall is determined, in part, by the adaptation of method of learning to the purpose of the total procedure, according to whether there is plenty of time or just an instant for observing the stimulus, and according to whether immediate or permament retention is the goal to be achieved.

Associative inhibition, at times, interferes seriously with recall. Suppose you learn to associate r-a-l:m-e-s and then you are instructed to learn to associate r-a-l:b-a-p. You will find that the first association obstructs the formation of the second. When the common first member of each pair is shown, inhibition results as the two syllables, m-e-s and b-a-p, get in each other's way, so to speak. In every-day experience, recall is rendered momentarily inefficient because the individual sets off on the wrong track in search of a word or a name. A person, for example, in trying to recall a man's name, was sure that it began with "H." He could not make any progress. Finally he allowed the matter to drop, the "H" association no longer blocked the path, and the name "Sawyer" flashed into his mind. Learning a thing wrong stands in the way of learning it right. When a later learning activity interferes with an earlier learned activity, the interference is known as retroactive inhibition.[1]

Two common experimental methods for studying recall are the Method of Retained Members and the Method of Paired Associates.

In the Method of Retained Members, more items are presented than the subject can possibly recall. The score is computed by the number of items successfully reproduced. Presentation is usually either visual or auditory.

In the Method of Paired Associates, a pair of items is presented, either visually or orally. When the series of pairs is completed, one member of each pair is given and the other is to be supplied by the subject. The order is shifted in the test series to prevent the learning of associates in serial order. Have someone read the series so that the following pairs will be presented one at a time.

pen—tree	type—hill
skate—desk	box—roof
book—light	dog—early
auto—grass	smoke—sharp
day—church	try—laugh
dirt—note	read—square

Now have the reader give you the first word of each pair, allowing you five seconds for naming the associate. Try the same experiment, making up a list of nonsense syllables.

4. Recognition. Recognition, as previously stated, is easier than recall. A "true-false" examination, therefore, must be worded with great care lest recognition be given precedence over

[1]See C. R. Griffith: *An Introduction to Educational Psychology*, pp. 439–444.

recall. "Who rescued John Smith?" is a more difficult question than "Pocahontas rescued John Smith—true or false?"

The capacity to recognize is usually sufficient for practical purposes, since the individual is thereby enabled to adjust himself to a situation in the light of his particular past experience. There is no wisdom in overburdening the mind with unnecessary luggage.

Recognition is characterized by the experience of "againness," a feeling of familiarity. The subjective feeling of certainty is no guarantee of the validity of recognition, as is illustrated in the familiar *déjà vu* illusion, where a person feels he has seen a thing before somewhere, though he has not actually done so. Recognition is the psychic indicator of the accuracy of recall. Recognition functions as a check upon recall, in that the item recalled is referred to time and place for a judgment based on the feeling of familiarity.

Recognition may be implicit, in which case the object arouses the experience of "againness," though the individual is unable to place it. Thus you may know that you have seen a person before, and yet not be able to recall just when or where you saw him. Recognition may be explicit, in which case the orientation of the object with respect to the past is carried out successfully. When implicit recognition becomes explicit, the baffled feeling gives way to one of relief.

In a typical experimental test of recognition, twenty-five items, such as words, pictures, or designs, are exposed to the observer. These twenty-five items are then mixed with twenty-five more, and the whole series of fifty items is submitted. The subject is told to indicate the items he has seen before. Errors consist of failure to recognize an item seen before, and false recognition of items not previously presented. The score is usually computed by deducting twice the number of errors from the total number of items shown.[1]

---

[1] See H. E. Garrett and M. R. Schneck: *op. cit.*, Part I, p. 126ff.

E. Can Memory Be Improved? Some psychologists assert that memory cannot be improved by training.

A man does not improve his memory. He merely figures out ways of holding certain things in mind. These are memory aids, not memory improvements. Such aids are called mnemonic aids. We all use them now and then. For instance, how could we get along without this one, "Thirty days hath September—?"

Perhaps you have felt the necessity of trying to recall the details of some past experience. On every item that you feel sure about you can state a reason in terms of some connection. These connections, which are called associations, are your memory aids.

Now if you know in advance that you will need sometime to recall the details of something, you will then and there establish the proper connections. You haven't improved your memory. You have only hooked up the facts you want to keep in mind.[1]

There is much confusion on the issue, which would be averted if we use the term "remembering" rather than the term "memory." The person described by Sprowls has improved his remembering as long as he remembers things better. Our question should, therefore, be revised to read: Can a person improve his remembering? And the answer is, obviously, Yes.

III. ANTICIPATING

Imagining directed toward the past we have designated as remembering; imagining pointing to the future we shall call anticipating. Pre-cognition differs from re-cognition in respect to its time-reference; the former being forward in its reference, the latter backward. It is important to keep this distinction in mind because the term "imagination" as used by the layman usually includes in its connotation only the forward reference. "Anticipating" is a more accurate term than "imagination" for describing the mental activity which

---

[1] Jesse Sprowls, in a syndicated news column. The Boston *Herald*, December 23, 1930.

is aiming at the prospective solution of a problem-situation. The financier, like the author, must build up his plot, imagining what other folks will do at certain moments and planning his own program in accordance with his predictions. Business requires no less imagination than writing fiction.

A. Thinking. Thinking consists essentially in remembering the past in an effort to utilize that experience in anticipating the future. Thinking is a delayed reaction, an inner rehearsal, which spares the individual the penalty of costly errors, by providing a plan for the economical guidance of performance when the ideas eventuate in action. The fundamental function of the mind is to act as an intermediary by which the wants of the organism may become satisfied. Its basic function is the anticipation of experience. Random ideas are checked long enough to be lived through mentally before they are expressed in overt adjustment. Adjustment is intelligent when anticipation of an act precedes its execution.

B. Foresight. Anticipation means foresight. The expert in any line of endeavor must anticipate the impending moves of those persons with whom he has to deal. The man who is eager for a raise in pay, for example, must regulate his office behavior with reference to the prospective reactions which he will probably evoke in his employer, and take care to select the psychological moment for presenting his petition in order to gain a favorable response. He must anticipate the employer's objections to his request, prepare his answers to those objections, and plan his objections to the employer's objections, so that the ultimate issue of the argument will be the raise desired.

Prediction and control, it was stated earlier, are the aims of science. Exact knowledge is desirable because it makes possible accurate anticipation. To see ahead is to facilitate the effective adjustments which depend upon planning for their successful execution.

The ability to anticipate the consequences of action is a suggestive index of a man's intelligence and character. Bringing the past to bear upon the present situation, a person suspends his impulses until he has had time to deliberate upon alternative courses of action. "Thinking it over" consists largely of a survey of the contingent results in the light of cause-effect relationships reviewed from the past. The capacity for thinking through an event to its consequences can be investigated by a Free Response Foresight Test, in which the subject is instructed to think of all the things that might happen in connection with such incidents as the following:

1. Whenever anyone picked on John, he would go tell his teacher.
2. John accidentally broke a street lamp with a snowball.
3. Jim was anxious to make good marks at school; so he usually studied instead of going out to play with the other fellows.[1]

Varying the procedure and the presentation of material, the subjects are given the opportunity to select the most probable and the most important consequences, and the reverse, and to decide what they would do if they were confronted with such situations. These various procedures were planned on the assumption that foresight implies:

1. The ability in any situation to think of a large number of consequences.
2. The ability to judge between consequences as to their probability.
3. The ability to judge between consequences as to their importance.
4. The ability to decide the best course of action to pursue on consideration of all the consequences likely to follow.[2]

Vernon Jones has worked out a similar procedure to secure evidence for Character Education. A true story from the

[1] H. Hartshorne, M. A. May, and F. K. Shuttleworth: *Studies in the Organization of Character*, pp. 43-44. Credit for the work is also due to Angus B. McLean and George S. Patterson.

[2] *Ibid.*, p. 240.

lives of great men and women, such as the following, is re-counted. Samuel Gompers, as a boy, was a close companion of a relative of his, a boy named Simon, who was ten months older but physically weaker. Samuel protected Simon from bullies, but he was unwilling to have Simon impose on him. The two boys were supposed to get the milk at a near-by dairy every day. Samuel thought they should take turns in carrying it, but Simon often refused to coöperate. One day Simon rebelled when Samuel insisted that it was his turn. Samuel felt it was time to give Simon a lesson in fair play. They both left the milk in the road and continued homeward, each de-manding that the other go back for it. The folks at home sent them after the pail. The milk was not to be found, for some animal had drunk it, and the pail was battered out of shape. "It's your fault," said Simon. "It's your fault," said Samuel. They were both whipped when they returned home. Later in the day they met, their eyes red from crying. "You made me get a whipping," said Simon. "You made us both get one," said Samuel. "Next time you will take your turn, I guess." "Not unless you do," said Simon.[1] What would you have done? "An attempt was made," says the author, "to stimulate the child to see relationships in the realm of choice, to stimulate him to see consequences of certain de-cisions, and to encourage him through thought questions to generalize. . . . The experimenter and the class set out to discuss any problems of choice suggested by the episode, and not to draw up a set of rules of conduct as a result of each discussion."[2]

The infantile mode of procedure is to act impulsively, and then to consider after the deed is done. The suspension of action for the purpose of anticipative deliberation is the mark

---

[1]See Vernon Jones: *What Would You Have Done?* Pp. 3–6. 1931.

[2]Vernon Jones: *Character Education through Cases from Biography*, p. 28, a Teachers' Manual to Accompany, *What Would You Have Done?*

of maturity. "We must learn to look forward to the consequences of pursuing a desire, not inward to its emotional appeal or backward to its traditional sanctity."[1] The rôle of anticipation will be considered further in Chapters XIII and XIV, when its importance for thinking and intelligent behavior will be more adequately indicated.

C. Constructive (Creative) Imagination. Constructive or productive imagination, in distinction to reproductive imagination, proceeds by recombining past experiences in new ways, modifying the elements, if necessary, to fit the new pattern. Most inventions are the culmination of a gradual evolution.

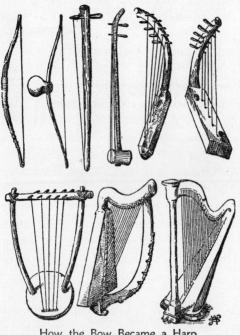

How the Bow Became a Harp

Stringed musical instruments and belt-driven rotative machinery are traceable, step-by-step, from the primordial bow and arrow. Some creative genius bridged the gap between the hand-thrown javelin and the bow and arrow. The twang of the bow produced a musical note, suggesting the conception of string music. The addition of a resonator, the multiplication of strings, and the improvement of the bow were natural steps

[1]Hugh Hartshorne: *Character in Human Relations*, p. 266. 1932.

in the evolution to the harp, and, by the creation of an enlarged sound-box, to the piano. Similarly, some inventive genius discovered that, as a means for drilling holes, his bow and arrow could be substituted for the tiresome method of twirling the drill between the palms of his hands. It must occasionally have happened while drilling in wood with the bow and a drill, the point of which had become blunted and rounded by use, that the resulting dry wood-dust burst into flame from the heat generated by the rapid rotation of the blunt drill. Thus was suggested the use of the bow and a

How the Bow Entered Industry

pointless arrow as a firemaking instrument—the fire-drill. Later, a lazy genius invented the four-handed fire-drill; still later, the elegant apparatus in which both the needed pressure and the twirling functions were combined in the down-stroke of a cross-bar. From the fire-drill to the lathe is a comparatively short step, merely involving a shift of position from vertical to horizontal, and from a portable to a stationary device. The potter's wheel is only the primitive lathe put back into the vertical position with the addition of a flywheel. The rotation of the potter's wheel is effected by the foot of the operator, thus leaving his hands free for shaping the clay. Modern rotative machinery is simply a further stage in the evolution.[1]

Whether anything can be imagined of which any part has never been perceived in the past, is an open question. The term "creative imagination" seems to imply that something distinctly new has been evolved by the functioning mind. The credulous person, in particular, likes to believe in mysterious inspirations which have produced something out of nothing. A careful study of creative productions reveals some interesting facts which suggest that a natural explanation may, indeed, be adequate.

Poetic genius is famous for its flashes of insight. Longfellow made this entry in his Diary:

I wrote last evening a notice of Allston's poems. After which I sat till twelve o'clock by my fire, smoking, when suddenly it came into my mind to write the "Ballad of the Schooner Hesperus," which I accordingly did. Then I went to bed, but could not sleep. New thoughts were running in my mind, and I got up to add them to the ballad. I feel pleased with the ballad. It hardly cost me any effort. It did not come into my mind by lines, but by stanzas.

The spontaneity of such a creation fosters the illusion that the poem "came right out of a clear sky," or more specifically, right out of nowhere.

But as evidence that such spontaneity is an illusion, it is worthy of note that the poet gets a poetic inspiration, and not a brilliant hunch for improving the weight-balance of bridges or for baking better biscuits. This fact that inspirations are confined to a special field of interest suggests that intuition depends, far more than is obviously apparent, upon accumulated effort. Inspiration is the fruition of labor. The mis-

---

[1]William H. Smyth: "What Is Invention?" *The Journal of the Patent Office Society*, reviewed in the *Literary Digest*, January 10, 1931.

leading factor is that the insight comes at unexpected moments when the material pondered over has lapsed into the subconscious regions of the mind, so that the source, being forgotten, may elude detection.

The creative process evolves through several successive stages:

(1) Preparation—first is the period in which the problem is investigated.

(2) Incubation—next, the mind goes over the information acquired in the first stage.

(3) Illumination—then, of a sudden, appears the inspiration, the hatching after the incubation.

The dependence of creative imagination upon forgotten past experiences has been beautifully revealed by Lowes' investigation of the long process of preparation and incubation which culminated in the inspired writing by Coleridge of "The Rime of the Ancient Mariner" and "Kubla Khan." Coleridge left a notebook through which Lowes traced his readings and related them to his poetic creations. "I have read almost everything," wrote Coleridge. The notebook is a hodgepodge of information, showing that the poet had been "reading with a falcon's eye for details in which lurked the spark of poetry."[1] "To follow Coleridge through his reading is to retrace the obliterated vestiges of creation."[2] Thus as his mind became steeped with travel lore, a reservoir was established as a source of his poetry. Let us take some samples.

Reading   There is a Tradition among them, that in November, 1668, *a Star appear'd below the Body of the Moon within the Horns of it.* (From Volume V of a work, *Philosophical Transactions.*)

---

[1]John L. Lowes: *The Road to Xanadu. A Study in the Ways of the Imagination*, p. 33. 1927. By permission of and by arrangement with Houghton Mifflin Company.

[2]*Ibid.*, p. 37.

Poetry

Till clomb above the eastern bar
The horned moon, with one bright star
Within the nether tip.

Reading

During a calm . . . some parts of the sea seemed *covered with a kind of slime;* and some small sea animals were swimming about . . . that had a *white*, shining appearance. . . . When they began to swim about, which they did, with equal ease, upon their back, sides, or belly, they emitted the brightest colours of the most precious gems. . . . Sometimes they assumed various tints of *blue*. . . . But . . . the colour was, chiefly, a beautiful, pale *green*, tinged with a burnished gloss; and, in the dark, it had a faint appearance of *glowing fire*. They proved to be . . . probably, an animal which has a share in producing . . . *that lucid appearance, often observed near ships at sea, in the night*. (From Cook's *Voyage to the Pacific Ocean*.)

Poetry

The very deep did rot: O Christ!
That ever this should be!
Yea, slimy things did crawl with legs
Upon the slimy sea.

About, about, in reel and rout
The death-fires danced at night;
The water, like a witch's oils,
Burnt green, and blue, and white.

Out of the Deep Well of experience, the Shaping Spirit of imagination creates the Magical Synthesis. Coleridge himself, in commenting on the genesis of nightmares, wrote: "The imagination . . . the true inward creatrix, instantly out of the chaos of elements or shattered fragments of memory, puts together some form. . . ."

Inspiration proceeds by the same paths in scientific hunches. A hunch is a unifying or clarifying idea which springs into consciousness suddenly as a solution to a problem in which we are intensely interested.   It follows a long period of study, but comes into consciousness at a time when the mind is not consciously working on the problem.   A hunch springs from a wide knowledge of facts.

Archimedes was taking a bath.   All at once he had a bright idea—a sudden flash of intuition.   Without stopping to pick up his clothes, he leaped up and ran through the streets of Syracuse, shouting, "Eureka! I have found it!"   He had discovered the law of floating bodies.

One scientist was studying the problem of how to improve circulation of oil in pipe coils.   The correct principle came to him like a flash, in church, when the preacher was announcing the text of his sermon.   Another scientist reports that most of his hunches come to him in the early morning while in bed thinking about some problem on which he has done considerable work.   He states that he does more work before getting up in the morning than after.   Still another scientist finds that most of his problems are solved at night while he is trying to go to sleep.   The experience is so common that he keeps a pad and pencil on a table near his bed, to jot down ideas.[1]

Hunches often come in the period between wakefulness and sleep because the drowsiness of the mind removes the interfering obstructions which operate in the waking hours when thought persists in starting off on the wrong tracks.

Inspiration is not a miracle but a natural phenomenon subject to scientific explanation.   Striking revelations take place only after a period of work; they complete or continue something already begun.   When the solution is complex, it does not come to the mind with all the details fully worked out; the key is at hand, but it has still to be used.   These revelations are rare.   Discoveries just as remarkable are made much more frequently in the ordinary way—that is, in answer, it seems,

[1]From a report by R. A. Baker to the American Chemical Society.

to continuous effort. If it is true that the solution of a problem may come unexpectedly and, at times, long after we have ceased to be actively engaged in its consideration, nevertheless, there is no satisfactory evidence in support of the assumption commonly made that it ever appears after the person has ceased to be interested in it. On the contrary, the solutions that come in the form of inspiration refer to problems which have not been finally dismissed, which have remained, as it were, in the "back of the mind," ready to force themselves upon the attention. Instances of inspiration do not seem to transcend the apparent capacity of the persons who get them.

Thinking does not proceed steadily and consistently to its goal, but by leaps and bounds. Inspiration is simply the fruition of purposive thinking which has faltered under the weight of a difficult problem, only to rest for a moment to regain its strength, and then to continue on its way to ultimate triumph.

CHAPTER XII

MENTAL CONFLICT

PSYCHOLOGY is primarily concerned with the activities that constitute our conscious experience. Experience, however, cannot be adequately understood until we probe into the tendencies that determine our mental reactions—until we comprehend the glandular basis of our moods, until we uncover those habitual dispositions which have dropped from our notice through long practice, and until we unearth those primitive longings for brutality and lust that usually elude awareness. The experience we know is determined to a large extent by factors ordinarily outside awareness. We must investigate this dim background, "the hidden recesses of the mind," to appreciate the significance of the fact that we are often motivated in our thoughts and actions by trends in our nature which remain, often discreetly, *incognito*. There are some persons who feel that our self-respect must inevitably suffer if we get to know our "real" selves too well, but we should steel ourselves to the truth, for even though it turn out that we are worse than we ever suspected, we may also find that we are better than we ever dreamed.

I. UNCONSCIOUS BEHAVIOR

While it is true that man is a thinking animal, many of his adjustments are worked out without much conscious reflection; such is the case particularly when factors either in the environment or within the mind involve elements repugnant to the personality. Behavior is often unconscious because peace of mind is better preserved if the motives remain unknown.

A. The Ego Ideal. Each of us sets up for himself an ideal which represents that pattern of life which will sustain self-respect and merit social approval, and this goal for self-realization we may designate as the ego ideal. The individual comes to measure himself against the ideal as a standard, and since human nature is beset with diverse tendencies some of which do not fit handily into the picture of respectability, he is forced to realize, only too often, that he falls short of his high aims. In order to maintain his self-respect and the admiration of his fellows, the individual must resort to devices which will serve to conceal his motives from the scrutiny of his own conscience and the censure of his associates. Thus it happens that subtle adaptations are effected which escape even his own detection.

B. Defense Mechanisms. Modern psychology has revealed the fact that many adjustments proceed outside the awareness of the individual. Indeed, such adaptations as constitute defense mechanisms—mechanisms, that is, which defend the ego against depreciation—must escape the light of consciousness if they are to succeed in fulfilling their purposes. There is no doubt that the human being is often unconscious of the motivation and meaning of his behavior. Problems which are vital to the personality are solved by devious means which elude detection. The solutions are frequently compromises which merely postpone the day of reckoning, providing a temporary peace of mind. Since the function of consciousness is to promote efficient adaptation, it is the part of wisdom to examine the means by which the mind succeeds in fooling itself, and to substitute for unthinking adjustments ones in which the value of thinking can be adequately capitalized.

1. Evidence from Abnormal Psychology. Evidence of the importance of mental mechanisms which function in a subtle manner is supplied by a study of the abnormal mind in which the normal person can see his own foibles in the spotlight of exaggeration. The lunatic is only a caricature of the normal person. It is said that the wise man and the fool seem much alike when they fall in love or try to explain hard times. We are all irrational. In view of our follies, it is really astonishing that we seem as rational to ourselves as we sometimes do.

2. **Evidence from Psychoanalysis.** Psychiatry, the study of mental diseases, has shed considerable light upon the workings of the abnormal mind, findings which are equally applicable in their fundamentals to the normal mind. Psychoanalysis, which is a special technique for the diagnosis and treatment of the psychopathological individual, has been especially fruitful in extending the range of psychological understanding, bringing into bold relief the psychology of illness.

Illness, psychoanalysis points out, affords peculiar satisfactions which may be denied in health. For the sick child, there is a relaxation of parental discipline. Everyone likes to be pampered. An ill child can in a day be spoiled beyond weeks of redemption. The solicitude of friends is gratifying to one who enjoys being the center of attention. To have undergone an unusual operation is to win notice and distinction. Unfortunate health habits are established whenever a person makes his sickness an occasion for some special dispensation, such as a trip to Bermuda, an indulgence foregone during times of well-being for reasons of economy. Neurotic individuals cultivate illness unconsciously to gain pleasurable ends, to win sympathy, to secure special consideration, to afford an excuse for some failure. Strangely enough such persons want to be ill, though they would never admit it to others or to themselves.

A large part of the material of this chapter would not be available, were it not for the discoveries of Sigmund Freud,

the founder of psychoanalysis.   Credit should also be given to
Bernard Hart, who in his *Psychology of Insanity* elaborated
the Freudian concepts and emphasized anew their applicability to the normal mind.

3. Evidence from Mental Hygiene. On March 28, 1841,
Dorothea Lynde Dix undertook to give Sunday-school instruction to the female inmates of the East Cambridge House of
Correction, in Cambridge, Massachusetts. There she was
brought into contact, for the first time, with the deplorable
conditions existing in the penal institutions of those days.
She found twenty women, among whom several were insane,
crowded together in one room in which no provision was made
for either bedding or heat. Shocked and outraged at the
conditions she encountered, Miss Dix determined to establish
asylums for the care of the insane. When the nineteenth
century opened, America had only one asylum; it was located
in Virginia. Single-handed, frail in health, but with in-
domitable energy and firm moral purpose, Miss Dix succeeded
in a few years in securing the establishment of no less than
thirty-two public and private institutions for the insane.
Through her efforts the way was prepared for the origination
of the Mental Hygiene movement which came into being
twenty-one years after her death.

In 1900 Clifford Beers of New Haven "lost his mind" and
entered upon a period of confinement in various hospitals and
asylums where he was subjected to brutal treatment of a most
inhuman sort. He vowed, if he ever regained his sanity, to
write a book describing his experiences, in the hope that the
public would be stirred to reform the institutional care of the
insane. Fortunately, Beers' hope was realized. Encouraged
by William James, who read his manuscript and urged him to
publish it, Beers issued his story, *A Mind That Found Itself*,
in 1908. The book attracted widespread attention.

With the coöperation of friends, Beers founded the Connecticut Society for Mental Hygiene in 1908. In 1909 the National Committee for Mental Hygiene was established. The movement has since grown into an international organization.

The original purpose of the Mental Hygiene movement was to take measures for humanizing the care of the insane. As the work progressed, it became apparent that the prevention of insanity was equally as vital as the cure. It was natural, therefore, that mental hygiene should branch out to include normal people, pointing the way to the means of achieving that efficiency and that happiness which insure the healthy mind against the dangers of breakdown. During the last twenty-four years the literature of mental hygiene has grown rapidly.

The material of this chapter is typical of the approach to mental life taken by the mental hygienists, whose main concern is to stimulate an interest in those problems of emotional adjustment which are of vital import in the attainment of happiness.

II. CONFLICT

One of the most obvious aspects of human nature is inconsistency, especially as we see it exhibited in the conduct of others rather than in ourselves. A famous astrologist who was consulted by international bankers before they committed themselves on important financial negotiations, died insolvent, in spite of the fact that she was well informed on the planetary portents concerning monetary prospects. A prominent banker, in his report for 1930 as chairman of the bank's governing board, recommended industrial pay reductions at about the same time his own salary was being increased from $218,000 to $250,000 yearly. George Bernard Shaw and H. L. Mencken both attacked marriage as an ignominious capitulation, and then yielded in shameful surrender, themselves. Alfred Nobel made a fortune in the manufacture of explosives, producing the most destructive forces that ever ravaged mankind, and then, at his death, devoted his wealth to rewarding the promoters of peace among nations and the benefactors of humanity in literature and science. It is small wonder that the minds of ordinary mortals are beset with confusion.

In behavioristic terms, conflict results from the evocation of incompatible reaction tendencies, either instinctive or learned. Dogs have been trained to react differentially to two figures such as an ellipse and a circle. If the ellipse is gradually altered until it nears the form of the circle, the dogs become so confused that they grow restless and start to howl.[1]

Watson claims that a person may be rendered psychopathological by building in conflicting habits.[2] Butler, too, points out that warring habits often result from misdirected habit training. He urges parents who inculcate ambition in their children also to instill habits of industry. Otherwise, the desire to get ahead in the world will clash with the tendency to "take things easy," and unhappiness will ensue.[3]

Reference has been made in Chapter II to the experiments of Lewin, a *Gestalt* psychologist, who places children in situations where conflict is generated. A toy in a dark room, for example, involves a positive valence and a negative valence. These reaction tendencies are obviously incompatible.

Luria induces conflict experimentally by various means. One method is to establish a set toward success in the subject by giving him some problems which he can solve, and then presenting a problem which is incapable of solution. Conflict results when the setting toward success meets an unsurpass-

---

[1]See I. P. Pavlov: *Lectures on Conditioned Reflexes*, Chapter XXXVI, "Relation between Excitation and Inhibition and Their Delimitations; Experimental Neuroses in Dogs."

[2]J. B. Watson: *Behaviorism*, pp. 295–300. Revised edition, 1930.

[3]J. R. Butler: *Human Nature. A Guide to Its Understanding*, Chapter VI, "Warring Habits."

able obstruction. Luria also induces conflict by suggesting during hypnosis two equally obligatory and opposed tendencies, for example, a plea to a medical student to perform an abortion and a warning not to go through with it. Affective reactions of restlessness and distress in the subject indicate the presence of an acute conflict.[1]

The ambivalence of human impulse affords some insight into the nature of mental conflict. Hatred, strangely, seems to be a natural component of love. It is possible, even natural, assert the psychoanalysts, to love and to hate the same person, particularly if the affection is unrequited. One woman told her husband that if there were not something within her that told her she loved him, she would be sure she hated him. Certainly, thwarted love often turns to hatred, and perhaps the ease of the transition from the one emotion to its opposite is explicable in terms of the fact that hatred is inherent in love.

The inconsistencies of conduct indicate that personality is a manifold complex affair, in which diversity is even more apparent than unity. The individual is made up of numerous selves, displaying one self in the home, another in the office, and still another on the golf course, as we have already noted in describing the specificity of habit. Frequently these selves conflict with each other, as may happen when the undergraduate away at college engages in dissipations scrupulously avoided at home. There are many different conflicting situations to which a person must adapt himself. The moral codes of his own generation may condone conduct of which his parents, his grandparents, or his parents-in-law vigorously disapprove. Since he is sensitive to the opinions of all the several persons with whom he associates, and since he craves the esteem of each and every one he cares about, it is clear that, in the effort to please them all, conflicts are inevitably

---

[1] A. R. Luria: *The Nature of Human Conflicts*, pp. 132–133: also Part Two, "Psychophysiology of the Conflicting Processes."

generated. To assert that an individual has many selves is simply to state that he has many interests in life. The different inclinations of the human being, because of their variety, may never be adequately systematized to produce a unified personality.

Christianity dramatized the conflict of good and evil engaging the human soul. When a little boy was asked by his Sunday-school teacher as to what one must do to be forgiven, he replied, "Sin!"

The fundamental conflict involves the adjustment of impulse to the demands of conscience. Ideas of right and wrong are inculcated by approval and disapproval. A code of conduct is thus developed, which, however it may differ among individuals, constitutes a categorical imperative. The violation of this imperative brings a sense of guilt with its attendant discomfort.

Since mental conflict produces a state of restless dissatisfaction, a drive is engendered toward resolving the stress in order to gain peace of mind. The so-called "mental mechanisms" which we are about to describe are different modes for the resolution of conflict. In contrast to some of our problems which are attacked by thinking, the way out of emotional strife is often traversed in an unthinking, unconscious fashion, so that the individual concerned may be at a loss to account for his own behavior until he has resorted to considerable reflection, and even then, the very subtlety of his adjustments may prompt him to a misinterpretation.

III.　THE RESOLUTION OF CONFLICT

A. Repression. Suppose two rough urchins fight every day on the way home from school, much to the chagrin of a dignified woman who witnesses their combat from the window of her home. In her distress, she will seek to prevent them from fighting. She may rush out and restrain one of the combatants by force—that would be repression; she may instruct the teachers to send them home over different routes so that they do not confront each other—that would be dissociation; or she may put whiskers on one or both of them so that they do not recognize each other when they do meet—that would be rationalization, or displacement, or one of the other deceptive mechanisms.

Repression is the process by which an element in the conflict is forcefully ejected from the conscious arena. Conscience is the bouncer who gives the "bum's rush" to undesirables. In times of depression, when it is unpleasant to contemplate the consequences of disastrous investments, it is a relief to dismiss the stock market from the mind, to refrain from thinking about it, to skip the financial page of the daily newspaper, to avoid friends who insist on brooding over declining quotations, and to turn a deaf ear to comrades who have a wonderful tip.

It is not always simple to succeed in repression. Inhibition of desire sometimes only serves to whet the appetite. Trying too hard to forget may defeat its own end. Thinking continually "I won't smoke" may suggest anew the delights of tobacco.

While repression may afford a temporary relief, its results are ultimately unwholesome. Banishing the forbidden desire relegates it to a region outside conscious control. In the recesses of the shadows, it can work havoc unnoticed. Just as prohibitions produce the bootlegger, so repression gives the mental outlaw an opportunity to work under cover. It would be far better to hale the criminal wish into the mental court where it can be regulated with intelligent justice. It is the part of wisdom to keep our tabooed urges in the open so that we can follow them and keep them under control.

Repression is, in a large measure, responsible for the success of the disguises under which many adjustments take place.

Driven under cover by repression, desires operate in ways unknown to the personality. The repressing forces of conscience encourage subtlety—and thus prepare the way for unthinking behavior.

B. Dissociation. Dissociation is another means of resolving a conflict. The antagonists are separated as a referee parts two fighters in a clinch. The combatants are not allowed to get at each other at all.

A common form of dissociation is the logic-tight compartment. If a person has a pet theory, upsetting evidence is ruled out of order. Our political convictions are notoriously inaccessible to argument. It is of no avail to try to convince a person that his candidate suffers from serious deficiencies. One might as well try to tip over the Rock of Gibraltar as to seek to persuade a loyal New Englander that the schedule of the protective tariff should be more concerned with the interests of the western farmer, or to lead a Southern Democrat to believe that the Republican party is responsible for the preëminence of the United States in the modern world. Logic cannot "crash the gate" where it is not wanted.

Science and religion are often kept in separate enclosures. The hard-headed scientist may believe the incredible when he thinks his soul is at stake. His intelligence is no guarantee against credulity when the hungers of the heart assert themselves. "Man does not live by bread alone." Swedenborg was a renowned scientist until, at the age of fifty-seven, he heard a call from the glory world, and discarding his scientific training, he devoted the rest of his days to fellowship with the angels, finally convincing himself that the "sciences contribute nothing to salvation, but rather confuse and distort ideas."[1]

In Swedenborg's case, the dissociation was chronologically

[1]Charles Ferguson: *The Confusion of Tongues*, Chapter XVI, "Swedenborgianism." 1929.

successive. It is possible, however, for a person to keep both science and religion alive simultaneously, with no effect exerted by one on the other. Religious teachings are often divorced from the practices of weekday life. The practical business man who is accustomed to dealing with "hard facts" in the commercial sphere may seek in religion spiritual rest rather than cerebral exercise, and, consequently, he is apt to approach religious matters with an ingenuous naïveté which would spell ruin for him in his business transactions.

Dissociation is a very natural state of affairs. We all get dissociated, more or less, except those people who cannot go to pieces because they never got assembled. The girl who goes about stockingless, with a fur neck piece added to her summer ensemble, is unorganized. She may never have had to go to the trouble of becoming disorganized. The person who weeps over the plight of the hero on the stage, although he knows the drama is just a play, is dissociated. The individual who forgets a name has disintegrated. Most people go to pieces only under stress, though others need less provocation.

C. Compensation. Compensation is a defence mechanism by which the individual, to guard against one extreme, goes to the other extreme. A person leans over backward to prevent falling forward. Just as the stock market goes too high when it rises and too low when it sinks, with respect to sound values, so the individual swings from one extreme to the other in seeking to maintain his psychic equilibrium. Excessive behavior is very apt to be defensive tactics of a compensatory nature. Many a high hat covers a low brow.

A troubled wife beseeches counsel:

My husband shows in every way his devotion and admiration for me and for our two lovely children whom he adores. But now and then some fair one appears and her forced attentions flatter his ego until he finds himself taking part in a small-sized affair. I always sense it, for at such times he is doubly nice to us, and I know this is not to deceive me, but because at heart he is truly ashamed of what he is doing.

Her insight probably is correct. Her husband's doubled devotion is unconsciously motivated. He may be unaware of the significance of his conduct.

Religious dogmatism is a compensation for harassing doubts. Fanaticism in one direction is an effort to defeat strong inclinations in the opposite direction. Prudery is not a sign of purity, but a revelation of licentious proclivities. Ultramorality is a defence against immoral tendencies.

Compensation is so subtle in its working that it often foils interpretation. Where compensation is concerned, behavior can only be understood in terms of "either—or." Either a man is good because he is really good, or he is good because he is really bad. A person who cannot take orders from those in authority was reared by parents who were *either* too strict, in which case he has transferred his seething rebellion toward other superiors, *or* too lenient, in which case he has never learned to obey commands.

Compensation also serves to overcome or to conceal inferiority. The person who has some peculiarity or defect which lowers him in the esteem of others is goaded by a feeling of inferiority to make a show of strength, either fictitious or real. A sense of insecurity provides the spur which stimulates him with a zest for winning the admiration of his associates by some superlative achievement.[1]

Compensation may be effected through "the neurotic fiction."[2] The individual may indulge in daydreams of greatness. He may strike a pose of audacity, concealing his cowardice under the display of bravado. The bluff may succeed. In

---

[1] See W. F. Vaughan: *The Lure of Superiority.* 1928.
[2] See Alfred Adler: *The Neurotic Constitution.* 1921.

any case, the goal is the restoration of his own self-respect, an end which may be achieved either in phantasy or reality.

The sense of inferiority may be more adequately allayed in the realms of reality. Compensatory activities may be anti-social or social in their consequences. On the one side is the criminal who seeks the spotlight of public attention by way of notoriety; on the other is the individual who devotes his life to the championing of the cause of justice on behalf of the laboring class of which he himself is a member.

Compensation may be direct. Years ago a child was born on a Missouri farm, who, from birth, was frail and weak. Before he was ten years old, he saw his father die a drunkard's death. His mother was wasting away with consumption. He, too, was doomed to a consumptive grave. Doctors could do nothing for him. They agreed he could not live. But he did. And he grew up to become a renowned Physical Culturist. This was Bernarr Macfadden.

Compensation may be vicarious. A girl who is not graceful enough to be popular on the dance floor may devote herself to writing poetry. A boy who lacks the physique to win glory on the gridiron may achieve distinction, instead, in the classroom. Failure in one field of endeavor for which a person is ill-adapted may spur him on to assuage his humiliation through success in another field of activity.

D. Displacement. Displacement is a change of outlet for an emotional drive, an indirect expression due to the blocking of the direct pathway. In Chapter VIII, displacement was discussed in connection with anger. It was pointed out then that indignation may not eventuate in murder, if civilized sentiments intervene, but instead may be displaced to a different outlet such as fighting the liquor traffic.

Repression of a wish does not annihilate the urge. Suppressed desires, facing censure, escape in disguise. Displacement is one of the most deceptive of all the mechanisms.

Elderly unmarried women, for example, denied a normal outlet for their sexual cravings, satisfy their longings through a morbid interest in births, marriages, and scandals.

The employment of euphemisms is a subtle form of displacement. The love of power is often disguised as "parental solicitude." American imperialism is masked as "protective benevolence." Japan is fighting a "defensive war" on Chinese soil.

Humor is often an excellent disguise for attitudes which would be shocking if they were given frank, direct expression. Mother-in-law jokes will nearly always provoke mirth, releasing venom that the young couple feel but dare not express to each other out of respect for filial loyalty. "Wisecracks" about the long-suffering of married persons affords a similar satisfaction.

When an emotion is displaced from a lower level to a higher one, it is said to be *sublimated*. Civilized modes of expressions are substituted for primitive ones. Sublimation is most often referred to in connection with the sex impulse, but of course it is just as applicable to other tendencies. Directing indignation at the eradication of a social evil such as child labor is considered a more cultured performance than setting out to destroy "the Hun." Similarly, the voyeurism of the sex impulse may be sublimated into physiological research, sadism into surgery, or exhibitionism into teaching. Carnal lust may be sublimated into social work, nursing, or Platonic friendship.

E. Projection. Projection is the process by which a person externalizes elements in his own personality by attributing them to other individuals or to the environment. Usually, the elements externalized are repugnant to the possessor because they degrade the ego. Instead of reproaching himself, the individual resorts to the more comfortable expedient of rebuking his neighbor. It is common for people to be especially sensitive to their own faults when they see them in others.

Peace of mind is often achieved by shedding the responsibility for failure. A poor workman blames his tools, the failing student blames his teacher, the unadjusted husband blames the institution of marriage. Faults are disowned. The lover who is untrue comes to suspect his beloved of infidelity. The person who cannot trust other people is the individual who distrusts himself.

The voice of conscience is often experienced in hallucinations, by means of which the person hears the voice of God whispering in his right ear and the voice of the Devil whispering in his left ear.

Delusions of persecution also involve projection. A man who is troubled by the unpardonable sin which he has committed thinks that people, who do not even know of his transgression, are talking about him and conspiring to punish him. The delusions are the externalization of his conscience.

Theology is replete with projection. Wishes become realities. The belief in a heavenly Father is the projection of the human family with the solicitude of the human father magnified into a God of love. The comfort to be derived from a belief in a God who cares deeply for each and every one of us is an inducement to translate the wish into a conviction about reality. Our faith is the product of our wishes. Yet such a view ignores the fact that there are many *objective* phenomena which suggest the operation of a divine intelligence in the world of nature, and which also suggest that our religious aspirations are more than mere wishes since they accord with the trend of evolution, as we see it in the order of things of which we ourselves are an integral part. To say that God is fictitious because our idea of Him is a projection of our wishful thinking is to reach a conclusion that is not justified by the evidence. Wishful thinking, indeed, may eventuate in sound conclusions. God may exist even though I like to think that He exists.

Projection is well illustrated in the case of the New Hampshire farmer who opposed the introduction of daylight saving time on the ground that God's time, he guessed, was good enough for him. Some people seem to think that God handed down the Ten Commandments to Moses in perfect King James English. One student refused to learn Greek because he felt that if English was good enough for Jesus Christ, it was good enough for him.

An individual's opinion may be so projected as to become the will of God. Thus a person who feels personally that gambling is wrong will condemn gambling because it is a violation of God's will, or justify negro slavery because it accords with the divine will.

F. Introjection. Introjection is the process by which an individual identifies himself with others, usually for the purpose of appropriating their desirable qualities. Frequently, the identification is made with some group the achievements of which reflect glory upon the individual members, some of whom contribute nothing, probably, to the collective success. Thus I may take pride in a football victory of *my* college or the attainments of a man who belongs to *my* fraternity. Boston, to any Bostonian, is the cultural center of the nation. Praise of *my* community is a subtle way of flattering *myself*. The fly on the axle of the thundering chariot boastfully shouted, "Lo, what a dust I raise!"

Introjection is practised by the spectator of a drama, who identifies himself with the characters and lives through their experiences himself. In Georovesti, Rumania, when a cinema theater was opened for the first time, gaping peasants watching the screen were so terrified as they saw a locomotive hurtle toward them that they stampeded and wrecked the building.[1]

Sir Bruce Bruce-Porter, prominent London physician, was treating a girl for a grave disease. The patient was reading a serial story in which the heroine was dying of the same disease.

---

[1] *Time*, February 9, 1931.

The story was obviously affecting her. Sir Bruce Bruce-Porter wrote the novelist and explained that, for the sake of his patient, the heroine of the story should, at all costs, be allowed to recover. The heroine got better—and the patient recovered, too.[1]

Empathy is another term for introjection. To empathize is to feel yourself into an object or the situation of another person. The sight of a Gothic arch is uplifting—it leaves the observer with a sense of aspiration. Similarly, the beauty of a colonial mansion is due in part to the feel-ing of strength which the observer derives from identifying himself with the stately pillars holding up the portico. Looking at the Leaning Tower of Pisa makes the be-holder feel tipsy. How does it affect you?

Riding in the seat of a car next to the driver, you have probably found yourself pressing your right foot on the floor board when an automobile darted suddenly into your path. At a track meet, the spectator kicks to help the high jumper over the bar, and at a football game the cheering section presses forward when the ball carrier plunges toward the goal line. It is easy to grow dizzy watching a man washing windows on a high building.

Sympathy is based on the capacity for introjection. An individual becomes dejected himself when he identifies himself with a person who has suffered some serious misfortune. It is especially easy to sympathize with a hero. Millions of people have been distressed by the Lindbergh kidnaping who never felt a tinge of pity when they heard of the abduction of some unknown child. So thoroughly do we, as human beings, feel ourselves into the lives of others, that we insist on our authors bringing their stories to a happy ending.

[1]The Boston *Post*, July 29, 1931.

It is exhilarating to watch a game when the performers are experts. The spectator performs the acts of skill himself and goes home with a sense of work well done. Our heroes must be clever and they must also be lucky, for we like to feel we are the darlings of fate.

G. Transfer. Transfer is the mechanism underlying the conditioned response. A person reacts toward one stimulus as if it were another stimulus with which the first, by experience, has become associated. Thus a girl who was jilted by a medical student developed a hatred for all doctors. A person who gets a reputation for humor can never be taken seriously. Mark Twain once attempted to make a solemn speech and his audience laughed hilariously. They transferred their response to the humorous Mark Twain over to the serious Mark Twain, reacting to the latter as if he were the former.

Since transfer has already been covered at some length in the discussion of the conditioned response, no further space will be given transfer here.

H. Rationalization. Rationalizing is thinking the aim of which is not to ascertain the truth but to satisfy a wish. Reason becomes the handmaid to prejudice. Henshaw Ward calls it "thobbing," since we "think out the opinion that pleases us and then believe it."[1] John Wesley described the process neatly when he asserted that "passion and prejudice govern the world—under the name of Reason."

When we reason to justify a desire or an action, we are rationalizing.[2] If you have some important work to do and a friend invites you to play golf on a course that you have always wanted to visit, you will convince yourself that health is a prime essential and conclude by believing that it is not merely a privilege to get out in the open, it is a duty you owe

---

[1]Henshaw Ward: *Thobbing.* 1926.
[2]See Ernest Jones: "Rationalization in Everyday Life," *Journal of Abnormal Psychology*, August–September, 1908.

yourself and your family—and even your country. So convenient a thing it is to be a reasonable creature, since it enables one to find or make a reason for everything one has a mind to do.

We rationalize because we have certain ideals which we like to believe are embodied in our lives, and when we do not measure up to those ideals, we have to reconcile our failures in order to preserve our peace of mind.

Fundamentally, we rationalize because we like to think of ourselves as rational creatures, a conviction which is seriously jeopardized by constant reminders of our irrationality.

Love, for example, is blind. The motivation is instinctive, and largely unconscious, and obviously, at least to impartial observers, irrational. Attracted by a cute lisp or a baby stare, a man will insist that his lady's charm lies in her keen intellect or her spiritual aspirations. The motivation being unconscious, it is easy for consciousness to supply flattering explanations in the form of rationalizations. Thus, in spite of contradicting evidence, the human being can hold to his pet conviction that his conduct is guided by reason. The reasons evolved to account for behavior are logically acceptable, but manufactured *ex post facto*, and untrue.

We are lazy but we like to think we are industrious.

The Real Reason

I love to lean upon my spade,
  As the day begins to close,
To smell the scent of fresh-turned earth,
  The fragrance of the rose.

I listen to the nesting birds,
  As they chirrup in the trees,
And watch the bonfire smoke ascend
  As gray wisps in the breeze.

I love to lean upon my spade—
I am like my fellow-men—
For when we're leaning on our spades,
We are not working then.[1]

The shiftless often evolve a sophisticated defence for their inertia, singing praises for the art of "taking things easy" as constituting the essence of good living.

The philosopher is especially apt, by virtue of his profession, to flatter himself that his views of the universal scheme of things are the result of cold cogitation, and yet nowhere can there be found a more fruitful supply of evidence for the subtle intrusion of bias into the reasoning process, all the more deceptive because the philosopher is disinclined to recognize the rôle of desire. "A good many of us," says Uncle Eben, "thinks we's standing up foh de truth when we's only bein' obstinate 'bout a personal opinion."

Rationalization is a very elusive process unless the thinker is alertly on his guard.

Rationalization is the process of constructing a system of ideas, the real function of which is to justify some preëxisting desire or belief, without any attempt objectively to examine that desire or belief with reference to its truth. . . . Every thoughtful person is conscious of how profoundly he is influenced by desires and beliefs originating in his physical organism or his early training. Rationalization of these desires and beliefs is a subtle foe of the philosophical spirit.[2]

Thoughtful persons may be conscious of the rôle of desire in philosophizing, as a general proposition, yet it is likely that they may not detect the particular occasions upon which their emotional dispositions give direction to their thinking.[3]

Rationalization has characteristic symptoms by which it

---

[1]*Pearson's Weekly.* By permission of *Pearson's Weekly.*

[2]E. S. Brightman. *An Introduction to Philosophy,* p. 9. 1925. Reprinted by permission of Henry Holt and Co.

[3]See J. H. Robinson: *The Mind in the Making,* p. 45. 1921.

can be detected by the careful observer. Exaggerated emotionalism is a mark of rationalizing. If someone says that two and two make four, nobody gets excited. But if someone says that all pacifists are cowards, somebody in the audience is liable to get excited.

A passionate fondness for our own opinions is another indicator of rationalization, a fondness for these opinions, not as ideas, but as an integral part of our very being. To have them disputed is to be insulted. Much of our reasoning consists in finding arguments for continuing to believe as we already do.

A third mark of rationalization is the conviction that our judgments are obvious, and that questioning them is merely to carry scepticism to an absurd degree. They are beyond argument. There can be no doubt as to their validity.

In considering the rôle of rationalization in thinking, it is easy to fall into the fallacy that rationalizing inevitably leads us to wrong conclusions. If we are honest in our thinking, we should suspect a conclusion arrived at by rationalization, but, at the same time, we should be prepared to accept it as valid if investigation reveals more sound reasons for holding to the same belief. "Sour grapes" may lead a person to think that a job he has lost was not good enough for him, anyway, and it may be true that a better position awaits him.

The grave disadvantage of rationalization, and all the other subtle adaptations, is that the resources of the individual get no chance to come into full play. If intelligence is to be of any value, it must be applied to the planning and directing of activity, and not be reserved for the justification of conduct subsequent to the performance.

It is obvious to the studious observer of conduct that the lines of distinction between the various subtle adaptations are vague. The mechanisms usually combine and interfuse in their functioning. Conflict motivates compensation, displacement, projection, rationalization, and so on. Rationalization implies dissociation, since one part of me succeeds in fooling "Me." Suppose I am attracted to a new job merely because there is a higher salary offered, but I do not want to confess my interest in money even to myself, so I say that I am called to "a larger field of service." In deceiving "Me," the rationalization acts as a disguise to escape the censor—it is, in other words, a displacement. If I reason that my failure in a task is due to your lack of coöperation, I am both rationalizing and projecting. "Sour grapes" is rationalizing and compensating. Thus it can be seen that it is impossible to draw sharp lines of cleavage among the different processes of subtle adaptation. The mind has worked out a variety of defence mechanisms which reinforce each other to preserve the personality from disturbing shocks.

I. Integration. Organization of the conflicting trends of personality is called integration. A unified personality is not a gift but an achievement. Integration requires an effort toward systematization of the habits which have developed for specific situations, and which, therefore, may be unrelated and inconsistent. Integration, as a remedy for, and a prevention against, conflicting and dissociating trends, is more effective than the subtle modes of adaptation which we have just described.

The assumption of responsibility is an effective integrating force in the evolution of personality. A child should be assigned a task in the family chores for which he is encouraged to feel an obligation. Work and responsibility are as indispensable for the development of character as food and exercise to the body. Purposeful activity requiring sustained effort in the interest of others contributes in an important way to the organization of personality. The child should be forced, as soon as possible, to assume the responsibility for watching the clock and for getting to school on time. It is through such little incidents that a sense of self-confidence is nourished. A child should learn how to work, how to value his services, and how to handle money. The discharge of these functions helps him to mature.

The adult, too, needs a job that gives him a sense of usefulness. The work should not be too easy or too hard. It should be difficult enough to challenge his full resourcefulness. Most of us shirk responsibility whenever we can respectably escape it, thus depriving ourselves of opportunities for building up personal stability.

Religion is another aspect of experience which contributes to integration in an important way. Religion supplies a philosophy which enables the individual to "see life whole," and an ideal around which the various trends of human endeavor can be integrated. Values worth striving for are posited as the goals to stimulate and to organize conduct. Religion, to achieve its full purpose, should penetrate every phase of life, lending every activity significance and meaning.

Integration is essential to that effective living which is the basis of happiness. The unity derived from a life well organized around interests which are valued enough to stimulate sustained effort for their fulfillment is the best insurance against the ravages of mental conflict. A great purpose is sure to generate a wholesome personality.

CHAPTER XIII

THINKING

M^{ANY} of our adjustments are made without full realization on our part of all the factors determining action. Thinking, however, is the process through which we seek consciously to organize experience. To "think of" is to be aware of an object; to "think about" is to relate that object significantly to other objects, to pass from apprehension to comprehension. Thinking proceeds by referring the past to the future, as we remember in order to anticipate.

I. THE FUNCTION OF THINKING

Putting two and two together, developing the implications of a situation, drawing conclusions, are apt phrases to describe the nature of thought. "To think is to bridge a gap in experience, to bind together facts or deeds otherwise isolated."[1] Experience is organizable because the mind is ever ready to recognize connections and to get understanding. When we cogitate, we deal with relations in such a way as to gain an appreciation of meanings. One item in experience signifies another, points to it through some definite relationship, as exemplified in the interpretation of signs. On the Atlantic coast "a salty smell" in the air means "east wind" and "east wind" signifies "rain." Conditioning occurs as the associations are repeated until the time arrives when the mind passes automatically from premise (east wind) to conclusion (rain).

It is difficult to ascertain how much intellectual understand-

---

[1] John Dewey: *How We Think*, p. 80. 1910.

ing may be involved in the conditioning process. Associative bonds are involved in the conditioning process and in the logical process; in the latter, the associative links must be consciously appreciated, while in the former they may or may not be outside awareness. When the advertiser pictures his low-priced car in front of a palatial residence, we may say that the reader is seduced into making the inference that the ownership of that particular make of car is a sign of good breeding, or we may say that he is conditioned in such a way as to react in the same differential manner to that car as he does to persons with prestige. Fortunately for the advertiser and the manufacturer, the inference, if such a process be involved, is drawn unconsciously, since even the briefest logical analysis of the situation reveals its absurdity. It is difficult to say just how much logic enters into human behavior. The relationships are there, in our experience, but they often proceed unanalyzed to affect our actions for better or worse. Logic can seriously affect the conditioning process if it will. The reader who pauses to pierce the illogic of the advertisement upsets the conditioning so subtly plotted by the advertiser. The advertiser, indeed, usually thinks for the consumer; it is a wise consumer who thinks for himself. Certain it is that a conscious examination of associative connections in our experience will promote comprehension. Intelligent action is, after all, the goal of thinking.

Necessity, so the proverb goes, is the mother of invention. Thinking is a last resort, forced upon us by a pressing problem. A feeling of perplexity resulting from the thwarting of some desire impels us to search for some solution. Thought begins with a question that requires an answer. The course of conduct, being blocked, variation is necessitated; alternatives are weighed. For example, the depression which disorganized business in 1929 compelled industry to search for new ways to profit. While many gave in to discouragement, the resourceful looked around for novel methods to defeat the slump.

Improved methods of distribution have helped a good many firms to do more business than ever during the depression. A hair-tonic concern recently had to enlarge its plant capacity by one-third and its sales are at a record volume, although it is still making the same sort of tonic it always has and makes no pretence of having anything new to put on the market. What that company did was to reduce the size of its bottles, thus bringing them down to a price that made them have a considerably wider appeal than the larger and more expensive bottles had had. Immediately the tonic was snapped up by chain stores and independent merchants, not only all over the United States but in foreign countries as well. I understand that a tobacco company had to put on a night shift to meet the demand for one of its products when it was presented to the public in a new kind of package. Other firms have found that it paid them to diversify the lines they were manufacturing. They have equipped their plants to turn out products allied to those they were already making and whose manufacture or sale was more or less closely related to the production or distribution methods they had already set up. This sort of thing has benefited not only the stockholders, but also the wage earners in these factories. For instance, a piano concern found that there was a lessened demand for its instruments. If nature had been allowed to take its course, many of its skilled cabinet makers, who had been in the firm's employ for many years, would either have been thrown out of work or would have had to be put on jobs where their specialized training would have been completely wasted. But nature did not take its course, for the management of this company realized that many people were buying other things than pianos. It put its cabinet makers to work on another line which was something that might seem to be entirely unrelated to the manufacture of pianos—motor boats, of all things! But the boats were sold, the cabinet makers held their jobs, and the profits of the company increased.

In the midst of the new, the precarious, the uncertain, and the obscure, the individual must pass from the known to the unknown in the process of discovery. Something present suggests something further until the mind is led on to the solution of the puzzle confronting it. Thinking is problem solving. There is an end to be attained, there are means to be used, there is a procedure to be organized.

Consciousness has a prospective function which is fulfilled by planning adjustment in the light of past experience. Thus the desire to control natural forces to promote our own ends is more efficiently satisfied. "Biologically the purpose of ideation is to prepare for action. . . . Conciousness is the life impulse in the process of becoming conduct."[1]

The immediate expression of an impulse is fatal to thinking. To yield to caprice is to be guided by the circumstances of the moment. Thought involves the inhibition of action, the suspension of judgment. Effective thinking depends upon a state of doubt which lends sustenance to a systematic and protracted inquiry.[2]

Planning is the integration of action through the organization of experience. Mental manipulation and exploration precede the execution of the plan. Mental experiment has the advantage of permitting the arrangement of a situation that the investigator might have to wait a long time for the course of natural events to produce and to repeat. There is economy in running through an experiment mentally before carrying it into execution. Through reasoning, the problem may be submitted to hypothetical conditions and the question proved (tested). Thus inferences may be checked and verified.

---

[1] L. L. Thurstone: *The Nature of Intelligence*, pp. 30, 12.
[2] Joseph Jastrow: *Effective Thinking*. 1931.

A fundamental advantage in thinking is derived from the attainment of general principles. Generalization spares the thinker the necessity of going through the gamut of cogitation with each separate occurrence of a typical event. Thus when the mathematician asserts that the sum of the angles of a triangle is equal to two right angles, he saves himself the bother of proving the statement each time he confronts the problem, provided of course that he is fully convinced of the truth of his proposition. A principle explains on a large scale. The ability to generalize is very important for intelligent living, since it facilitates that process which is popularly described as "learning from experience." The individual who learns his lesson and brings his experience to bear upon relevant situations which later arise has availed himself of a valuable resource for adjusting to the changing demands of his environment. Ordinarily specificity is only too characteristic of behavior. The person fails to see the connection. The result is departmentalized conduct, inconsistency, conflict. Children must be guided in seeing relationships between the decisions made in their various activities, if we are to expect the decision made in one situation to transfer to another. "We must be concerned with the ideas and ideals which children get from their activities as well as with the activities themselves."[1]

II. HOW THINKING PROCEEDS

Introspection, unfortunately, has not shed much light upon the exact nature of the thought process. Some psychologists insist that thought consists of a succession of images, and some psychologists maintain that images are unnecessary, even superfluous. Evidently there is disagreement. Probably thinking sometimes involves images and sometimes gets along without them.

Thinking usually makes use of symbols in order to escape

[1]Vernon Jones: *Character Education through Cases from Biography*, p. 3.

the necessity of dealing directly with things. The employment of number symbols permits the transaction of financial operations without the actual handling of coins and bills. Suppose, for example, that you owe me $10 and I owe you $20. We can settle the debts by my presenting you with twenty one-dollar bills and your returning ten of them. But it is much simpler to calculate by means of symbols that if I pay you $10, not necessarily doing so concretely, our mutual obligations will be discharged.

The most useful symbols are words through which it is easy to deal with things without the manipulation of the concrete objects. Language developed from the urge to communicate thought. We can think without words, but we can think better with them. The formulation of thought in words is a great aid to its clarification. Many persons think most effectively when they think out loud. Verbalization facilitates the evolution of an idea. Watson even goes so far as to say that all thinking is simply subvocal speech.[1] This assertion is somewhat belied by the fact that some people find their thinking proceeding faster than their vocal organs can function. The public speaker must think ahead of his tongue in order to be sure that his delivery will progress without interruption. Certainly speech and thought are intimately related, but they are not equivalent.

The importance of language for thinking is observable in developing children. The acquisition of words increases the span of the budding mental life, and the child learns that the utilization of words saves him effort in the attainment of his desires. Names come to be associated with the various objects with which he has to deal. The rudimentary nature of his vocabulary parallels the obscurity of his thinking. The man with whiskers is Grandpa. So is every other man with whiskers. The dog is a bow-wow. So is every other animal.

[1] J. B. Watson: *Behaviorism*, Chapter X.

Only gradually do objects become more definitely distinguished, as ideas evolve into concepts. The concept of an object is all that the object comes to mean to the individual who contemplates it. Eventually it is discovered that only particular sorts of animals may be properly designated dogs. Then, too, there are collies, bulldogs, spaniels, each of which may be identified, and all of them dogs. "Dog" thus becomes a general term applicable to a certain class of animals. When this stage has been reached, thinking can be expanded so that it is no longer limited to thinking of things as concrete objects. Ultimately the mind is able to think in terms of abstractions. "Justice" can then be conceived, covering a host of different acts which resemble each other in so far as they are "just." A definition is the verbalization of a concept, expressed in such a way as to embrace all cases coming within its scope. This very sketchy description of several stages in the evolution of thought is intended to indicate that words are an important tool for the thinking process.

Whether images, verbal or otherwise, constitute the stream of thought has been the subject of an extensive controversy. Titchener maintained that thought consists of images, whereas the Würzburg school of psychologists asserted that much of the process is imageless. According to the latter group, all thinking involves unconscious and therefore unintrospectable factors, impalpable bits of knowledge, determining tendencies, which are imageless. Evidence for this point of view may be observed in two simple experiments.

$$1:4::8:?$$

Did you have an image of 32 or did it come without imagery?

cold	—hot	high	—low
big	—small	few	—many
light	—heavy	smooth	—rough

$$black \quad — \quad ?$$

When you came to black, why did you think of white? The answer lies in the fact that the attitude set up by the preceding antonyms, though imageless, was determining your thinking activity. When "white" came to your mind, did it appear as an image or was it imageless?

Spearman states that images are almost entirely absent in his own thought. His thinking is imageless and wordless. His investigations have convinced him that there is no correlation between excellence of imagery and excellence of thought. The proponents of the Titchenerian view are usually those persons whose mental life is rich in imagery, while the supporters of the Würzburg doctrine are those whose mental life is, we might say, defective in imagery. Each accuses the other of being unable to introspect. Images are not indispensable, in fact, they are not even of any appreciable assistance to thinking.[1] In contrast to Titchener's description of thought, Spearman's discussion only mentions images in a casual way, while concentrating upon the comprehension of relations in which imagery is notable by its absence.

In summarizing the controversy, we may say that the thinking process often consists of images, but this is not always the case, for thought can get along without them and sometimes does so more effectively.

III. BELIEF

The products of our thinking are beliefs which function as definite determiners of conduct. A belief is an act in the making. When a belief has become thoroughly emotionalized, it becomes a conviction-provoking loyalty. A belief, to be effective, must be tied up to the emotions; otherwise a person may believe that it is morally wrong to gamble in the stock market and yet proceed to practice speculation. Such a per-

---

[1] C Spearman: *The Nature of Intelligence and the Principles of Cognition*, p. 192. 1923.

son thinks one way but feels another.   It is the affective nature which gives potency to beliefs.

Beliefs are formed and held because they satisfy.   Desire plays a large part in their formation and retention.   Prepossession engenders credulity.   Conclusions exert a magnetic influence, reinforcing anticipation.   Desire begets hope, hope expectation, expectation belief.

Right belief and credulity refer to habits of mind as well as to standards of evidence.   "Thinking straight is essential to seeing straight.   The evidence grows out of the attitude far more than the attitude results from the evidence."[1]   Some people are so entrenched in their own convictions that they resist the truth.   It is easy for an anti-vivisectionist, for example, to discredit the value of animal dissection in the progress of medical research.

Most people believe too much rather than too little.   Credulity is rampant.   Ours may be a scientific age, yet this era is the heyday of the fortune tellers.   One million three hundred thousand radio listeners in a year responded by mail to Evangeline Adams's tri-weekly broadcasts.   In New York City twenty-five million dollars a year cross the palms of clairvoyants.   Millions of adult Americans believe that the future can be foretold.   Many others are casting about for some excuse to believe.

The most striking aspect of the belief in astrology is the ease with which so many people accept the premise on which the system stands.   Persons who are otherwise intelligent, who habitually draw reasonably correct conclusions from given data, never balk, somehow, at the notion that stars give off something that makes human beings what they are and what they are to be.   They stake their fortunes on a supposition they do not even try to test, accepting without question the statement that a heavenly body makes them tall or short, rich

[1]Joseph Jastrow: *The Psychology of Conviction*, p. 113.   1918.

or poor, well or ill.   Persons who make sure that a radio works before they buy it will nevertheless pay money to anyone who promises to decide the most important issues of their lives. "It is a gaudy paradox that a race whose name is a by-word for shrewdness, caution, and practical guile should give over in droves to a footless will-to-believe.   Most successes in prophecy are remembered, failures forgotten.   The stock answer is, that the stars are never wrong, but that astrologers may be, which is admittedly an argument to end all argument."[1]

The richest field for the study of credulity lies in medical quackery, whether it be a movie star who attributes her perfect teeth to eating "Ootsies" (which were not even invented until long after her molars had matured), or a distinguished foreign physician who recommends yeast for a specific ailment in such a way as to allow the advertiser to seduce the public into believing that a cure for staphylococcic infections must be a panacea for all ills.

The tenacity of belief in the fact of disquieting evidence is illustrated in spiritism, a thriving cult in modern times.   Two little girls, Kate and Margaret Fox, of Hydesville, New York, learned how to crack their big toes.   Their parents and neighbors took the sound for spirit rapping.   The Fox sisters capitalized on their discovery, giving demonstrations as mediums in public performances.   For forty years they were regarded widely as gifted with special powers of revelation.   They feared to expose their trickery because they dreaded the wrath of the religious mob and the anger of their sister Leah who had used the girls to make money.   In 1888 they summoned the courage to show a New York audience how it was done.   Reuben Briggs Davenport wrote a book on the inspiration he derived from the exposé entitled *The Death-Blow to Spiritualism.*

[1]Travis Hoke: "The Heyday of the Fortune Tellers," *Harper's Magazine,* January, 1932.

It was an amusing title: the death-blow produced very few results.　Spiritualism went merrily on.[1]

Logical attainment in one direction is no bar to extravagant conclusions in another.　Natural intelligence is no barrier to the propagation of error.　The person who believes in miracles, exceptions to the causal order, appeals to testimony which under normal circumstances he would himself distrust.　Beliefs are so complicated by personal values as to encourage uncritical judgment.　The dissociated mind falls readily into the acceptance of inconsistent convictions.　The "bonus" bill, for example, seems a dreadful thing to nice men who sold the Government $10 articles at $640 during the War.　Most of us accept the conventional fallacies.　We believe that Nero fiddled while Rome burned, though Nero was not in town, and there were no fiddles in those days.　We believe what we are told to believe.　The newspapers build up myths around popular heroes, to which the public gives ready credence.　The press helped to create the impression that Mary Pickford and Douglas Fairbanks were the ideally mated couple by publishing glimpses of the happy home, and photographs in which they always posed together, a simple device testifying to the good business sense of Mary who is shrewd in the affairs of the world.　The modern newspaper has made and unmade heroes at will.[2]　The modern publicity agent can assure stardom to mediocrity, depending upon his own wiles and upon the gullibility of the public.[3]

With so many factors predisposing us to embrace absurdity, it is surprising that our conduct makes sense at all.　It is certain that the achievement of a logical mind requires long discipline in exact science until habits of careful inquiry and

---

[1]C. W. Ferguson: *The Confusion of Tongues.*

[2]Silas Bent: *Ballyhoo.*　1927.

[3]D. Freedman and Harry Reichenbach: *Phantom Fame: the Anatomy of Ballyhoo.*　1931.

cautious conclusion become second nature. A discussion of psychology and logic will indicate some of the means that may be employed to insure sound thinking which is essential to sane living.

IV. PSYCHOLOGY AND LOGIC

Psychology touches Logic intimately in the study of rationalization. Thinking is largely characterized by emotional interest in conclusions. For example, Eddington deduces religion from the fact that atoms do not obey the laws of mathematics, while Jeans deduces it from the fact that they do.

The fact that a person is rationalizing does not prove that his conclusions are erroneous, but it should render them subject to suspicion, in the sense only that they should be investigated. It is well known that errors in observation may often be traced to intense emotional slants. The scientist who becomes attached to his theories fails to notice facts which contradict them. He is predisposed against giving due weight to the objections of his opponents. Many interminable disputes never lead to any result, just because of the passionate enthusiasm of those who take part in them. The perverting influence of an intense emotional slant on the judgment of a matter calling for cool philosophical deliberation is illustrated in the reaction provoked in a learned reader by Spinoza's *Tractatus Theologico-Politicus:* "It is a Book full of curious, but abominable discoveries, the Learning and Inquiries whereof must needs have been fetched from Hell. Every Christian, nay, every Man of Sense, ought to abhor such a Book. . . . I have read that Book of Spinosa with application from the beginning to the end; but I protest at the same time before God, that I have found no solid arguments in it, nor anything that could shake, in the least, my belief of the Gospel. Instead of solid reasons, it contains mere suppositions". . . .[1]

[1]From Frederick Pollock: *Spinoza; His Life and Philosophy*, Appendix, p. 403. 1899. By permission of The Macmillan Company, publishers.

The metaphysician, according to Rignano, starts with the desired conclusion and goes back in search of the necessary premises from which it may be deduced. It is common practice among philosophers to present reality in conformity with certain intimate and profound aspirations. What matters most of all to the thinker is not the truth, but rather the object of his faith.[1]

An error often committed by psychologists is the assumption that in disclosing the origin of a philosophical doctrine they are casting discredit on its validity. It is natural that a person's philosophy should be an outgrowth of his own peculiar experiences, through which a solution is sought for emotional problems confronting him. A man who has suffered misfortune may find solace through faith in a loving God. The psychologist may dismiss the belief by contemptuously labeling it wishful thinking, and then dashing to the conclusion, logically unwarranted, that, since trust in a Heavenly Father is satisfying, it must be an unfounded hope, an illusion—there really is no God, after all; the believer must be mistaken. This error, known as the genetic fallacy, is frequently committed by psychologists.[2] It serves as a pointed reminder of the fact that psychology must conform to the standards set by Logic if it is to be intelligently applied.

Psychology describes how we incline to think; Logic how we must think if we would think correctly. Knowledge of the rules of straight thinking and attention to the pitfalls common to the cogitative activities of human kind combine to promote adherence to the principles underlying the intelligent regulation of life. Logic is not merely a theoretical study, as the naïve assume; on the contrary, it is one of the most vital sciences. Empirical thinking observes the sequences of events without checking against a control. Thus a person attributes

---

[1] See E. Rignano: *The Psychology of Reasoning*, p. 229. 1923.
[2] Sigmund Freud: *The Future of An Illusion*. 1928.

the cure of his cold to a bottle of pills, when any number of other factors may have been responsible, such as diet, sleep, sunshine, or just the plain curative resourcefulness of nature. As empirical observations accumulate, folklore is developed, which curiously enough often passes for common sense. An amusing example of such uncontrolled empiricism is the saying: "Stuff a cold and starve a fever." Originally the counsel read: "If you stuff a cold, you'll later have to starve a fever." To such trivial variations we entrust our lives.

Reasoning is a mental experiment. Sound reasoning must be subject to the rigorous conditions of scientific control. Scientific thinking observes the rules of logic which are the canons of science. It is vital that we learn to think straight. Crooked thinking is costly. The tendency to go to extremes in health fads leads people to believe that if a little of something is good, a lot of it is better. One man, advised to drink a quart of milk daily, complained to the physician that his stomach was upset. Investigation revealed he was consuming a gallon of milk a day on the theory that he was assuring himself of four times the benefit of one quart. Another man whose physician directed him to take a bottle of mesothorium water, was so convinced of its curative power that he continued the treatment for a year on his own responsibility, assuming that if a little was good, more would be better. He drank unheard-of quantities of the water. Symptoms appeared which led to an examination, and his bones were found to be loaded down with mesothorium. He died of an overdose of mesothorium, but it might be more accurate to say that he died of faulty logic.

Scientific thinking depends upon a certain type of evidence afforded only by controlled observations. The fact that a person gets well under a certain mode of treatment proves nothing, for he may have recovered without it or even in spite of it. Is quinine good for colds? The scientific test is to give quinine to one group of persons suffering from colds and to avoid its use with another group also afflicted with colds, to keep accurate records of the recoveries, and then to determine, by a comparison of the records for the two groups, whether quinine is useless, beneficial, or harmful. This simple method of testing the value of drugs did not come into use until the nineteenth century, and there are plenty of people today who govern their selection of remedies for their ills without any resort to controlled observation. The scientific method has penetrated modern thought to only a slight extent, whether it be in medicine, politics, economics, religion, or ethics.[1]

The achievement of sound thinking is important. It depends, at the outset, upon a recognition of the fact that mental data are not isolated but connected. Reasoning is the process by which the mind passes from a given fact to other facts implied through logical relations. The farmer's wife who said to the druggist, "Now, be sure and write plain on them bottles which is for the horse and which is for my husband. I don't want nothin' to happen to that horse before the spring plowin'," suggested certain implications which may not have been intended. The individual infers, "carries over," in going beyond what is surely known to something else accepted on its warrant. He draws conclusions, or better still, he leaps to them. The demands of Logic are satisfied when the inferences are made with due respect for consistency. By following such methods as Logic suggests, for Logic is the "logy" or method which guides our thinking and experiment, we reach conclusions as sound as it lies within our capacities to achieve.

Reasoning has to start with some assumption, proved or unproved, some premise or hypothesis, which must be believed and asserted. The fundamental problem of Logic, then, is to seek valid premises upon which, as a basis, reasoning may proceed. Induction is the method by which a general principle is derived from a study of particular cases—from the fact that

---

[1]See Howard W. Haggard: *Devils, Drugs, and Doctors*, pp. 350–351. 1929.

each time there is a ring around the moon, it rains, it may be concluded that, as a general rule, it will rain when there is a ring around the moon; deduction is the method by which the rule is applied to a particular case—since there is a ring around the moon, it is going to rain now. The problem of induction is to establish the truth of the premises from which deductions are to be made. Classification is the intermediate link between the inductive and deductive procedures.

There are three inductive methods which deserve mention here, since they constitute the principles guiding scientific experiment in any field of investigation:

1. The method of agreement.

Suppose three men are successful in business and it is found that:

Brown left school after the eighth grade and he is intelligent;

Jones graduated from high school and he is intelligent;

Smith graduated from college and he is intelligent.

Conclusion: Success is due to intelligence and not to education.

2. The method of difference.

Suppose Smith is the only one of the three who succeeds and it is found that: Brown graduated from high school and he is intelligent;

Jones graduated from high school and he is intelligent;

Smith graduated from college and he is intelligent.

Conclusion: Success is due to the college education.

3. The method of concomitant variations.

Suppose Brown is fairly successful, Jones is more successful, and Smith still more successful and it is found that:

Brown graduated from grammar school;

Jones graduated from high school;

Smith graduated from college.

Conclusion: Success is proportional to the length of school training.

The above examples, of course, are offered on the assumption that all other conditions remain constant. In reality, there is the possibility that a plurality of causes may be operating in any given instance, and, therefore, that it is important that the various methods be employed as checks upon each other. The agreement, for example, may have been a matter of coincidence; negative instances may have been overlooked; more ultimate (less obvious) causes may have been responsible, such as family pull or an optimistic outlook. Procedure must be thorough if results are to approximate validity.

The collection of instances in induction must be carried out with due respect for certain requirements. It is obvious that life is too short to allow for the enumeration of all possible instances. Samples, therefore, are selected. The sampling must be fair. There is a strong tendency to choose the instances to suit a given bias. Thus negative instances are readily ignored. The man who insists that rich people are stingy fails to notice cases of generosity on the part of the wealthy. Then, too, there is the danger of taking the exceptional as typical. Thus the advertisement of the man who made $110 the first day selling corn poppers gives the impression that he made $110 every day. The instances must be significant. When a lawyer was informed that three persons had seen his client commit the crime, he replied: "That's nothing. I can produce 300 witnesses who didn't see him do it." Enough instances must be covered to give a fair sampling, otherwise the particularistic fallacy may be indulged in by generalizing on the basis of inadequate evidence. Thus a person may consider all Chinamen crooked because he was once cheated by his laundry man.[1] "All Indians walk in single file," reported the traveler. "How do you know?" queried the listener. "Well," was the retort, "the only one I ever saw, did." Such is the logic upon which our prejudices are born and nourished.

Faulty classification, "drawing the line," is reponsible for a number of fallacies. Thus a person may insist that a man must be either sane or insane, not realizing that variation is

[1]See E. S. Bogardus: *Fundamentals of Social Psychology*, p. 288. 1924.

continuous, sanity and insanity merging into one another very gradually, all of us partaking in some degree of each. Speaking more exactly, a person's behavior is more or less sane or insane—it is all a relative matter. It is convenient to classify people into sheep and goats, the blessed and the damned, but human nature does not fall readily into such discrete categories. If an individual is "bad," we tend to think of him as all "bad," and so atheists are not allowed to testify in some courts on the ground that all atheists are liars. Type psychology is based on unsound logic, involving several fallacies. There is the fallacy of false simplicity which leads the uncritical to believe that traits are discontinuous and simple in organization, the mistake just described above. There is the fallacy of verbalism which consists in believing that naming a thing constitutes proof of its existence as an entity. There is the fallacy of the particular case which a person commits when he finds what he is looking for when it really is not there.

One of the most common dangers in induction is hasty generalization. Being impatient, we rush to conclusions before there is enough evidence in to justify judgment.

Overassertion is another mistake likely to be committed in induction. The conclusion drawn from a sampling of cases should be in terms of tendencies rather than absolutes—that is, an investigation may indicate that there is a tendency for a given religious sect, we shall say, to be hidebound; it is saying too much to assert that all members of that sect are inevitably hidebound.

Deduction consists in showing the relations of propositions to each other. Deductive reasoning starts from premises which are propositions, proved or assumed, serving as a ground for a conclusion. The more general premise, which contains the predicate of the conclusion, is called the major premise; the more particular premise, which contains the subject of the conclusion, is called the minor premise. The major term and the minor term are logically related to each other through the middle term which is common to both, in such a way as to imply a conclusion. The three propositions, the major premise, minor premise, and conclusion, constitute a syllogism, the syllogism being the unit of deductive inference. If the premises are true and the reasoning is valid, the conclusion must be true. Syllogistic proof presupposes the truth of its premises.

He must be intelligent because he is a college graduate.

Deductive arguments are not always formulated syllogistically, for in practice part of the argument is omitted, but arguments are more apt to conform to the laws of Logic if they are exposed in the clear light of the syllogism. Take the example above:

All college graduates are intelligent.
(major premise)
He is a college graduate.
(minor premise)
He must be intelligent.
(conclusion)

The middle term is "college graduate." The absurdity of the major premise at once becomes apparent, invalidating the argument at its initiation. It is helpful to preface the major and minor premises with the word "if," thus calling into question the validity of the premises for the purpose of checking them before the argument proceeds. *If* all college graduates are intelligent—but they are not, and that is that. Special care must be taken to be sure that the meanings of terms and relations remain unchanged throughout the syllogism.

Whoever obeys laws submits to a governing will.
Nature obeys laws.
Therefore, nature submits to a governing will.

The syllogism is invalidated by the fact that the term "laws" is used in two different senses.

Illogical conclusions might often be avoided by a full, accurate statement of the syllogism. A very common error is the following:

Great men have been ridiculed.
I am ridiculed.
Therefore, I am a great man.

All great men do not coincide with all who have been ridiculed, and I may be in the class of the ridiculed without entering the class of the great. From the fact that great men are often unpopular, some people are so fatuous as to mistake their own unpopularity for a sign of greatness. The attractiveness of the conclusion encourages the perpetration of such an illogical bit of reasoning.

Another prominent deductive fallacy is the *petitio principii*, or begging the question. Some psychologists, for example, may argue that mind is not real because it cannot be measured. They assume that only the measurable is real, which is just the point that is in question. There are some logicians who contend that deduction inevitably begs the question, since the major premise assumes what is necessary for the conclusion.

The *argumentum ad hominem* is another favorite, consisting in an attempt to establish or to discredit a proposition by appealing to the emotions and prejudices of the audience. Thus a debater may cast aspersions upon the character of his opponent in order to undermine his argument. This technique sometimes takes the form of *tu quoque*, so vividly described in the popular phrase, "So's your old man." Many arguments in politics degenerate into "mud-slinging." Another form of the *argumentum ad hominem* is the *argumentum ad verecundiam* which is an appeal to prestige. It may be a citation of Biblical authority or the mention of some person of respectability to carry a point. Testimonials of prominent society folk who recommend Whatsits Bread because it supplies the vitamins necessary to vigorous health illustrate the technique. Still another *argumentum ad hominem* is the *argumentum ad populum* which is characteristically an appeal to the emotions of the rabble such as is employed by orators at holiday celebrations. It should be noted that the *argumentum ad hominem* is fallacious only when the argument is irrelevant to the topic under consideration.

A sound argument must, by all means, be fair. Absurdities are believed and uttered daily by the majority of the human race. One cannot refute theism by refuting absurdities held by theists any more than one can refute atheism by refuting absurdities held by atheists. It is an axiom that no idea is refuted unless it is refuted in its best form.

With this brief review of some of the principles of Logic in mind, let us examine more at length two prevalent cases of faulty reasoning—analogy and causation.

Analogies, to be valid, must be comparisons in respect to vital similarities. Unfortunately, analogies are often employed with little regard for this demand. The use of an analogy is based on the assumption that because N has the properties A and B which belong to M, it must also have the property C which belongs to M. But things which are alike in some respects differ in others. The Communists are in favor of revolution. Should a person who commends the American Revolution be logically compelled to espouse Communism? The points of resemblance must be real and basic, the more the better, with no point of crucial difference. The critical question may be put thus: Are the two items similar in precisely those respects that are significant? When a person has suffered some dreadful misfortune, a friend may console him with the suggestion that "lightning never strikes twice in the same place." Is that a fair analogy? If you want to keep young, advises a doctor, live as the young do. Perhaps, too, you can get rich if you live as the rich do, but, unfortunately, it does not work that way.

To the naïve person, the argument by analogy is apt to carry conviction, even though the points of resemblance are few and unessential. Superstitious thinking is based on the most strained and remote analogies. Thus it has been thought that a person born in the summer will be taller because the days are longer; that lungwort will cure pneumonia because the leaves resemble the surface of the lungs; that bear's grease will prevent baldness; that a person born under the planet Jupiter will be jovial, Jove being the Greek name for Jupiter—Jupiter, Jove, jovial—such is the logic of the "science" of astrology. Consolation for misfortune is derived from the fact that "it's a long lane that has no turning," or "every cloud has a silver lining," or "it's always darkest before dawn."

The following analogies have been gathered from various sources. Examine them carefully to determine whether they are legitimate.

The salaries of school teachers should not be cut during the depression because the lower pay will make it impossible for the schools in the emergency to train the youth to maintain the ideals which have guided our people in the past. As well should we expect the householder, when a fire is raging in the next block, to cancel the insurance on his home.

———

Nobody can be healthful without exercise. For a state an honorable war is the true exercise. A foreign war is like the heat of exercise, and serves to keep the body politic in health.

———

Attempting to deal with unemployment by plunging into naval building is about as sensible as would be an attempt to improve medical standards by loading the water supply with typhoid germs.

———

The News wants peace as ardently as any signer of any antimilitary petition ever circulated, but it does not believe that the way to check a forest fire is to cut off the water supply, or that the way to prevent disease and physical injury is to abolish all anti-toxins and to destroy all surgical instruments.

Billiard cushion shows why fresh——Gas is better. . . . "See," . . . says the scientist, "the newer and livelier the billiard cushion, the more pep it gives the ball. Gasoline is like that—the fresher it is, the more pep and power it gives a car."

The popular logic of causation also deserves examination. If one event follows another, the temporal sequence is interpreted as cause and effect. Thus the wealth of the United States is attributed to the superior intelligence of the Nordic settlers, neglecting the consideration of the fertile lands, the mineral resources, and other like factors; or the poverty of Russia since the World War is blamed on Bolshevism, disregarding the blockades, the droughts, and the war losses. In inductive reasoning this error is known as the fallacy of *Post hoc, ergo propter hoc;* in deductive reasoning, *Non sequitur.*

Examine the following samples of reasoning from cause to effect:

If the Republican party is going to take the credit for the prosperity of the Coolidge era, they should be willing to shoulder the blame for the depression of the Hoover era.

After Princeton's disastrous season in football in 1931, President Hibben resigned. Two days after Harvard lost the football game to Yale in 1932, for their second consecutive defeat, President Lowell resigned. It was a good thing for President Angell that Yale won that game, for the victory redeemed a poor season at New Haven.

When Mr. O'Toole visited Niagara Falls, he was much impressed with the power house in which, he understood, was "the machinery what pumps the water for the falls."

In 1835 the appearance of Halley's comet was followed by death and destruction over the whole world. Immediately after the comet became generally visible in the old world the bubonic plague, generally known as the "black death," broke out in Egypt. In the city of Alexandria alone 9000 persons died in a single day. By the Moslems this calamity was generally attributed to the influence of the comet.

Knowledge of the laws of Logic is no guarantee against fallacious reasoning. Prejudice may confound the thinking of the best informed. A learned man may defend unsound views with fool-proof logic.[1] At the same time it should be noted that true conclusions may possibly be supported by unsound arguments. While the study of Logic cannot assure straight thinking, still, no one will deny its advantages in the encouragement of accurate reasoning. It is something to be headed in the right direction.

V. EDUCATION FOR THINKING

Straight thinking is not a gift but an achievement. Training in Logic is not the whole story. There must be not only a knowledge of the rules but also a strong desire to apply them. Almost anybody who is set to detect error will see the flaws in the following:

Will Rogers: I did not register to vote. If this country is not run right, I won't be to blame.

You wouldn't eat a green orange, why drink unripe ginger ale?

It is wise to vote for the party in power because they represent Experience; it is unwise to vote for the party out of power because they represent Experiment.

But would almost anybody, without being warned to beware, notice the fallacies so neatly hidden in some of these statements? The answer must be an unequivocal "No." People generally are not alert in such matters, especially because they are not interested so much in truth as they are in the reinforce-

[1] R. H. Thouless: *Straight and Crooked Thinking*. 1932.

ment of their own biases. Our minds fall into traps readily in judging even the plainest things, so that we are capable of coming to wrong conclusions about self-evident facts.

The success of Democracy depends upon the straight thinking of the citizens who are forced by the exigencies of politics to consider the merits of various public questions. It is obvious, even to the casual observer, that the decisions of the average citizen are the products, not of sound thinking, but of emotional attitudes touched off by stereotyped catchwords. Economic issues are not weighed; they are espoused or opposed. Such words as "dole," "gold standard," and "inflation" provoke violent emotional reactions in people who have little conception of the real meanings of these terms or the social effects that might follow their incorporation in political practice. Consider "inflation." The word is a bogey and "the very people who would gain most by it have been taught to fear it."[1] The vested interests, who tend to be in charge of the government by virtue of their opulence, are, in general, the losers by "inflation" and, therefore, they induce the gullible masses to believe that "inflation" is bad for everybody by playing upon their fears. Arguments are offered that if we inflate, we must inevitably carry it too far; and these arguments are supported by citing what happened in this country after the Civil War and in Germany after the World War, both analogies being fallacious. Reginald McKenna, head of the largest bank in England, pointed out the unfairness of the latter analogy when he made the following comment: "I confess the thought of inflation does not alarm me. I attribute such fear of inflation, as is being expressed, to the German post-war experience, but the present situation bears no analogy, for the German inflation came on top of a previous war inflation."[2] It is a trick of politicians to invent bugaboos and then to demolish

---

[1] Gilbert Seldes: *The Years of the Locust*, p. 145. 1933.

[2] The Boston *Herald*, February 7, 1933.

them for the entertainment of the populace. "Inflation" is one of the bogies. The average citizen does not know whether it is proposed to inflate his currency, his credit, or his ego. All he knows is that he wants a stable currency, but he is opposed to any measure for stabilizing it. The term "inflation" is enough to condemn any proposal regardless of its merits. Clear thinking on economic issues, or on any other issues, is rare because the average voter is so easily baited by slogans to cheer for the policies of the party in power, even though he cuts his own throat in doing so.

Education can do something toward the encouragement of straight thinking. The appreciation of the importance of correct reasoning is one step in the right direction. "For a great many people to believe the earth to be flat would do no particular social damage, but for a great many people to believe that waste is good for trade, machinery bad for labor, that the foreigner can and should send us plenty of money but no goods, are ideas (all but universal in Europe) which cause immeasurable misery and suffering."[1]

The educational procedure must be considerably revamped if the training of students in ratiocination is to be effectively conducted. There must be less emphasis on facts, more on their interpretation and evaluation. Critical understanding must be inculcated through the practice of the scientific spirit in which curiosity is kept alive and a sense of evidence is instilled. Discrimination must be encouraged in the accepting of authorities. The student must be warned that the teacher's say-so is not the final word and that the textbook is not infallible. The examination system has been developed in such a way as to place a premium upon memorizing, in order to facilitate the mechanical process of marking. Thus the pupil is asked: Is this so? not, what do you think of it? History, to take an example, should be studied through a variety of

[1]Norman Angell: *The Public Mind*, p. 209. 1928.

sources. There should be several textbooks written from different points of view. A course in American History should include a study of the Revolution by an Englishman.[1]

The educational method of encouraging critical study may be appropriately illustrated by indicating two weaknesses to which scientific psychology is liable. The thinking student will keep in mind, in evaluating modern experimental psychology, the dangers of oversimplification and artificiality.

Too often in our day the scientist solves the mysteries of life by ignoring them or by simplifying nature until it becomes comprehensible. Science, says Knight Dunlap, always prefers the simplest hypotheses.[2] The lure of simplicity has distorted the perspective of scientists, in many cases, so that they can no longer see the complications which are staring right at them in the phenomena under observation.[3] It is the habit of science to thrust in the background that which it is unable to measure and understand, which is the same as saying that it is the habit of science to be unscientific. The cocksureness of the scientist, in psychological terms, is a compensation for his own underlying uncertainties.

The urge for simplification has seduced psychology into errors. The law of parsimony (economy of hypothesis) has been stated for psychology in Morgan's Canon: "In no case may we interpret an action as the outcome of the exercise of a higher psychical faculty, if it can be interpreted as the outcome of the exercise of one which stands lower in the psychological scale."[4] In practice the simplest adequate interpretation has given way to the simplest interpretation whether it is adequate or not.

Morgan, in laying down his principle of economy, intended it chiefly as a warning against the anthropomorphic interpreta-

---

[1]H. A. Overstreet: *Influencing Human Behavior*, Chapter XI, "The Problem of Straight Thinking." 1925.

[2]Knight Dunlap: *Freudianism, Mysticism, and Scientific Psychology.* 1920.

[3]Joseph Jastrow in *Feeling and Emotions*, pp. 436-437. 1928.

[4]C. Lloyd Morgan: *An Introduction to Comparative Psychology*, p. 53. 1903.

tion of animal behavior. Anthropomorphism means that the human being explains animal behavior in terms of human experience, converting the animal into a human being for purposes of description. The dog lover who reads his own feelings into canine experience illustrates the anthropomorphic tendency. "See, Rover is dejected, he feels sorry for what he did—his conscience is bothering him." Montaigne described the cogitations of a fox who speculated as to whether he would cross a river where the ice was thin. After hearing the running water, the fox indulged in the following logic: "Whatsoever maketh a noise moveth, whatsoever moveth is not frozen, whatsoever is not frozen is liquid, whatsoever is liquid yields under any weight." In reacting against this sort of anthropomorphism, psychologists have gone to the other extreme, becoming obsessed with an undue feeling of caution. When a German police dog responded to such verbal instructions as "jump over the sofa"—or "go into the back room," a psychologist commented thus on the abilities of the dog: "Animals may obey commands as sounds rather than words. Personally we are of the opinion that the dog has learned to associate certain sounds, rather than words in the human sense, with the proper objects and commands." When he was asked whether he thought the dog could think, he continued: "I wouldn't say that. We can't say that people do."

The same urge for simplicity has carried over into the interpretation of human behavior. Since consciousness baffles the psychologist, there is no consciousness—man is just a machine. Such an attitude is a betrayal of science, for the scientific method demands the recognition of *all* the discoverable facts pertinent to any problem. Herrick writes: "Our subjective experiences are very real to us, and before throwing them into the discard we may well inquire in an unprejudiced attitude whether they are not genuine factors in a rigidly scientific study of man. . . . We must . . . recognize con-

scious acts, that is, processes which we know best introspectively, as by far the most important agencies of control of
human behavior."[1]

In addition to the error of oversimplification, psychology
has trespassed on fact in claiming too much for the experimental method.[2] In fleeing the armchair psychology of me-
dieval philosophers, psychologists have relied upon experiment
to win scientific recognition. We must note, however, that
only a limited range of experience can be submitted to the conditions of laboratory testing. It is one thing to study animals
or human beings under the natural conditions of everyday life,
and another to observe them under experimental controls in
the laboratory. "When we used to experiment upon the emotions in the psychological laboratory, we had all the equipment
for it except the emotions."[3] Laboratory psychology often
runs the risk of being artificial. It is difficult to set up the
conditions in an experiment so accurately that they duplicate
exactly the natural situation, and because of this difficulty it
is not safe to predict from one's behavior under one set of conditions just what he will do under another. A psychologist
studied religious emotions by playing hymns on an organ in a
laboratory and asking his listeners to report on their feelings
under the sway of the music. People do not experience religion under such conditions.

Some years ago a psychologist conducted a research on joy.
A whole series of experiments was carried out "to determine on
a biological or organic basis why events happen in pleasant
emotions as they are known to happen."[4] For the purpose of

[1]C. J. Herrick: *Fatalism or Freedom*, pp. 46–47. 1926. Reprinted by permission of W. W. Nodon & Co.

[2]See H. Prinzhorn: "The Value and Limits of the Experimental Method in
Psychology." *Character and Personality*, 1933, I, pp. 251–258.

[3]E. R. Wembridge: "Emotion in the Courtroom," *American Mercury*, 1929,
17, 48–53.

[4]The report of this actual research on joy is taken from a critical article written
by H. T. Peck: "Scientific Joy," *Cosmopolitan Magazine*, 1901, 30, 389–392.
By permission of H. T. Peck and the *Cosmopolitan Magazine*.

the experiments, fourteen young and impressionable persons were selected, nine of them being men and five of them being women. The conditions were that they should all be made to feel simultaneously the emotion of joy—first in a moderate degree, and then by easy stages with greater and greater intensity, while the psychologists kept tab on them to see what they would do. But how were these emotions to be excited in them in such various degrees, and yet by precisely the same means? By gifts of money.

No other sort of object seemed to serve those requirements so well as gifts of money. No very wealthy persons being among the subjects, the acquisition of money would be as great a source of joy to one as another, and considerable to all.

But here arose a difficulty which would have seemed to the unscientific mind to be insuperable. The psychologists did not have the money to give to the subjects. How then was it possible to make the subjects joyful by such gifts? That was easy. Imagination supplied this necessary deficiency. The gifts were hypothetical gifts. The subjects were rounded up and seated comfortably, and were then asked to imagine that to each of them had been given a specified sum of money. The fact that there was no actual cash in the transaction was not to dampen their joy, for they were directed to employ "repeated auto-suggestion."

Those conditions being understood, one after another hypothetical gifts of ten dollars, one hundred dollars, one thousand dollars, ten thousand dollars, and one hundred thousand dollars, respectively, were made to the subject. What would he or she do under these various circumstances?

The experiments finally reached their end. The facts were all recorded. The symptoms were all noted down. Then the psychologist gathered them all together and dealt with them in the statistical way which psychologists employ when they wish to arrive at definite results.   There seems to be some ground for doubting, however, whether alleged results derived from the fictitious emotions excited by the hypothetical gift of an imaginary ten-dollar bill should be glorified as Science simply because the experiment is conducted by an eminent psychologist in a reputable Psychological Laboratory.

VI.   OUR NEW WAYS OF THINKING

The Aristotelian Logic was the prevalent mode of thinking until very recent times.   The shift to new modes of thought is fundamentally due to the development of statistics.   The change is from an absolute, final truth to a changing, growing probability.   The difference between the two Logics rests fundamentally upon the difference between an Aristotelian "class" and a statistical "group."   "All soldiers are brave," meant, for the Aristotelian Logic, that there is a quality, "bravery," which appears incarnate in each and every soldier, if the statement is true.   In so far as soldiers are members of the class of heroes, they are all alike.   It also followed that there is a quality called "not-bravery," or "cowardice," which no soldiers have.   "All soldiers are brave" would mean in statistical logic that if you arranged each and every soldier in order of bravery, assuming that bravery is something measurable, you would find a few who were always brave and a few who were never brave.   You would find that in between the extremes of these two contrasting groups was an overwhelming mass of individuals whose differences were less and less noticeable, the so-called "average" doughboys, who neither courted danger nor shunned it.   "All soldiers are brave," then, would mean not that absolutely each and every soldier is brave and to the same degree brave, but that on the whole soldiers are brave.

The Greek believed that all animals fall into fixed and permanent groups called "species."   Within any group the individuals are all alike. When the group's characteristics are known, the characteristics of the individuals are automatically known. One had only to classify and all was done, for once an object was classified its nature was known. What was done with exceptions? They were either called "accidental" if they were slight, or "monstrous" if they were great. Individuals may range from the idiot to Einstein. Einstein, if his reputation is justified, is just as monstrous at one end of the scale as the poor cretin at the other. He varies almost as far from the median. He varies, however, in a good direction. There is no feeling that his variation is something either diabolical or divine. It is to be expected.

Justice used to be conceived as blindfolded. No longer is this so. *Justice* treats no two individuals alike, for it weighs not the criminal but the peculiar conditions which brought him forth. Moral standards must be refashioned and made relative to individual needs and capacities. Standards represent the "normal" only in the sense of a statistical "average." So long as humanity *on the whole* acts in a given way, society will have its standards.

Statistical records tell us only about group tendencies. They do not justify an interpretation of the probable conduct of any specific individual. An observer watches a vast throng pushing through an amusement district. By the law of averages he knows that a certain proportion will attend one theater, other proportions other theaters. But he cannot tell which person will enter any particular theater. Many of the people themselves could not enlighten him. The prediction of group tendencies is very useful. The plotting of fashion changes, for example, is helpful to the manufacturer who contemplates the introduction of a new style. Some specific person cannot be counted upon as a prospective customer, but the consuming public, in general, can be relied upon, with a fair degree of probability, to fall in line.

Science must take account not only of uniformity but also of variation. Whereas variation was shocking in Greece and had to be explained away, uniformity is shocking today and equally suspect. The newer procedure is to get a wide selection of samples, to analyze the differences and likenesses, to draw conclusions which are to be recognized as mere approximations. Facts are only probabilities. All measurement involves three independent variables:

1. the thing to be measured
2. the measuring instrument
3. the observer.

A number of readings is taken and the average computed. The average is then called *the* reading. Measurements are approximations, and, therefore, should not be venerated as absolute.

Definitions are arbitrary, convenient; not true, or false. The Aristotelian will criticize a book by saying that it is a good book, but that it is not a novel. What of it? What is a novel? Your answer will be neither true nor false, but merely a matter of convenience.

Thus the newer Logic is introducing a different way of looking at things. Modes of thought have changed. Attitudes have altered. A new spirit has been engendered which is tolerant of the exceptional, which appreciates the relative nature of judgments, which has turned from absolutes to probability.[1]

[1]George Boas: *Our New Ways of Thinking*. 1930.

CHAPTER XIV

INTELLIGENT ADJUSTMENT

B<small>Y THE</small> majority of the populace physical prowess is esteemed more highly than preëminent intelligence. Brawn carries more prestige than brains. The athlete is glorified while the intellectual is lost in the shuffle. By the bestowal of its admiration society creates its own heroes—football stars, prizefighters, home-run kings, and marathon dancers. It is obvious to the thoughtful observer that athletes do not make contributions to the advancement of civilization commensurate with the applause awarded them. A chimpanzee is three or four times as strong as the huskiest athlete. It is folly, therefore, for man to covet brute strength when his special gift lies in the supremacy of mind.

I. THE IMPORTANCE OF INTELLIGENCE

One of the fundamental tenets of the American faith is the belief that industry and thrift are the sole prerequisites of success. "Never forget that all the recipe any man needs to make a million dollars is hard work." Such a doctrine, of course, is sheer nonsense. There are probably many people who work hard and who fail to achieve any perceptible results, simply because they lack the intelligence to direct their efforts in the most fruitful channels. The small farmer who toils from dawn till darkness with outmoded tools is more cursed with fatigue than wealth; the husband who putters around the house when he should be improving himself for advancement in the office is penny wise and pound foolish. Hard work has its place but many people would not have to labor so strenuously if they were blessed with more intelligence, or if they made use of the intelligence available to them.

One of the most vital problems of society is to discover persons of high intelligence, and to evolve political means of securing their rise to office, for the price of stupidity is multiplied beyond computation when dullness is enthroned in high places.[1] If psychology can determine the nature of intelligence and then develop procedures for testing it, a long step will be taken toward capitalizing the human resources at our disposal. We need men of the highest mental caliber not only in political office, but also in all positions of leadership—in banking, industry, law, medicine, teaching, and the ministry. Not all of the hopes which were centered upon the fruitfulness of intelligence testing have as yet been realized, but progress has been made in improving its usefulness. Too much was expected in the enthusiasm of first discovery; experience has given us the wisdom to evaluate the import of intelligence in a larger perspective. The findings of psychological research into the problems of intelligence have proven their value.

II.   WHAT IS INTELLIGENCE?

Intelligence is not a thing, but it is a term used to describe the degree of efficiency with which the organism succeeds in adjusting itself to the environment. On the physiological level, it must be recognized that bodily processes function intelligently without any conscious direction, that is, they function in such a way as to promote the most effective adjustment of the organism to the environmental demands, whether it be the mending of a broken bone, the repair of an injured nerve fibre, or the healing of an open wound.[2] Living matter is

---

[1] See W. B. Pitkin: *A Short Introduction to the History of Human Stupidity*, pp. 112–115. 1932.

[2] See W. B. Cannon: *The Wisdom of the Body*. 1932.

characterized by a capacity for adapting itself to changing conditions in ways conducive to its self-preservation.

On the psychological level, intelligence refers to the success achieved by the individual in consciously organizing his attitudes and capacities to meet the various problems involved in living. In the interest of accuracy, it might be wise to avoid the use of the noun "intelligence," and to substitute the adverb "intelligently" whenever the term is called for. Thus it would be proper to say that Jones behaves intelligently, not that Jones has intelligence; that is, Jones does the right thing at the right time. If the top of his toothpaste tube, for example, is fumbled over the washbowl, Jones does not chase the top all over the bowl but places his hand over the drain to prevent the elusive object from escaping through the outlet. In other words, Jones handles the problem with a high degree of effectiveness. If Jones does as well in most situations, he conducts himself intelligently. How is Jones' efficiency to be explained? The simple answer is that he has intelligence, and there the analysis stops because a word has solved the whole puzzle, whether or not there exists something to correspond to the verbal designation. The more exact answer is that Jones' mind functions in such a way as to secure the maximum of efficiency, because certain definite capacities are successfully integrated. The answer is incomplete. It is merely a challenge to investigate further. What is there about Jones' mind which makes it possible for him to act more intelligently than someone else? The problem is very complex; the solution, therefore, will be very complicated.

An analysis of intelligence shows that the term ordinarily involves:

An inborn capacity to learn;

A capacity for abstract thinking;

Mental alertness;

Sound judgment;

Good taste;

Emotional balance;

and

General adaptability.

We shall examine these factors in order.

A. An Inborn Capacity to Learn. The physical basis of intelligence, according to one theory, is the number of nervous connections made possible by original nature.[1]

Since intelligence depends upon the physical structure of the brain that is inherited, it seems fitting to assume, as many psychologists do, that intelligence consists of a native capacity to assimilate and to profit by experience.   One bit of evidence in favor of the view that intelligence is native is the approximate constancy in the growth of ability with respect to increasing age.   A bright child, generally speaking, becomes a bright adult; a dull child, a dull adult.   Another bit of evidence is the transmission of intelligence through heredity.   One famous study is a survey of the descendants of Martin Kallikak.   During the Revolutionary War, Kallikak met a feeble-minded girl by whom he became the father of a feeble-minded son.   In 1912 there were 480 known direct descendants of this temporary union, 143 of them known to be feeble-minded, many of them of illegitimate birth, and many of them alcoholics or prostitutes.   Returning from the War this same Martin Kallikak married a respectable girl of good family.   Among the 496 individuals in direct descent there are no feeble-minded persons, no illegitimate children, no prostitutes, no criminals; they are, for the most part, distinguished persons, including doctors, lawyers, judges, educators, traders, and landholders.[2]

In spite of those psychologists who define intelligence in terms of native capacity, there is evidence to support the view

---

[1]See E. L. Thorndike, *et al.: The Measurement of Intelligence.* 1926.

[2]H. H. Goddard: *The Kallikak Family.* 1914.

that environment plays an important rôle in the determination of intelligence. Sherman and Henry made a study of five communities in the Virginia mountain region, of varying levels of culture, in which they considered the relation of intelligence to the cultural background. The communities studied were four hollows located approximately one hundred miles west of Washington, D. C., in the Blue Ridge Mountains, and a small village at the base of the Blue Ridge about the same distance from Washington to the southwest. All the children were of the same ancestral stock. Intelligence tests were given to more than half of the children of the five communities. The results of the intelligence tests of mountain children living in varying degrees of isolation appear to confirm the belief that the expression of intelligence as measured by standardized tests depends upon the opportunities to gather information, and upon the requirements made upon the individual by his environment. The young children of the various Hollows do not differ greatly in intelligence, whereas great differences are found between the older children of the different Hollows. The only plausible explanation of the increasing difference with increasing age is that children develop only as the environment demands development. The intelligence of the children is found to be highest in the communities highest in the scale of social development, and to be lowest in the communities of lowest social development.[1]

Assuming that intelligence is a native capacity for learning, psychologists have been interested in ascertaining, by tests, what a person can learn rather than what he has learned. The aim of the tests is to discover inborn capacity as distinct from acquired knowledge. What a person has learned is some index, of course, as to what he can learn. But it would be unfair to measure native capacity in terms of knowledge, because people differ so widely in the sorts of environments to

[1] See M. Sherman and T. R. Henry: *Hollow Folk*. 1933.

which they are exposed, and because these differences are dependent to such an extent upon the vicissitudes of life that experimental control is out of the question. The psychologist, therefore, aims to present situations which involve a minimum of advantage in experience, in order to discover the native learning capacity for various sorts of material. Whether it is possible to eliminate the factor of experience is certainly debatable. At any rate, the psychologist seeks to reduce this factor to a minimum.

The intelligent person learns from experience. He profits by his mistakes. The person who behaves intelligently learns, among other things, to control his desires in the light of the consequences which he foresees as evolving from his present actions.

Learning is only one aspect of the remembering process, and the remembering process is only one of many mental processes. Learning, therefore, taken by itself, does not exhaust intelligence. Binet once said: "Memory is a great simulator of intelligence. It is a wise teacher who is not deceived by it." The educational program is so arranged as to place undue stress on memorizing, so that the high-ranking student is often the "grind" who mechanically learns by heart the material to be covered in the examinations, but who is suspected of not deserving the label "intelligent" by his less conscientious classmates. Nevertheless, there is a high positive correlation between memory and intelligence, for which there is a psychological basis in the fact that memory capacity involves mental organization to a high degree.[1]

An inborn capacity to learn, however it manifests itself, is one of the factors involved in intelligent behavior.

B. A Capacity for Abstract Thinking. The intelligent person is outstanding in his ability to think abstractly. It is

---

[1] H. P. Haiti: "Memory and Intelligence," *Indian Journal of Psychology*, 1931, 6, 169–181.

common to consider a philosopher as being more intelligent than a mechanic, no matter how expert the mechanic is in his own line. "An individual is intelligent in proportion as he is able to carry on abstract thinking."[1] The abstract thinker deals with concepts rather than concrete objects. He reasons well because he can grasp relations, because he can plan ahead, because he can organize what he has learned, and can apply his knowledge effectively. If two men possess equally rich stores of knowledge, the more sagacious one will be more gifted in selecting from the facts at his finger tips those facts that are relevant to the particular problem at hand. Suppose these two men are lawyers. They both are well versed in law. The more intelligent one of the two is the one who can select from all the cases of which he is cognizant only those specific cases which are immediately applicable to the situation of his client; he not only knows the precedents, but he also appreciates their full significance in their bearing upon the legal problem which he is attacking. The factor which constitutes his superior intelligence is his ability to generalize or, to use a phrase from Francis Bacon, it is his ability to recognize similitudes. It is this same capacity which underlies the inventiveness of the constructive imagination, the knack for combining facts in new ways so as to improve upon the old. Take, for example, the brilliant medical discovery of Auenbrugger. He was the son of an innkeeper, and in his boyhood it was his chore to look after the wine casks. He learned to estimate the amount of wine in the kegs by tapping them on top: if the resounding note was low, it meant that the wine was nearly gone; if the note was high, it meant that the wine was still plentiful. Later in life Auenbrugger became a doctor. One of his patients died. The autopsy revealed a chest full of fluid—pus. The problem flashed into Auenbrugger's mind: How could a doctor discover

---

[1] L. M. Terman: "Intelligence and Its Measurement: A Symposium," *Journal of Educational Psychology*, 1921, 12, 127–136.

fluid in the chest while the patient was still alive?   In groping
for an answer to that query, his mind went back to his boyhood, to the days when he tended the wine casks.   The connection dawned on him.   The chest with fluid in it was much
like a wine cask.   It had a rigid opaque wall; there was air
above and fluid below.   He took patients and began tapping
their chests.   The procedure worked perfectly.   He could find
fluid, and he could also find the solidifications of tuberculosis
and pneumonia.   Auenbrugger applied his experience because
he was intelligent enough to appreciate a relationship between
two problems, and to draw a generalization which linked the
solutions.   He recognized a similarity which would have
escaped the notice of a less intelligent person.   The ability
to put two and two together constituted one aspect of Auenbrugger's intelligence.   Therein lay his inventiveness.

C. Mental Alertness.   Mental alertness is another factor
in the makeup of intelligence.   The intelligent person takes
an interest in events.   He keeps himself well informed because
he feels a zest for life and an eagerness to participate in the
solution of its manifold problems.   The intelligent player in a
game of contract bridge plays the game in a "heads-up"
fashion, that is, watches the cards carefully as they fall, so that
he will not nonchalantly play the wrong card.   Some people
are bright enough to play bridge well, yet they do not enjoy
the game enough to pay attention.   They are stupid bridge
players simply because they are not alert in that particular
situation.   Intelligence must be judged by performance, not
by potentiality.   If an individual absentmindedly boards the
wrong train, his behavior is stupid, no matter how bountifully
he may be blessed with brains.   To take full advantage of his
capacities, the human being must concentrate on the present
problem.   He must be alert every moment.   He must "keep
his wits about him."

Some people remain in blissful ignorance of the world about

them. College students often manifest an inordinate lack of curiosity. When a class is asked who discovered insulin, it is rare to find more than one or two in the group who know, in spite of the fact that the men responsible for this contribution to medical progress are outstanding benefactors of humanity. It is even more enlightening to repeat the question a week later and to learn that the same state of ignorance still prevails, none of the class showing enough interest to investigate the problem. They do not care.

Insensitiveness to the environment is due, in some cases, to defective sense organs. Many people have eyes defective enough to render reading distasteful to them, so that they grow up ill-informed. Pitkin found that many business men give up virtually all cultural reading because their eyes are tired by the time they have covered the assignments of the daily grind at the office. They make no pretense of keeping abreast of the times, even by a thorough perusal of the news-papers. Thus they gradually dull their sensitivities to world trends and human relations.[1]

What has been said of the eyes is equally applicable to the ears, though the eyes are probably the more important sense as far as the intellectual life is concerned. Sensory incapacities combine with deficient powers of attention to render observation ineffective. Since intelligent action depends to a large degree upon accurate observation, insensitivity contributes its part to the promotion of incompetence. Mental alertness, whether conceived in terms of efficient sense organs or in terms of a wide-awake intellect, must be considered as one factor in the total structure of intelligence.

D. Sound Judgment. The intelligent direction of conduct demands something that transcends mere knowledge, something that cannot be gained from books or lectures, something which we usually designate as wisdom. The idea is well

[1] W. B. Pitkin: *op. cit.*, pp. 138-140.

expressed by a friend of mine who is a farmer and who has not had a higher education: "I'd rather have common sense than brains." People who are blessed with wisdom are found in all walks of life. They always seem to know just what the situation calls for. They do not blunder at the critical moment and then discover afterward what they should have done. They execute the correct response without the necessity for long cogitation. The passage of time only serves to confirm them in the confidence which dictated the initial decision. Even when they have time to think things over, they arrive at the conclusion which exactly fits the solution of the problem. They comprehend the human equation in its relation to the events with which they are dealing. Their judgments are sound, which is equivalent to stating that their adjustments are intelligently planned and executed.

The popular mind draws the distinction between knowledge and wisdom in its suspicion of "book larnin'." The average citizen looks upon the professor as a theorist who inevitably becomes a bungler when it comes to the hard facts of the workaday world. A good example is found in the popular reaction to the brain trust organized by President Roosevelt. Many hard-headed business men feel that the professors should confine themselves to the classroom where their ideas may remain harmless. The theories furnish interesting material for speculation, but they do not work in practice. Professors of Economics teach Free Trade, but men of the world know that Free Trade is impractical. Professors of Ethics teach Pacifism, but realists know that Pacifism does not work. It is not surprising, therefore, that the entrance of the professoriate into politics is regarded, in many quarters, with considerable alarm. Professors may know a lot, so the opinion runs, but they are not wise in the affairs of men.

Wisdom is, to some degree, the product of experience, though it is not everyone who becomes wiser through experience.

Sanity and balance are achieved only by those persons who are quick to appreciate the significance of events, who are ready to weigh issues with a sense of proportion, and who are prepared to relate every happening to their perspective of the whole. It is not so much the experience a person has that counts—it is what he does with it. Intelligent living results when there is a happy combination of knowledge with the ability to apply that knowledge effectively to ends which are judiciously chosen.

E. Good Taste. The intelligent person appreciates the higher values of life. He turns to the editorial page of the newspaper rather than to the "funnies" and sports; he prefers the stage to the movies; he dials his radio to bring in a lecture or a symphony rather than a jazz band or a play-by-play description of a marathon dance; he reads the best books instead of trifling away his time in the perusal of trashy literature; he avoids the trivial in conversation; he prefers a discussion of art to an analysis of the stock market. What a person does in his leisure moments is generally considered as one index of his intelligence.

The intelligent person cultivates intellectual tastes as opposed to the vulgar, vacuous, sensuous delights of the masses. He reads the *Atlantic Monthly* more avidly than the Sunday Supplement, and he derives more satisfaction from Plato's *Dialogues* than he does from an evening of bridge.

F. Emotional Balance. Poise is necessary if ability is to function to the best advantage. Students frequently insist that they know more than they have shown on the examination, and that their poor exhibitions are due to the fact that they go all to pieces under the stress of a test. Some individuals become so unnerved by the realization that they are taking an intelligence test that they cannot do justice to themselves. The answer to such excuses is that one factor in intelligence is the ability to keep cool under trial. Success in life often depends upon the knack of doing well when shining really counts: appearing at one's best in an interview or making a convincing speech in a critical situation. Capacity is of no avail if it fails to function when it is most needed. A quarter-back who scintillates in practice, but who chooses the wrong plays in the crucial game, is not a great football player. The student who allows an examination to "rattle" him is not a success, in so far as the educational system measures success by its clumsy methods of testing, and in so far as progress in life, too, is determined by clumsy judgments based on periodic trials of the individual's mettle. Courage is requisite to the full capitalization of ability, and as such must be considered a factor in intelligence. Poise is sometimes as important as knowledge for passing the tests we all have to pass in our competitive existence.

Freedom from prejudice is likewise significant for intelligence since the biased mind may fail to make the best use of the mental resources at hand. An individual may commit a serious blunder because he has closed his mind to certain facts that must be recognized if the situation is to be effectively met. A prejudiced opinion is seldom intelligent. Prepossessions may thwart even the best minds by blinding them to the most obvious facts. Effective adjustment must be based on a knowledge of the truth rather than on sentimental notions. Strong prejudice may impede the application of intelligence so seriously as to render it useless, and even harmful, for the consistent pursuit of folly is a definite insurance of disaster.

The importance of emotional balance is well illustrated in habits of stubbornness. The term "habits" is used purposely because stubbornness is not a general trait but a specific habit. A person is stubborn only in certain situations; at other times, he is just persistent. When a man tries to put on a tire chain that is too short, and pulls on it peevishly instead of surveying the situation and pausing to insert an extra link, his stupidity is largely the product of his obstinacy. The man who stays in a rut all his life is often honored by a banquet for his faithful service, though, if the truth be known, his long record is merely a monument to his unintelligent doggedness. Traditions of perseverance and stick-to-it-iveness often make it difficult to quit a given line of endeavor, even though the odds are overwhelmingly against further plodding. The fear of being called a quitter or "a rolling stone" keeps a person from doing the intelligent thing, giving up what he is trying to do, and attempting something else for which he may be better fitted.

Thus it becomes obvious that intelligent progress in life depends to a considerable extent upon the development of emotional habits which promote the use of ability to the utmost advantage.

G. General Adaptability. The final factor in our analysis of intelligence is general adaptability. Intelligence is a matter of modifiability and variability. The intelligent person learns from experience to meet a wide variety of situations adequately. He can deal with novel situations successfully. He can do a variety of things and do them all well. In such a category belongs Albert Schweitzer whose manifold accomplishments in theology, music, and medicine recall the many-sided genius of Leonardo da Vinci.[1] The breadth of his mind constitutes his versatility.

The intelligent individual excels in the catholicity of his talents, feeling at home in the classroom, on the athletic field, or in the drawing room. If a person is intelligent, he will not only do well in one sort of activity, but he will also do well in other sorts of activity, because he possesses some general ability that is applicable to various kinds of tasks. This general intelligence accounts for the positive correlation among the different intellectual traits of the individual.

Educational policy in universities dedicated to the pursuit

[1]See Albert Schweitzer: *Out of My Life and Thought; An Autobiography.* 1933.

of the liberal arts has been based on the conviction that the training of general intelligence through cultural studies is the most adequate method of preparing the student for any vocation. In recent years many courses have been introduced into university curricula which provide specific training for specific occupations, such as *ad hoc* courses in journalism, advertising, accounting, and selling. Many educators feel that the true purpose of a university is being defeated by such courses. Flexner made a thorough survey of American, English, and German universities in an effort to clarify educational aims, and his investigation revealed a lamentable state of confusion. Flexner suggests that universities should not train a man for a specific trade, but should train his intelligence, which then can be applied to any field of endeavor. It is not the business of universities to introduce the student to all future and possible details, but to train him in fundamentals so that he can later solve his own problems.

Education—college education, liberal education, call it what you will—should, one might suppose, concern itself primarily during adolescence and early manhood and womanhood with the liberation, organization, and direction of power and intelligence, with the development of taste, with culture . . . on the assumption that a trained mind, stored with knowledge, will readily enough find itself even in our complex world.[1]

Thus Flexner advocates formal discipline: train the mind culturally, and the reward will be a perfected instrument applicable to any vocation, whether it be plumbing, selling bonds, or the practice of law.

Thus speak the proponents of the view that there is a general intelligence.

Opposing such a view are those psychologists who stress specificity, the specificity of habit or the specificity of ability,

[1]Abraham Flexner: *Universities, American, English, and German*, pp. 53, 63. 1930.

and who insist that there is no intelligence, but that, instead, there are intelligences. Evidence of specificity is familiar to the observant person.

Authors frequently go on the lecture platform and draw large audiences because people assume that if a man can write well he can also speak well. Their expectations, however, often prove ill founded, for writing and speaking seem to be distinct abilities.

The scholar is often blessed with abstract intelligence, though lacking concrete intelligence, that is, the mechanical ability for handling things with agility and skill, whether it be a football or a sparkplug.

The scholar is likewise apt to be lacking in social intelligence. The intellectual seldom becomes renowned as a social lion. It is exceptional, as William James pointed out, for the philosopher and the lady-killer to inhabit the same tenement of clay. The bright person is often "hard to get along with" because he cannot understand why everybody else is so stupid. The lack of social intelligence frequently renders the professor an easy mark for swindlers. A professor in New York City, for example, was duped into paying a crook $25,000 for a quarter interest in the Philadelphia advertising firm of N. W. Ayer and Son, one of the largest in the world—a scheme that was as preposterous as the selling of the Brooklyn Bridge to gullible investors. And a Boston professor, along with some other prominent Easterners, turned over the major portion of his life's savings to a stranger who promised him a share in the spoils to be recovered from a treasure ship sunk years before off the coast of Nova Scotia.[1] The itch to get something for nothing may plunge the bright and dull alike into folly.

The fact that a man has ability in one field of activity is no guarantee that he is just as capable in other lines of endeavor. It may be misleading, therefore, to call a person

---

[1] The Boston *Herald*, September 25, 1930, and November 14, 1932.

intelligent, since it may result in saying, absurdly, that an intelligent individual does stupid things. In the interest of accuracy, therefore, it is advisable to reserve the term "intelligent" for a description of specific behavior in specific situations. Sometimes the individual behaves intelligently; sometimes, stupidly. He may lead his class in mathematics and trail his class in Latin.

Special abilities which are encountered commonly are the linguistic, the mathematical, the artistic, the musical, and the mechanical. It is an everyday observation that a person may excel in one of these skills and be deficient in the rest.

Vocational guidance, which consists in finding the right man for the right job, tends to favor the view that mentality is a group of distinct abilities. If ability were so general that anybody could succeed in any occupation equally well, there would be no call for vocational guidance. There is an inclination, therefore, among those who are engaged in giving counsel on such matters to stress the specificity of ability, and, accordingly, to examine the client with a view toward discovering a special talent for some definite occupation. Johnson O'Connor, a leader in vocational guidance, asserts that intelligence is not an indivisible entity such as adaptability, but a combination of distinct mental functions. "Abilities," he says, "are not cosmopolitan, intelligence not general; genius is confined to specific crafts and arts."[1] In advocating human engineering, he states, "The world must learn not only that each occupation has its individual requirements, but that every human being has his specialized function."[2] Certain deficiencies may definitely disqualify a person from some pursuits, though constituting no handicap at all for others. Manual

---

[1]Johnson O'Connor: *Born That Way*, p. 112. 1928.
[2]Johnson O'Connor: "A Study of Human Nature," the *Atlantic Monthly*, 1932, 150, 722–732.

awkwardness, for example, is detrimental to a pianist, surgeon, or instrument assembler, but not to a lawyer.

It is difficult to realize, says O'Connor, how distinct abilities are from each other. He has devised certain tests for the diagnosis of ability. Among them is a test of assembling pins, in which the task is to pick up pins from a tray and insert them into holes; another involves the checking of numbers; still another calls for the solution of a jig-saw puzzle in three dimensions, the assembling of a wiggly block. The ability to assemble pins and the ability to check numbers are independent of one another and scatter among men according to laws of chance, and the same statement holds for the relation of the wiggly block to the other two tests. "Capacity to check numbers is independent of ability to assemble the blocks; the two are separate brain functions, never reached by the same training. . . . Aptitude for the one and the other are . . . completely independent. . . . The cause of excellence in number checking differed from that which gave power to analyze concrete structure."[1] The positive correlation that some psychologists find in respect to their various tests O'Connor attributes to the fact that their tests are fundamentally similar in that they are all of the paper and pencil variety. O'Connor believes that his tests are more accurate and in the light of the results he has obtained from giving his battery of tests he concludes, "Anything enabling its possessor to grade well in all tests might reasonably be called general intelligence. But no such condition appears."[2]

The view that the mind includes a host of highly particularized and independent abilities, with no correlation at all between any two tests except in so far as they involve identical elements, is associated with the name of Thorndike, though he is not as insistent upon the specificity of ability as he used to

[1]Johnson O'Connor: *Born That Way*, pp. 87–88.
[2]*Ibid.*, p. 113.

be. Other psychologists, however, are definitely committed to the position that mental abilities are unrelated. Kelley points out that certain capacities—some memory functions, for example—are independent variables, so that the score in one gives no prediction as to the probable score in another.[1] Memory for digits does not indicate memory for faces; memory for spoken numbers is no index of memory for printed numbers. There is no memory; there are only memories.

There has been a sustained controversy over the correlation of mental abilities. Many psychologists feel that too much stress has been laid on the specificity of ability. There are specific skills, no doubt, but transfer of training does occur. Evidence is too limited to assert dogmatically, as some have done, that transfer only occurs through identical elements. Certainly there is no scientific basis for the doctrine of formal discipline which has actuated our educational practice, and there is just as little scientific basis for some of the views critical of formal discipline, too. "Practice effects are found everywhere. They are the bane of laboratory psychology, which must always be watchful lest they confuse results. In some cases, there seem to be effects of practice on practice; learning itself seems to be learned."[2] The above statement of Dunlap's is supported by Stratton, who likewise notes the possibility of transfer, and who maintains that children trained to be neat in arithmetic are neat also in geography.[3]

A group of English psychologists, led by Spearman, find a positive correlation between mental abilities, which they explain by reference to a general factor underlying all kinds of mental operations, designated as "g." In any problem calling for the play of intelligence, two factors operate: one factor

---

[1] T. L. Kelley: *Crossroads in the Mind of Man.* 1928.

[2] Knight Dunlap: *Habits*, pp. 112-122. 1932. By permission of Liveright Publishing Corporation.

[3] G. M. Stratton: "The Mind as Misrepresented to Teachers," the *Atlantic Monthly*, March, 1921.

being a specific ability, the second factor being a general ability common to all the specific functions. Sometimes "g" is described as the ability to educe relations, sometimes as a mental energy transferable from one mental operation to another. In short, "g" represents a common factor corresponding to what we have called general intelligence.[1]

Whether you accept the viewpoint which stresses specificity or the viewpoint which emphasizes the general nature of ability, intelligence is a matter of versatility. In the former case, a person is intelligent who possesses a repertoire of numerous special abilities; in the latter case, a person is intelligent who is blessed with enough "g" to allow him to adapt himself readily to a wide variety of situations. In either case, he must be versatile. In testing practice it makes little difference in the answer whether you pool cognitive operations or average special abilities, as will become clear when we consider intelligence testing.[2]

H. Summary. Intelligence involves a host of factors, some of which have been mentioned, such as:

1. An inborn capacity to learn.
2. Abstract thinking.
3. Mental alertness.
4. Sound judgment.
5. Good taste.
6. Emotional balance.
7. General adaptability.

The above list is not intended to be exhaustive. It suffices, however, to indicate the complexity of the subject. Some of the factors cited are ignored by some psychologists; still others might be added by some psychologists; furthermore, psy-

---

[1] See Charles Spearman: *The Abilities of Man.* Also *The Nature of Intelligence and the Principles of Cognition.* 1923.

[2] See W. F. Dearborn: *Intelligence Tests: Their Significance for School and Society.* 1928.

chologists differ in the weighting of the various factors, some stressing the learning capacity, some the aptitude for abstract thinking, and some the general adaptability. In some cases, the conception of intelligence has been narrowed down to fit the limitations of testing, so that a particular test may be considered as an adequate measure of whatever the psychologist decides to call "intelligence." It is obvious that a number of the factors we have noted are not easily subject to accurate measurement. Usually, therefore, they are passed over in favor of those factors which can be more readily measured.

In fairness to all the several aspects of the problem, it seems justifiable to state that an individual qualifies as intelligent if his mind functions effectively; that is, if he can concentrate his attention on what he is doing, if he perceives clearly the essential elements in a situation, if he learns rapidly and remembers with facility, if he can look ahead and anticipate accurately, if he can think straight and weigh his conclusions judiciously, if he can organize his mental processes around ends that are important to his welfare, or, to put it succinctly, if he can adjust himself successfully to any sort of demand imposed upon him in the course of his everyday life.

III. INTELLIGENCE TESTING

To the uninitiated it may seem that an intelligence test is any collection of forty or fifty questions to which the eminent psychologist giving the test happens to know the replies, but to the initiated an intelligence test represents a standardized interview carried out according to a standardized procedure, and interpreted according to norms established by long painstaking investigation.

The measurement of ability must proceed by comparing one person's ability with another's. One man is more or less intelligent than another. A preliminary step in the formulation of a test must be the determination of a standard. The psychologist must select certain tasks which he considers as indicative of intelligence and then ascertain whether his results correlate positively with other estimates of intelligence. The procedure, in general, is to decide, at the start, who are intelligent and who are stupid, checking by means of all the available criteria, such as the teachers' estimates, school records, and similar measures; then a test is devised and administered to the individuals concerned; if the intelligent persons tend to excel in the test and the stupid persons tend to do poorly, then the test may be considered valid in proportion to the degree of positive correlation. Only by applying the test to a wide sampling of individuals under standardized conditions can the test be adequately validated. A given test differentiates the intelligent from the stupid with reference to a standard which the tester conceives to be definitive of intelligence.

Historically, the interest in testing intelligence grew out of the practical necessity of distinguishing readily the pupils in school who could be relied upon to make normal progress from those pupils who were apt to meet failure. It was natural, therefore, that the standard of intelligence should be formulated in terms of scholastic success. Those pupils who were ranked high by their teachers in their classroom work were taken as representative of intelligence, and tests which revealed their superior abilities were considered as valid measures of intelligence; comparable results for the pupils ranked as stupid by their teachers, of course, were involved in the process of validation. Thus a test was devised which served as a ready measure of aptitude for scholastic tasks, and this aptitude was called intelligence. The early tests were designed for scholastic use, and most of the tests evolved since that time have been planned with the same end in view. Consequently, it is not surprising that intelligence testing has stressed those functions which count heavily in school success.

A. History. In 1904, Alfred Binet, a French psychologist, was appointed a member of a commission to formulate recommendations for the administration of the special classes for dull children in the public schools of France. The appointment afforded him an opportunity to try out some tests he and Simon had been developing. Their dominant interest was to devise some accurate means of discriminating between the normal child and the feeble-minded child. Galton's studies on the subject of individual differences prepared the way for the development of the project undertaken by Binet.

Binet emphasized three characteristics of the thought process:

1. its tendency to take and maintain a definite direction;
2. the capacity to make adaptations for the purpose of attaining a desired end;
3. the power of self-criticism, as involved in comparing oneself to a model to determine whether one is correct or not.[1]

As Binet felt his way in this pioneer investigation, he experimented with a wide range of tests, such as time orientation, three or four kinds of memory, apperception, language comprehension, knowledge about common objects, free association, number mastery, constructive imagination, ability to compare concepts, to see contradictions, to combine fragments into a unitary whole, to comprehend abstract terms, and to meet novel situations. In 1905 a rough graded series of tests was completed, which was revised in 1908 and again in 1911. Binet proceeded on the assumption that the percentage of passes on the series of tests should increase with age and that children known on other grounds to be bright should pass more tests than children of the same age known on other grounds to be dull. Arranging the tests in the order of difficulty, he dis-

---

[1]See L. M. Terman: *The Measurement of Intelligence.* 1916.

covered that on the average a child of a certain age could perform successfully tasks of a certain degree of difficulty. The main problem was to determine the age level of a given test, that is, to discover at what age a "normal" child could pass a test. The easiest test was formulated for a three-year-old child; the tests for the four-year-old child were designed to be too difficult for the three-year-old child and just difficult enough for the four-year level. A test was located at that particular year level where two-thirds to three-quarters of unselected children of that particular age were able to perform the task successfully. Thus the norm was established for that age. The tests had to be tried out on children of different ages and made easier or more difficult to fit the age in view more exactly. Each particular test was scored as passed or failed. The raw score for the individual was the number of tests passed. The raw score, on the average, increased with age, so that, in general, children of eight attained a higher score than children of five, and so on along the scale. Each raw score was the norm for some age, and that level was called the mental age. In the normal child mental age and chronological age were identical; in the dull child the mental age was below the chronological age; in the bright child the mental age was above the chronological age. Binet recognized that a comparison of the mental ages of two children was valid only when both had the same schooling and the same common background of experience.[1] The tests were standardized without differentiating between the sexes. Binet endeavored in his revisions to improve his scale by seeking tests that resembled school work as little as possible, since he was aiming to measure intelligence rather than knowledge. The tests were not intended to uncover special talent. Later investigations have shown that Binet's tests were too easy in the lower ages and too difficult in the upper range of the scale. Binet

[1] See Henry E. Garrett: *Great Experiments in Psychology*, p. 10. 1930.

himself was engaged in revising his scale at the time of his death in 1911.[1]

BINET'S 1911 SCALE

Age III.
1. Points to nose, eyes, and mouth.
2. Repeats two digits.
3. Enumerates objects in a picture.
4. Gives family name.
5. Repeats a sentence of six syllables.

Age IV.
1. Gives his sex.
2. Names key, knife, penny.
3. Repeats 4 digits.
4. Compares two lines.

Age V.
1. Compares two weights.
2. Copies a square.
3. Repeats a sentence of ten syllables.
4. Counts four pennies.
5. Unites the halves of a divided rectangle.

And so on for ages VI, VII, VIII, IX, X, XII, XV, and Adult.

Binet's scale was successful in weeding out the dull from the bright pupils in the French schools. The testing gave consistent results which proved significant in practice with respect to the purpose which Binet and Simon had in mind.

The news of Binet's intelligence scale soon reached America. H. H. Goddard, director of research at the Training School for the Feebleminded at Vineland, New Jersey, learned of the progress in intelligence testing in France. He experimented with the tests and found they differentiated well between the different grades of feeble-minded children. He translated the tests into English, made the necessary adaptations, and re-standardized them on American children. In the early stages of the development in America, normal children were tested

---

[1] See Joseph Peterson: *Early Conceptions and Tests of Intelligence*, pp. 117–214. 1925. Also see Rudolph Pintner: *Intelligence Testing: Methods and Results*. New edition, 1931.

only for the purpose of standardization, for the main interest lay in the detection of those persons who possessed subnormal intelligence. Goddard's introduction of intelligence testing to this country aroused a widespread interest which has steadily increased.

Binet and Simon had instituted the use of mental age in the measurement of intelligence. As testing progressed, it became obvious to a German psychologist, William Stern, that mental age was not accurate enough as an index of a person's intelligence. The information that a child's mental age was five did not shed any light on his relative brightness without some reference to his chronological age. A mental age of five in a three-year-old child signified one thing; a mental age of five in a nine-year-old child signified quite another. The vital datum, felt Stern, must relate mental age to chronological age, and so in 1912 Stern proposed that intelligence be described in terms of the ratio of mental age to chronological age. This ratio was called the *intelligence quotient*, later abbreviated to I.Q.

$$I.Q. = \frac{M.A. \quad \text{(mental age)}}{C.A. \quad \text{(chronological age)}}$$

The percentage is omitted in stating the I.Q., so that a boy of nine who has a mental age of nine is said to have an I.Q. of 100. Thus:

$$I.Q. = \frac{9}{9} = 1.00$$

Move the decimal point two places to the right:

$$I.Q. = 100.$$

Such a person is normal, that is, he has the intelligence that can be expected in an average boy of his age. While the mental age describes an individual's intelligence level at a given time, the I.Q. goes further by describing the rate of mental development. An I.Q. of 125, for example, indicates that a person's intelligence has grown 25% faster than the average individual. Any person with an I.Q. over 110 may be considered superior; any person with an I.Q. below 70 may be suspected of feeble-mindedness. The I.Q. was a notable contribution to intelligence testing, since it furnished a convenient mode of summarizing the relative status of an individual's intelligence. Stern's proposal was adopted by Terman when he undertook the revision of the Binet-Simon scale.

In 1916 Lewis M. Terman, professor of psychology at Leland Stanford University, published the "Stanford Revision of the Binet-Simon Tests," known more familiarly as the "Stanford-Binet," the result of long, arduous investigation. Terman was convinced that the number of tests in the Binet-Simon scale was inadequate, that the scale should be lengthened out at both ends to get down to the lower levels and up to the higher levels of mental ability more accurately, that the tests in the upper age levels were too difficult, that some of the tests should be ranked in different order, and that the instructions for the administration of the tests were too indefinite to insure a standardized procedure. He spent six months training examiners and six months supervising them in testing. Forty new tests were tried out on a group of 1,000 school children of average social status. Finally, ninety tests were selected from the Binet-Simon material and from the new material for the revised examination.

The Stanford-Binet test includes a number of tests arranged for each of these ages—3, 4, 5, 6, 7, 8, 9, 10, 12, 14, 16, 18. The spacing of the ages is not arbitrary, but the result of careful experiment. The age at which the person passes all the tests for that age is called his basal year. Any tests he passes at higher levels are credited so much to be added to the basal year, in obtaining the mental age. From the mental age and chronological age, the I.Q. can be readily computed.

The tests include a wide variety of tasks which are to be performed under the directions of the examiner, such as counting pennies, naming colors, repeating digits from memory, giving the differences between familiar objects, indicating the similarities between familiar objects, defining words, arranging cubes in their order of weight, explaining absurdities, interpreting fables (generalizing), solving arithmetical problems, distinguishing abstract terms, and repeating the thought of a passage read by the examiner.[1]

Special training is required for administering the test. The examiner must gain the coöperation of the person to be tested, he must know the instructions by heart, and he must be skilled in the scoring of the answers. Definite standards are furnished for scoring.

The Stanford-Binet and other tests of a paper and pencil sort which stress verbal ability cannot be used successfully with deaf children, foreign children, or children with speech defects. To take care of this class of individuals Performance Tests have been developed, involving such tasks as fitting pieces into a form board and completing pictures from which parts have been omitted. One of the best known of the scales is the Pintner-Paterson Performance Scale. The picture completion test in the lower right-hand corner of the illustration on p. 526 involves the fitting of the blocks with the objects depicted on them into the appropriate spaces in the picture to combine the separate activities into a meaningful pattern.

Measures of infant intelligence must obviously be predominantly performance tests. Arnold Gesell, in connection with his program at the Yale Psycho-Clinic, has been perfecting an intelligence scale for the infant and the preschool child. Gesell has standardized twelve developmental levels for the first twelve months of life, by noting whether the infant, at certain stages of his growth, can sit up, manipulate objects

[1]See L. M. Terman: *The Measurement of Intelligence.*

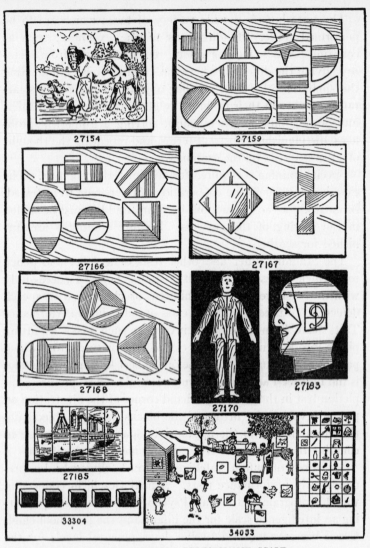

27154 27159 27166 27167 27168 27170 27183 27185 33304 34053

PINTNER–PATERSON PERFORMANCE SCALE

(Reproduced by courtesy of the C. H. Stoelting Company.)

526

with one hand, manipulate objects with both hands, and so on.[1]

Charlotte Bühler, Professor of Child Psychology at the University of Vienna, has also developed some excellent measures for infant intelligence. In planning her Baby Tests Doctor Bühler has tried particularly to fit the situations to the natural interests of the infant. She feels that the common conception of intelligence employed in testing places too much emphasis on the ability to think or the capacity for learning. Consequently, she directs her investigation beyond mere intelligence to the personality as a whole. Her test items are designed to measure the individual in all the varied aspects of his life, which she classifies for convenience into bodily control (B), mental ability (M), social development (S), and manipulation of objects (O).

Some Tests of Bodily Control:

Holding the head up in the prone position..Age: 2 months.

Extricating himself from a diaper placed over his head while he is supported in a sitting position...................7 months.

Sitting alone................................8 months.

Standing with support......................10 months.

Climbing up on to a chair..........This test is one item in a series allocated at the period of 1 year 9 months to 1 year 11 months 29 days; represented as 1;9—1;11 (+29).

Some Tests of Mental Ability:

Looking for the source of a sound.............3 months.

Memory test—a box containing a ball is given the child for five minutes, the box is then taken away, and is returned after thirty seconds without the ball. The child is expected to look for the ball, and to turn in astonishment to the examiner......10 months.

Imitating beating a drum with two sticks...1;3—1;5 (+ 29).

Searching for the reflection behind a mirror. 1;6—1;8 (+ 29).

Some Tests of Social Development:

Response to an adult's glance..................2 months.

Organized play—the child is seated on a bed, his hands are held

---

[1]See Arnold Gesell: *Guidance of Mental Growth in Infant and Child.* 1931.

while he is pushed gently into the dorsal position, then lifted into the sitting position, three or four times each way. The examiner accompanies the movements with the words "up" and "down," and the child is expected to enter laughingly into the game, to follow the movements willingly, or to reach of his own accord for the examiner's hands in order to raise himself to the sitting position again

1;0—1;2 (+ 29).

Some Tests for the Manipulation of Objects:

Defence reaction to the withdrawal of a toy......5 months.

Crushing, rolling, or tearing a piece of white writing paper placed in the child's hand, or changing the form of the paper in some other way..7 months.

Putting blocks back into a box...........1;3—1;5 (+ 29).

Placing blocks on top of one another.....1;9—1;11 (+ 29).

A profile may be drawn by plotting the scores as shown on the developmental profile.[1] Thus the examiner can indicate graphically in what respects a child may be retarded or accelerated in his growth. The evidence may prove valuable in determining whether a child should be left in his own family or given to foster parents, whether he should be placed in an institution for normal or feeble-minded children, or whether he is to be considered worthy of adoption by interested people.

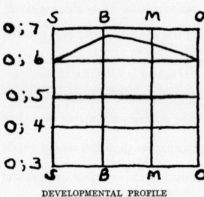

DEVELOPMENTAL PROFILE

Excellent photographs of infant behavior under test conditions are now available in talking pictures, providing a vivid record of the work of Gesell and of Bühler for classroom dem-

[1]Charlotte Bühler: *The First Year of Life*, p. 201. 1930. By permission of John Day and Company, Inc.

onstration. One striking feature of the Gesell film is the comparison of the activities of the same child at two different stages of development in the same situation, with the two records running simultaneously side by side.

The intelligence tests which we have so far described have been developed for use in examining the individual. During the World War the pressure of time provided a great stimulus to the promotion of group tests. Of these, the best known is the Army Alpha.

In April, 1917, the American Psychological Association appointed a committee of five psychologists, specialists in mental testing, to work under Robert M. Yerkes as chairman, in the devising of a test which would serve the following purposes:

(a) to aid in segregating the mentally incompetent,
(b) to classify men according to their mental capacity,
(c) to assist in selecting competent men for responsible positions.[1]

The committee surveyed all the available tests and selected their material with certain objectives in view:

1. to make it as independent of school information as possible;
2. to secure a wide range of difficulty, arranging the tests under each task in their order of difficulty;
3. to provide for easy objective scoring, eliminating subjective estimates by the scorer;
4. to involve a minimum of writing so that slow writers would not be penalized;
5. to produce a number of forms of the complete examination equal in difficulty in order to prevent coaching;
6. to set a time limit which would permit only the fastest examinees to complete the assigned task.

The Army Alpha examination was devised for general application; the Army Beta examination was planned for those who, for various reasons, were so handicapped in the matter of language as to require a performance test.

[1] C. S. Yoakum and R. M. Yerkes: *Army Mental Tests*, p. xi. 1920.

In standardizing the Alpha examination, the test was administered to elementary and high school children, students in colleges and officers' training camps, over 5,000 enlisted men, and inmates of various institutions for the feeble-minded. Its validity was checked against all the available criteria: among the students and the feeble-minded, by school grades, teachers' estimates, and other intelligence tests; among the soldiers, by officers' ratings, the rank attained, ability displayed in training, and previous civilian accomplishments.

During the period of 1917–1918 about 1,750,000 men were tested, a gigantic accomplishment and a great boom, on the whole, to the development of intelligence testing.

The Alpha examination comprised:

1. following directions;
2. arithmetical problems;
3. practical judgment;
4. synonym—antonym;
5. disarranged sentences;
6. number series completion;
7. analogies;
8. general information.

After the War, the examination was used extensively in universities, where it did not prove so satisfactory, chiefly because the test had been devised for a wide range of ability in the army, whereas the range of ability is much narrower among college students who constitute a selected group of a superior order. F. L. Wells has revised the Alpha examination with this factor and other factors in mind. Military references have been eliminated. The material has been brought up to date. A simple addition test has been substituted for the original Directions of test I, and a relatively elaborate Directions test for the Information of test VIII. The Wells revision has been adapted for use among women as well as men, and has been planned for "that intensive psychometric study of superior individuals which is the practical purpose involved in the present studies. The advantages of the present revision are essentially those of convenience in administration, which is what was aimed at. The revision takes about four minutes less time to give and about two-thirds as long to score. The relative simplicity of the scoring processes may be also conducive to fewer scoring errors. . . . From the standpoint of correlation the ultimate desideratum is maximal relationship not with Army Alpha but with something ('intelligence') of which Army Alpha, like other tests, is an admittedly imperfect measure. The concept of this something is still so vague that only crude validation of an intelligence test is possible. During the year that the old and new tests have functioned side by side in individual, quasi-clinical examinations, their scores stand the pragmatic test about equally. It is well known that under such conditions it still makes rather less difference what tests are used than who uses them."[1]

A sample of the Revised Alpha examination will clarify its nature.[2]

1. Addition
    $3 + 4 = \ldots$
2. Arithmetic
    How many are 5 men and 10 men?. . . .
3. Common sense
    Why do we use stoves? Because 1, they look well. 2, they keep us warm. 3, they are black. . . . (2)
4. Synonym—antonym
    good—bad. . . . . (o)pposite
    little—small. . . . . (s)ame
5. Disarranged sentences
    A eats cow grass. . . . (+)
    Arrange in right order; if it is true, mark +; if it is false, mark —.

---

[1] F. L. Wells: "Army Alpha-Revised," *The Personnel Journal*, 1932, X, 411–417. By permission of The *Personnel Journal*.

[2] By permission of the Psychological Corporation, Room 2045, Grand Central Terminal Building, New York.

6. Number series completion

2 4 6 8 10 12... $\overset{14}{...}$ $\overset{16}{...}$

7. Analogies

TABLE GREEN

sky—blue   grass—   ....(G)....

WARM BIG

See what the relation is between the first two words and write in the ( ) at the end of the dotted line the first letter of the word in heavy type that is related in the same way to the third word.

8. Directions

Write the smallest of these numbers backwards.

13   21   64   18   16 ..$\overset{31}{......}$..

B. Uses. The value of these various intelligence tests, only a few of which have been enumerated, is manifold. The detection of feeble-mindedness and the sorting of ability in the army have already been mentioned. Testing has been employed in the schools for grouping pupils according to their several abilities, so that the instruction may be adapted more accurately to the capacities of the students. Often a test is valuable in tracing school difficulties, the evidence being used to determine whether failure is due to lack of ability or to other factors such as poor instruction or lack of effort on the part of the pupil. Testing has been a valuable source of data in clinics for the discovery of mental defects, permitting the exact adjustment of treatment to the needs of the individual, and in vocational guidance, aiding the examiner in advising the occupation suited to the talents of the appplicant. There are many other uses for intelligence tests. The expert examiner can analyze the various assignments and supplement his general advice with specific recommendations for the case involved. While the tests were first used for the detection of the subnormal, there has been much emphasis of late on the discovery of genius (supernormal), for the effective training of genius is of vast importance to society.

C. Criticism. The results of intelligence testing can only be considered valid when they are interpreted with a critical understanding. The tester must be aware of the importance of uniformity in administration and scoring, of the influence of variable experience under differing environments, and of the significance of the language factor in the prevailing paper and pencil procedure. He must appreciate the fact that, at best, a psychological test is only a rough measure of "intelligence."

What are some of the factors which must be kept in mind in the evaluation of intelligence testing?

1. Equivocation. The psychologist assumes, on the basis of certain premises involved in its standardization, that he is constructing a test of "intelligence." The fact that he calls the object of his investigation "intelligence" does not mean that it actually is intelligence he is measuring. The score on the test merely indicates what the score on that particular test is. If, for example, a child proves by the Stanford-Binet to have a mental age of ten, the result does not signify that he has a mental age of ten, but only that he has a Stanford-Binet mental age of ten, according to the norm of that particular scale. Two psychologists construct two different tests, and they both claim they are measuring intelligence. But are they both measuring the same thing? The assumption that they are both measuring the same thing involves the fallacy of equivocation, for while the two tests are equivocal (both being called "intelligence tests"), they are not necessarily equivalent.[1]

2. Sampling. The psychologist who constructs an intelligence test must select certain tasks for the examinee, in ac-

---

[1] H. M. Johnson: "Some Fallacies Underlying the Use of Psychological Tests," *Psychological Review*, 1928, 35, 328–337.

cordance with his own particular conception of intelligence. The problem as to what abilities the test aims to measure and as to what their respective relations to intelligence are, constitutes an ambiguity of content. Selection of material, too, is determined somewhat by convenience, since tasks usually are chosen not only to suit a verbal paper and pencil test which is easy to administer in a short time, but also to yield data which are readily measurable.

3. Performance. An intelligence test measures performance—not capacity—in the test situation, and the very fact that the testee realizes he is under the pressure of an examination may militate against his doing himself justice. A test reveals, not what a man can do, but what he does do.[1] We sometimes say of a person who has committed a blunder that he knows better. In the given situation, however, his performance is what counts.

Some psychologists insist that an intelligence test measures an inborn capacity for learning. Such an achievement, however, is impossible. A test can only measure what the individual has learned, not what he can learn; it can reveal acquisition, not natural capacity. Any reference to inborn ability is merely an inference based upon performance. Actually, from what the individual shows he has acquired, the psychologist can estimate his capacity to acquire further; by plotting the course already traversed, the psychologist can predict the prospects of further progress.[2]

Brigham found, in surveying the data of the Army Alpha examinations administered during the War, that the intelligence ratings of immigrants were directly proportional to the length of residence in the United States. This evidence means either that the newer immigrants are more stupid than the

---

[1] J. H. McFadden: "The Will-o'-the-Wisp Intelligence," *Psychological Review*, 1932, 39, 225–234.

[2] Knight Dunlap: *Old and New Viewpoints in Psychology*, p. 22. 1925.

older immigrants, or that the Army Alpha measures what the individuals have acquired in their new environment rather than their innate abilities. Possibly, both conclusions are justified.[1]

If it is impossible to demarcate inborn and environmental effects with any absolute finality, there are two paths open to the tester who wishes to approximate a measure of fundamental capacity. First, he can endeavor to equalize environmental influences by choosing common tasks for which everybody has had some training, such as tying a bow knot. "The wisest procedure at present is to equalize environmental forces by using a wide variety of data with which all individuals have had adequate experience, and to make as correct allowances as we can for what we cannot equalize."[2]   Second, the psychologist can strive to present novel situations which may circumvent the effects of training, though this mode of procedure is subject to serious limitations. "Intellectual tasks, success in which requires zero training and is uninfluenced by any kind or amount of training, do not exist and cannot exist, at least not in shape to measure appreciable amounts of intellect."[3]

Performance, further, depends considerably upon the attitude of the testee, whether he is coöperative, whether he is embarrassed, whether he is ill, or whether he is trying to do his best. If he is not exerting his maximal effort, his potentialities will be underestimated. The examiner, of course, is supposed to secure coöperation by tactful preparation and to note any of the above factors which appear to be affecting the results. Complete control of these aspects of the situation is impossible. Again, it seems that in practice the criterion of intelligence must be performance, not potentiality. Perhaps

[1] C. C. Brigham: *A Study of American Intelligence*. 1923.
[2] E. L. Thorndike, *et al.*: *The Measurement of Intelligence*, p. 462.
[3] *Ibid.*, p. 436.

some of the confusion would be avoided if we restricted ourselves, as suggested before, to the use of the adjective or adverb and avoided the noun, so that we should speak not of "intelligence" but of "intelligent performance," or say that in the test situation the individual "behaves intelligently."

4. Complications of Level, Scope, and Speed. The performances of individuals in intelligence tests vary in the level of difficulty achieved, some people being able to do harder tasks than others; in the number of tasks covered at a given level, some people being able to solve more kinds of problems, excelling others in the scope of their comprehension; in the speed of accomplishment, some people being able to work faster than others. Level and extent are positively correlated to a high degree, but level and speed are not so highly correlated, though the coefficient is positive. How are these factors, level, extent, and speed, to be weighted?

Many students feel that it is unfair in measuring intelligence to require speed, since they feel sure that they could do the tasks correctly if they were allowed the necessary time. There are several answers to this objection. One is that speed is conceived as an element in intelligence. If two persons perform a task correctly, and Jones completes the task in half the time it takes Smith, then Jones is the more intelligent. The time element, according to some psychologists, plays an important rôle in intelligence tests, since speed of reaction probably correlates highly with intelligence.[1] Another answer is that not all tests require speed, and that the time limits on group intelligence tests are probably quite fair to the majority of persons. In general, according to Pintner, it is advisable to set generous time limits, placing emphasis on difficulty or level.[2]

[1] H. Peak and E. G. Boring: "The Factor of Speed in Intelligence," The *Journal of Experimental Psychology*, 1926. 9, 71–94.

[2] R. Pintner: *op. cit.*, p. 534.

The Army Alpha scores show a positive correlation with the amount of schooling, that is, the more schooling the examinees have completed, the better their scores. The conclusion might be drawn that the Army Alpha examination—as charged against others too—is really a measure of scholastic aptitude rather than a measure of intelligence, but the situation is not

A-FRESHMAN **B-FRESHMAN** **A SENIOR** **B SENIOR**

Illustrations from *Hygeia* (Chicago)

FOUR HIGH-SCHOOL YEARS TELL THE STORY

The boy on the left, in the black trousers, represents the students with low intelligence who enter the freshman class in an Eastern high school. The boy in the checked trousers represents the freshmen students with high intelligence. At the right we see how many of the original groups are left in the senior year. Four years of schooling have not improved their intelligence. The seniors are more intelligent because 80 per cent. of those with less brains have left school.[1]

simple enough to justify such a conclusion. It seems reasonable to suppose that the more able men made the highest scores on the Army Alpha, and that they also had the most schooling; for education is a highly selective process, in which only the more intelligent survive through the higher schools. To a large extent, it may be fair to assert that the Army Alpha, like other tests, measures both schooling and intelligence.

[1]By permission of *Hygeia* and D. A. Laird.

5. Verbal Facility. Most intelligence tests, being paper and pencil tests, set a premium on a special type of intellect which may be designated as literary intelligence, involving skill in the use of language. In general, intelligence tests measure academic ability, since their sponsors are usually professors of psychology who naturally incline to stress the line of endeavor in which they themselves excel. If tests were devised by carpenters and automobile mechanics, the emphasis would be diverted to mechanical ability. An investigation at Harvard showed that professors of language, though presumably no more intelligent than professors of chemistry and physics, excelled the latter in their undergraduate scores on the Army Alpha.

There are a number of pertinent comments respecting the verbal emphasis, worthy of mention. Terman states that verbal intelligence is of a higher order than mechanical intelligence or other kinds of intelligence, since it is the basis of conceptual capacity, the essence of understanding, the foundation of all great discoveries. Intelligence tests, therefore, should concentrate on the most important kind of ability, the aptitude for language.

In so far as intelligence tests have been used predominantly as measures of scholastic aptitude, it seems justifiable that they should stress the language ability which contributes more than any other factor to school success.

Furthermore, officers scored consistently higher than native-born white soldiers for each grade of education. That is, an officer would tend to score higher in a test than a private, though they had both completed only the grammar school. At each educational level, the scores were, in order of ranking: officers, native-born whites, foreign-born whites, Northern negroes, Southern negroes. "These regular and consistent gaps in Alpha performance, for a constant amount of schooling, bear significant testimony to the part played by native ability."[1]

[1] H. E. Garrett: *op. cit.*, pp. 45–46.

6. Scoring. The validity of an intelligence test involves the method of scoring. Tests are made objective to facilitate easy and rapid correction. In the valuation, the answer is either right or wrong. But "wrong" may be "just wrong" or "decidedly wrong," though no distinction is made between gradations of error. In an arithmetic problem, for example, one man may get the wrong answer through a mere mistake in calculation though he comprehends the problem, while another man may get the wrong answer because he does not grasp the problem at all. No distinction is made in the scoring. They are both "wrong."

Then, too, the units of measurement are arbitrary. Test scores are translated into mental ages and I.Q.'s with so many months credited for the accomplishment of one task and so many for another. On the average, the gradation may be valid though it may work out inequitably in specific cases. Further, suppose A scored 125 in the Army Alpha, B, 150, and C, 175. Is the difference between A and B equal to the difference between B and C in terms of intelligence? An absolute acceptance of their equivalence would be unwise.

M.A. and I.Q. are useful measures where children up to high-school age are concerned, but they are of doubtful value for persons of Senior High-school level, college students, and superior adults. Other standards of comparison must be used when college students and adults are compared to others in their respective groups.

In computing the I.Q. on the Stanford-Binet, 16 is taken as the C.A. for anybody 16 or over, since Terman feels that intelligence has attained its full growth by that time. Intelligence matures rapidly in the early years of life, advances more and more slowly till the teens, and ceases to progress somewhere between 14 and 16. A person at 16, or so, will do as well in an intelligence test, therefore, as he ever will. Since the I.Q. is based on the ratio of M.A. to C.A., it would ob-

viously be unfair to compute the I.Q. in terms of a C.A. over
16 if the M.A. does not increase beyond that age. The average M.A. of the American soldiers was computed to be about
14, which seemed scandalous to those persons who were not
aware of the complete maturation of intelligence at 16, more
recently allocated by psychologists as nearer 14.

But does intelligence stop growing at 14 or 16? Those
psychologists who believe it does, state that people may gain
in experience after that age but not in fundamental ability.
Such an assumption, however, supposes that a psychological
test can differentiate native endowment from subsequent ac-
quisitions, which is practically impossible. "Nature sets certain general limits, but for each individual there is a margin of
safety or a range of accomplishment which is a function of the
environment, and the extent of which can only be ascertained
by individual effort under the most favorable conditions."[1]

Is intelligence improvable? On the whole, test results have
indicated a constancy of the I.Q., which coincides with the
everyday observation that bright children grow into bright
adults and dull children into dull adults. If A, B, and C rank
1, 2, and 3 in intelligence at the age of 5, the probability is they
will still rank in that same order at the age of 10. If a child of
3 has an I.Q. of 110, he will probably have an I.Q. of approximately 110 when he reaches 14. A constant I.Q. depends
upon constancy in environmental conditions, constancy in
schooling, constancy in culture or home conditions, and constancy in health. "A radical change in any of these conditions
may affect the rate of individual mental development."[2] Intelligence is improvable, within limits, according to Dearborn.
A dogmatic negative rests on the unjustifiable assumption that
innate capacity can be isolated. Slightly below average performance may be improved through environmental changes to

[1] W. F. Dearborn: *op. cit.*, p. 309.
[2] *Ibid.*, p. 28.

somewhat above average performance. A superior environment may raise the I.Q. 10 points or so.[1] "Some children do change in I.Q. as they grow, because of illness, sudden and great changes in environment when very young, and from other obscure causes, but the number so changing is small. The usual picture is one of steady regular growth of intelligence giving a constant I.Q. We cannot hold out the hope to the parents of the child of low I.Q. that he will suddenly change for the better at the mystical ages of seven or fourteen. More likely is it that his I.Q. will remain low, in spite of all that can be done."[2]

7. Summary. In view of all the factors we have surveyed, we may conclude that intelligence tests have much practical value if they are intelligently administered and intelligently interpreted.

IV. DISTRIBUTION OF INTELLIGENCE

Individual differences in intelligence approximate the normal curve in their distribution. About 1% of the general population has an I.Q. below 70, about 1% an I.Q. over 130:

I.Q. below 70	1%
70–79	5%
80–89	14%
90–99	30%
100–109	30%
110–119	14%
120–129	5%
over 130	1%

This perfect curve, of course, is only approximated in practice.

A composite picture of the "average man" has been drawn by Harry L. Hollingworth, a Columbia psychologist, on the

---

[1]Gardner Murphy and Lois Murphy: *Experimental Social Psychology*, p. 107. 1931.

[2]R. Pintner in *The New Generation*, p. 437. 1930. By permission of The Macaulay Company.

basis of the evidence collected during the War from the intelligence examinations. The average man is, of course, an abstraction, a central point that we all approach to some extent. His vocabulary includes about 7,500 words. He can probably tell you what is meant by "nerve," but he will have difficulty with "coinage"; he understands "insure" and "shrewd," but he is not clear about "dilapidated" and "philanthropy." He may know from actual experience, but he can not explain, the difference between poverty and misery. He can give three differences between a President and a King, but the difference between evolution and revolution seems to him not worth mentioning. If he has a whole minute for the problem he will get the correct answer when asked how many pencils can be bought for 50 cents if two pencils cost 5 cents. He can also find out how much seven feet of cloth will cost at 15 cents a yard. But he is completely lost when asked how many boxes there are in a collection in which one large box holds four small boxes, each containing four smaller ones. He can repeat seven numbers he hears, but if asked to repeat eight, he leaves out one of them. He can repeat simple sentences such as "It is nearly half-past one o'clock; the house is very quiet, and the cat has gone to sleep." But if complicated instructions are given him, he will not be able to remember them all. The average man leaves school at the eighth grade. He has a smattering of local geography, knows a little bit about history, and knows a few elementary facts of physiology. In spite of the fact that he is to be accepted as a citizen, he has no general knowledge of civics, science, politics, or literature. He is able to speak one language only. On a standardized intelligence test he makes about the same score as does an average boy of fourteen. He never develops the intelligence required for satisfactory high-school work. In industry he is likely to drift into the skilled trades, but is not likely to have an occupation superior to that of his father. After a short period of training he can become a plumber, a carpenter, a mechanic. He marries at an early age, and has from three to five children.

Frederick Osborn of the American Museum of Natural History and Frank Lorimer of the Eugenics Research Association have administered a battery of mental tests in a nationwide survey of intelligence. Generally speaking, they found that the city child has a higher intelligence quotient than his country cousin. The widest, the most consistent, and the most interesting differences in intelligence revealed in their study lay in the distribution of the population by occupational groups. The children of professional men have, when considered in large numbers, consistently the highest intelligence quotient; the offspring of business and clerical fathers ran second; the skilled and semi-skilled workmen next, the unskilled laborer next, and the children of the farmer are to be found in the rear.[1]

One impression that has resulted from the wide application of intelligence testing is the tremendous range of differences among individuals with respect to their mental capacities.

At one end of the distribution curve of intelligence are the feeble-minded who constitute a grave social problem, since they turn so readily to crime if the proper safeguards

COLLEGE GIRL-8TH GRADE GIRL- PROSTITUTE

THE CAUSE

Many delinquents are subnormal mentally, as this picturegram indicates.[2]

---

[1] The *Literary Digest*, June 3, 1933.

[2] Picturegrams taken from D. A. Laird: "Brains, A Matter of Relativity," *Hygeia*, 1929. 7, 369–372. By permission of D. A. Laird and *Hygeia*.

are not taken in their training. In juvenile courts about one out of three children charged with delinquency is subnormal mentally. About one out of every four wayward girls is deficient in brains. Furthermore, the care of the feeble-minded imposes a severe financial burden upon the community. In Massachusetts, for example, about one-fifth of the annual budget is devoted to this item.

Feeble-mindedness is largely hereditary.[1] The feeble-minded are usually classified:

Idiot   —M.A. of 2 years or less
Imbecile—M.A. of 3–7
Moron —M.A. of 7–12

Since the feeble-minded tend to propagate their own kind, and since they tend to multiply rapidly, eugenicists have suggested segregation, colonization, and sterilization as remedial measures. Certainly it is incumbent upon the majority to provide a special environment for the mental defective where he can adapt himself, preferably an institution designed for that purpose.

It is cruelly unfair to expect the feeble-minded individual to adjust himself to the demands of ordinary society, because he lacks the particular level of intelligence fixed by social necessity. As Binet put it, "A French peasant may be normal in a rural community but feeble-minded in Paris." The defective is intelligent enough to live successfully in a simple environment. It is only just, therefore, to see to it that that simple environment, in the form of institutional care, is provided for him.

The mental defective is not simply slow. He is incapable. He cannot be trained to perform well a task beyond his mental level. It is important, therefore, to determine the level of intelligence demanded by certain tasks, to ascertain the mental level of the individual, and then to relate the two accordingly.

---

[1] H. H. Goddard: *Feeble-mindedness. Its Causes and Consequences.* 1923.

Intelligence testing has made an important contribution to the procedure of selection and the adaptation of training.

The mental defective is incurable, but he is teachable within limits.[1] It is folly to try to teach him reading and writing in the public school, as the effort will be wasted, and such a policy will be apt to discourage the pupil and to convert him into a disciplinary problem. He can be taught specific habits—how to eat with a fork instead of his fingers, how to dress, how to comb his hair, and how to obey commands without resorting to tantrums—all of which may promote healthful recreation and social contacts.[2] Vocational training should be confined to simple tasks of a manual sort, and routine work should be planned to absorb his energy.

Moral training is especially important, since the mental defective is apt to become a menace if he remains in society. Eleanor Wembridge has written delightfully of this problem. She tested some morons:

If two pencils cost five cents, how many can you get for fifty cents?
> Flora: 25 because 2 into 50 is 25.
> Lucille: 100 because 2 times 50 is 100.
> Annie: 5 times 50, because 5 cents times 50 cents is 5 times 50—whatever that is.
> Chuck: 10—You get 2 for 5 and 2 times 5 is 10.

Such persons should not be expected to conduct their financial affairs with prudence; nor should they be expected to be prudent in other matters involving ethical issues. There can be little appreciation of moral principles.

The fable of the crow who was flattered into dropping her meat in order to sing was interpreted:
> "That's like Lucille. These flappers. It don't pay to be led by flappery."

---

[1]See S. L. and L. C. Pressey: *Mental Abnormality and Deficiency*. 1926. See also H. Woodrow: *Brightness and Dullness in Children*. 1919.

[2]Leta S. Hollingworth: *The Psychology of Subnormal Children*. 1924.

The fable of Hercules and the wagon provoked:
"It teaches how to drive cars."
"Don't go in holes."
"Learn about the roads."
"Unharness oxen."
"Always put wheels on your shoulders."
"Shouldn't go with boys in a machine because they make you walk."
"Shows how to be nice to a horse."
"It teaches a lesson all right."

A moral appeal to principles must fail where such a low grade of intelligence is concerned. Training must be based on the inculcation of blind obedience to conventions, such as "a woman's place is in the home," for Queen Victoria knew her morons. The limitations of the defective must be constantly kept in mind, for "we are not sauntering with Socrates in Athenian groves. We are sitting with Jenny in jail."[1]

At the other end of the intelligence scale are the geniuses. The term "genius" is used here, not to describe the possessor of a special talent for poetry or music, but to denote persons with an I.Q. over 135 or so. The geniuses have been as grossly misunderstood as the mental defectives by the general public. Child prodigies are generally regarded as frail, sickly, nervous, eccentric, maladjusted, one-sided, hard to get along with, lacking in moral and emotional balance, liable to break down mentally and nervously, to "peter out," and either to die young or else to land in the penitentiary or in the school for the feeble-minded or in the hospital for the insane. One American editor asked Wiggam to write an article showing why it is that nearly all great geniuses had been very dull children! All of these popular notions have been disproved by a research conducted under the leadership of Terman, over a period of

---

[1] Eleanor Wembridge: *Life Among the Lowbrows.*　1931.　By permission of and by arrangement with Houghton Mifflin Company.

fifteen years, in which 1,000 gifted California children have been subjected to thorough mental and physical examinations. The results have been published in three volumes under the title, *Genetic Studies of Geniuses*. All the techniques of psychological and medical science have been used in the study of these children of unusual mental superiority, and in following them into adult life for the purpose of comparing final achievement with early promise. The research has also included an investigation of 300 of the world's most eminent individuals (popularly called geniuses) of the past 400 years for the purpose of finding out how their careers from childhood on compare with the modern generation.

After selecting the children with much care, Terman and his associates studied their mental, physical, and personality traits exhaustively. They found that the children came from homes superior in parental care and cultural influences. Seventy-three families in the group yielded two subjects each, and nine yielded three or more. Nearly a quarter of the members of the Hall of Fame are known to be related to one or more of the subjects. Gifted children come predominantly from families in which superior ability and achievement have been evidenced. There was an appreciable negative correlation between the I.Q. of the child and the number of children in the family.

Anthropometric measurements showed that the gifted children were above the standards for American-born children with respect to average height and weight, lung capacity, width of shoulders, and strength of muscles, and were in general physically superior to children taken at random in the school population. The popular notion which caricatures the man of great intellect with a puny body is thus definitely disproved by overwhelming evidence.[1]

Nearly all the gifted children are in a school grade consider-

[1]See D. G. Paterson: *Physique and Intellect*. 1930.

ably below that which corresponds to their mental age. No evidence was found for the widespread belief that gifted children actually dislike school. No evidence, to speak of, was found to warrant the belief that the superior intellectual attainments of the group were due to artificial stimulation by the parents. In fact, in many cases, the parents were not even aware of the child's superiority.

The Stanford Achievement Test, a four-hour examination affording a dependable measure of the child's proficiency in all of the leading subjects of the elementary school education, exploded the common belief that the abilities of gifted children are excessively specialized or one-sided, for the scores revealed an exceptional regularity in the various subjects.

The group manifested an interest in the more abstract subjects such as literature, dramatics, and arithmetic, and a lack of enthusiasm for the manual subjects such as penmanship, manual training, and sewing. The gifted children read on a wide range of topics, concentrating on science, history, biography, travel, informational fiction, poetry, and drama, and devoted less time to books of adventure, mystery, and emotional fiction.

The play interests and social interests appeared normal. It is the exception and not the rule for the gifted child to be regarded by his playmates as queer or peculiar. Faults of character are unquestionably less common among intellectually superior children in general.

A follow-up study shows that early promise is realized as the child matures. Unfortunately, many schools attempt to meet the needs of the brightest children by granting extra promotions. Other educators, with more insight into the situation, favor the establishment of special classes for the gifted.[1]

---

[1] Material largely gleaned from Terman's article, "Talent and Genius in Children," in *The New Generation*, pp. 405-423.

V. THE EMPLOYMENT OF INTELLIGENCE

Intelligence is of no practical value unless it is used.

Suppose we find that a person has a certain I.Q.   Can we be sure that he will use his ability?   That will depend on what we might call his G.Q., or Gumption Quotient, which will tell how much backbone he has, how much he will sacrifice for his education, how many headaches he will bear, how long he will stick to a challenging mental task.

The responsibility for failing to "use our heads" lies largely in our emotional training.   Emotional excitement tends to obscure clear thinking, and thus to nullify the advantages of intelligence.   Man lives not by bread alone, but principally by such catchwords as scofflaw, killjoy, copperhead, carpet-bagger, scalawag, pacifist, scab, slacker, and profiteer, terms which serve to determine his attitudes so effectively as to exclude intelligence.   Medical men did not attack microbes with emotional phrases but with patient research.   Political questions, however, are settled by orators who sway men's minds by stirring their emotions, realizing that people cannot think straight under high emotional tension.

Poetry, romantic prose, and emotional oratory are all of inestimable value, but their place is not where responsible decisions must be made.   The common (almost universal) use of emotional words in political thinking is as much out of place as would be a chemical or statistical formula in the middle of a poem. . . .   Let us think calmly and scientifically about war, and then actively oppose it with all the passion of which we are capable.[1]

Many persons are convinced in each presidential election that if their particular candidate is defeated it is only a question of time before the day of doom will descend.   Reactionaries feel that it is best to stick to the tried-and-true measures because anything in the way of an experiment is dangerous.

[1]R. H. Thouless: *Straight and Crooked Thinking*, p. 19.   Reprinted by permission of Simon and Schuster, Inc.

But as Justice Brandeis said, in his dissenting opinion in the Oklahoma Ice Case, "If we would be guided by the light of reason, we must be bold." Boldness, unfortunately, is too often confused with rashness, and condemned accordingly by people who fail to realize that boldness is as important for the solution of our social problems as intelligence, since timidity discourages the practice of thinking.

The lack of social-mindedness is responsible for much wasted intelligence. We are so self-centered that we do not pause to consider how we might plan to help the other fellow whose welfare is so intimately linked with our own. We destroy in a Fourth of July bonfire enough fuel to warm the homes of the poor in the community for an entire season, thus expressing our patriotic fervor with no regard for our less fortunate neighbors who are compelled to paw through the rubbish in the city dumps to secure the bits of wood to heat their houses. Similar waste is encouraged in industry by the producer whose interest in profits exceeds his interest in the welfare of the consumer, so that ingenuity in production is dedicated to inventing new ways of manufacturing an article that will wear out in the shortest feasible time.

Intelligence has been devoted to the development of the physical sciences to the neglect of the social sciences, a fact which is well symbolized by the anomalous situation in Chicago when the Fair of 1933 was opened by a beam of light from Arcturus forty light-years away, during a time when municipal mismanagement and corruption rendered it impossible to collect taxes or to pay school teachers.

Science must be motivated by love if the human struggle is going to achieve a more intelligent level of existence. "Men sometimes speak," says Bertrand Russell, "as though the progress of science must necessarily be a boon to mankind, but that, I fear, is one of the comfortable nineteenth-century delusions which our more disillusioned age must discard.

Science enables the holders of power to realize their purposes more fully than they could otherwise do. If their purposes are good, this is a gain; if they are evil, it is a loss. . . . This is why the heart is as important as the head. By the 'heart' I mean, for the moment, the sum-total of kindly impulses. Where they exist, science helps them to be effective; where they are absent, science only makes men more cleverly diabolic."[1]

The world suffers from the machinations of the intelligent who lack the kindly impulse, but it suffers as well from the blunders of men who "mean well" but whose stupidity is only rendered the more dangerous by their utter spirit of benevolent devotion. Human nature will destroy us unless it is disciplined by knowledge. Emotion must be definitely under control if intelligence is going to be of any avail.

In the midst of a profound economic depression, many counselors are urging that nature be allowed to take its course, that other depressions have come to an end sooner or later without resort to radical panaceas, on the assumption that economic cycles are inevitable, and that there is no use in trying to stop them. A new spirit, however, is developing, which is inspiring a determination in us to remain no longer the victims of circumstance, but to become the masters of our destinies. It is beginning to dawn on us that our own wrongheadedness is responsible for our recurrent hard times. We are coming to realize that events may be brought within our control if we are willing to subordinate our passionate self-interest to the pursuit of ends that have social value, and if we are willing to capitalize the intelligence that is available to us in the achievement of those ends. Such a goal has been the hope of science since the days of Francis Bacon. It is an ideal within our grasp if we are determined to make the effort necessary to its realization.

---

[1]Bertrand Russell: *Icarus, or the Future of Science*, p. 57. 1924. Reprinted by permission of E. P. Dutton & Co.

PROJECTS AND EXPERIMENTS

INTRODUCTION

The student will derive more value from the elementary course by supplementing his study of the textbook with additional reading and experimentation. Various references have been provided in the footnotes which will give the student a bibliography to guide him in his outside reading. Further references are supplied under *Projects*. The material in this section is intended to offer suggestions for research. The student will be expected to plan projects of his own and to carry them out, so that he may gain a practical knowledge of the various phases of psychological investigation. The section on *Experiments* will supplement the experiments included in the body of the text.

The student will find the following books helpful:

H. B. English: *A Student's Dictionary of Psychological Terms*. *1934*. The Antioch Press, Yellow Springs, Ohio.

H. C. Warren: *Dictionary of Psychology*. 1934. Houghton Mifflin Company.

PROJECTS

CHAPTER I

1. For the history of psychology, consult the following:

   G. S. Brett: *A History of Psychology*. Three volumes. 1912, 1921.

   Max Dessoir: *Outlines of the History of Psychology*. 1912.

   W. Durant: *The Story of Philosophy*, pp. 29–40, 405–408. 1926.

   W. S. Hulin: *A Short History of Psychology*. 1934.

   W. McDougall: *Body and Mind. A History and a Defense of Animism*, Chapter I, "Animism and the Ancient World." Fifth Edition, 1920.

   G. Murphy: *Historical Introduction to Modern Psychology*. 1929.

2. Is Psychology a science?

   Grace Adams: *Psychology: Science or Superstition?* 1931; "The Rise and Fall of Psychology," *Atlantic Monthly*, January, 1933.

   Henshaw Ward: *Builders of Delusion. A Tour Among Our Best Minds*. 1931.

   H. P. Weld: *Psychology as Science. Its Problems and Points of View*. 1928.

   H. Wickham: *The Misbehaviorists. Pseudo-Science and the Modern Temper*. 1928.

   Compare issues of the *American Journal of Psychology* with issues of *Everyday Psychology and Inspiration*.

3. Describe some instances of animism in modern life.

555

4. For the study of Common Sense Psychology, consult:

Angelo Patri's syndicated news columns.

Angelo Patri: *The Questioning Child and Other Essays*.   1931.

The Voice of Experience.   1933.

Listen to the radio program of "The Voice of Experience."

E. T. Webb and J. J. B. Morgan: *Strategy in Handling People*.   1931.

5. For a survey of non-scientific Psychology consult:

M. Fishbein: *Fads and Quackery in Healing; An Analysis of the Foibles of the Healing Cults with Essays on Various Other Peculiar Notions in the Health Field*.   1932.

F. C. Haddock: *Power of Will*.   1907.

J. Jastrow: *Fact and Fable in Psychology*.   1900;   *Wish and Wisdom; Episodes in the Vagaries of Belief*.   1935.

S. Zweig: *Mental Healers*.   1932.

6. For an exposition of the synoptic principle, see:

E. S. Brightman: *An Introduction to Philosophy*, Chapter I, "The Philosophical Spirit."   1925.

CHAPTER II

1. What does the scientific viewpoint contribute to life?

C. E. Ayres: *Science, the False Messiah*.   1927.

B. Russell: *The Scientific Outlook*.   1931.

2. What is the relation of science to religion?

K. F. Mather: *Science in Search of God*.   1928.

3. Pavlov's mechanistic psychology has been taken as the basis of the new Russian education.   See:

I. P. Pavlov: *Lectures on Conditioned Reflexes*.   1928.

V. M. Bekhterev: *General Principles of Human Reflexology; Introduction to the Objective Study of Personality.* 1933.

A. P. Pinkevitch: *New Education in the Soviet Republic.* 1929; *Science and Education in the U. S. S. R.* 1935.

4. For a description of the extrovert and introvert, see:

B. M. Hinkle: *The Recreating of the Individual,* Chapter V, "A Study of Psychological Types." 1923.

C. G. Jung: *Psychological Types; or the Psychology of Individuation.* 1923.

J. Oppenheim: *Behind Your Front.* 1928. Evaluate the data presented.

M. Freyd: "Introverts and Extroverts," *Psychological Review,* 1924, 31, 74–87.

CHAPTER III

1. For a survey of the different viewpoints in Psychology, consult the following:

J. C. Flügel: *One Hundred Years of Psychology, 1833–1933.* 1933.

E. Heidbreder: *Seven Psychologies.* 1933.

W. McDougall: *Energies of Men,* Chapter II, "Schools of Psychology." 1932.

C. Murchison, Editor: *Psychologies of 1925.* 1926; *Psychologies of 1930.* 1930.

R. S. Woodworth: *Contemporary Schools of Psychology.* 1931.

2. For an exposition of the Gestalt Psychology, consult:

G. W. Hartmann: *Gestalt Psychology; A Survey of Facts and Principles.* 1935.

H. Helson: "The Psychology of *Gestalt,*" *American Journal of Psychology,* 1925, 36, 342–370; 494–526. 1926, 37, 25–62; 189–223.

K. Koffka: *The Principles of Gestalt Psychology.* 1935. "Perception: An Introduction to the *Gestalt-Theorie,*" *Psychological Bulletin,* 1922, 19, 531–585.

3. Collect illustrations of tied images (closure).

4. For an exposition of Behaviorism, see:

J. B. Watson: *Behavior: An Introduction to Comparative Psychology.* 1914. *Behaviorism.* Revised edition, 1930; "What Is Behaviorism?" *Golden Book*, April, 1928; "How We Think: A Behaviorist's View," *Harper's Magazine*, June, 1926; "Memory as the Behaviorist Sees It," *Harper's Magazine*, July, 1926; "The Myth of the Unconscious," *Harper's Magazine*, September, 1927; "The Heart or the Intellect," *Harper's Magazine*, February, 1928.

Rosalie Rayner Watson: "I Am the Mother of a Behaviorist's Sons," *Parents' Magazine*, December, 1930.

5. Compare the three editions of Woodworth's *Psychology*, 1921, 1929, 1934.

6. Compare the following textbooks:

E. B. Titchener: *A Text-book of Psychology.* 1921.

J. R. Angell: *Psychology.* 1908.

J. B. Watson: *Psychology from the Standpoint of a Behaviorist.* 1924.

W. McDougall: *Outline of Psychology.* 1923.

R. H. Wheeler: *The Science of Psychology.* 1929.

CHAPTER IV

1. What effect will the movies have on our educational technique?

P. J. Rulon: *Sound Motion Picture in Science Teaching.* 1933.

2. Is reading disability due to sensory deficiency or to faulty training?

D. D. Durrell: "Confusions in Learning," *Education*, February, 1932.

3. How far does reading depend upon auditory sensitivity?

G. L. Bond: *The Auditory and Speech Characteristics of Poor Readers*. Teachers College *Contributions to Education*, #657. 1935.

4. How far does reading depend upon visual sensitivity?

P. Fendrick: *Visual Characteristics of Poor Readers*. Teachers College *Contributions to Education*, #656. 1935.

5. What is the rôle of the receptors in the response mechanism?

E. D. Adrian: *The Basis of Sensation*. 1928.

CHAPTER V

E. D. Adrian: *The Mechanism of Nervous Action: Electrical Studies of the Neuron*. 1932.

C. M. Child: *Physiological Foundations of Behavior*. 1924. *The Origin and Development of the Nervous System from a Physiological Viewpoint*. 1921.

A. Forbes: "The Mechanism of Reaction," *Handbook of General Experimental Psychology*, C. Murchison, Editor. 1934.

G. T. Ladd and R. S. Woodworth: *Elements of Physiological Psychology; a Treatise of the Activities and Nature of the Mind, from the Physical and Experimental Points of View*. Revised edition, 1911.

J. D. Lickley: *The Nervous System*. New edition, 1931.

R. S. Lillie: *Protoplasmic Action and Nervous Action*. Second edition, 1932.

W. McDougall: *Physiological Psychology*. 1905.

L. T. Troland: *Principles of Psychophysiology; a Survey of Modern Scientific Psychology*. 1929.

CHAPTER VI

1. What physiological processes underlie motivation?

   L. T. Troland: *Fundamentals of Human Motivation.* 1928.

2. For a study of physical processes involved in action, see:

   W. J. Crozier and H. Hoagland: "The Study of Living Organisms," *Handbook of General Experimental Psychology*, C. Murchison, Editor. 1934.

   J. F. Fulton: *Muscular Contraction and the Reflex Control of Movement.* 1926.

   C. R. Griffith: *Psychology and Athletics; a General Survey for Athletes and Coaches.* 1928.

   A. V. Hill: *Muscular Activity.* 1926.

CHAPTER VII

1. For a study of attitudes, see:

   G. W. Allport: "Attitudes," Chapter XVII in *A Handbook of Social Psychology*, C. Murchison, Editor. 1935.

   D. Katz and F. H. Allport: *Students' Attitudes.* 1931.

2. Write an essay characterizing the following stereotypes: the dude, the capitalist, the chef, the mannequin, and the southern belle.

3. How do we form our political opinions?

   W. F. Vaughan: "An Experimental Study in Political Prejudice," *Journal of Abnormal and Social Psychology*, 1930, 25, 268–274.

4. Our American democracy is based on faith in the common sense of the common people. Taking yourself as a sample, investigate the sources of your political opinions. In the light

of your findings, do you think such a faith can be intelligently justified?

5. Prepare arguments for and against the *New Deal*. Do you find the arguments accumulate on one side more readily than on the other? Is such a tendency an indicator of prejudice on your part?

6. Is an open mind an asset or a liability?

Roger Lewis: "I Have My Doubts," *Atlantic Monthly*, Dec., 1927.

7. Should education aim at the indoctrination of what the teacher considers the "proper" bias, or should it aim at the cultivation of individual judgment, allowing the student to solve controversial issues according to his own lights?

H. E. Barnes: "Education versus Enlightenment," *The New Generation*, V. F. Calverton and S. D. Schmalhausen, Editors. 1930.

8. For an exposition of the *inferiority complex*, see:

E. Bagby: *The Psychology of Personality. An Analysis of Common Emotional Disorders*, Chapter VIII, "Inferiority Complexes." 1928.

Lee Dodd: *The Golden Complex; a Defence of Inferiority.* 1927.

E. R. Groves: *Understanding Yourself. The Mental Hygiene of Personality*, Chapters X to XIII. 1935.

W. F. Vaughan: *The Lure of Superiority.* 1928.

9. Is religious thinking entirely wishful?

H. E. Fosdick: *As I See Religion*, pp. 129–159. 1932.

10. How may good tastes (emotional habits) be developed? How can the child be trained to prefer good books to trash and classical music to jazz?

11. For a discussion of moral knowledge in children, consult:

H. Hartshorne, M. A. May, and F. K. Shuttleworth; *Studies in the Organization of Character*, especially Chapters IV–X, 1930.

CHAPTER VIII

1. What satisfactions are vital to happiness? What do people want?

Popular Mechanics says that the toy, "dancing Jim Crow," yielded its inventor $75,000 a year, while the man who invented the roller-skate realized more than a million dollars. Rubber tips for lead pencils yielded the man who thought of them $100,000 a year, and $2,500,000 was realized by the inventor of shoe laces. The ordinary umbrella earned more than $10,000,000 for its inventor, and the man who made the first steel writing pens received an enormous fortune. The inventor of the metallic heel-plate for shoes sold 143,000,000 a year, and realized more than $1,500,000 in royalties.

What simple devices can you think of that might reap the inventor a fortune today?

2. The interest in horse racing has increased during the depression. Why?

3. The argument has been advanced that inventors like Watt, Faraday, Marconi, and Edison were actuated solely by the profit motive. Without the incentive of financial gain they would not have labored at their tasks. Do you agree with this point of view?

4. Why do people work? Compare the conceptions of motivation entertained by advocates of capitalism and advocates of communism. Which is sound? Are they both sound in some respects? How?

5. What satisfactions do people expect to derive from their work?

> Whiting Williams: *What's on the Worker's Mind.* 1920.
>
> Kirby Page: "What Is the Profit Motive?" *The Christian Century*, March 20, 1935.

6. How can a person appeal successfully to people's wants?

> H. A. Overstreet: *Influencing Human Behavior.* 1925.

7. Study the urges exploited by advertisers.

8. What is the rôle of tropisms in animal behavior?

> Jacques Loeb: *Forced Movements, Tropisms, and Animal Conduct.* 1918.
>
> H. S. Jennings: *Behavior of the Lower Organisms.* 1931.

9. What is the rôle of emotion in behavior?

> C. A. Ruckmick: "Why We Have Emotions," *Scientific Monthly*, 1929, 28, 252–262.
>
> P. Bard: "Emotions: I. The Neuro-humoral Basis of Emotional Reactions," *Handbook of General Experimental Psychology*, Chapter VI, C. Murchison, Editor. 1934.
>
> W. B. Cannon: "The James-Lange Theory of Emotions," *American Journal of Psychology*, 1927, 39, 106–124.

10. How may we utilize our emotional resources to give our lives more vigor?

> E. Jacobson: *You Must Relax; a Practical Method of Reducing the Strains of Modern Living.* 1934.
>
> W. James: *Memories and Studies*, "Energies of Men." 1911.
>
> Jules Payot: *The Education of the Will.* 1909.
>
> W. B. Pitkin: *More Power to You! A Working Technique for Making the Most of Human Energy.* 1933.
>
> B. Sidis: *The Foundations of Normal and Abnormal Psychology*, Part I, Chapter XXXI, "The Principle of Reserve Energy." 1914.

11. What is the relation of values to motivation?

    A. C. Garnett: *The Mind in Action. A Study of Motives and Values.* 1932.

12. What are some of the emotional adjustments involved in married life?

    R. L. Dickinson and L. Beam: *A Thousand Marriages.* 1931.

    R. V. Hamilton: *A Research in Marriage.* 1929.

    E. R. Groves and Gladys Groves: *Sex in Marriage.* 1931.

13. Collect instances in which the term *instinct* is abused.

14. For an exposition of maturation, consult:

    L. Carmichael: "Origin and Prenatal Growth of Behavior," *A Handbook of Child Psychology*, Chapter II, C. Murchison, Editor. Second edition revised, 1933.

    A. Gesell: "Maturation and the Patterning of Behavior." *Ibid.*, Chapter IV.

15. Johann Sebastian Bach's father, four generations of grandfathers, and four of his sons were all musicians, and most of them were distinguished musicians. How do you explain this?

16. It is often said that human nature cannot be changed. Is it true?

17. When should children begin the study of various school subjects?

    E. C. Deputy: *Predicting First Grade Reading Achievements.* Teachers College *Contributions to Education,* #426. 1930.

    Ernest Horn: "A Basic Writing Vocabulary," University of Iowa *Monographs in Education*, First Series, #4. 1926.

    A. I. Gates: "Psychology and Education," *Psychology at Work*, Chapter III, P. S. Achilles, Editor. 1932.

E. L. Thorndike: *Arithmetic by Grades*.

E. L. Thorndike and J. H. Wohlfarth: *Growth in Spelling*. 1929.

CHAPTER IX

1. Study fixation and regression in your own experience. Consult:

Van Wyck Brooks: *The Ordeal of Mark Twain*. 1920.

2. Study positive and negative adaptation in your own experience.

3. Collect examples of bad habits established in children by their elders. Consult:

S. Blanton and M. G. Blanton: *Child Guidance*. 1927.

4. In what respects do you feel the need of reëducation? How would you proceed with such a program?

H. W. Frink: *Morbid Fears and Compulsions. Their Psychology and Psychoanalytic Treatment*, Chapter X, "The Theory and Mechanism of the Psychoanalytic Cure." 1921.

5. What habits do you possess that are particularly specific? Do they produce disorganizing effects on your personality?

6. Read some fables and draw the morals. Are the generalizations justified? Consult *Aesop's Fables*.

7. How would you break yourself of the fear of speaking in public?

8. What counsel would you give to a student who is so afraid of examinations that he cannot do himself justice?

9. How effective is the preaching of a sermon for the reformation of human emotions?

10. Are posters and dramatics effective in promoting "health" and "safety" habits?

11. What should you do if a child lies to you?

12. How far is a culture a matter of habit patterns?

R. Benedict: *Patterns of Culture.*   1934.

CHAPTER X

1. Are there any situations in which it is hard for you to pay attention?   Why?

2. How can the teacher vary the presentation of his material to hold the interest of his students?   What plan could be evolved to improve the teaching of: Psychology, Chemistry, History, and Economics?   Consult:

H. C. McComas: "Some Types of Attention," *Psychological Monographs*, 1911, 13, # 3.

W. B. Pillsbury: *Attention.*   1908.

3. For an extended discussion of *meaning*, see:

C. K. Ogden and I. A. Richards: *The Meaning of Meaning.* 1923.

4. How can reading be improved?   Consult:

A. I. Gates: *The Improvement of Reading.*   Revised edition, 1935.

CHAPTER XI

1. How do people differ in their imagery?

C. H. Griffitts: "Individual Differences in Imagery," *Psychological Monographs*, Volume, 1928, 37, # 3.

2. Keep a record of your day-dreams. What do they reveal concerning your goal in life?

> Alfred Adler: *Understanding Human Nature.* 1927.

3. What movies remain vivid in your memory? Why?

4. Question some children regarding the impressions they gain of certain movies. Attend a Saturday matinee performance arranged especially for children. Do you consider the program wholesome?

> W. W. Charters, Chairman: *Motion Pictures and Youth: The Payne Fund Studies.* 1933.

5. What is a psychogenetic disorder?

> J. A. Jackson and H. M. Salisbury: *Outwitting Our Nerves: A Primer of Psychotherapy.* Second edition revised and enlarged, 1932.

6. For a discussion of physiological memory see:

> W. B. Cannon: *The Wisdom of the Body.* 1932.

7. Is a puzzle-box a fair test of an animal's intelligence?

> Michael Joseph: "The Intelligence of Cats," *Harper's Magazine,* May, 1935.

8. For a discussion of forgetting, see:

> S. Freud: *Psychopathology of Everyday Life.* Thirteenth impression, 1926.

9. How effective is our system of punishing the criminal? How could our penal system be made more scientific?

> S. S. Glueck and E. Glueck: *One Thousand Juvenile Delinquents, Their Treatment by Court and Clinic.* 1934.
>
> Lewis E. Lawes: *Twenty Thousand Years in Sing Sing.* 1932.

10. For a discussion of transfer, consult:

> C. H. Judd: *The Psychology of High School Subjects.* 1915.

W. S. Monroe, J. C. DeVoss, G. W. Reagan: *Educational Psychology*, Chapter VII, "Transfer of Training." 1930.

H. O. Rugg: *The Experimental Determination of Mental Discipline in School Studies.* 1916.

E. L. Thorndike: "Mental Discipline in High School Studies," *Journal of Educational Psychology*, 1924, 15, 1–22; 83–98.

H. Woodrow: "The Effect of Type of Training Upon Transference," *Journal of Educational Psychology*, 1927, 18, 159–172.

11. For helpful advice in the matter of learning, consult:

M. E. Bennett: *College and Life. Problems of Self-Discovery and Self-Direction*, Part III, "Learning in College." 1933.

C. R. Griffith: *Psychology of Coaching. A Study of Coaching Methods From the Point of View of Psychology*, Chapters II–III. 1932.

H. D. Kitson: *How to Use Your Mind*, Chapter VI, "First Aids to Memory: Impression." 1921.

12. Teaching others to learn involves the building up of associations. With this thought in mind, how may biography be used in the teaching of History?

13. Study your dreams. Are they all cases of wish-fulfillment?

F. V. Markey: "Imagination," *Psychological Bulletin*, 1935, 32, 212–236.

CHAPTER XII

1. Write an essay entitled, *How I Solve My Conflicts*.

2. Collect illustrations of the various mechanisms for the resolution of conflict.

H. W. Frink: *Morbid Fears and Compulsions. Their Psychology and Psychoanalytic Treatment*, Chapter IV, "The Mechanisms of Psychopathological Manifestations." 1921.

3. Apply the principles of mental hygiene to some biographies. Consult the Psychographs of Gamaliel Bradford; for example, his *Damaged Souls*. 1931.

> Lucile Dooley: "Psychoanalytic Studies of Genius," *American Journal of Psychology*, 1916, 27, 363–416.

4. What are the sources of mental conflict in our American culture? Can you suggest any remedies? Are remedies desirable?

> M. Mead: *Coming of Age in Samoa*. 1928.

5. What is the rôle of guilt (conflict) in religious experience?

> A. J. Russell: *For Sinners Only*. 1932.

6. Desirable intellectual and social traits tend to correlate positively. Does this mean that compensation is exceptional?

7. A man wants to buy a new car, but he realizes the purchase would impose a strain on his budget. Work out some rationalizations that would help him in this trying situation.

CHAPTER XIII

1. Analyze the faulty reasoning involved in some of our superstitions.

2. Collect some illogical advertisements.

3. Collect illustrations of arguments involving analogy or causation.

4. Does the study of Latin improve mental powers? Suppose it is found that students who take Latin excel in Geometry those students who do not take Latin, what conclusion is likely to be drawn? Is it justified? Why not? Plan an experiment

with controlled conditions to demonstrate a sound answer to the questions just propounded.

5. Prison inmates are low in intelligence. What does this signify concerning the intelligence of criminals?

6. Sun-bathing is bad for the body because the tanning process is nature's effort in self-defense against the rays of the sun. Is this a sound conclusion?

7. A man decides that he will save money by purchasing a new automobile to replace his old one. Would he not save still more money if he bought two new cars? Discuss the problem raised by such a question.

8. Contrary to common belief, college athletes live longer than average men of the same age and circumstances, according to a study of longevity made by the Metropolitan Life Insurance Company. The histories of 4,976 men who had distinguished themselves in intercollegiate sports were tabulated over a period of 20 years for this report. Strangely enough, the highest mortality was recorded by the baseball players, with crew men next, then track men, and last football players. The most surprising fact is the extraordinarily favorable showing of men who won letters in more than one sport. What is the moral?

9. Can thinking be promoted by education?

　　C. R. Griffith: *An Introduction to Educational Psychology*, pp. 246–255. 1935.

10. What changes in pedagogy would you consider advisable for encouraging critical judgment in the various courses of the college curriculum?

11. What are the social implications of independent thinking on the part of citizens? Will social chaos be a consequence?

> H. S. Gray: *Character "Bad": The Story of a Conscientious Objector.* 1934.
>
> B. Russell: *Freedom Versus Organization.* 1934.

12. Collect examples of the various inductive and deductive fallacies. Analyze them.

13. For an exposition of thinking in children, see these references:

> Jean Piaget: *The Child's Conception of Causality.* 1930. *The Child's Conception of the World.* 1929.
>
> Jean Piaget, *et al.: Judgment and Reasoning in the Child.* 1928. *Moral Judgment of the Child.* 1932.

CHAPTER XIV

1. Is good health a factor in intelligence? Show how fatigue or indisposition may interfere with the effective performance of your task, with the result that your ability is not fully realized. Indicate how vigor and "pep" contribute to business success.

2. Describe how emotional factors may render intelligence ineffective.

3. Investigate the attitudes of people toward intelligence tests. Are their judgments based on knowledge of the facts or on ignorant prejudice?

4. What friends have you considered especially intelligent? Why?

5. Name all the colors you can think of. Is a high score on such a test an indication of superior intelligence? Discuss.

6. Are intelligence and wealth positively correlated?   Discuss the various factors involved in the study of such a problem.

7. Does reading ability affect the score on an intelligence test?

> D. D. Durrell: "The Influence of Reading Ability on Intelligence Measures," *Journal of Educational Psychology,* September, 1933.

A STUDY OF THE JOURNALS

It is suggested as a valuable project that the student investigate the various psychological periodicals published in English, and acquaint himself with their contents and aims.

American Journal of Psychology
Journal of Genetic Psychology
Psychological Review
Psychological Monographs
Psychological Index
Psychological Bulletin
Archives of Psychology
Journal of Abnormal and Social Psychology
Psychological Clinic
Journal of Educational Psychology
Psychoanalytic Review
Journal of Experimental Psychology
Journal of Applied Psychology
Journal of Comparative Psychology
Comparative Psychology Monographs
Genetic Psychology Monographs
Psychological Abstracts
Journal of General Psychology
Journal of Social Psychology
British Journal of Psychology

ADDENDA

For questions that may suggest further projects, consult:

A. Ralston and C. J. Gage: *Present Day Psychology; An Objective Study in Educational Psychology.* 1931. Questions will be found at the end of each chapter.

C. E. Seashore and R. H. Seashore: *Elementary Experiments in Psychology*, Chapter V, "Status in Psychology." 1935.

H. C. Warren and L. Carmichael: *Elements of Human Psychology*, Appendix V, "Review Questions." Revised and enlarged edition, 1930.

R. S. Woodworth: *A Revised Standardized Examination on Woodworth's Psychology.* Third edition, 1934.

EXPERIMENTS

Procedure:

Some experiments will be described which can be performed by the individual student, or by the students in pairs, or by the students in groups, or by the class under the guidance of the instructor.   Experiments will begin with Chapter II.

In writing up the experiments the following outline is suggested:

> Purpose
> Materials
> Methods of procedure
> Record of data
> Introspection—if it is involved
> Interpretation of results

Psychological Supplies:

> C. H. Stoelting Company
>> 424 North Homan Avenue
>> Chicago, Illinois
> Marietta Apparatus Company
>> Marietta, Ohio

Bibliography:

F. C. Bartlett: *Remembering.   A Study in Experimental and Social Psychology.*   1932.

E. G. Boring: *A History of Experimental Psychology.*   1929.

W. B. Cannon: *A Laboratory Course in Physiology.*   1925.

M. Collins and J. Drever: (1) *A First Laboratory Guide in Psychology.*   1926; (2) *Experimental Psychology.*   1926.

G. W. Crane: *Class Demonstrations and Experiments* to accompany *Psychology Applied.*   1934.

J. F. Dashiell: *Experimental Manual in Psychology.* 1931.

A. Ford: *Group Experiments in Elementary Psychology.* 1931.

W. S. Foster: *Experiments in Psychology.* 1923.

S. I. Franz and K. Gordon: *Psychology Workbook. References, Demonstrations, and Experiments.* 1932.

H. E. Garrett: *Great Experiments in Psychology.* 1930.

H. E. Garrett and M. R. Schneck: *Psychological Tests, Methods, and Results.* 1933.

J. P. Guilford: *Laboratory Studies in Psychology. A Manual and Workbook for Students.* 1934.

L. W. Kline and F. L. Kline: *Psychology by Experiment.* 1927.

H. S. Langfeld and F. H. Allport: *An Elementary Laboratory Course in Psychology.* 1916.

E. S. Marks, E. L. Horowitz, *et al.: Psychology Work-Book.* 1933.

M. Metfessel and H. Musgrave: *Instructor's Guide for Demonstrations of Psychological Experiments.* 1933.

M. Metfessel and H. Musgrave: *Student's Guide.* 1933.

C. Murchison, Editor: *A Handbook of General Experimental Psychology.* 1934.

G. Murphy and L. B. Murphy: *Experimental Social Psychology.* 1931.

C. S. Myers: *A Textbook of Experimental Psychology with Laboratory Exercises.* 1911, 1925.

H. H. Remmers and G. C. Brandenburg: *A Syllabus Work-Book For a Two-Level Plan of Instruction in Elementary Psychology.* 1932.

C. A. Ruckmick: *The Mental Life. A Survey of Modern Experimental Psychology.* 1928.

E. C. Sanford: *A Course in Experimental Psychology.* 1897.

C. E. Seashore: *Elementary Experiments in Psychology.* 1908. "Elementary Psychology: An Outline of a Course by the Project Method." *University of Iowa Studies,* First Series No. 153, April 15, 1928.

C. E. Seashore and R. H. Seashore: *Elementary Experiments in Psychology.* 1935.

G. M. Smith: *Workbook in Psychology*. 1934.

D. Starch: *Experiments and Exercises in Educational Psychology*. 1930.

P. M. Symonds: *Psychological Diagnosis in Social Adjustment. Including an Annotated List of Tests, Questionnaires, and Rating Scales for the Study of Personality and Conduct.* 1934.

E. B. Titchener: *Experimental Psychology*, four volumes. 1901–1905; "Class Experiments and Demonstration Apparatus," *American Journal of Psychology*, 1903, 14, 439–455.

W. C. Trow: *Manual to Accompany Educational Psychology*. 1932.

W. L. Valentine: (1) *A Psychology Laboratory Manual.* 1933. (2) *Readings in Experimental Psychology.* 1930.

H. C. Warren and L. Carmichael: *Elements of Human Psychology*, Appendix VI, "Suggested Class Demonstrations." 1930.

G. M. Whipple: *Manual of Mental and Physical Tests*. 1914.

For the sake of convenience, references to the books included in the bibliography will be made by citing the names of the authors.

CHAPTER II

1. A Few Experiments.

J. McKeen Cattell: "Some Psychological Experiments," *Science*, January 1 and January 8, 1926.

2. Psychophysical Methods.

Valentine (1), pp. 5–15.

3. Method of Impression.

Langfeld and Allport, # 74.

4. Method of Expression.

Ibid., # 78.

5. Conditioned Response.

Use a bell and electric shock to evoke finger withdrawal. Guilford, pp. 103–104.

6. Reaction Time.

Chain reaction method. Fourteen students stand in a circle holding hands. The members of the group are instructed to pass along a squeeze felt in the left hand to the right hand of the next person. The timer says ready, waits a few seconds, starts the stop-watch, and squeezes the hand of the person to his right. The timer stops the watch when the squeeze is felt in his left hand, having completed the circle. Make five trials. In computing the reaction time, divide the group reaction time by the number of persons in the group, counting the timer twice. Take an average of the five trials for the reaction time.

Seashore and Seashore, Chapter XXXVII, "Reaction Time."

7. Individual Differences.

Starch, Chapter I, "Individual Differences."

8. Errors in Observation.

The Subject (S) attempts to reproduce a straight line of a given length three hundred times, drawing the horizontal line by free hand, and with visual aid alone. Measure the errors, and compute the constant and variable errors, the mean deviation, and the probable error. Represent the performances of S on a distribution curve. Guilford, pp. 229–231.

9. Correlation.

Correlation of speed and accuracy. Determine Speed by a Tapping Test, and Accuracy by a Dart-Throwing Test (throwing darts at a target). Correlate the scores.

See Langfeld and Allport, #56, for an experiment on correlation.

Correlating two accuracy tests. Use a Steadiness Test and a Dart-Throwing Test. Correlate the scores.

10. Correlation of Speed and Accuracy.

Study the following keyboard for three minutes.

T Q J L A V N G W
1 2 3 4 5 6 7 8 9

D R K M P C U F O
10 11 12 13 14 15 16 17 18

X E Z S Y H B I
19 20 21 22 23 24 25 26

When the instructor says, "Go," you are to substitute the numbers for the letters in the following passage. When you have finished, speak your name so that the experimenter can write it on the board. Your names will be recorded in the order in which you finish.

Summer breezes raise your hopes high and bring promises of better days. Soon you will be leaving, with joy, the days of the depression. Where lesions of the cortex may be involved, the person may be crazy, and will, therefore, be allowed no say in settling the question of how his wants are to be satisfied. In such a case a query will be gagged. Leave us in the van now and go on to what you were doing before.

Correct for errors and compute the accuracy score. Correlate the score in accuracy with the score in speed.

11. Finding the coefficient of correlation by the Pearson Method.

$$Formula: \text{r} = \frac{\Sigma xy}{n\sigma x . \sigma y}$$

r — coefficient of correlation.

Σ sigma — the sum.

x — the difference between the score of an individual and the average score on Test I.

y — the difference between the score of an individual and the average score on Test II.

Thus, Σxy equals the sum of the products of the difference between each individual score on Test I and the average of the Test I scores (x) multiplied by the difference between each individual score on Test II and the average of the scores for Test II (y).

n — the number of cases; *i.e.*, the number of individuals taking the tests.

σx — the standard deviation of the scores of the group on Test I.

σy — the standard deviation of the scores of the group on Test II.

Multiply the number of cases by the standard deviation of the scores of Test I, and then multiply the product thus obtained by the standard deviation of the scores of Test II. This equals nσx.σy. Let us work out the formula using the following scores.

Tested Individuals.	Scores for Test I.	Scores for Test II.
A	10	9
B	6	8
C	7	6
D	5	4
E	2	3
5—Total no. of cases	30—Total	30—Total

NOTE.—In arithmetical and algebraic procedures, attention must be paid to the plus and minus signs. In multiplying two plus or two minus items, proceed thus: -2 times$-2 = +4$. In multiplying items with different signs a minus answer is obtained, as -2 times $+2 = -4$.

Now we are ready for the computation. Solve the denominator of the formula first. The denominator is nσx.σy, which is *the number of cases times the standard deviation of x; this product multiplied by the standard deviation of y.* Obtain these standard deviations. Proceed as follows for each test: Test I—add up the scores, giving 30 for the sum. Find the *mean* by dividing the sum of the scores by the number of cases; *i.e.*, divide 30 by 5 yielding 6. List, item by item, the plus or minus amount by which each score of Test I differs from the mean. For example, A's score on Test I is 10. The mean is 6. 10 less 6 yields $+$ 4. Do this for all the items of both tests. The following difference table will result.

	x	y
A	4	3
B	0	2
C	1	0
D	-1	-2
E	-4	-3

Square each difference just obtained:

	x^2	y^2
A	16	9
B	0	4
C	1	0
D	1	4
E	16	9

Total: 34   Total: 26

Now divide each total by the number of cases (5) giving approximately 7 and 5 for the two tests with which we are working. Obtain the square root of each.[1] The square root of 7 is 2.6 and the square root of 5 is 2.2. Multiply these two items by each other (2.6 times 2.2) which gives 5.72. Multiply this figure by the number of cases (5). This procedure gives us 28.60 which is the denominator of the formula.

Now work out the numerator of the formula, Σxy. The *differences for each individual* in the x and y columns of the *difference table are multiplied together*. For example, Individual A shows a difference of 4 on Test I in the x column of the difference table, and a difference of 3 on Test II in the y column. Multiplying 4 by 3 we obtain 12. Do this for each case and total these products of multiplication, giving 26 as shown below. 26 is the numerator of the formula. In practical work careful attention must be given to plus and minus signs in working out these items. The procedure just completed is tabled below:

xy

12

0

0

2

12

26

The final step is obtaining the coefficient of correlation by *dividing the numerator* (26) *by the denominator* (28.6) which gives us +.91. +.91 is the coefficient of correlation between Test I and Test II. This is a significant correlation.

---

[1]The student is advised to make use of square root tables for this step.

12. Finding the coefficient of correlation by the Spearman Method.

Below are two sets of scores obtained by individuals on two different tests of personality traits. Determine the coefficient of correlation by means of the following formula:

$$r = 1 - \frac{6\Sigma(d^2)}{n(n^2-1)}$$

Scores for Trait I.[1]	*Scores for Trait II.*
39	66
48	47
65	73
35	95
74	58
61	18
65	93
42	10
42	91
52	80
93	70
20	10
66	98
70	5
81	96
67	66
60	90
65	95
35	37

The solution of this problem will be found on pages 610–611.
See other statistical problems in later chapters of this section.

---

[1] In the above series of scores it will be noted that some scores appear more than once, as, for example, under Trait I we find the score 42 appearing twice. When this occurs it is necessary to give equal rank to each score, and yet the total of the ranks must remain the same as if all the items were different. In this case the score 42 represents the 14th and 15th items. The next number in rank is 16. 14.5 is the position on the scale that is midway between 14 and 15. Both scores will then receive the rank of 14.5.
We note that there are three scores of 65. They occupy the positions of 7, 8, and 9. The midpoint is 8 and the three scores receive this rank. The next score is given the rank of 10.

13. Personality Tests.

Character Education Inquiry (C. E. I.) Tests.

Tests of Honesty and Trustworthiness.

See H. Hartshorne and M. A. May: *Studies in Deceit.* 1928.

Tests of Coöperation; Inhibition; Persistence.

See H. Hartshorne, M. A. May, and J. Maller: *Studies in Service and Self-Control.* 1929.

Test of Moral Knowledge and Attitudes.

See H. Hartshorne, M. A. May, and F. K. Shuttleworth: *Studies in the Organization of Character.* 1930.

See also: Garrett and Schneck; Symonds; Murphy and Murphy, especially Chapters X–XI.

14. *Mechanics of the Brain.* (Motion picture).

Pavlov's experiments on the conditioned reflex. 35mm. only. Six reels. It can be rented from the Amkino Corporation, 723 Seventh Avenue, New York City.

CHAPTER III

1. Introspection.

Plan an introspective experiment and carry it out: (a) in the Titchenerian style, and (b) in the *Gestalt* style.

2. Gestalt.

Demonstration of the phi phenomenon. See L. Carmichael and H. Schlosberg: "A Device for the Demonstration of Certain Illusions of Motion," *American Journal of Psychology*, 1928, 40, 128–129. Motion picture—M. Metfessel and W. Joel: *Types of Apparent Movement (including the phi phenomenon).* 16 mm. One reel, 241 feet. C. H. Stoelting Company.

Prepare visual material to test the grouping of stimuli.

Consult: *Psychologies of 1925*, p. 168ff., C. Murchison, editor. *Gestalten.* Consult: Ford, #35.

An experiment in *tonal memory*. The experimenter (E) informs the students that he will play a series of notes on the piano. The subjects are to count 1, 2, 3, 4, 5, etc., each number to correspond to one of the notes. Then a series of notes will be played which will repeat the first series except for one change. The students are to count the second series and to determine by number which note is changed. There should be some practice before the actual experiment begins. Instructions will be given as follows: "I will play a series of ten tones, one of which will be altered in the second presentation. Determine by number which note is changed." E will then play the following sequence of notes on the piano:

First presentation: D A E C# B E♭ F F# A E♭

Second presentation: D A E C# B♭ E♭ F F# A E♭

Instructions: "Now we will try a series of sixteen tones.

First presentation: C C D B C D E E F E D C D C B C

Second presentation: C C D B C D E E F E♭ D C D C B C

3. Extrovert—Introvert.

D. A. Laird: *Colgate Mental Hygiene Tests, Personal Inventory C 2.* 1925 (*Hamilton Republican*, Hamilton, New York).

C. A. Neymann and K. D. Kohlstedt: *Diagnostic Tests for Introversion and Extroversion.* 1928. (C. H. Stoelting Co., Chicago, Illinois.)

E. S. Conklin: *Introversion-Extroversion in Terms of Interest.* 1928. (University of Oregon, Eugene, Oregon.)

4. *Illusions of Movement.* (Motion picture.)

The Phi Phenomenon. 16mm. only. Fifty feet. Adelbert Ford, Lehigh University, Bethlehem, Pennsylvania.

CHAPTER IV

1. Absolute Pitch.

Instructions: I will play a note on the piano. You are to name the note by letter.

E then plays the note on the piano, and records the answers

given by the subjects who write their answers down and hand them in.

> C. H. Wedell: "The Nature of the Absolute Judgment of Pitch," *Journal of Experimental Psychology*, 1934, 17, 485–503.

2. C. E. Seashore's Test for Musical Talent.

> Records by the Columbia Phonograph Company.
> C. E. Seashore: *The Psychology of Musical Talent.* 1919.

3. Color Blindness.

> Ishihara's *Test for Color Blindness.* C. H. Stoelting Company, Chicago, Illinois.

4. Tactual Localization.

While S's eyes are closed, E touches S on the forearm with a pencil point. S is then to touch the same point with another pencil immediately afterwards, with his eyes still closed.

Estimate the error.

For many interesting experiments on sensation, requiring a minimum of apparatus, consult Sanford.

5. Two-Point Limen for Touch.

S closes his eyes and extends his bare forearm. E determines the two-point limen for the tip of the index finger by applying evenly the points of an æsthesiometer (or hairpin), using the *method of limits* described in Chapter II. With the points of the æsthesiometer separated at the distance of the two-point limen on the finger tip, E applies the stimulus in a uniform fashion to the following areas of the skin, S stating whether the sensation is of one or two: wrist, forearm, forehead, tip of nose, cheek, lip, back of neck, back of hand.

Determine the two-point limen for the back of the hand, and apply the points to the areas in reverse order. S reports his sensations, whether he feels one or two points.

6. Kinæsthesis.

Place a yardstick horizontally on a table. E places his finger on the end of the yardstick next to zero, picks out a number visually on the yardstick, then closes his eyes and moves his finger to the point on the yardstick which he has selected. The reports are recorded and the errors are estimated.

A variation of this method is to allow E to move his finger along the yardstick to a point he selects, with his eyes open; then he closes his eyes and tries to duplicate the movement.

The same methods may be used with the yardstick in a vertical position.

See Ford, #28.

7. Past-Pointing.

S is seated in a rotating chair. E stands in front of him with his arm extended, and pointing his index finger. S reaches forward and touches E's finger. He then closes his eyes and lowers his arm. After a moment he raises his arm and tries to touch E's finger. S is then rotated about six revolutions. The chair is stopped with S facing E. S touches E's finger with his eyes open, closes his eyes, drops his hand and then tries to touch E's finger again. Note the direction of the error.

The rotation should be in the plane of the horizontal canals.

W. Howell: *A Textbook of Physiology*, p. 406. 1924.

A further reference for experiments on Chapters IV–VI: Cannon.

CHAPTER V

1. Phrenology.

Measure the skull with head calipers and compute the cephalic index, according to instructions to be found in Garrett and Schneck, Part I, pp. 14–16.

2. Patellar Reflex.

S sits in a chair with his legs crossed. E applies a smart blow just below the knee-cap of the upper leg. The reflex movement will occur in response.

3. The Blinking Reflex.

E moves his closed fist in the direction of S's eyes, stopping just short of S's face. The blinking reflex will be observed.

4. Pupillary Reflex.

E observes the size of S's pupils in normal light. E then flashes a light steadily into one of S's eyes and observes the reduction in the size of the pupil.

5. *The Nerve Impulse.* (Motion picture.)

Animated diagrams illustrating the discoveries of Lucas, Forbes, Lillie, and others. 16mm. only. Two hundred and ten feet. Adelbert Ford, Lehigh University, Bethlehem, Pennsylvania.

CHAPTER VI

1. Strength Test.

S squeezes a dynamometer with his right hand. E records the score without announcing it. Each member of the group is given one trial. The scores are then arranged in order and posted on the board without any names being assigned. Each S then takes a trial before the group, and his score is posted at once in a second column with his name assigned. After all the scores are posted in the second column, each S is given one more trial and the scores are posted in a third column with the names assigned.

E then writes the names beside the scores in the first column.

Is there any indication that performance is improved by rivalry? What other factors may enter into the changes in score?

2. Endurance Contest.

Using an ergograph, apply the same method described for the dynamometer.

3. Motor Reactions in Penmanship.

Give a spelling test. Then measure the speed of handwriting. Is there any correlation of real significance between the scores?

Give the tapping test and correlate the score with the score in the speed of handwriting. What is the significance of the relationship revealed?

4. Tapping Test.

To be performed in pairs. One tapping, the other timing.

Draw on a piece of paper three three-inch squares. S holds a pencil over the first square one foot from the paper. At the signal "Go" given by the timer, S is to tap in square one as rapidly as possible for ten seconds, after which interval the timer will say stop. After a brief pause, S proceeds to square number two at the signal, stops at the signal, rests, and proceeds to square number three in the same fashion.

Count the dots. Compare the records of the members of the class. Plot a distribution curve.

CHAPTER VII

1. Set in Learning.

Dashiell, LVII. Also Foster, #6.

2. Set in Discrimination.

Metfessel and Musgrave: *Instructor's Guide*, pp. 67–69.

3. Observational Set.

Expose the king of hearts for thirty seconds, instructing S to study it. Remove the card and tell S to reproduce the following points: Draw the rectangle. Locate K or K's. Locate the heart or hearts. Locate approximately any hands that are showing. Is the king's neck visible? What is the color of the crown? What color of ink is used in representing the eyes of his royal highness?

E then tells S that he is about to expose the queen of hearts and the same questions will be asked after the card is removed.

Is the performance of S superior when he knows what to look for?

4. Ethical Sets.

Seashore and Seashore, Chapter IV.

S. C. Kohs: *Ethical Discrimination Test.* (C. H. Stoelting Co.)

S. C. Kohs: "Ethical Discrimination Test," *Journal of Delinquency*, 1922, 7, 1–15.

5. Scientific Attitude.

> D. L. Zyve: *Stanford Scientific Aptitude Test.* 1930. (Stanford University Press, Stanford University, Cal.)

6. Æsthetic Attitude.

> Consult A. R. Chandler: *Beauty and Human Nature; Elements of Psychological Æsthetics.* 1934.

7. Sets and Values.

> G. W. Allport and P. E. Vernon: *A Test for Personal Values.* Consult *Journal of Abnormal and Social Psychology,* 1931, 26, 231–248. Also E. Spranger: *Types of Men.* 1928.

8. Social Attitude.

E prepares a list of ten statements concerning *Anarchism,* such as "Anarchists are unpatriotic." The statements are to be marked *true* or *false.* When the list is completed, E hands the subject a sheet headed by the instruction: "Write a brief exposition of the principles of Anarchism."

Check the exposition with the actual meaning of Anarchism. Is there any relationship between prejudice and ignorance in the subject's attitude? Consult:

> L. L. Thurstone and E. J. Chave: *The Measurement of Attitude.* 1929.
>
> L. L. Thurstone: "Attitudes Can Be Measured," *American Journal of Sociology,* 1928, 33, 529–554.
>
> Seashore and Seashore: Chapter XXXVIII.

9. Inferiority and Introversion.

> Edna Heidbreder: *Personal Traits Rating Scale.* 1927. (C. H. Stoelting Company, Chicago, Illinois.)

10. Social Attitudes.

> H. Hartshorne, M. A. May, and F. K. Shuttleworth: *Studies in the Organization of Character,* Chapter III, "Tests Used to Measure Social Attitudes." 1930.
>
> Murphy and Murphy, Chapter XI, "Social Attitudes and Their Measurement."

CHAPTER VIII

1. What Do People Want?

Imagine yourself a publisher, selling books to the general public. Which one of each pair of book titles below would you select in order to sell a greater number of volumes? Place a check mark before one of each pair.

1. Battles of a Seaman
2. Privateersman

1. Ten O'Clock
2. What Art Should Mean to You

1. The King Enjoys Himself
2. The Lustful King Enjoys Himself

1. Pen, Pencil, and Poison
2. The Story of a Notorious Criminal

1. The Truth about Patent Medicine
2. Patent Medicine and the Public Health

1. The Art of Controversy
2. How to Argue Logically

1. The Art of Courtship
2. The Art of Kissing

1. An Introduction to Einstein
2. Einstein's Theory of Relativity Explained

1. Nietzsche: Who He Was and What He Stood For
2. The Story of Nietzsche's Philosophy

1. Quest for a Blonde Mistress
2. Fleece of Gold

1. Markheim's Murder
2. Markheim

1. How to Improve Your Conversation
2. The Secret of Self-Improvement

1. Eating for Health (Vitamins)
2. Care of the Skin and Hair

1. The Facts about Fascism
2. The Truth about Mussolini

1. The Mystery of the Iron Mask
2. The Mystery of the Man in the Iron Mask

Key for correcting your answers. The correct numbers for the pairs will be given in order: 1, 2, 2, 2, 1, 2, 2, 2, 2, 1, 1, 1, 2, 1, 2.

From G. W. Crane: *Psychology Applied*. 1932. By permission of the Northwestern University Press.

2. Ascendance—Submission.

> G. W. Allport and F. H. Allport: *A Scale for Measuring Ascendance, Submission, and Personality. The A-S-Reaction Study*. 1928. (Houghton Mifflin.)
>
> G. W. Allport: "A Test for Ascendance-Submission," *Journal of Abnormal Psychology*, 1928, 23, 118–136.

Interpreting Emotional Expression.

> Kline and Kline, Chapter XI.
>
> F. H. Allport: *Social Psychology*, Chapter IX, "Social Stimulation—Facial and Bodily Expression." 1924.
>
> C. Landis: "The Expressions of Emotion," Chapter XIII in *The Foundations of Experimental Psychology*, C. Murchison, Editor.

Have some member of the group who is adept at acting assume the facial expressions depicting various emotions. Instruct the members of the group to choose from a list of terms supplied them the particular term which fits each expression. Do the members of the class agree in their interpretations?

Professor Leonard Carmichael and Shearly O. Roberts of Brown University called in Professor Thomas Crosby Jr., of the Brown Department of English, an actor of the old school, to portray various emotions by means of hand gestures. The members of the class set down the names of thirty-five different emotions such as fear, hate, entreaty, surprise, anger, etc. Then Professor Crosby stood behind a dark curtain, rolled up his sleeves, thrust his arms through holes, and began the gestures which, in his judgment, best expressed each of the thirty-five emotions. Photographs were taken of which ten will be used in the experiment to follow. In the experiment at Brown the majority of the students recognized thirteen out of the thirty-five emotions depicted, and got most of them approximately right. Some of the students, in making up their minds, first placed their hands in the position shown in the pictures. Then they began to get the feeling of what was intended. It is suggested that the subjects employ this method in interpreting the photographs which follow on pages 592–593.

The descriptive terms are to be chosen from the following list:

scolding	worship
determination	anger
stubbornness	entreaty
contemplation	assurance
grief	sympathy

The key for the correct interpretations will be found on page 611.

(Pictures used in a study of manual expression in relation to emotional and other states, by Leonard Carmichael and Shearly O. Roberts of the Department of Psychology, Brown University.)

4. Emotional Stability.

S. L. Pressey: *X-O Tests for Investigating the Emotions.*   1920. C. H. Stoelting Company, Chicago, Illinois.

S. L. Pressey: "A Group Scale for Investigating the Emotions," *Journal of Abnormal and Social Psychology*, 1921, 16, 55–64.

5. *The Study of Infant Behavior.*   (Motion picture.)

Sound film. Gesell's studies at the Yale Psycho-Clinic. 16mm. and 35mm. Two reels. *Life Begins.* Sound film. More of Gesell's studies. 16mm. and 35mm. Seven reels. Both of these films may be procured from Electrical Research Products, Inc., 250 West 57th Street, New York City.

CHAPTER IX

1. Force of Habit.

Put your watch in the wrong pocket, or, if it is a wrist watch, on the wrong wrist. Keep a record of the mismoves you make until the new habit is established.

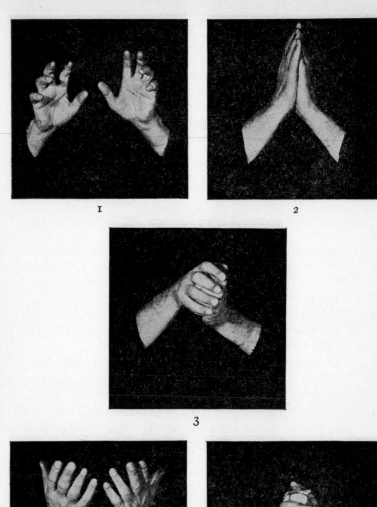

1   2

3

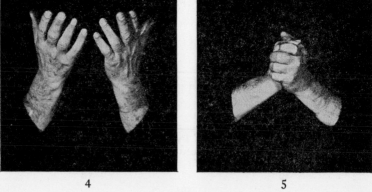

4   5

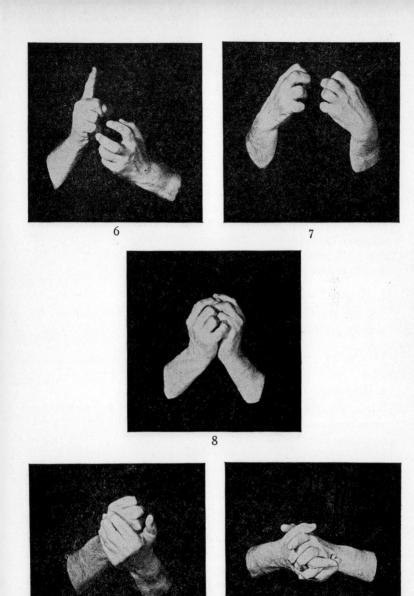

6   7

8

9   10

2. Breaking a Habit.

Break yourself of some habitual craving for a certain period, such as smoking, chewing gum, or eating candy. What is your technique?

3. Negative Adaptation.

Use a wink reflex stimulator procurable from the C. H. Stoelting Company, Chicago, Illinois.

S is seated in a position enabling him to adjust himself to the head-rest with his nose almost touching the glass plate of the apparatus. The soft hammer is released by E one hundred times at irregular intervals while S makes no attempt to inhibit the wink reflex. E notes whether the stimulus evokes a complete wink reflex, an incomplete wink reflex, or no wink reflex at all.

4. Negativism.

Study the experiments reported by Murphy and Murphy, especially pp. 164–168.

CHAPTER X

1. Meaning.

Run through a telephone directory and select at random the letter combinations at the top of the pages so that you get a list something like the following:

And-And
Bou-Bow
Cha-Cha
Dow-Dow
Fit-Fit
Gar-Gar
Hot-Hou
Mac-Mac
Naz-Nei
Par-Par
Rad-Ram
Sum-Sut
Was-Wat
You-Zan

Write down the ideas suggested by the above combinations.

Sample of what can be done: I suppose all the politicians are listed under *Bla-Bla.* *Don-Don* and *Dun-Dun* why don't you don-don like you dun-dun before? *Hot-Hou,* is it hot enough for hou? *Loo-Lou* and *Luv-Luc,* Loo-Lou, I still Luv you, any Luc? (With apologies to Dahl.)

2. Thematic Apperception.

E reads the following sentence: "We were strolling down the lane."

E asks the members of the group to describe the scene in great detail.

Have the members read their descriptions and discuss the different interpretations in terms of personal background.

This is a sample of the *Thematic Apperception Test* that is being used in various forms for the diagnosis of personality.

3. Vocabulary Test for Determining Meaning in Terms of Background.[1]

I	II	III
Cooking	*Meat-Buying* (What part of what animal?)	*Flowers* (how they look)
1. Shortening	1. Brisket	1. Zinnia
2. Sauté	2. Flank	2. Monk's hood
3. Casserole	3. Chuck roast	3. Calendula
4. Basting	4. Short rack	4. Syringa
5. Soufflé	5. Sirloin	5. Sweet alyssum
6. Trussing	6. Top of the round	6. Verbena
7. Hors d'œuvre	7. Cube steak	7. Lobelia
8. Bisque	8. Rib roast	8. Lupin
9. Crouton	9. Pot roast	9. Delphinium
10. Suet	10. Lamb fores.	10. Columbine

[1]Contributed by Donald Durrell.

IV	V	VI
Music	*Livestock*	*Dressmaking*

IV	V	VI
1. Fugue	1. Guernsey	1. Tunic
2. Arpeggio	2. Holstein	2. Jabot
3. Concerto	3. Ayrshire	3. Smocking
4. Counterpoint	4. Suffolk	4. Felling
5. Rondo	5. Southdown	5. Shirring
6. Chromatic scale	6. Chester White	6. Bodice
7. Minor chord	7. Tamworth	7. Organdie
8. Motif	8. Duroc Jersey	8. Yoke
9. Coda	9. Clydesdale	9. Bolero
10. Pianissimo	10. Belgian	10. Picot

VII	VIII	IX
Economics	*Woodworking*	*Automobile* (what they are and what they do)

VII	VIII	IX
1. Malthusian doctrine	1. Mitre-box	1. Differential
2. Gresham's Law	2. Dowel pin	2. Universal joint
3. "Closed shop"	3. Half-lap joint	3. Transmission
4. Boycott	4. Rip-saw	4. Cam shaft
5. An "acceptance"	5. Cross-cut-saw	5. Wrist-pin
6. Balance of trade	6. Expansion bit	6. Distributor
7. Marginal utility	7. Joiner	7. Vacuum tank
8. Underwriting	8. Tri-square	8. Connecting rod
9. "Preferred stock"	9. Draw-knife	9. Crank-shaft
10. "Single tax"	10. Jack-plane	10. Wheelbase

X

Sports

1. Lateral pass	4. Par	7. "Crawl"
2. Offside	5. Volley	8. Half-nelson
3. Mashie	6. American twist	9. "Spare"
		10. Fielder's choice

4. Word Completion Test.[1]

DIRECTIONS.—Below is a list of incomplete words. In each case you are to complete the three letters given with those necessary to make the first word that occurs to you. For example:

CHA — CHARLES
STE — STEP
BRE — BREAD

Please perform this test as rapidly as possible.

MEL	WIN	BUT
LAM	PUD	PIC
BAT	STE	GRA
LAR	RAD	CER
CHI	CHA	LET
POR	SPI	BRE
WAT	PAR	SAL
BEA	WAT	FLO

5. Sound Localization.

Station five experimenters so that one is situated one yard to the left of S, another one yard to the right, another one yard in front, another one yard in the rear, and another with his hand one yard above S. Each E is provided with a berry-capper. A plan is devised to determine the order in which the stimuli are presented. The experimenters in turn click the cappers and S calls out "front," "back," "right," "left," and "above."

Tabulate the judgments of direction in the following fashion:

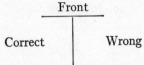

Compute the percentage of correct judgments in each direction. Complete fifty trials, ten from each direction.

Kline and Kline, pp. 171–174.

---

[1]Supplied by Lowell Trowbridge.

6. Drawing Project.[1]

DIRECTIONS.—Below are twenty lines. Kindly complete each unfinished sketch to represent any subject you wish. You may label the sketches, if you wish. This is not a test of artistic skill, so please do the sketches as rapidly as possible. For example:—

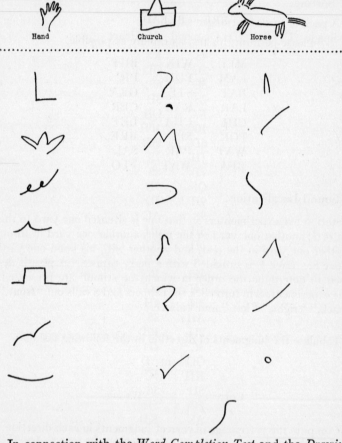

In connection with the *Word Completion Test* and the *Drawing Project*, do you observe that sets provided in the instructions influenced the meanings involved in the process of completion (closure)?

[1]Supplied by Lowell Trowbridge.

7. Light and Shade in the Perception of Visual Distance.

Demonstration with the boiler picture. Consult:
   J. F. Dashiell: *Fundamentals of Objective Psychology*, p. 386a.
   1928.

8. Sorting.

A pack of cards is arranged as follows:
S: Spade   C: Club   D: Diamond   H: Heart

4S	KS
2C	QD
8C	6S
2S	3D
KC	QH
10C	10H
6D	9C
JH	7S
7D	8S
QS	9D
9H	JD
9S	AC
8H	3H
6H	5C
7C	8D
JS	10S
7H	6C
2H	4H
AH	3S
2D	10D
3C	4D
QC	AD
KH	4C
5D	5S
JC	5H
AS	KD

Sort the cards, putting the four s's together, the four 3's together, and so on through the four aces. When you have completed this task, arrange the cards in suits running from 2 to ace. Say "Done" when you have finished.

Time the performance for each member of the group.   Plot the scores on a distribution curve.

9. Visual Illusions.

Procure the movable figures of the Müller-Lyer illusions from the C. H. Stoelting Company, Chicago, Illinois.   Instruct S to adjust one of the figures to equal the other as nearly as he can estimate by visual means.   Take the measurements.

For further experiments on visual illusions, see:

Langfeld and Allport, #43.

Seashore and Seashore, Chapter XXII.

Seashore, Chapter XIV.

Myers, Part I, Chapter XXII.   (1911.)

E. B. Titchener: *Experimental Psychology*, Volume I, Experiment #44.   Motion picture—M. Metfessel and H. Musgrave: *Measurement of Müller-Lyer Illusion*.   16 mm.   One reel, 47 feet.   C. H. Stoelting Company.

10. Fluctuation of Attention.

Show the Rubin figure-and-ground pattern to a number of people and tabulate which aspect of the pattern is seen first as figure.   Is the distance of the S from the stimulus a factor?

Prepare other S's by showing them a silhouette in black before presenting the Rubin stimulus.   What happens?

Try out the pattern in different colors.

Use the reversible staircase figure.   Have S fixate his gaze upon a median point.   Let him practice in reversing the perspective for one minute.   Then E times S for two minutes to see how many reversals he can effect, S counting the reversals to himself and reporting the total to E.

After a short rest have S fixate upon a cross located in the center of the diagram and attempt to prevent the reversals.   S is to count the number of reversals which occur in spite of his efforts to prevent them.

Langfeld and Allport, #57.

Valentine (1), pages 119–120.

Motion picture—M. Metfessel and N. Warren: *Range of Visual Perception*.   16 mm.   One reel, 50 feet.   C. H. Stoelting Company.

11. Division of Attention.

S is to speak the alternate letters of the alphabet, A, C, E, G, etc. When S reaches Y he is to begin over again immediately, this time starting with B, D, F, and H. S continues for one minute while E keeps time and makes a record, by tallying, of the number of letters uttered by S.

S then counts on paper, writing every third number, 1, 4, 7, etc., to 100, then continuing with 2, 5, 8, for one minute.

S then combines the two tasks, while E tabulates the letters uttered, for one minute. The record of the numbers is on the paper.

Guilford, pages 206–207.

12. Degree of Attention.

Distraction. Arrange the members of the class in pairs. One member of the pair performs the task, the other member times the operation.

At a signal from E, S multiplies:

$$4\ 7\ 8\ 9\ 6\ 3\ 7\ 5\ 6\ 2\ 9\ 8\ 9$$
$$7\ 5\ 2\ 4\ 9\ 7\ 5\ 9\ 8\ 6\ 9\ 6\ 7$$

The instructor then reads the following passage slowly while the same members time and the same members multiply these figures:

$$9\ 8\ 9\ 2\ 6\ 5\ 7\ 3\ 6\ 9\ 8\ 7\ 4$$
$$7\ 6\ 9\ 6\ 8\ 9\ 5\ 7\ 9\ 4\ 2\ 5\ 7$$

The instructor meanwhile is reading: "Multiplication is a simple process, but it is easy to make mistakes, such as calling 9 times 7 equal to 62, or 7 times 9 equal to 64. 8 times 4, of course, is not 36, any more than 5 times 6 is 33. Carrying over the numbers may involve errors since 8 may be carried over instead of 7, and the result will thus be incorrect. A long number like 4789637562989 is only as long as 7524975983967 but 6834592178364 is three digits short of a number like 2684286573179287. If the correct answer to a problem is 999666333777, then the answer 999666333776 is just far enough off to be wrong, and a miss is as good as a mile. If you were owed $7,896,437, you would not be satisfied with $7,596,437, would you?"

Does the distraction prolong the time?

See Marks and Horowitz, Experiment #XXVI.

13. Perceiving Time Intervals.

Dashiell, p. 95.
Myers, Chapter XXIII.

14. Reliability of Testimony.

Aussage Experiment. Collins and Drever (2), pp. 183–185.

15. Catching Attention.

Write the Barron G. Collier Agency, 220 West 42nd St., New York City, for some copies of street-car advertisements. Study the attentional value of the colors employed.

> G. W. Crane: *Psychology Applied*, Chapter VIII, "The Fields and Functions of Advertising."

> See also an experiment in Starch, Chapter XIV.

> Motion picture—H. Musgrave and M. Metfessel: *Determiners of Attention.* 16 mm. One reel, 76 feet. C. H. Stoelting Company.

Intensity. E reads a list of twenty three-syllable words, one word per second, in an even tone. S is to write down the words when the list is completed.

E reads another list, speaking three of the words in a louder tone. S writes down the list as before.

E reads another list, speaking three of the words in an audible whisper. S writes down the list as before.

E tabulates the three lists on the board, starring the emphasized words.

Tabulate the number of S's, remembering each word.

From the table make three graphs on the same base for comparison.

> Kline and Kline, pp. 106–107.

16. Span of Attention for Touch.

Use marbles and exposure board according to instructions in Kline and Kline, pp. 119–120.

CHAPTER XI

1. Reading.

Children are now taught to read silently in order to improve their rate of reading. Read a passage from a book as you naturally would do. Introspect your imagery. Are you slowing yourself down by using voci-motor verbal imagery?

Read a passage as fast as you can. Are you conscious of an effort to suppress voci-motor verbal imagery?

For an experiment on *reading efficiency* see Remmers and Brandenburg, Lesson #1.

2. Imagery.

Langfeld and Allport, pp. 131–136.

For some excellent experiments on imagining and remembering, see Bartlett.

3. Ideational Types.

Titchener: *Experimental Psychology*, Volume I, Experiment #XXXVI.

4. Imaginative Design.

Franz and Gordon, pp. 181–183.

5. Dream Interpretation.

Collect ten suitable cartoons and delete the labels. Submit them to S for interpretation.

H. M. Frink: *Morbid Fears and Compulsions*, p. 68ff.   1921.

Keep a pad and a pencil at your bedside. Record your dreams. Interpret them.

6. Accuracy of Observation and Memory.

A student in the front row is given the following account to expose for the person behind him to read. As soon as the account is read the second person writes the account from memory and shows his account to the student behind him and so on around the class. The last person then reads his account to the class. The original account is as follows:

Peoria police are closing in on a man about twenty-five years old, six feet tall, weighing about 170 pounds, dressed in a gray tweed suit with a double-breasted coat, who killed a store keeper named Kevinsky at the Main St. A & P store, wounded a policeman, and escaped with $325.42, at 2:30 A. M. on Thursday, May 16.

7. Aussage Experiment.

Prepare a picture or stage a scene which will include a number of items to be observed during a brief period.

Narrative: S writes a description.

Deposition: E prepares some leading and misleading questions which will fall into six categories similar to the following:

1. *Determinative:* What color was the dog?
2. *Completely disjunctive:* Was there a dog in the picture?
3. *Incompletely disjunctive:* Was the dog black or white?
4. *Expectative:* Was there not a dog in the picture?
5. *Implicative:* What color was the cat? (There is no cat.)
6. *Consecutive:* Was it spotted or striped? (Referring to the above cat.)

Note the four types of errors involved in the reports:

1. Omission
2. Erroneous insertion
3. Substitution
4. Transposition

Which method, narrative or deposition, is more accurate?

Study the newspaper accounts of the Lindbergh trial, particularly the questions asked of the witnesses called to testify.

> G. M. Whipple: "The Obtaining of Information," *Psychological Bulletin*, 1918, 15, 233–247.

> Motion picture—M. Metfessel and N. Warren: *Reliability of Memory*. 16 mm. One reel, 40 feet. C. H. Stoelting Company.

8. Whole and Part Learning.

> Kline and Kline, pp. 253–255.

ç. Perseveration.

The members of the class are instructed to write down for five minutes words beginning with the letter "r."

The instructor then lectures for ten minutes, suddenly turns on the class and instructs them to write down for one minute in another column any more words the members may think of beginning with the letter "r."

Call for introspective reports as to what happened during the ten-minute lecture.

10. Primacy, Frequency, Intensity, Recency, and Recall.

Starch, pp. 108–134.

11. Paired Associates.

E prepares a series of twenty photographs containing faces and names. Each picture is exposed for ten seconds while E pronounces the name distinctly two times.

Repeat.

Then for retroactive inhibition have S's work on arithmetical problems for five minutes.

E then exposes the pictures in the same order, each for ten seconds. S is to write the name associated with each face.

12. Controlled Association.

Perform a cross-word puzzle. Record introspectively the steps involved in the solution.

Crime detection. Prepare an experiment involving the commission of a "crime" and its detection by means of a Controlled Association Test.

Foster, Experiment #XX.

J. A. Larson: *Lying and Its Detection.* 1932.

Seashore and Seashore, Chapter XXV.

13. Associative Inhibition.

Talk or write nonsense for five minutes. Introspect. Do you have any difficulty in performing the task?

Motor habits. Give the tapping test to determine the speed of S's.

Group the members, if possible, into those who play cards and into those who do not play cards.

Have the players and the non-players deal one hundred and four cards, beginning with the left and dealing to the right. Time the performance.

Time the players and the non-players while they deal the cards in the reverse direction.

Are the *players* comparatively more slowed by the unaccustomed operation?

For another experiment on associative inhibition, consult Trow, pages 120–122.

14. Transfer (Inhibition or Facilitation).

Practice on the test shown on page 37 until the performance is perfected.

Try it with the other hand. Is there any transfer of practice effect?

Perform the task in the opposite direction. Determine the influence of the previous practice.

Change the size of the diagram and perform the task in the various ways described. What do you get?

15. Anticipating.

Describe an historical situation which is little known to the members of the class. Ask them to write down what events were likely to follow. Discuss. Then describe what did follow.

16. Foresight.

H. Hartshorne, M. A. May, F. K. Shuttleworth: *Studies in the Organization of Character*, p. 43ff.

CHAPTER XII

1. Conflict.

Pat a dog gently, and in a friendly tone, say, "Nice Rover" (or the dog's name). While you continue to repeat softly, "Nice Rover," gradually increase the intensity of the patting until you are imparting vigorous blows. Does the dog's behavior reveal the presence of conflict?

For some excellent experiments on conflict, consult:

    A. R. Luria: *The Nature of Human Conflicts*, especially pp. 213–234. 1932.

2. Empathy.

Present some pictures suitable for arousing empathy. Have S record his reactions.

3. Integration.

    H. Hartshorne, M. A. May, F. K. Shuttleworth: *Studies in the Organization of Character*, Part IV, "The Significance of Integration."

4. Projection and Introjection.

Use a *Thematic Apperception Test* which you may plan as follows:

Tell S that you are going to give him a test of creative imagination. Present a picture with some person in it who resembles S in age or appearance or situation, somebody with whom he can identify himself readily. Ask him to create a story around the theme of the picture.

S will probably identify himself with the character in the picture and will probably project his own personality into the evolution of the theme. Thus the story which he tells about the picture will really be a story about himself. The inhibitions which would ordinarily prevent him from revealing his innermost thoughts and longings do not function in the Thematic Apperception Test because S is not aware of the real purpose of the experiment.

The theme is interpreted according to the same principles as are employed in the interpretation of dreams.

This method of personality diagnosis is being used successfully by Murray and Morgan of the Harvard Psychological Clinic.

CHAPTER XIII

1. The Concept and Its Development.

    Guilford, pp. 242–247.

2. Cause and Effect.

> H. Hartshorne, M. A. May, F. K. Shuttleworth: *Studies in the Organization of Character*, p. 38ff.

3. Reasoning.

E fastens two pieces of heavy twine to the ceiling, long enough to just reach the floor and far enough apart so that S cannot reach either string if he holds the other at the same time. A table, a chair, a yardstick, and a clamp are placed in the proximity of the twine. S is told he may use any of the implements he desires.

E instructs S to tie the ends of the two strings together. E times the solution. If S solves the problem, E suggests that he try to attain the goal by other methods.

> Valentine (1), pp. 217–218.

4. Subvocal Talking.

Add the following column, saying the numbers "under your breath." Have E time you.

Rest a minute. Then add the following column, keeping your tongue motionless between your teeth. Have E time you.

1 7 4 8 6 2	9 3 1 5 2 7
9 3 1 5 2 7	7 7 9 8 5 6
3 5 4 3 2 9	5 2 7 7 6 1
8 8 1 9 7 3	1 7 4 8 6 2
5 9 8 9 1 2	4 3 6 8 6 2
5 2 7 7 6 1	7 9 9 5 3 6
7 9 9 5 3 6	3 1 9 6 6 8
6 5 7 8 9 3	8 8 1 9 7 3
4 3 6 8 6 2	3 5 4 3 2 9
9 4 9 8 3 5	1 6 9 5 4 3
8 5 5 6 9 4	9 4 9 7 3 5
3 1 9 6 6 8	5 9 8 9 1 2
6 7 5 8 3 9	6 5 7 8 9 3
1 6 9 5 4 3	8 5 5 6 9 4
7 7 9 8 5 6	9 8 9 8 9 8

Does the performance of the second task require more time? Why?

CHAPTER XIV

1. Effect of Practice on Intelligence Score.

Give an Intelligence Test and record the scores.
Provide practice on taking Intelligence Tests.
Give the first test again. Score it. Is there any improvement?
If there is, how can you account for it? What factors are involved?

2. Problems Involved in Correlation.

Administer *Wells' Revision of the Army Alpha Intelligence Test.*
Record the scores.
Correlate with these scores the following scores:
Ratings of intelligence of the members of the class by the members of the class.
Score of the *Minnesota Mechanical Ability Test.*
Score in terms of time on the solution of a Jig-Saw Puzzle.
The same with a bridge puzzle for bridge players only.
Success in playing checkers.
Marks in various courses in the curriculum.
(Is the concept of "G" confirmed?)
See Collins and Drever: (1) #27, pp. 93–97.
Information on current events:
O'Connor *English Vocabulary Test.*
(Procurable from the Stevens Institute of Technology.)
Social Intelligence Tests (Revised form)
by Moss, Hunt and Omwake.
Otis Group Intelligence Scale (Advanced Examination).
(Procurable from the World Book Company, Yonkers, N. Y.)

3. Picture Performance Scale.

Serial pictures are to be arranged in the proper order to tell the story.
J. Tuckman: "A Picture Performance Scale," *Journal of Educational Psychology*, 1935, 26, 17–29.

Most of the material used by Tuckman consisted of Soglow's pictures in the *New Yorker*.

It is possible to use pictures found in O. Soglow: *Little King*. 1934.

4. *Stages of Child Growth*.   (Motion picture.)

Sound film.   Bühler's studies.   16mm. and 35mm.   Two reels. Electrical Research Products Inc., 250 West 57th Street, New York City.

SOLUTION OF CORRELATION PROBLEM
(Page 581)

$$r = \frac{6\Sigma(d^2)}{n\,(n^2 - 1)}$$

Trait I (scores)	Trait II (scores)	R (rank in I)	R_2 (rank in II)	D_r (difference in ranks)	D_r^2 (square of difference)
39	66	16	11.5	4.5	20.25
48	47	13	14	1	1
65	73	8	9	1	1
35	95	17.5	3.5	14	196
74	58	3	13	10	100
61	18	10	16	6	36
65	93	8	5	3	9
42	10	14.5	17.5	3	9
42	91	14.5	6	8.5	72.25
52	80	12	8	4	16
93	70	1	10	9	81
20	10	19	17.5	1.5	2.25
66	98	6	1	5	25
70	5	4	19	15	225
81	96	2	2	0	0
67	66	5	11.5	6.5	42.25
60	90	11	7	4	16
65	95	8	3.5	4.5	20.25
35	37	17.5	15	2.5	6.25
					878.50

$$r = 1 - \frac{6 \times 878.5}{19\,(19^2 - 1)}$$

$$r = 1 - \frac{5271}{19\,(361 - 1)}$$

$$r = 1 - \frac{5271}{6840}$$

$$r = 1 - .77$$

$r = + .23$ This is too low to be considered a significant correlation.

KEY TO INTERPRETATION OF HAND GESTURES
(Pages 590–593)

1. Posed as Anger
2. Posed as Worship
3. Posed as Grief
4. Posed as Entreaty
5. Posed as Assurance
6. Posed as Scolding
7. Posed as Stubbornness
8. Posed as Sympathy
9. Posed as Determination
10. Posed as Contemplation

INDEX OF NAMES

INDEX OF SUBJECTS